PREVENTING AND HEALING CLIMATE TRAUMAS

Using extensive research, interviews with program leaders, and examples, *Preventing and Healing Climate Traumas* is a step-by-step guide for organizing community-based, culturally tailored, population-level mental wellness and resilience-building initiatives to prevent and heal individual and collective climate traumas.

This book describes how to use a public health approach to build universal capacity for mental wellness and transformational resilience by engaging community members in building robust social support networks, making a just transition by regenerating local physical/built, economic, and ecological systems, learning how trauma and toxic stress can affect their body, mind, and emotions as well as age and culturally tailored mental wellness and resilience skills, and organizing group and community-minded events that help residents heal their traumas. These actions build community cohesion and efficacy as residents also engage in solutions to the climate emergency.

This book is essential reading for grassroots, civic, non-profit, private, and public sector mental health, human services, disaster management, climate, faith, education, and other professionals, as well as members of the public concerned about these issues. Readers will come away from this book with practical methods—based on real-world examples—that they can use to organize and facilitate community-based initiatives that prevent and heal mental health and psycho-social-spiritual problems and reduce contributions to the climate crisis.

Bob Doppelt coordinates the International Transformational Resilience Coalition (ITRC), a global network working to prevent and heal the mental health and psycho-social-spiritual problems generated by the climate emergency.

D1572245

"The health of our planet is inherently connected to our well-being. Preventing climate trauma and supporting holistic healing and resilience in the ways that our diverse communities interact with the stresses of climate change is quickly becoming one of the biggest challenges of our generation. Bob Doppelt's new book offers an essential blueprint towards building a healthier future in the places where we live."

Antonis Kousoulis, *director for England and Wales,*
Mental Health Foundation, UK

"The world is beginning to experience an epidemic of climate change-related mental and emotional distress that, regrettably, is likely to become a pandemic. Developing community-based approaches to promoting mental and emotional resilience in the face of climate change is one of humanity's most pressing imperatives. In this book, one of the world's leading experts, Bob Doppelt, shares his deep insights into how we rise to this challenge."

Edward Maibach, *MPH, PhD, Distinguished University Professor and director of*
the George Mason University Center for Climate Change Communication

"I strongly encourage everyone to read this wonderful book because it emphasizes the importance and the magic of community work. It is about time we evolve from individualistic models of mental health care that focus on what is wrong with a person. The teachings this book provides will help us, our loved ones, and our communities face the climate change mental health crises successfully in a just and equitable way."

Carissa Cabán-Alemán, *MD, associate professor,*
Herbert Wertheim College of Medicine, Florida International University, and
member of the Climate Psychiatry Alliance

"This is the book we've been waiting for. Frankly setting out the frightening and challenging effects of climate change, Bob Doppelt's book also gives us hope that by coming together as communities, we can help ourselves mitigate some of the worst impacts on our own lives and the lives of our families and our neighbours. This is an essential read for policy makers, practitioners, and community organisations."

Fiona Garven, *director of the Scottish Community*
Development Centre, Glasgow, Scotland

"The obvious consequences of climate change—extreme weather events, droughts, floods—sit among the clearer results of manmade global warming. This important new book from Bob Doppelt helps us mitigate the often invisible outcomes of global warming, including anxiety, depression, PTSD, and trauma. Drawing on psychology, spirituality, and bottom up, community-based resilience practices, this monograph can help us build the capacity to manage mental wellness, recover from current and forthcoming shocks, and ensure equitable outcomes."

Daniel P. Aldrich, *director of the Security and Resilience Studies Program at*
Northeastern University, and author of Building Resilience and Black Wave

"Bob Doppelt is a recognized international leader on the human impact of climate change. His knowledge and wisdom illuminates *Preventing and Healing Climate Traumas*. This is a must read for anyone interested in conceptualizing new systems of support for our worldwide community."

Elaine Miller-Karas, *cofounder of The Trauma Resource Institute*

"Ultimately, the responsibility for preventing and healing climate trauma falls to family, friends, and neighbours, the three supportive social units of our lives. As a municipality we are making way for this prevention and healing by resourcing and organizing the irreplaceable capacity of neighbourhoods to foster mental wellness and resilience. This new book by Bob Doppelt will serve us well as in this regard."

Howard Lawrence, *Abundant Community Edmonton coordinator, Neighbourhoods Services, City of Edmonton, Canada*

"In this book Bob Doppelt presents a compelling argument that damage to person's mental health and overall well-being is occurring in reaction to the ever-increasing climatic disasters and that we have well-understood approaches for building population level resilience to mitigate these effects. It is critical that we implement these science-based approaches to increase our communities' ability to more healthfully react to the inevitable increase in climate trauma. Bob provides the call to action."

David Shern, *PhD, senior associate in the Department of Mental Health, Bloomberg School of Public Health, Johns Hopkins University, and vice chair of the Campaign for Trauma-Informed Policy and Practice*

"Bob Doppelt's new book offers high-impact recommendations on how to bring community resilience to the forefront of the climate change crisis. Bob excels at describing the impact a community-based approach has on cultivating the power of the collective spirit in addressing the health of our communities. Read it now and put it into action!"

Theresa Barila, *founder and board president emeritus of the Community Resilience Initiative*

"Bob Doppelt is a leader in the movement to build effective community responses to climate change and prevent its most severe mental health impacts. This book contains solid information and insights that can be readily applied by community leaders, practitioners, and policymakers."

Howard Kurtzman, *PhD, former senior science advisor (retired) to the American Psychological Association*

"Bob Doppelt is one of my heroes: a man who was far out ahead of the curve anticipating the psychological and social consequences of climate change and climate trauma. Read his new book because you and your loved ones are going to need the information that is in it."

Sandra L. Bloom, *MD, associate professor of health management and policy, Dornsife School of Public Health, Drexel University; cofounder of the Sanctuary Model and founder of Creating Presence*

"Bob Doppelt's book sets out principles for challenging our growing global climate emergency. We can't address a crisis of this magnitude with the same methodologies we've been using—we need to rescue those drowning AND address why they're drowning in the first place. As Bob notes, this means focusing on community-level strategies that start with healing and foster resilience in our systems, communities, neighborhoods, and families."

Ruben Cantu, *associate program director for community trauma, mental health, and violence prevention, Prevention Institute*

"We are at a crossroads in our country in terms of how we understand and respond to mental health. At a time when the eco-anxiety of young people is at an all time high, we need concrete, research-based strategies to support them in navigating in a rapidly changing world. Bob's book lays out a clear framework on how to do it and should be required reading for anyone working on adaptation and mitigation strategies for our climate."

Lil Milagro Henriquez, *executive director and founder, Mycelium Youth Network*

"If you are in the fight against climate change, it can actually be easier to face what is happening and the damage that is surely coming. But for most people, that is not the case, and a new type of community action is needed. A key chapter in this important book tells us to 'begin building community capacity for mental wellness and transformational resilience,' and that about says it all. The book describes how to do that. It is needed today and will be even more so in the years to come."

James Gustave Speth, *former dean, Yale School of the Environment*

"As much as I wish we didn't need this book, at this point I am not sure we can live without it. A practical guide to understanding what we must do to prepare ourselves for the reality of the climate crisis, Bob's book outlines concrete, accessible strategies we can implement now, to build upon the incredible resilience that is in all of us, individually and even more so, collectively. I am beyond grateful for this engaging, thought-provoking, well-researched, powerful resource."

Ann DuPre Rogers, *LCSW, executive director, Resources for Resilience™, coauthor, Reconnect for Resilience™*

"Bob Doppelt's new book weaves together intersections of prevention science and environmental science to elevate a self-healing journey where social connection is key, raising hope comes with concrete action steps, and resilience helps us move forward with increased community-wide wellness to mitigate the impacts of toxic stressors and traumas we increasingly face as humanity, including harsh environmental and climate events. This book is hope raising...and we need it."

Kristi Slette, *executive director, Whatcom Family and Community Network*

"Bob Doppelt has surfaced a critical problem that is grossly under addressed by climate solutions. He listened to the voice of the communities and the traditions of our ancestors that have taken us through the storms of the past and identified that it is only through strong community bonds and caring relationships and systems that we can weather present and future climate catastrophes."

Jacqui Patterson, *founder and executive director, The Chisholm Legacy Project*

"To build transformational resilience and hope amidst a global cataclysm, traditional diagnostic constructs and individual-based mental health treatments will not suffice. A community/population-based strategy is necessary, one with a focus on prevention. Bob Doppelt's insightful approach outlines the complex dilemma of climate change and mental health and provides a pragmatic template for guiding communities toward wellness."

Andrew J. McLean, *MD, MPH, chair of the Department of Psychiatry and Behavioral Science, University of North Dakota School of Medicine and Health Sciences*

"In this sobering and insightful book, Bob Doppelt provides us with an immersion in the facts of our climate challenges and then the community-based ways we can rise to this moment in our collective human history to make the necessary changes in how we live while building our relationships with each other and with nature. The power of this book rests in its emotional intensity, bringing us from the realization of our fear and loss, to the empowerment and hope of potential growth."

Daniel J. Siegel, *MD, New York Times bestselling author of* IntraConnected: MWe *(Me plus We) as the Integration of Self, Identity, and Belonging; executive director, Mindsight Institute; clinical professor, UCLA School of Medicine*

PREVENTING AND HEALING CLIMATE TRAUMAS

A GUIDE TO BUILDING RESILIENCE AND HOPE IN COMMUNITIES

Bob Doppelt

Routledge
Taylor & Francis Group

NEW YORK AND LONDON

Cover image: Itsanan Sampuntarat/Getty

First published 2023
by Routledge
605 Third Avenue, New York, NY 10158

and by Routledge
4 Park Square, Milton Park, Abingdon, Oxon, OX14 4RN

Routledge is an imprint of the Taylor & Francis Group, an informa business

Library of Congress Cataloging-in-Publication Data
Names: Doppelt, Bob, author.
Title: Preventing and healing climate traumas: a guide to building resilience and hope in communities/Bob Doppelt.
Description: New York: Routledge, 2023. | Includes bibliographical references and index. | Identifiers: LCCN 2022041918 (print) | LCCN 2022041919 (ebook) | ISBN 9781032200217 (hardback) | ISBN 9781032200200 (paperback) | ISBN 9781003262442 (ebook)
Subjects: LCSH: Climatic changes—Psychological aspects. | Community psychology. | Community mental health services. | Resilience (Personality trait)
Classification: LCC RA790.55 .D67 2023 (print) | LCC RA790.55 (ebook) | DDC 362.1—dc23/eng/20221004
LC record available at https://lccn.loc.gov/2022041918
LC ebook record available at https://lccn.loc.gov/2022041919

ISBN: 9781032200217 (hbk)
ISBN: 9781032200200 (pbk)
ISBN: 9781003262442 (ebk)

DOI: 10.4324/9781003262442

Typeset in Baskerville
by codeMantra

This book is dedicated to all the people willing to see and act on truths that overcome the ignorance, delusion, and dissociation that created the global climate emergency and can set humanity on a socially, economically, and ecologically regenerative path.

CONTENTS

Acknowledgments   ix

About the Author   xi

Introduction   1

Part I A Public Health Approach is Required to Build Population-Level
Capacity for Mental Wellness and Transformational Resilience for the
Long Climate Emergency   17

1 Climate Overshoot "101"   19

2 The Causes and Consequences of Individual, Community, and Societal Traumas 36

3 Elements of a Public Health Approach to Enhancing Mental Wellness and
Transformational Resilience for the Long Climate Emergency   54

Part II Organizing and Operating Community-Based Initiatives that Build
Universal Capacity for Mental Wellness and Transformational Resilience   73

4 Get Organized   77

5 Begin Building Community Capacity for Mental Wellness and
Transformational Resilience   100

6 Establish RCC Goals, Objectives, Strategies, and Action Plans   116

Part III The Five Foundational Areas RCCs Must Emphasize to Enhance
Universal Mental Wellness and Transformational Resilience for the
Climate Emergency   127

7 Build Social Connections across Boundaries in the Community   129

8 Ensure a Just Transition by Creating Healthy, Safe, Just, and Equitable
Climate-Resilient Local Physical/Built, Economic, and Ecological Conditions   147

9 Cultivate Universal Literacy about Mental Wellness and Resilience   170

10 Foster Engagement in Specific Practices that Support Mental Wellness and
Resilience   183

11 Establish Ongoing Opportunities for Residents to Heal Their Distresses
        and Traumas   203

12 Continually Track Progress, Learn, Improve, and Plan for the Long Term   215

        Conclusion: The Need for a Global Movement to Enhance Universal
        Capacity for Mental Wellness and Transformational Resilience for the
        Civilization-Altering Climate Emergency   228

Index   *235*

ACKNOWLEDGMENTS

This book is the outcome of many years of research and practice by numerous individuals and organizations around the world. I have merely tried to integrate the incredible work they have done into a framework and plan of action to use a public health approach to build population-level capacity for mental wellness and resilience for the climate emergency.

I would like to give a great big thanks to people in the US, Canada, UK, and other nations who took the time to speak with me about the different forms of community resilience-building initiatives they are involved with. After the interview, many often sent more information and answered additional questions. They include: Ruben Cantu, Prevention Institute; Teri Barila, Walla Walla Community Resilience Initiative; Kristi Settle, Whatcom County Family & Community Network; Jim Diers, first director of the Seattle Department of Neighborhoods; Rich Harwood, the Harwood Institute; Howard Lawrence, Abundant Community Edmonton; Seth Saeugling, Rural Opportunities Institute; Ann DuPre Rogers, Resources for Resilience; Lil Milagro Henriquez, Mycelium Youth Network; Jerry Tello, National Compadres Network; Joe Christal, Metropolitan Alliance for the Common Good; Judith Landau, ARISE Network; Risa Wilkerson, Healthy Places by Design; Steve Wilson, World Laughing Tour; Dr. Robert Enright, Aristotelian Professorship in Forgiveness Science, University of Wisconsin-Madison; Mebane Boyd, Resilient Communities Office, N.C. Partnership for Children; Daniel Homsey, SF Neighborhood Empowerment Network; Dr. Kiffer Card, University of Victoria, School of Public Health; Dr. James Gordon, Center for Mind-Body Medicine; Barbara Garbarino, Putnam Resilient Children Resilient Communities; Violet Saena, Climate Resilient Communities; Michelle Colussi, Building Resilient Neighborhoods, BC; Luis Manriquez M.D. Assistant Clinical Professor, Washington State University College of Medicine; Amee Ravell, Asian Pacific Environmental Network; Mia Patricia and Chris Ausura, Rhode Island Health Equity Zone; Susan Silber, NorCal Resilience Network; The Rev. Paul Abernathy, Neighborhood Resilience Project; The late Terry Patton, Integral Psychologist; Norma Servin-Lacy, Northern Valley Catholic Social Service; Tina Pearson and J'vanete Skiva, New Hanover County Resilience Task Force; Linda Anderson Stanley, Equal Justice Works; Robin Saenger, Peace4Tarpon; Michelle Colussi, Victoria BC Building Resilient Neighborhoods, Dr. Ken Thompson, Visible Hands Collaborative; Jacqui Patterson, The Chisholm Legacy Project; Jane Stevens and Gail Kennedy, PACEs Connections; Eddie Garcia, Coalition to End Social Isolation and Loneliness; Fiona Garven, Director, Scottish Community Development Centre; Kosha Joubert, The Pocket Project in the EU; Dr. Antonis Kousoulis, Director for England and Wales, Mental Health Foundation; Dr. Jude Stansfield, Public Mental Health and Healthy Communities, Public Health England; Gavin Atkins, Head of Communities, Mind, UK; Isabel Young, The Young Foundation UK; Talia Levanon, Israel Trauma Coalition; and Lisa Petraschuk, Ministry of Health, New Zealand.

I also want to thank those engaged in some of the leading research used in this book. In addition to reviewing their research, many of these individuals took the time to speak with me about their work: Dr. William Eaton, Department of Mental Health, Johns Hopkins University Bloomberg School of Public Health; John McNight, ABCD Institute at DePaul University; Peter Block, the Abundant Community; Dr. Pauline Boss, author of *Ambiguous Loss*; Dr. Tony Biglan, Oregon Research Institute; Dr. Diana Fishbein, National Prevention

Science Coalition; Dr. Susan Clayton, College of Wooster; Helen Berry, inaugural Professor of Climate Change and Mental Health at the University of Sydney in Australia; and Dr. Michael Ungar, Director, Resilience Research Centre, Halifax Nova Scotia. The research completed by the Mobilizing Action for Resilient Communities (MARC) program (which includes some of the communities described in this book) and the Community and Regional Resilience Institute (CARRI) was also helpful. Please accept my sincere apologies if I forgot to include someone or an important piece of research in this list.

I would also like to thank the team that helped get the ITRC research into these issues off the ground in early 2019: Dr. Carissa Cabán-Alemán, Florida International University; Dr. Jura Augustinavicius, John's Hopkins University; Amélie Doyon and Alison Paul, Canadian Red Cross; Ea Suzanne Akasha International Red Cross Reference Centre for Psychosocial Support; Dr. Nicolas Bergeron, former President of Doctors of the World Canada; Dr. Sandra Bloom, Drexel University; Dr. Joseph Prewitt, American Red Cross; Amélie Doyon Canadian Red Cross; Dr. Erika Felix, University of Santa Barbara; Dr. Theopia Jackson, Saybrook University and Association of Black Psychologists; Dr. Katie Hayes, Health Canada; Dr. Maryam Kia-Keating University of California, Santa Barbara; Dr. Andrew McLean, University of North Dakota School of Medicine and Health Sciences; Alison Paul, Canadian Red Cross; Dr. Daryl M. Rowe Professor Emeritus, Pepperdine University; and Dr. Ruth Zúñiga, formerly with Pacific University.

A special call out goes to the members of the International Transformational Resilience Coalition (ITRC) National Steering Committee and Federal Policy Team who helped promote the need for community-based approaches to mental wellness and resilience, as well as policies to support and fund the initiatives: Laura Porter, ACEs Interface; Dr. Mandy Davis, Trauma Informed Oregon; Anna Lynn, State of Minnesota; Elaine Miller-Karas, Trauma Resource Institute; Dr. Howard Kurtzman, American Psychological Association (now retired); Dr. Patricia Foxen, formerly with UNIDOS U.S.; Steven Hoskinson, Organic Intelligence; Dr. Lise Van Susteren, Climate Psychiatry Alliance; Dr. David Pollack, Oregon Health Sciences University (Emeritus) and Climate Psychiatry Alliance; Dr. Natasha DeJarnett, University of Louisville; Surili Sutaria Patel, private consultant; Dr. Joseph Keller, formerly with the American Psychological Association; Tia Taylor Williams, Director, American Public Health Association; Cara Cook, Alliance of Nurses for Healthy Environments; Jesse Kohler, Campaign for Trauma Informed Policy and Practice (CTIPP); Dr. David Shern, CTIPP and National Association of State Mental Health Directors; Katherine Catalano, American Public Health Association; Scott Barstow and Corbin Bernstien, American Psychological Association; Lee Westgate, National Association of Social Workers. Dr. Elizabeth Hasse and others with the American Psychiatric Association also deserves great thanks. I want to give a special thanks to Sarah Butts with the National Association of Social Workers for the extra time and effort she gave to supporting our work and advancing community-based resilience-building programs and policies.

I want to personally thank Anna Moore, my editor at Routledge Publishing, for her continual support and helpful recommendations, Nancy Schenck who did the first edit of this book, and Kerry Lutz, who did the graphics.

Finally, I send my deepest appreciation to my best friend, playmate, love of my life, and wife of 38 years, Peggy Bloom, for the patience, support, and excellent editorial advice she provided throughout the entire process of writing this book.

Many thanks to all of you.

ABOUT THE AUTHOR

Bob Doppelt coordinates the International Transformational Resilience Coalition (ITRC), a global network of mental health, social service, climate, and other organizations committed to preventing and healing the mental health and psycho-social-spiritual problems generated by the climate emergency. He is trained in both counseling psychology (M.S.) and environmental science (M.S.) and has combined the two fields throughout his career. He is also a Graduate of the International Program on the Management of Sustainability, in Ziest, The Netherlands, and a Mindfulness-Based Stress Reduction Instructor. For many years, Bob directed the Climate Leadership Initiative at the University of Oregon, which was one of the first organizations in the US to assist private and public entities to develop climate mitigation and adaptation plans. He also taught systems thinking and global warming policy at the university. Through his work on climate adaptation, Bob realized that the mental health and psycho-social-spiritual impacts of the climate crisis were a major but largely unaddressed problem. This led him in 2013 to organize the ITRC. Due to his many years of work, in 2015, Bob was named one of the world's "50 Most Talented Social Innovators" by the World CRS Congress.

Bob is the author of a number of books on the interface between individual, group, community, and social change and ecological regeneration including:

- *Transformational Resilience: How Building a Culture of Human Resilience Can Safeguard Society and Increase Wellbeing* (2016, Routledge), which just months after publication was called "My go to book for hope" in *Psychology Today* in a post by Marc Bekoff PhD.
- *From Me to We: The Five Transformative Commitments Required to Rescue the Planet, Your Organization, and Your Life* (2012, Routledge).
- *The Power of Sustainable Thinking: How to Create a Positive Future for the Climate, The Planet and Your Life* (2008, Routledge), which in the summer of 2010 *Audubon Magazine* deemed one of the "eleven most important books on climate change."
- *Leading Change Toward Sustainability: A Change Management Guide for Business, Government, and Civil Society* (2003, Routledge), which just six months after publication was called one of the "ten most important publications in sustainability" by a GlobeScan survey of international sustainability experts.

Information about Bob Doppelt's books and activities can be found at: www.bobdoppelt.com

Information about the International Transformational Resilience Coalition (ITRC) can be found at: www.itrcoalition.org

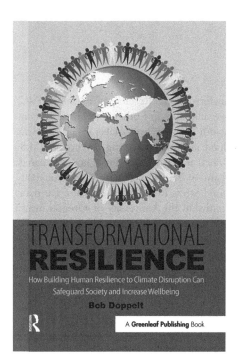

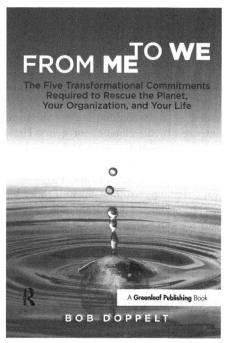

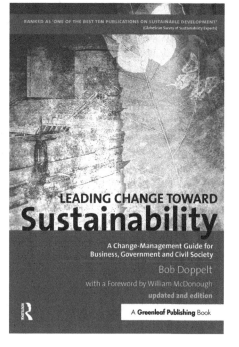

INTRODUCTION

The thermometer outside our home registered 85 degrees. We were in the midst of a record drought in western Oregon, and a Red Flag Warning was issued to beware of wildfires. This would have been normal had it been in late summer or fall when wildfire season historically occurs in the region. But it was only April 16, 2021, when 50-degree temperatures and pouring rain are the norm.

The surprising conditions put my wife, me, and our friends and neighbors on edge, fearful about what would happen as the spring gave way to summer and fall. During the previous September, the Holiday Farm wildfire incinerated the small town of Blue River and destroyed at least 400 homes and 20 commercial sites in the McKenzie River Valley, which is just a few miles from where we live.[1] Multiple wildfires burned throughout the state at the time, forcing more than 500,000 people—over 10 percent of the state's population—to evacuate.[2] Even in areas that were not facing immediate fire danger, wildfire smoke was a major threat, triggering "very unhealthy" air quality alerts that urged everyone to stay indoors to prevent respiratory health problems.[3]

After the wildfire ended, a number of residents of the McKenzie Valley developed severe anxiety, depression, and other mental health problems. Statewide, over 35 percent of first responders fighting the wildfires were at risk of developing post-traumatic stress disorder (PTSD). Other citizens throughout the state were also greatly distressed. As one Oregon resident told NBC News, "It's kind of hard to have good mental health days when your world is, literally, on fire."[4]

The alarming events that occurred in Oregon mirror the disruptions to the global climate system, regional weather patterns, and ecological systems happening across the US and worldwide, and the effects they have on people.[5] They show that everything is interconnected and that impacts in one system can produce cascading effects in many others.

On Earth Day 2021, just a week after the Red Flag Warning in Oregon, President Joe Biden boldly committed the US to slashing greenhouse gas emissions by 50 percent by 2030 compared with 2005 levels. Leaders from a number of other nations offered more modest commitments.[6] Although much needed, these pledges are coming very late in the game and, even if successful, will not prevent severe impacts to the planet and every aspect of society.

As they attempt to aggressively cut emissions, the US and all other nations must therefore make an equally bold commitment to rapidly prepare all adults and youth for the relentless psychological, emotional, and spiritual suffering generated in the new epoch we are entering that I call the "Traumacene."[7] This is the multi-decades or longer period in which individual, community, and societal distresses and traumas generated directly and indirectly by the climate emergency will occur on a scale never before seen in modern times.

This book explains how the widespread distresses and traumas generated during the long climate emergency can be prevented and healed by returning the responsibility for fostering mental wellness and resilience to neighborhoods and communities where it existed for most of human history and has the greatest chance of success.

DOI: 10.4324/9781003262442-1

It argues that, for decades, the dominant view held in the US and many other industrialized nations has been that mental health and psycho-social-spiritual problems result primarily from personal genetic, biological, or family dynamics. Accordingly, the chief antidotes have been fairly standard approaches to individual and family clinical treatments and direct human service programs delivered by licensed professionals. This work is typically done in isolation from the social, cultural, physical/built, economic, and ecological factors that overwhelming research shows play major roles in creating personal and family problems.

However, just as the climate emergency is often described as a "wicked" problem—one that results from numerous factors that interact in new and surprising ways to defy standard solutions—the pervasive distresses and traumas it generates are also "wicked" problems that cannot be resolved through conventional professionally delivered individualized clinical treatment services. That's because they result from multiple accumulating forces that interact in surprising ways to disrupt all aspects of human society. No standard individualized measures, and no single profession, organization, or program can prevent or heal these types of widespread problems.

Effective responses must be at the scale of the challenges that lie ahead. They must also address the interconnectedness of personal, family, social, economic, and ecological traumatic stressors. This means effective solutions will emerge only through ongoing interactions among a wide and diverse coalition of people. Those solutions must be based on first principles. The chief goal should be to prevent severe distresses and traumas during the long climate crisis by building population-level capacity for mental wellness and what I call transformational resilience. Methods to help people heal the psychological and emotional suffering they experience and regain their capacity for mental wellness and resilience should be embedded within the community prevention activities. Clinical treatment for severely traumatized individuals should complement and support the community prevention and healing activities, not be the dominant focus.

Accordingly, this book contends that entire neighborhoods and communities must be engaged to prevent and heal the distresses and traumas generated during the long climate mega-emergency. Local residents, groups, and organizations must come together to plan, implement, and continually improve age and culturally accountable, multipronged (or multisystemic) strategies that help *all* adults and youth enhance their capacity for mental wellness and transformational resilience during ongoing adversities. Actions to eliminate greenhouse gas emissions, adapt to climate impacts, and build more socially, economically, and ecologically healthy, safe, just, and equitable climate-resilient conditions should be integrated into these efforts to establish a holistic approach.

If whole-community initiatives are launched throughout industrialized nations and worldwide, the indomitable human spirit and capacity for resilience can be activated. People will realize they are inextricably connected to everyone and everything else and begin to care for each other and the planet. A powerful sense of collective purpose and efficacy will emerge that empowers people to create innovative ways to establish more just, equitable, and ecologically regenerative systems that, over time, reduce the climate crisis to manageable levels and restore humanity's faith in the future.

This book is written for:

- Community leaders striving to improve local health and wellness, address inequities and injustices, reduce violence or political polarization, or address the climate emergency and other challenges;

- Volunteer neighborhood and grassroots leaders seeking to enhance local social, economic, and ecological conditions;

- Mental health and other direct human service professionals focused on preventing and healing widespread mental health and psycho-social-spiritual problems;

- Educators seeking to teach students how to respond constructively to the climate emergency and other stressful situations and use adversities as learning opportunities;

- Disaster response, faith and spirituality, climate change and environmental leaders, and other professionals desiring to learn self-care skills and understand what they can do to prevent and heal mental health and psychosocial problems generated during emergencies;

- Students interested in learning how to enhance their capacity for mental wellness and transformational resilience and engage in actions that can meaningfully address the climate emergency and other challenges;

- Government personnel involved with efforts to enhance mental health, physical health, or social, economic, physical/built, and ecological conditions;

- Elected officials interested in programs and policies that can prevent and heal mental health, psycho-social-spiritual, and related physical health problems, or empower community members to establish healthy and safe and equitable local conditions.

ORIGINS OF THIS WORK

I was trained in both counseling psychology and environmental science.[8] My first professional job was counseling troubled youth and their families. After a few years, however, I felt the approaches I learned in graduate school were inadequate for the job. The dominant reason was that they focused only on the dynamics between parents and their children and neglected the historic and intergenerational, as well as ongoing economic, social, racial, and environmental traumas that interacted to produce family and child dysfunction.[9] These concerns, and the resulting burn out I experienced, led me to leave the mental health field and focus exclusively on ecological issues.

Twenty-five years later, I ended up directing the Climate Leadership Initiative (CLI), which was affiliated with the University of Oregon. During this time, the field of climate science was rapidly advancing, and I had the opportunity to interact with many top climate scientists.

The CLI initially focused on both climate mitigation, which is action to reduce greenhouse gas emissions, and climate adaptation, which is action to prepare for and adapt to the impacts of a disrupted climate system. We helped nonprofit, private, and public organizations throughout the US develop climate action plans and, like most other organizations working on these issues, we primarily focused on the external technological and physical changes involved with mitigation and adaptation.[10]

The limits of our work, however, and a glaring hole in the climate field as a whole, became evident to me after Hurricane Sandy slammed the East Coast of the US in 2012, producing high levels of severe anxiety, depression, PTSD, and other mental health problems.[11] I knew the climate emergency was going to get far worse and feared that unless we got ahead of these problems, millions of people in the US, and billions worldwide would experience significant distresses and traumas. This was of great concern because no other health problems come close to generating the extent and persistence of personal, family, social, economic, and political troubles as those caused by mental health and psycho-social-spiritual maladies.

In addition, I was concerned that the traumas generated by the impacts of the long climate crisis would activate a vicious cycle of frightened people further damaging the earth's ecological systems as they tried to protect themselves from climate impacts, which would circle back to increase the ecological damage that caused their stresses and traumas.[12]

Further, traumatized people can't resolve complex problems like the climate emergency. They tend to retreat into a self-protective survival mode that produces denial and dissociation and creates opposition to anything that seems threatening. Included can be things like changes in consumption patterns that will be needed to reduce greenhouse gas emissions and regenerate ecological systems. This made me worried that left unaddressed, widespread climate distresses and traumas would make the changes required to reduce the climate emergency to manageable levels all but impossible.

These concerns led me to reenter the mental health field, this time with a focus on how the direct and indirect impacts of the climate crisis would undermine individual and collective mental wellness and resilience, and how those impacts could be prevented and healed. I summarized my early work, which focused primarily on the benefit of everyone learning "Presencing" (or self-regulation) and "Purposing" (or adversity-based growth) skills in the book *Transformational Resilience: How Building Human Resilience to Climate Disruption Can Safeguard Society and Increase Wellbeing*,. I also organized the International Transformational Resilience Coalition (ITRC), a network of mental health, social service, climate, faith, and other organizations and individual professionals, to work on the issues.

During our first few years, the ITRC ran conferences and held workshops and webinars to raise awareness of the coming rush of climate change-generated mental health and psycho-social-spiritual problems. We also trained people in how to teach age and culturally appropriate resilience skills to others.[13] This work took place within the context of the existing mental health and social services systems of the US and other industrialized nations.

It eventually became evident, however, that the approaches that dominate these fields were shaped by narrow perspectives about the causes of, and solutions to, widespread mental health and psycho-social-spiritual problems. The limited assumptions and beliefs produced a crisis and illness-focused system operated by credentialed professionals who treat individuals and families, mostly one-at-a-time, only after they show symptoms of psychopathology, and often with medication.

No society, however, has ever fostered widespread mental wellness and resilience by merely fixing deficits or treating traumatized individuals one-at-a-time. And, a large body of research exists on the benefits of a more holistic approach that builds population-level—or universal—capacity to prevent and heal distresses and traumas. In the US, and most other industrial nations, however, the current system remains firmly rooted in the professionally run, individualized, deficit and pathology-based mental health treatment and direct human services approach.

This realization spurred an intensive two-year investigation into approaches that can enhance the entire population's capacity for psychological, emotional, and spiritual wellness and resilience during relentless climate adversities, as they engage in actions that help reduce the crisis to manageable levels. This book describes the findings.

THE LOOMING CLIMATE OVERSHOOT

The first step in grasping the need to rapidly shift the responsibility for preventing and healing mental health and psycho-social-spiritual problems back to communities is to come to grips with the reality that humanity is in the midst of a multi-faceted mega-emergency that will profoundly alter every aspect of civilization.

As will be described in greater detail in Chapter 1, average global temperatures have already risen by more than 1.8 degrees Fahrenheit (1.04 Celsius) since the Industrial Revolution began in the mid-1800s. The earth's surface temperatures have been getting progressively warmer during each of the last three decades, and July 2021 was the hottest month ever recorded in human history. Arctic summer sea ice has declined by about 40 percent since records began, and sea levels have been rising every year since the early 1990s.[14]

As the impacts seen worldwide already show, any temperature increase above pre-industrial levels harms people and the planet. Climate science has determined that if average global surface temperatures rise more than 2.7 degrees Fahrenheit (1.5 Celsius) above those of the mid-1700s, extremely grave and possibly irreversible impacts to the planet and society will be activated.[15] Scientists often call this "climate overshoot," which is the term I will use throughout this book.

Unfortunately, even if President Biden's efforts are successful and US emissions are quickly and significantly slashed—which will be a monumental challenge—numerous factors make it almost certain that temperatures will still overshoot the dangerous 2.7 degrees Fahrenheit (1.5 Celsius) threshold. The Intergovernmental Panel on Climate Change (IPCC) said in April 2022 that limiting warming to that level will require global emissions to peak within by 2025 and then be reduced by at least 43 percent by 2030.[16] Although this is technically possible, achieving it will be extremely difficult if not impossible because, as previously stated, the climate crisis is a wicked problem. Some problems are very challenging but can be resolved by applying standard interventions over a specific period of time. These can be considered "ordinary" problems. The global climate emergency, on the other hand, is a wicked problem because it has multiple causes that interact in ways that generate many known, and often even more surprising harmful impacts.

Humans have never dealt with this type of complex global issue before, so approaches developed to resolve previous, more limited social, economic, environmental, and political problems in many cases aren't very helpful. Every solution can adversely affect some population, sector, or nation, which makes it difficult to identify just and equitable responses or obtain the political consensus and firm commitments required to make meaningful changes. In addition, some proposed fixes end up producing unintended consequences that make things worse. And the ultimate benefits of many solutions will not be felt for a decade or more. This makes it very difficult to determine the effectiveness of many proposed remedies.[17]

Indeed, the authors of the IPCC 2022 report acknowledged that it *is* likely global temperatures will shoot beyond the 2.7 degrees Fahrenheit (1.5 Celsius) extreme danger threshold. In May 2022, just a month after the IPCC released its report, the World Meteorological Organization said there is almost a 50-50 percent chance that temperatures will at least temporarily overshoot the 2.7 degrees Fahrenheit (1.5 Celsius) extreme danger threshold within the next five years.[18] Other assessments have also determined that the overshoot is likely to occur before 2030, or soon afterward. Climate overshoot is thus imminent. When it occurs, it will continue for the decades or longer that it takes humanity to stop adding more greenhouse gases to the atmosphere, and remove a great deal as well, regenerate ecological systems that sequester carbon and support biodiversity, and cool global temperatures back down to manageable levels.[19]

Preventing temperatures from rising far above the 2.7 degrees Fahrenheit (1.5 Celsius) extreme danger threshold, and then bringing them back down to manageable levels many years in the future, is thus likely the best that global emission cutting efforts can now hope to achieve. Until this happens, we must plan for unrelenting harmful impacts.[20]

THE CLIMATE CRISIS MIXES CASCADING DISRUPTIONS TO ESSENTIAL SYSTEMS WITH MORE FREQUENT, EXTREME, AND PROLONGED DISASTERS

The COVID-19 pandemic offers a tiny preview of some of the consequences of the rapidly accelerating climate mega-emergency. As in the pandemic, continuous and often surprising compounding disruptions will occur in the ecological, social, and economic systems people rely on for food, water, power, shelter, jobs, incomes, health, safety, and other basic needs. These impacts will, at least initially, affect low-income populations, black and indigenous people of color (BIPOC), and older residents the hardest because they tend to live in more vulnerable locations, have limited resources available to protect themselves beforehand, and have fewer means to recover after an event. Soon, however, no one on the planet will be immune from the incessant pileups of often overwhelming and harmful—or toxic—psychological, emotional, and spiritual stresses generated by a disrupted climate system.

A small example is the historic heat wave that baked my town in the US Pacific Northwest in June 2021. I have a home orchard composed of apple, pear, and plum trees. The extreme heat burned about a third of the fruit so badly that they split open and had to be thrown away. My experience mirrored the research of the US Agriculture Department that found after the heat wave, 68 percent of Washington state's spring wheat and 36 percent of its winter wheat were in poor condition. The record heat also shriveled wheat kernels and reduced the nutrition level of some other crops.[21] Not only will the availability of wheat for food supplies be reduced, the incomes of farmers and the communities where they reside will be impacted. This illuminates that, as the climate emergency intensifies, the availability and costs of food, water, and other necessities will be affected, producing many types of toxic stresses for people everywhere.

Unlike the pandemic, however, the toxic stresses created by the climate crisis will be mixed with more frequent, extreme, or prolonged wind, rain, and snow storms, wildfires, heat waves, floods, droughts, and other acute disasters. Disasters can traumatize 20–40 percent of those who are directly impacted, 10–20 percent of disaster response workers, and 5–10 percent of the general population who are not directly affected but know someone who is or view the events from afar.[22]

Again, in the near term, low-income populations, BIPOC communities, single women with children, and older people will often be hardest hit by climate disasters. But as the climate emergency accelerates no one will be safe.

Between 2011–2021, more than 90 percent of Americans lived in a county that was affected by a climate change disaster. More than 656 people died due to disasters, and the financial cost totaled more than $104 billion (US). And this figure does not even include the exceedingly high costs of wildfires, extreme heat, and drought experienced in the western US.[23]

Disasters already directly impact more than 47 million Americans every year, and the Oakridge National Lab projects that number will at least double by 2050.[24] This indicates that one third or more of the US population will be directly impacted every year.

Similar numbers of people will be impacted in other nations.[25] The United Nations Office for the Coordination of Humanitarian Affairs, for example, projects that by 2050 over one billion people living in 31 countries will be severely impacted by disasters and other environmental catastrophes.[26] This projection is likely low as climate scientists have consistently found their models underestimate the impacts of a disrupted climate system.

More details will be provided in Chapter 1 about the impacts of the mixture of cascading disruptions to essential systems and acute disasters generated by the global climate crisis. What is important now is to realize there is little time left to prepare people for the impacts that will accelerate for years. If humanity remains unprepared, the psychological, emotional, and spiritual distresses and traumas, as well as the social, economic, ecological, and political harm they cause, will occur at levels no nation is prepared to address. The Traumacene will be in full force.

THE RESULT WILL BE WIDESPREAD DISTRESS AND INDIVIDUAL, COMMUNITY, AND SOCIETAL TRAUMAS

In a short post-script to his book *Man's Search for Meaning* titled *The Case for Tragic Optimism*, Holocaust survivor and Austrian psychologist Viktor Frankl suggested that the human experience will always include tragedy and grief.[27] Spiritual traditions such as Buddhism also emphasize that from the pain of childbirth to the loss of family and friends during our lives, and the inevitable death we all experience, life is filled with suffering.[28]

However, unless major initiatives are launched to prevent and heal them, the long climate emergency will generate tragedy, grief, and suffering on a scale that is far beyond anything that can be considered a normal part of human life. In many ways, this will require us to redefine what it means to experience mental health or psycho-social-spiritual problems.

Billions of people, for instance, are likely to experience heightened anxiety, depression, grief, anger, helplessness, hopelessness, and other forms of distress. Much of this, however, will be natural reactions to dysfunctional external conditions, not symptoms of psychological or emotional disorders. Rather than remaining focused on diagnostic labels the mental health field has established to understand and treat pathology, it will be essential to adopt an expanded approach that defines the distresses people experience during the long climate emergency as perfectly normal reactions to threatening conditions. Redirecting their distress with effective understanding, skills, and supports can motivate people to demand the transformational changes required to minimize the crisis.

In addition to great distress, the climate emergency is certain to produce adversities that will generate psychological, emotional, and spiritual maladies that mental health professionals currently define as trauma. As will be discussed in greater depth in Chapter 2, although there are different ways to define trauma, the effects of the Traumacene can be thought of as generating three interrelated types: individual, community, and societal.

Individual trauma can be defined as a psychological and emotional reaction to an event or series of events that a person perceives as threatening their physical, mental, social, or spiritual well-being.[29] This form of trauma overwhelms an individual's ability to cope and shatters their deeply held assumptions that the world is a relatively fair, orderly, and manageable place. These reactions can produce a range of harmful mental health and psycho-social-spiritual reactions.[30]

Community trauma can be thought of as an event, series of events, or conditions that produce not only widespread individual traumas, but also unhealthy, unsafe, and unjust social, cultural, economic, built/physical, and environmental conditions in a specific geographic area that traumatize everyone residing there.[31] Community trauma can also be defined as events that affect people with shared identities, such as Internet-based, religious or spiritual, or refugee groups. Like individual trauma, the impacts can undermine how the community views the world, and their sense of meaning, purpose, and hope for the future. The consequences can include widespread mental health and psycho-social-spiritual problems.

Societal trauma goes beyond a specific geographical area or group with a shared identity to affect entire cultures, nations, or humanity as a whole. The COVID-19 pandemic is an example. Just as individual and community traumas generate hopelessness that shatters the core assumptions and beliefs people hold about the nature of the world and their role in it, the societal trauma generated by the pandemic disrupted the way billions of people worldwide perceive the meaning of events and the purpose of their lives.[32] The consequences of the societal traumas generated by the long climate emergency will be immeasurably worse.

One of the greatest challenges in addressing these distresses and traumas will be the confusing nature of what is happening and how to respond. As the climate emergency worsens, people will in some ways feel they are dealing with challenging but ordinary events. A major windstorm or flood will occur, for example, and afterward people will go about repairing damaged facilities. If someone died during the event, they will hold a funeral ceremony and then bury the body or scatter the ashes. This ritual will help survivors come to terms with the reality that a permanent loss has occurred, the normal grieving process can begin, and then, they can move on with their lives.

At the same time, these same people will be dealing with never-before-experienced relentless compounding adversities caused by external forces that have no easy fix, closure, or end point. Those who survive a damaging windstorm or flood, for example, might soon experience another disaster, leaving them confused about whether to rebuild damaged structures because they could be destroyed again in the next disaster. As they deal with these confusing emotions, they might also experience food shortages or job losses, see their family and friends harmed by a climate disaster, or witness other calamities occurring elsewhere on TV or social media.

The uncertainty of what will happen next and the ambiguity of how to deal with the incessant adversities and losses caused by never-ending external forces that are out of their control will cause many people to feel hopeless and become immobile, frozen in grief. This is called complicated grief and it inhibits a person's ability to reach closure, complete the mourning process, and move on with their lives.[33] This is merely one of many examples of the "wicked" psychological, emotional, and spiritual consequences of the global climate crisis.

Unless we quickly expand the way widespread distresses and traumas are prevented and healed, the interactions between them will often be horrific. Again, the COVID-19 pandemic offers a modest example. The fear and grief caused by the sudden onslaught of virus-caused illnesses and deaths, constant worry about being infected, social isolation, lost jobs and incomes, school closures, and other impacts of the viral pandemic added to and aggravated many other festering toxic stresses to produce a pandemic of mental health and psycho-social-spiritual problems. The widespread social distress and disconnection people experienced intensified unresolved past traumas like historic racism and economic inequalities and created dangerous us-vs.-them polarization among people. In many locations, these forces have undermined social cohesion, produced socially unjust and inequitable norms, practices, and policies and led to interpersonal and institutional violence.

Left unaddressed, far more harmful reactions can be expected as global temperatures rise to extremely dangerous levels. Everyone's health, safety, security, and well-being will be undermined, as will the social efficacy required to slash emissions, restore ecological systems, and reduce global temperatures to manageable levels.

PREVENTING AND HEALING WIDESPREAD CLIMATE DISTRESS AND TRAUMAS REQUIRES NEW THINKING AND EXPANDED APPROACHES

After we realize that humanity is in the midst of a rapidly accelerating civilization-altering mega-emergency that will produce unprecedented scales and forms of harmful distresses and traumas, the next step is to determine whether the approaches that dominate the mental health and human services fields today can address these challenges. This requires examining the goals of the existing systems and the underlying assumptions and beliefs that produce them.

Some people believe that intense storms, wildfires, floods, and other disasters are the primary threats posed by the climate emergency and that improving disaster preparedness and disaster mental health programs should be the primary focus. Encouraging people to create emergency kits, plan escape routes, and in other ways prepare for disasters is important. But traditional approaches to disaster preparedness have not worked all that well.[34] One of the primary reasons is that they are typically disconnected from efforts to build the individual and collective resilience needed to prevent and heal the distresses and traumas generated by recurring adversities.

Disaster mental health interventions are designed to stabilize people during and immediately after single-event disasters that end and then give them time to recover. However, as temperatures overshoot the threshold that activates extremely dangerous impacts, people will be exposed to a relentless mixture of compounding disasters and toxic stresses that provide little or no time to recover. Even with improvements, disaster mental health programs are not designed to address these types of challenges.

Both disaster preparedness and disaster mental health programs will remain important, but will become much more effective if they become embedded within a far more comprehensive holistic approach.

As previously stated in most industrialized nations today, the dominant approaches to addressing mental health and psychosocial problems are for licensed professionals to treat individuals and families, mostly one-at-a-time, after they show symptoms of pathology, often with pharmacological treatments. This method is also utterly inadequate for the challenges that lie ahead.

There are many reasons why this is so. The COVID-19 pandemic, for instance, exposed the fact that the number of mental health professionals is already far less than the quantity needed to assist all the people who experience mental health problems. There will never be anywhere close to the total required to help the billions of people who will be traumatized as the climate crisis accelerates. Clinical treatment can also be expensive, and even people who have insurance often do not have sufficient funds to cover the co-pays. In addition, many people won't engage because they see therapy as only for the mentally impaired or weak, as a luxury for the rich, as conflicting with their religious or spiritual beliefs, or they fear being stigmatized if others learn they are in treatment. And most therapists are located in wealthier areas, not low-income communities or rural regions.

Further, in the US and other industrialized nations, most mental health diagnosis and treatments are shaped by the perspectives of white people and discount or completely ignore the emotional and spiritual dimensions of historic and intergenerational, as well as ongoing racial traumas. They also mostly ignore traditional healing methods that are fundamental to BIPOC residents. These omissions, combined with lower quality of care, lack of accessibility, racism, and other inequities drive disparities in many mental health and direct service systems that adversely affect BIPOC residents and produce deep-seated mistrust that causes many to reject involvement in the system.

In addition, clinical treatment and direct service professionals are trained first and foremost to focus on the individual in front of them. They diagnose that individual's symptoms and decide which treatment should be used. In contrast, the climate emergency will affect everyone and require responses that prevent and heal distresses and traumas experienced by the entire population, not just one person. We need to think and respond through a population lens, not an individual one.

Following from the above, the dominance of the expert-led individualized approach has caused most public and private philanthropic funds to be funneled to high-cost professional services, rather than to more cost-efficient community-based initiatives that help entire populations build and sustain their capacity for mental wellness and transformational resilience during persistent adversities. Almost all of the leaders of community-based initiatives I spoke with when completing the research for this book said lack of funding was the issue they struggled with the most. Yet, despite the monetary investment in professional services, few problems ever seem to be significantly reduced. This indicates that something beyond the professionally delivered clinical approach is needed.[35]

Most significant is that, as previously stated, the clinical treatment and direct service approaches assist individuals and families only after they show symptoms of pathology. They do not help everyone prevent mental health and psycho-social-spiritual problems before they occur.[36] Howard Lawrence, Coordinator of Abundant Community Edmonton operated by the City of Edmonton, Canada, which you will learn more about in the chapters to come, shared an analogy with me that might prove helpful here. Mental health and human service… "agencies are like a garage where people go to repair defective parts," he said. "Neighborhoods are like a garden where you tend the soil and grow everyone's capacity for health and wellness."[37]

To prevent and heal widespread mental health and psycho-social-spiritual problems generated by the climate emergency, we need to plant and nurture thousands of gardens—that is, actively engage neighborhoods and communities worldwide—not just "repair" individuals. (Note that in the remainder of this book when I will use the term "community," this should be interpreted to also include "neighborhoods.")

Please do not misinterpret these points. I'm not criticizing the purpose, intention, or importance of mental health and direct human service professionals or their organizations. I was trained as a counseling psychologist, have many friends in these fields, and know the people drawn to them have a deep desire to help others. The point is that unbeknown to many, the dominance of these expert-led approaches have today contributed to a profound shift in the way people view the causes of, and solutions to, mental health and psycho-social-spiritual problems. The result is that many now think they lack the capacity to prevent and heal their own psychological, emotional, and spiritual distress, and thus also discount the central role they, and their fellow neighborhood and community members, can play in preventing and healing the distresses and traumas others experience.

The noted pioneer in clinical psychology, Dr. George Albee, once said, "No epidemic has ever been resolved by paying attention to the treatment of the affected individual."[38] This will absolutely be true regarding the pending epidemic of mental health and psycho-social-spiritual problems generated by the climate crisis. To re-emphasize, as the climate emergency accelerates, clinical treatment and direct service programs will remain very important. But the fact that they have been the dominant approach for decades does not mean they should continue to dominate in the future. In fact, they will become much more effective if they become embedded within a much more comprehensive and holistic population-level approach.

The wicked problem of a disrupted climate system requires that the responsibility for preventing and healing mental health and psycho-social-spiritual problems be shifted back to neighborhoods and communities where they naturally belong and have the greatest likelihood to succeed. Broad-based collaborative approaches must be organized to foster and sustain everyone's capacity for mental wellness and resilience. This requires expanding the thinking, goals, and approaches beyond individualized treatments to empowering entire communities to continually engage in actions that help all adults and youth strengthen their capacity to prevent and heal distresses and traumas, as they also engage in actions that help reduce the climate emergency to manageable levels.

This is possible because, in my experience, people in communities all over the industrialized world are desperately searching for significant changes. They are just waiting to be asked to engage in something as big and meaningful as the problems they face. Converting responsibility from trained professionals back to neighborhoods and communities can create a powerful sense of collective purpose and social efficacy that empowers residents to build universal capacity to prevent and heal distresses and traumas and establish the health, safe, just, equitable, and ecologically regenerative conditions that so many know is needed and deeply desire.

TRANSFORMATIONAL RESILIENCE IS REQUIRED FOR THE CLIMATE EMERGENCY

Building a local culture in communities that builds universal capacity for mental wellness and resilience is not about helping people adjust to existing harmful or unjust conditions or "bounce back" to previous conditions after adversities. Research has found that when people have sufficient understanding, skills, social supports, resources, and other "protective factors," their innate capacity for resilience and self-healing can be activated. Positive learning, growth, and healthy hope can arise from events they previously perceived as distressing and traumatic.[39]

For this reason, as you have already read, when the term "resilience" is used throughout this book, I am referring to "Transformational Resilience." This is the capacity to transform the way we perceive and respond to distressing events by calming our body, mind, and emotions, and using the adversities as catalysts to move forward in life with new meaning, purpose, and healthy forms of hope.[40]

Transformational Resilience involves using painful experiences as learning opportunities to move beyond the way we perceived and dealt with adversities in the past to imagine and advance toward a new future that is substantially more constructive and positive than previous conditions. By focusing on transformational resilience, the indomitable human spirit and fierce determination can be activated to make what previously seemed impossible become reality. The climate crisis can inspire people to establish socially, economically, and ecologically healthy, just, and regenerative systems.

It is not easy, however, for an individual to develop this capacity on their own. It is as much, or more, the outcome of collective dynamics as it is one's personal capacities. This, again, points to why whole-community initiatives are needed, not just individualized interventions.

A PUBLIC HEALTH RESPONSE IS URGENTLY NEEDED

Mobilizing communities to "future-proof" everyone's capacity for transformational resilience for the incessant hardships generated by the wicked climate mega-emergency will require the use of a public health approach.[41]

A public health approach focuses on the entire population, not just those individuals deemed at high-risk or that show symptoms of psychopathology—although they must be given special supports and resources. It addresses health and social problems by fortifying existing protective factors and forming additional assets that help everyone push back against the forces that undermine their capacity for mental wellness and transformational resilience. It also prioritizes preventing problems, not merely treating them after they appear, by shifting norms, attitudes, habits, and behaviors that produce unhealthy outcomes.

In addition, a public health approach challenges people to view health and resilience from a holistic perspective. This means recognizing that most mental health and psycho-social-spiritual problems result from interactions occurring between personal, family, social, economic, physical/built, and ecological factors. The capacity for mental wellness and resilience cannot be separated from the conditions in which people live, work, and develop. This leads to the understanding that comprehensive multipronged strategies are needed to address the complex interrelated issues, not a few siloed and fragmented programs focused on single populations, issues, or geographic areas.

The growing interdisciplinary field of prevention science expands the public health perspective by showing that it is possible to prevent mental health and psycho-social-spiritual problems and that the capacity for wellness and resilience can be enhanced.

Further, there is a growing consensus that the most effective way to prevent and heal widespread distresses and traumas is to engage a broad and diverse set of individuals, groups, and organizations in communities—with a special emphasis on populations that are typically underrepresented or marginalized, or in other ways oppressed in jointly designing and implementing just and equitable, age and culturally appropriate activities that build a local culture of mental wellness and transformational resilience.

My research found that to achieve this goal will require a focus on five interconnected foundational areas. The five core areas include:

- Build robust social connections across geographic, economic, and cultural boundaries in communities.
- Ensure a "just transition" by creating healthy, safe, just and equitable climate-resilient local physical/built, economic, and ecological conditions.
- Cultivate universal literacy about mental wellness and resilience.
- Foster regular engagement in specific practices that support mental wellness and transformational resilience.
- Establish ongoing age and culturally appropriate opportunities for residents to heal their trauma.

These five foundational areas are interactive. They all should be emphasized when focusing on any particular one. Building social connections across cultural, economic, and geographic boundaries, for example, should also be a priority when community members engage in creating more equitable and just climate-resilient physical/built, economic, and ecological conditions, and when they participate in each of the other foundational areas. When taking this approach, the emphasis should be on bringing about new possibilities, not fixing deficits or treating individual symptoms of pathology.

THIS BOOK OFFERS A FRAMEWORK COMMUNITIES CAN USE TO BUILD UNIVERSAL CAPACITY FOR MENTAL WELLNESS AND TRANSFORMATIONAL RESILIENCE AS THEY ENGAGE IN CLIMATE SOLUTIONS

While there is increasing awareness of the need to expand to whole-community approaches to prevent and heal widespread distresses and traumas, until now no comprehensive framework has been offered to help people organize and operate these initiatives—especially as it relates to the long climate emergency. Although no community-based initiative addresses all of the five foundational areas, as I will describe in the chapters to come, my research found numerous ones in the US and other countries that focus on one or more of the key areas involved with an effective approach. I have brought all of the central focuses together into an inclusive framework—and plan of action—communities can use to establish the social infrastructure needed to build universal capacity for mental wellness and transformational resilience, as they also reduce their contribution to the climate crisis and prepare for and adapt to the impacts.

It is no longer possible to prevent relentlessly harmful climate impacts. The way out of the suffering people will experience is not to deny what is happening as this will only make things worse. The reality must be honestly recognized, the distresses and traumas it causes must be surfaced and released, and people must be helped to reframe the way they move through the challenging times that lie ahead. To achieve this, communities must be empowered to build a local culture that enables all residents to balance the ability to mourn what is lost with the recognition that it is still possible to live meaningful and fulfilling lives as they help heal the planet.

If this occurs, the global climate mega-emergency can become humanity's greatest teacher about what is required to live together on an ecologically finite planet. Billions of people can find new meaning, purpose, and healthy hope for the future, and many will be inspired to create innovative solutions to the climate crisis and the many challenges that result from it. The transformations that result can set humanity on a positive regenerative path.

THIS BOOK IS ORGANIZED INTO THREE SECTIONS

Part I describes why the responsibility for fostering mental wellness and transformational resilience must be returned to neighborhoods and communities to prevent and heal the distresses and traumas generated by the climate emergency and engage residents in solutions to the crisis.

Part II of this book describes, with examples, how to organize the social infrastructure in communities I call a Resilience Coordinating Coalition (RCC) needed to engage a wide and diverse set of individuals, groups, and organizations in designing, implementing, and continually improving actions that build universal capacity for mental wellness and transformational resilience.

Part III of this book goes into detail, with examples, about how RCCs can engage residents in each of the five interrelated foundational areas involved with building universal capacity for mental wellness and transformational resilience.

The Conclusion describes what will be needed to build a global movement to enhance population-level capacity for mental health and transformational resilience for the climate emergency.

With this information as background, let's dive into the issues.

NOTES

1 Duvernay A. (September 24, 2020). Coming home after the fire, many find much of McKenzie Valley unrecognizable. *The Register Guard*. Obtained at: https://www.registerguard.com/story/news/2020/09/24/coming-home-after-holiday-farm-fire-residents-find-little-left-standing/3502983001/

2 AP News. (September 20, 2020). *Latest: 500,000 People in Oregon Forced to Flee Wildfires*. Obtained at: https://apnews.com/article/kate-brown-fires-us-news-wa-state-wire-ca-state-wire-8e4e0818146a72c713de625e902f9962

3 Penaloza M. (September 14, 2020). 'It's A Bit Surreal': Oregon's air quality suffers as fires complicate COVID-19 fight. *National Public Radio*. Obtained at: https://www.npr.org/2020/09/14/912701172/its-a-bit-surreal-oregon-fights-smoke-from-record-wildfires-during-a-pandemic

4 KLCC Radio. (February 23, 2021). Impacts of wildfires affecting resident's mental health. (October 3, 2020). *NBC News*. Obtained at: https://www.nbcnews.com/news/us-news/impact-wildfires-affecting-residents-mental-health-n1241752; other information obtained from '*What Destruction Feels Like*,' *PTSD Takes Heavy Toll on First Responders*. Obtained at: https://www.klcc.org/disasters-accidents/2021-02-23/what-destruction-feels-like-ptsd-takes-heavy-toll-on-first-responders

5 See, for example, the new report by U.S. EPA (May 2021). *Climate Change Indicators in the U.S.* Obtained at: https://www.epa.gov/climate-indicators

6 Mason J. and Volcovici V. (April 23, 2021). U.S., other countries deepen climate goals at Earth Day Summit. *Reuters*. Obtained at: https://www.reuters.com/article/us-global-climate-summit-idAFKBN2C9198

7 I am indebted to Eric Garza who, to my knowledge, was the first person to use the term "Traumacene" in his article *Awakening to the Traumacene* which was published in *Age of Awareness* in May 29, 2019. Obtained at: https://medium.com/age-of-awareness/awakening-to-the-traumacene-8d5dcb92ea7f

8 In the mid-1970s I received an M.S. in Counseling Psychology (with a focus on family therapy) and an M.S. in Recreation and Park Management (which at that time was one of the few degrees focused on ecology) from the University of Oregon.

9   This issue was brought home to me when I was charged with counseling a Native American teen who had a history of crime and threatened to kill someone. His father was imprisoned for murder, his mother was an alcoholic, and he grew up in a tribal area with extremely high poverty. I had learned nothing in my counseling psychology graduate program that helped me understand or know how to offer meaningful assistance for the intergenerational or current traumas the teen experienced.

10 Among other activities, the UO Climate Leadership Initiative that I directed worked with the U.S.F.S. PNW Research Station to complete the first climate impact assessment for the State of Oregon, helped organize the Southeast Florida Regional Climate Change Compact, established the American Society of Adaptation Professionals (ASAP), created the Climate Masters program, hosted the Climate Access communications forum, completed leading edge research, and engaged in many other initiatives as well.

11 Schwartz R.M. et al. (2015). The impact of Hurricane Sandy on the mental health of New York area residents. *American Journal of Disaster Medicine*. Obtained at: https://www.wmpllc. org/ojs/index.php/ajdm/article/view/304; and Calma J. (2017). How New York City is tackling a mental health crisis spurred by Hurricane Sandy. *Grist*. Obtained at: https://grist. org/article/how-new-york-city-is-tackling-a-mental-health-crisis-spurred-by-hurricane-sandy/

12 This fear has proven accurate as, for example, government agencies and landowners fearful of wildfires cut down the forests near them, which releases carbon into the atmosphere, dries out the soil, harms biodiversity, diminishes the capacity to carbon sequestration, and worsens the climate emergency.

13 The International Transformational Resilience Coalition (ITRC): http://www.theresourceinnova-tiongroup.org/intl-tr-coalition

14 National Oceanic and Space Administration. (August 13, 2021). *It's Official: July Was the Earth's Hottest Month on Record*. Obtained at: https://www.noaa.gov/news/its-official-july-2021-was-earths-hottest-month-on-record

15 Carbon Brief. (December 2020). *Analysis: When Might the World Exceed 1.5C and 2C of Global Warming*. Obtained at: https://www.carbonbrief.org/analysis-when-might-the-world-exceed-1–5c-and-2c-of-global-warming

16 Intergovernmental Panel on Climate Change (2022). *Climate Change 2022: Mitigation of Climate Change*. Obtained at: https://report.ipcc.ch/ar6wg3/pdf/IPCC_AR6_WGIII_SummaryForPolicymakers.pdf

17 Murtugudde R. (December 2019). 10 reasons why climate change is a 'Wicked' problem. *The Wire*. Obtained at: https://thewire.in/environment/climate-change-wicked-problem

18 World Meteorological Organization. (May 9, 2022). *WMO Update: 50:50 Chance of Global Temperature Temporarily Reaching 1.5°C Threshold in Next Five Years*. Obtained at: https://public.wmo. int/en/media/press-release/wmo-update-5050-chance-of-global-temperature-temporarily-reaching-15%C2%B0c-threshold

19 Kaoru T. et al. (2019). *Effects on the Earth System of Realizing a 1.5 C Warming Climate Target after Overshooting to the 2C Level*. Environmental Research Letters. Obtained at: https://ui.adsabs.harvard. edu/abs/2019ERL....14l4063T/abstract

20 Intergovernmental Panel on Climate Change (2022). *Climate Change 2022: Mitigation of Climate Change*. Obtained at: https://report.ipcc.ch/ar6wg3/pdf/IPCC_AR6_WGIII_SummaryForPolicymakers.pdf

21 Ingwersen J. (July, 2021). 'Wither Away and Die:' U.S. Pacific Northwest heat wave bakes wheat, fruit crops. *Reuters*. Obtained at: https://www.reuters.com/world/us/wither-away-die-us-pacific-northwest-heat-wave-bakes-wheat-fruit-crops-2021-07-12/

22 Goldman E. and Sandro G. (March 2014). Mental health consequences of disasters. *Annual Review of Public Health*. Obtained at: https://www.annualreviews.org/doi/abs/10.1146/annurev-publhealth-032013-182435

23 James C. K. (January 2002). More than 4 in 10 Americans live in counties affected by climate disasters in 2021. *EcoWatch*. Obtained at: https://www.ecowatch.com/americans-climate-disasters-2021.html

24 The Oakridge National Lab. (May 2020). *Simulations Forecast Nationwide Increase in Human Exposure to Extreme Climate Events*. Obtained at: https://www.ornl.gov/news/simulations-forecast-nationwide-increase-human-exposure-extreme-climate-events#

25 Asia Development Bank. (2015). *Global Increase in Climate Related Disasters*. Obtained at: https://www. adb.org/publications/global-increase-climate-related-disasters

26 Reliefweb. (September 2020). *Ecological Threat Register 2020*. UN Office for the Coordination of Humanitarian Affairs. Obtained at: https://reliefweb.int/report/world/ecological-threat-register-2020

27 Frankl V. (2006). *Man's Search for Meaning. The Case for a Tragic Optimism*. Boston, MA: Beacon Press.

28 For decades I have been immersed in Buddhist philosophy and practices.

29 American Psychological Association. (2013). *Recovering Emotionally from Disaster: Understanding the Emotions and Normal Responses that Follow a Disaster or Other Traumatic Event Can Help You Cope with Your Feelings, Thoughts, and Behaviors.* Obtained at: https://www.apa.org/topics/disasters-response/recovering

30 Janoff-Bulman R. (1992). *Shattered Assumptions: Towards a New Psychology of Trauma.* New York, NY: Free Press.

31 Substance Abuse and Mental Health Services Administration. (2014). A treatment improvement protocol: Trauma-informed care in behavioral health services. Obtained at: https://pubmed.ncbi.nlm.nih.gov/24901203/

32 Vollhardt J.R. (2012). "Collective victimization" in *Oxford Handbook of Intergroup Conflict*, ed. Tropp L. Oxford, UK: Oxford University Press.

33 Shear K. (2012). Grief and mourning go awry: pathway and course of complicated grief. *Dialogues of Clinical Neuroscience;* and Shear K., *Managing Grief after Disaster.* U.S. Department of Veterans Affairs. Obtained at: https://www.ptsd.va.gov/professional/treat/type/manage_grief_disaster.asp#four

34 See for example: Uscher-Pines L. et al. (June 29, 2012). *Why Aren't Americans Listening to Disaster Preparedness Messages?* Rand Corporation Blog: https://www.rand.org/blog/2012/06/why-arent-americans-listening-to-disaster-preparedness.html

35 I am indebted to John McKnight and Peter Block for pointing this out to me in conversations I had with each of them in 2021. They are the authors of numerous books and articles on this and other important related topics. For more information see: https://www.peterblock.com/; and https://johnmcknight.org/

36 See for example: Stoerkel E. (2020). What is a strength-based approach? (Incl. activities and examples), *PositivePsychology.com*; Saul J. (2014). *Collective Trauma Collective Healing.* London and New York, NY: Routledge Publishing; and the large body of research on Positive Psychology.

37 Personal communication January 30, 2021.

38 Albee G. W. (1983). Psychopathology, prevention, and the just society. *Journal of Primary Prevention*, 4(1), 5–40.

39 See, for example: Joseph S. (2013). *What Doesn't Kill Us: The New Psychology of Post-Traumatic Growth.* New York, NY: Basic Books.

40 As described in my book: Doppelt B. (2016). *Transformational Resilience: How Building Human Resilience for Climate Disruption Can Safeguard Society and Increase Wellbeing.* London and New York, NY: Routledge.

41 To my knowledge the phrase "future-proof wellbeing" mental wellness was first used by Mungi N. et al. (2012). *The Wellbeing and Resilience Paradox.* The Young Foundation UK. Obtained at: https://youngfoundation.org/wp-content/uploads/2012/10/The-Wellbeing-and-Resilience-Paradox.pdf

PART I

A Public Health Approach is Required to Build Population-Level Capacity for Mental Wellness and Transformational Resilience for the Long Climate Emergency

INTRODUCTION TO PART I

Until mental health and psycho-social-spiritual problems significantly increased during the COVID-19 pandemic, most nations downplayed the magnitude and significance of the psychological and emotional troubles their citizens experienced. People who exhibited symptoms of problems were often ignored or shunned by family, friends, and society at large. When individuals who exhibit symptoms of problems could no longer be overlooked, they were encouraged to get treatment from a licensed mental health professional. However, due to a vastly insufficient number of trained clinicians, the high cost of services, where they are located in the US, and other factors even in the best of times, only about a third of the people who needed mental health treatment were able to obtain it.

The COVID-19 pandemic then came along and caused suffering to visibly skyrocket. In the US, as the fears of being infected, toxic social isolation, job and income losses, and other traumatic stresses caused by the pandemic persisted, the number of people who experienced mental health and psycho-social-spiritual problems could no longer be ignored. Demand for services climbed sharply, as did related drug and alcohol problems and deaths. Mental health and substance abuse treatment systems became so overtaxed that just 10 percent of the people who needed assistance could receive it. Indeed, as I write this in the summer of 2022, the US mental health system appears to be nearing a breaking point.

Rather than innovating and developing new and expanded ways to prevent and heal mental health and psycho-social-spiritual problems, major mental health and human services organizations urged the Biden Administration and Congress to provide additional funding to expand what they were already doing. Training more clinicians and providing greater access to treatment services will help more people. However, doing more of the same cannot address the scale and scope of the psychological and emotional problems Americans experience. Many other nations find themselves in similar situations.

These problems will become far worse as the global climate mega-emergency accelerates. Unless industrialized nations quickly expand their approach to preventing and healing mental health and psycho-social-spiritual problems beyond individualized treatment, the combination of climate-generated disruptions to ecological, social, and economic systems everyone relies on for basic needs, and more frequent, extreme, and prolonged disasters will produce unprecedented assortments and magnitudes of individual, community, and societal distresses and traumas. The method that is urgently needed is a public health approach to mental health, and Part I of this book goes into detail about why this is needed and what it involves.

DOI: 10.4324/9781003262442-2

Chapter 1 describes how human activities produced what is actually a "climate-ecosystem-biodiversity emergency" and how in short order it will alter every system, structure, and function of human civilization. Chapter 2 then describes the psychological, emotional, spiritual, and behavioral problems generated by those impacts that will produce a pandemic of individual, community, and societal distresses and traumas if expanded approaches are not rapidly instituted to prevent and heal them. Chapter 3 goes on to describe the principles and practices involved with a public health approach that engages whole neighborhoods and communities in activities that strengthen the entire population's capacity for mental wellness and transformational resilience for unrelenting traumas and toxic stresses as they engage in solutions to the climate mega-emergency.

CHAPTER 1

Climate Overshoot "101"

Intense. Prolonged. Record-breaking. Unprecedented. Abnormal. Dangerous. That was how the US National Weather Service described the event.[1] "We are not meant for this" is what Jay Inslee, the Governor of Washington State, told MSNBC news.[2]

Just ten weeks after the alarming red-flag wildfire warning was issued in mid-April for the part of western Oregon where I live, record-smashing heat engulfed the US Pacific Northwest and British Colombia in Canada.

For three consecutive days in late June, temperatures climbed to over 100 degrees Fahrenheit (37.7 Celsius), 30 degrees hotter than normal for that time of year. It hit 111 degrees on the second day, June 27, in my hometown, far and away the hottest temperature ever recorded. Portland, Oregon, reached an all-time high of 116 degrees.

Hundreds of people died because of the extreme heat. Most of the small town of Lytton, BC, burned to the ground, and residents were forced to flee their homes at a moment's notice, many without any belongings.[3]

Soon afterward, scientists released a report declaring that human-induced climate disruption made the off-the-charts heat "at least 150 times more likely to happen." They also said it may have been triggered by an unexpected "nonlinear" climate response that was compounded by the record regionwide drought.[4] "I think it's by far the largest jump in the record that I have ever seen," said Fredi Otto, a University of Oxford climate researcher who coauthored the study. "It was way above normal bounds," said Geeta Jan van Oldenborgh, another coauthor from the Royal Dutch Meteorological Institute. He added, "If global warming has pushed the climate past the heat wave tipping point, we are worried about these things happening everywhere."[5]

Indeed, these types of never-before-seen temperature extremes and other weird, abrupt, and intense weather events are occurring at alarming rates all around the globe. This book is not about climate science. But it is important for you to understand what is happening so you can clearly grasp the need to quickly build universal capacity for mental wellness and transformational resilience and connect those efforts with actions that reduce the climate crisis to manageable levels.

The information that follows is likely to be disturbing and cause you to stop reading. But I urge you not to deny or dissociate from it, as you will repeat the reactions millions of people have had that produced our current predicament. Please take some deep breaths as you read it to calm yourself, think about the implications, and consider how you can help address the challenges speeding our way in your home, professional life, and community.

DRIVERS OF CLIMATE OVERSHOOT

Back in 1859, Irish scientist John Tyndall discovered how what we now call greenhouse gases work. Building on previous discoveries, he showed that gases such as carbon dioxide absorb thermal radiation in the atmosphere and emit them in many directions, including

DOI: 10.4324/9781003262442-3

back toward the earth. The gases form an insulating blanket around our planet that retains warmth.

Almost 40 year later, in 1896, Swedish physicist/chemist Svante Arrhenius found that burning fossil fuels would add carbon dioxide to the atmosphere and thicken the insulating blanket of gases that surround the earth.[6] Thus, for well over a century, humans have known about the greenhouse effect, which is what happens when human activities release carbon dioxide and other gases into the Earth's atmosphere and, much like a greenhouse, trap more heat radiating from Earth back toward space, increasing surface temperatures.

Carbon dioxide (CO_2) is the most common greenhouse gas and the most long-lived cause of the climate emergency. It is released through natural processes such as respiration and volcanic eruptions. However, human activities such as burning fossil fuels, deforestation, and land use changes have generated about 75 percent of the additional CO_2 that is now warming the earth's atmosphere.[7]

Methane (CH_4) is another greenhouse gas that, per unit of mass, is about 80 times stronger than carbon dioxide over a 20-year period and 28 or more times as powerful over 100 years in trapping heat when it reaches the atmosphere.[8] However, it does not remain there as long as CO_2. Methane is produced through natural sources such as the decay of organic waste and ruminant digestion and human activities including the decomposition of wastes in landfills and agriculture practices such as rice cultivation and domestic livestock manure management. CH_4 has accounted for about 15 percent of anthropogenic warming.[9]

Another influential greenhouse gas is nitrous oxide (N_2O). It is produced by the natural circulation of nitrogen among the atmosphere, plants, animals, and microorganisms that live in soils and water. It is also produced by human activities with the most impactful being the use of nitrogenous fertilizers, as well as fossil fuel combustion, nitric acid production, and biomass burning.

Chlorofluorocarbons (CFCs) are still other potent greenhouse gases that disrupt the Earth's climate system. They are human-made synthetic compounds generated by industrial activity for use in several applications, such as air-conditioning, refrigeration, blowing agents in foams, insulations and packing materials, propellants in aerosol cans, and solvents. The production and release of many CFCs are now largely being phased out due to regulations by international agreements because of their impact on the Earth's ozone layer.

Some air pollutants are also disrupting the Earth's climate. Pollution from vehicle exhaust, smokestacks at factories, refineries, chemical plants, power plants, and emissions from agriculture and other sources produce ground-level ozone. Ozone pollution, or smog, can also result from paints, cleaners, solvents, and motorized lawn equipment. One of the impacts is that ozone pollution created in the Northern Hemisphere is transported toward the Arctic during winter and spring months, warming the region.[10]

The concentration of carbon dioxide, methane, and nitrous oxide that naturally occur in the Earth's atmosphere, together with water vapor, has for the past 12,000 years kept surface temperatures at just the right level to allow civilization as we know it to develop. However, the massive amounts of these and other greenhouse gases humanity has released into the atmosphere since the industrial revolution began in the mid-1700s and especially since the end of World War II, has intensified the greenhouse effect so much that the Earth's climate system, as well as ecological systems and the biodiversity they support, are now being profoundly disrupted.[11]

No relief is in sight. Despite much of the world spending at least part of 2020 under lockdown or working from home due to the COVID-19 pandemic, global greenhouse gas levels reached a record high that year. US emissions rose by 6.2 percent the following year.[12] Humanity now generates over 50 billion tons of greenhouse gas emissions annually.[13] The current level of atmospheric carbon dioxide is 50 percent higher than it was before the Industrial Revolution began, and levels haven't been this high in three to five million years, when average global temperatures were 3.6–5.4 degrees Fahrenheit (2–3 degrees Celsius) warmer than today.[14]

It is important to know that climate science has unequivocally determined that solar activity, volcanic eruptions, and natural variations have played little to no role in disrupting the Earth's climate system. It is the staggering increase of atmospheric greenhouse gases and the degradation of ecosystems that sequester carbon (more about this to come) that are disrupting the planet's climate system and heating up the earth.[15]

THE CURRENT TEMPERATURE RISE IS ALREADY PRODUCING RECORD IMPACTS GLOBALLY

The atmospheric warming Arrhenius predicted is now evident. In 2021, the excessive human production of greenhouse gases had caused global average surface temperatures to rise by slightly more than 1.8 degrees Fahrenheit (1.04 degree Celsius) above preindustrial levels. The average, however, obscures the fact that temperatures have not increased uniformly across the globe. More than one-fifth of the world's population lives in regions that have already experienced warming of more than 2.7 degrees Fahrenheit (1.5 Celsius) for one or more seasons.

A rise in temperatures of a few degrees might not seem like a big deal. But just like in the human body, a small increase in temperatures has major impacts on the Earth. During the Mesozoic era, for instance, which was the age of the dinosaurs, average temperatures were only about 7.2 degrees Fahrenheit (4 Celsius) warmer than today, crocodiles lived in what we now call the Arctic Circle, and no ice caps existed on the planet.[16]

The current 1.8 degrees plus Fahrenheit (1.04 Celsius) temperature increase is already causing serious damage worldwide. In May 2021, for example, the US Environmental Protection Agency (EPA) issued a report documenting how climate disruption is making life harder for Americans by threatening their health, safety, homes, and communities. "There is no small town, big city, or rural community that is unaffected by the climate crisis," said Michael Regan, the EPA administrator. "Americans are seeing and feeling the impacts up close, with increasing regularity."[17]

Regan's comment applies globally as well. Europe experienced its hottest summer ever recorded in 2021, and temperatures in the Mediterranean smashed previous records by large margins.[18] In July of that year, record flooding in Germany and Belgium killed at least 150 people.[19] Climate scientists determined the floods were up to nine times more likely because of climate disruption.[20] Australia experienced its hottest June on record in 2021—despite being hit with a blast of cold arctic air during the same month.[21] Record-shattering floods have occurred in South America and Southeast Asia. Devastating cyclones have occurred in Africa, South Asia, and the West Pacific. Due to climate disruption, Africa is experiencing food insecurity, population displacement, and great stress on water resources, along with devastating floods and an invasion of desert locusts.[22] I completed this book in mid-summer of 2022, and by the time it is published, there are certain to be many more record-damaging events driven by the climate mega-emergency.

In March 2022, the Intergovernmental Panel on Climate Change (IPCC) issued its gravest warning yet, stating that "The cumulative scientific evidence is unequivocal: Climate change is a threat to human well-being and planetary health." The report said that unless drastic cuts in greenhouse gases swiftly occur, the Earth will warm by 4.3 degrees Fahrenheit (2.4 Celsius) to 6.3 degrees Fahrenheit (3.5 Celsius) by the end of the century.[23]

Further, the IPCC report said that with every one-tenth of a degree rise in human-caused warming, more people will die, and unless human-caused warming is limited to just a couple of tenths of degrees more, the Earth will degrade in 127 different ways, with some being "potentially irreversible."[24]

To restate this: *ANY* increase in global temperatures from this point forward will cause more deaths and destroy more of the ecological systems that make life possible and unfortunately, temperatures will continue to rise.

THE COMMITMENTS OF THE PARIS CLIMATE ACCORD WILL NOT PREVENT CLIMATE OVERSHOOT

In December 2015, the Paris Agreement was signed by 196 Parties as a legally binding international treaty on climate change. It aims to limit warming to "well below" 3.6 degrees Fahrenheit (2 Celsius), while pursuing efforts to keep temperature below 2.7 degrees Fahrenheit (1.5 Celsius) compared with preindustrial levels. The emission reduction commitments of the signers, however, come nowhere close to the amount needed to limit global temperatures to those levels. And the Paris Agreement includes no concrete or enforceable measures to reduce emissions.

Further, the 3.6 degrees Fahrenheit (2 Celsius) limit is a purely political goal that is open to negotiations, not a scientific target. In contrast, scientists have determined that the rise in average global surface temperatures must be limited to no more than 2.7 degrees Fahrenheit (1.5 Celsius) above preindustrial levels. This is a firm scientific cap. Any temperature rise beyond this will generate relentless damaging and possibly irreversible impacts to the planet and society.[25] This was affirmed by one of the world's foremost climate scientists, Johan Rockström, the director of the Potsdam Institute for Climate Impact Research who said, "A rise of 1.5 C is not an arbitrary number, it is not a political number. It is a planetary boundary."[26]

Unfortunately, as stated in the Introduction, temperatures are now almost certain to overshoot that threshold (I include the word "almost" only because the future can never be completely known. However, most climate scientists will privately say there is no chance of preventing climate overshoot, while publically they try to present a somewhat rosier picture). The growth rate of global emissions slowed from 2.1 percent in the early part of this century to 1.3 percent between 2010 and 2019. But this means emissions are still rising, not dropping, just at a somewhat slower rate. The IPCC 2022 report voiced "high confidence" that unless global emissions are cut by 43 percent by 2030, temperatures will shoot beyond the 2.7 degrees Fahrenheit (1.5 Celsius) threshold. The co-chair of the IPCC's report, James Skea, told the Associated Press: "If we continue acting as we are now, we're not even going to limit warming to 2 degrees [Celsius], never mind 1.5 degrees."[27]

Just a month later, in May 2022, the World Meteorological Organization issued a startling report stating there is a 50-50 chance that temperatures will overshoot the ominous 2.7 degrees Fahrenheit (1.5 Celsius) threshold within the next five years, with the likelihood increasing with time.[28] They also said there is a 93 percent likelihood that least one year between 2022 and 2026 will become the warmest on record.[29]

One of the reasons is that carbon dioxide can stay in the atmosphere for hundreds of years. In addition, there is up to a 40-year delay between when emissions enter the atmosphere and temperatures rise. The 2021 report by the Intergovernmental Panel on Climate Change said that even under their lowest emission scenario, global surface temperatures will continue to increase until "at least" mid-century.[30]

Research has also determined that, based on capacity, 49 percent of the fossil-fuel-burning energy infrastructure now in operation worldwide has been installed just since 2004. Because of the size of the financial investments involved, most facilities stay in operation for at least 40 years. This makes it unlikely the facilities will be shut down and their emissions curtailed in time to prevent climate overshoot.[31]

Further, even if the US and other nations meet their new greenhouse gas reduction goals—which, unfortunately, is a very big if—humanity will merely be slowing, not halting the release of emissions into the atmosphere, let alone removing large quantities of what we have added., As I will discuss in a moment, this will also be necessary to limit warming to 2.7 degrees Fahrenheit (1.5 Celsius) above preindustrial levels.

The US generated almost 6,000 million tonnes of emissions in 2005.[32] While very important, reducing this by 50 percent in ten years as President Biden pledged to do will mean the US will still release significant amounts of greenhouse gases into the atmosphere every year for the next decade and add 3,000 million metric tons even in 2030.

THE BATHTUB ANALOGY EXPLAINS THE DYNAMICS

The "bathtub analogy" developed by Dr. John Sterman from the Massachusetts Institute of Technology helps explain what is happening.[33] The Earth's atmosphere operates much like a bathtub. The faucet puts water (in this case greenhouse gases) into the tub (the atmosphere). A drain (in this case ecological processes that sequester carbon) removes the water (greenhouse gases) from the tub (the atmosphere). The tub will eventually overflow if the amount of water entering the tub is greater than the amount emptying out the drain. Similarly, the tub will empty only if the water is discharged faster than addition water is added through the faucet.

Today, human activities are putting massive amounts of greenhouse gases into the tub while at the same time reducing the capacity of the drain to remove it by degrading the capacity of vegetation, soils, and the oceans to sequestration it. The tub therefore keeps filling and warming the planet. When the water spills over the top of the bathtub—that is, when emissions rise so high that they cause temperatures to overshoot the 2.7 degrees Fahrenheit (1.5 Celsius) extreme danger threshold—all life on earth will be profoundly and possibly permanently disrupted (Figure 1.1).

To reiterate, the excessive levels of emissions in the bathtub are already causing series harm worldwide, and every small rise in quantity will produce more deaths and destruction. It is also now almost certain that the bathtub will overflow this decade or soon thereafter. No matter when it occurs, climate overshoot will likely continue for decades or even centuries, until humanity makes the changes required to cool temperatures back down to manageable levels.[34] Life will not end. But with each slight increase in temperatures, everyone will experience more traumas and toxic stresses, and for many people, conditions will become life-threatening.

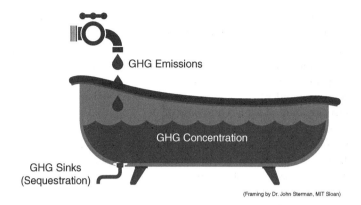

Figure 1.1 Greenhouse Gas (GHG) Bathtub Analogy

Reducing the climate emergency to a manageable level will be even more challenging than one might imagine because the rise in global temperatures is linked to the worldwide degradation of ecological systems and extinction of biodiversity. The US National Academy of Science said, "Climate disruption is transforming ecosystems on an extraordinary scale, at an extraordinary pace. As each species responds to its changing environment, its interactions with the physical world and the organisms around it change, too. This triggers a cascade of impacts throughout the entire ecosystem."[35]

These impacts are contributing to what most biologists agree is the human-caused "sixth mass biological extinction event" that is now underway.[36] Some researchers have projected that under the current emission path, abrupt "collapses of ecosystems" and "catastrophic" biodiversity loss will begin before 2030 in tropical oceans and then spread to higher latitudes.[37] From food production to ample supplies of clean air and water, the impacts will affect every aspect of society.[38]

In addition, the degradation of ecological systems and depletion of biodiversity diminishes the capacity of trees, grasses, and other plants to sequester carbon dioxide through photosynthesis and store it in tree trunks, branches, foliage, roots, and soils. This activates chain reactions that feed back to increase atmospheric carbon.

To be completely accurate, then, the looming climate overshoot is caused by an interconnected global climate-ecosystem-biodiversity crisis. This was stated very clearly by the United Nation's Convention to Combat Desertification (UNCCD) in April 2022 when they released a report that made the case that the climate crisis, biodiversity loss, and land degradation are integrally linked. Ibrahim Thiaw, executive secretary of the UNCCD said, "We cannot stop the climate crisis today, biodiversity loss tomorrow, and land degradation the day after. We need to tackle all these issues together."[39]

Although it must be a centerpiece, reducing the impacts of this civilization-altering mega-emergency to manageable levels will require much more than achieving "net-zero emissions," which is what 4,000 governments and private firms around the world have pledged to do.[40] It will likely require the near elimination of fossil fuel use and a complete shift to clean renewable forms of energy. At the same time, large swaths of forests, watersheds, streams, soils, estuaries, oceans, and other ecological systems will need to be protected and regenerated worldwide.

In addition, even though no safe or effective technologies exist yet to accomplish this—and might never be found—to reduce the climate crisis to manageable levels, greenhouse gases will also need to be withdrawn from the atmosphere and safely stored for hundreds of years underground or dissipated in some way.

From food production and distribution to the plastics used in almost every process and product today, the use of fossil fuels is deeply embedded within almost every aspect of modern economies. Swiftly and dramatically cutting emissions, let alone almost completely eliminating the use of fossil fuels, will therefore require vast unprecedented changes in resource extraction, manufacturing, trade, finance, banking, transportation, forestry, agriculture, material consumption, and other local, national, and international systems, along with associated shifts in the social, economic, political, and religious norms, values, and ideologies that support and promote the existing systems.

This is why the global climate-ecosystem-biodiversity mega-emergency has been defined as such a "wicked" problem. Humanity has never made these types of rapid massive complex systems changes before on a global scale. Solutions to any specific aspect of the crisis often undermine other elements, as well as the people or industries that rely on them. Some proposed solutions produce unintended consequences that make the problem worse, which makes it very difficult determine how effective any intervention will be.

Even if the path forward was clear, making the changes in the time that is available to prevent climate overshoot will require a never-before-seen, well-coordinated, mass global mobilization that is far greater than even what the US did when it entered World War II. And the mobilization will likely need to be sustained for decades.[41] While technically possible, there is nothing on the horizon that comes anywhere close to achieving it.

As stated in Introduction, limiting the extent of the climate overshoot and then reversing it decades (or centuries) down the road is likely the best that the emission cutting efforts of the US and other countries can now hope to achieve. Until this happens, we must plan for unrelenting harmful impacts.

IS POPULATION GROWTH THE PRIMARY PROBLEM?

Population growth did not, by itself, cause the global climate mega-emergency. Africa, for example, has 16 percent of the world's population, but emits just 4 percent of global emissions. Again, the crisis is caused by the massive burning and use of fossil fuels, degradation of ecological systems, and biodiversity extinction happening worldwide. Continued population growth can, however, overwhelm efforts to address the problem. For instance, emission reductions in commercial and residential buildings produced by energy efficiency measures can be offset when larger and more buildings and homes are constructed to accommodate a growing population. If they are powered by fossil fuels, the emission reductions achieved when people purchase more energy efficient vehicles can be overwhelmed if more cars and trucks swamp the roads and travel longer distances.

It is also true, however, that humanity today uses as much ecological resources as if we lived on 1.75 Earth's. According to the Global Footprint Network, we are consuming nearly twice the amount of resources than the planet can support sustainably. Most of the overconsumption occurs in the industrialized nations.[42] This underscores that the US, EU, Japan, and other industrialized countries in particular will need to double down on efforts to reduce their ecological footprints as we await the time when global population growth plateaus and possibly even shrinks a bit.

OVERVIEW OF THE CIVILIZATION-ALTERING IMPACTS OF THE CLIMATE MEGA-EMERGENCY

Now that you have a basic understanding of what is disrupting the Earth's climate and eco-logical systems and the dim hopes of preventing climate overshoot, it is important to under-stand the civilization-altering consequences. As mentioned at the start of this chapter, the synopsis offered here can be emotionally difficult to read. However, it is imperative for every-one to come to grips with the challenges we face because only then can we grasp the urgency of establishing new methods to prevent and heal the distresses and traumas they generate.

It is also important to understand that what is offered here undoubtedly does not describes all the impacts of the global climate-ecosystem-biodiversity mega-emergency. Just as the historic heat wave experienced in the US Pacific Northwest and western Canada in June 2021 surprised climate scientists because they did not realize the record drought would create a positive feedback that magnified temperatures, the impacts of a disrupted global climate system are certain to often interact in surprising ways and produce never-before-seen alarmingly new consequences.

THE BIO-PHYSICAL IMPACTS OF THE CLIMATE-ECOSYSTEM-BIODIVERSITY MEGA-EMERGENCY

- *Hotter Temperatures and More Extreme Heat Waves*: As previously noted, a disrupted climate system is both raising global average temperatures and producing more frequent, intense, and prolonged heat events. Even if emissions are reduced, tem-peratures will continue to rise and studies show the probability of record-shattering heat waves will continue to increase.[43] The 2021 report by the Intergovernmental Panel on Climate Change said that extreme heat waves, such as the deadly one that occurred in June of that year in the Pacific Northwest and western Canada, are already about five times more likely to occur with the current temperature increase of just over 1.8 degrees Fahrenheit (1.1C) above preindustrial levels. A 3.6 degrees Fahrenheit (2C) increase will increase the likelihood by 14 times. Heat waves will also get hotter.[44]

- *More Intense and Larger Wildfires*: Wildfires are a natural part of many landscapes and at normal scales help replenish the soils and strengthen forests. However, as seen on the West Coast of the US and Canada, in Australia, and elsewhere around the world, hotter temperatures, longer droughts, the ability of tree killing pests to sur-vive warmer winters, and other dynamics produced by a disrupted climate system will increasingly generate wildfires that are far more intense and larger than would naturally occur. Between 2011 and 2020 wildfires in the US more than doubled the amount of acreage consumed compared with the years 1983–1992.[45] A U.N. report issued in early 2022 said that catastrophic wildfires could increase by a third globally by 2050 and by more that 50 percent by the end of the century.[46]

- *More Frequent, Extreme, and Prolonged Storms and Floods*: Although it is difficult to assign a specific cause to any particular storm, evidence is growing that connects extreme weather events with climate disruption. Warmer temperatures add more energy to the atmosphere, which increases the frequency and intensity of windstorms. More heat also increases evapotranspiration, which is the transfer of water from the ground and vegetation into the air through a combination of evaporation and transpiration. Studies have found that evapotranspiration increased globally by 10 percent between 2003 and 2019 with the main driver being warming of the earth's land surface. The frequency of heavy downpours has consequently increased by about 30 percent globally, and they contain about 7 percent more water.[47] Warmer ocean temperatures and higher sea levels are also causing hurricanes to grow stronger and produce more rain, with a larger percentage of storms reaching the dangerous 3, 4, and 5 categories. This trend will increase as temperatures climb.[48] In addition, the disrupted climate system is causing "weather whiplash," which means wild swings between dry and wet extremes.[49]

- *More Frequent and Severe Droughts*: Climate disruption is causing more frequent and extreme droughts in many parts of the world, such as the one that plagued the Western US in the early 2020s. Severe droughts that used to occur an average of once per decade are now occurring about 70 percent more frequently. A study released in January 2022 found that the drought that has parched the American West for the past two decades was the driest 22-year period in at least 1,200 years. The authors attributed most of the cause to human-induced climate disruption. They also said the drought is likely to continue until at least the end of the decade.[50] If temperatures rise by 3.6 degrees Fahrenheit (2C) above preindustrial levels, major droughts will occur between two and three times more often.[51] Although drought does not have the same immediate impact as a major storm, they rank second in billion-dollar weather disasters in the US over the past three decades.

- *Rising Sea Levels and More Powerful Tidal Flooding and Storm Surges*: Climate disruption is activating a rise in sea levels. This is because hotter temperatures are expanding the volume of water that already exists in the oceans. The amount of ocean water is also increasing because many glaciers worldwide and the ice sheets in Greenland and Antarctica are melting at record rates. Sea levels are estimated to rise by two to seven feet (0.6–2.1 meters) or higher by the end of the century.[52] This will cause some islands, such as Kiribati in the central Pacific Ocean, to completely disappear and others to be frequently inundated. Higher sea levels will also worsen high tide flooding and storm surges. By 2050, some of the world's great coastal cities are consequently projected to be partially or completely flooded including London, Panama City, Bangkok, Mumbai, Shanghai, New York City, and the San Francisco Bay Area, to name a few.[53] One study estimated that by 2050, regions housing over 300 million people worldwide will be affected by coastal flooding. In addition, high tides may permanently flood coastal areas that are home to 150 million people.[54]

- *Ocean Acidification*: Increased carbon dioxide not only affects the Earth's atmosphere, it also has direct chemical effects on the world's oceans. The oceans have absorbed between a third and a half of all the CO_2 generated by humans since preindustrial times. This has slowed the rate of atmospheric warming. But the increased CO_2 also dissolves in seawater and has caused the oceans to become approximately 30 percent more acidic.[55] The rate of acidification is now about 10 times faster than at any time in the past 55 million years. The impacts of acidification will extend all the way up the marine food chain, including to aquaculture and will impact ocean food sources and protein levels.

- *Slowing Atlantic Circulation*: In addition to rising sea levels and ocean acidification, researchers have found the system of currents in the Atlantic Ocean that helps control temperatures in the Northern Hemisphere is showing signs of instability due to human-induced climate disruption. The Atlantic Meridional Overturning Circulation (AMOC), which is often described as a "conveyor belt" that takes warm surface water from the tropics and distributes it to the north Atlantic, helps maintain the energy balance in the Atlantic Ocean. In 2021, scientists warned that it could be "close to a collapse from a strong circulation to a weak circulation," although the threshold for such a collapse is still uncertain. If a collapse occurs, it will have profound implications for not only the Northern Hemisphere, but for the entire planet's weather systems and all life on earth.[56]

- *Habitat Degradation and Loss and Biodiversity Extinction*: Research found that 70 percent of the land on the planet has already been altered by humans.[57] Only 62 percent of the land that could be forested worldwide remains forested and, due to human activities, that total is disappearing fast.[58] In addition, 40 percent of the land worldwide is degraded. Forest loss and degradation, combined with hotter temperatures, droughts, wildfires, and other climate impacts, are adversely affecting or destroying habitats that species depend on to survive. Habitat loss, combined with the use of pesticides, has caused insects to decline by 75 percent over the past 50 years globally, with potentially catastrophic consequences. These and other factors have also caused the number of mammals, birds, reptiles, amphibians, and fish to fall by half worldwide since the 1970s.[59]

- *New and Surprising Impacts*: It must be noted again that the impacts described here include only those that have already been observed and thus can be projected. Many new and surprising impacts should be expected in the future due to feedbacks that scientists cannot yet observe or include in models. For example, only recently did researchers find that exposure to elevated levels of fine particle pollution found in wildfire smoke led to thousands of cases of COVID-19 and more coronavirus-related deaths.[60] The record drought and heat generated by climate disruption activated a positive feedback that increased the scale and intensity of wildfires, which produced elevated levels of smoke, which increased the health impacts of COVID-19. Numerous other unforeseen and startling impacts like this can be expected as temperatures climb.

THE HUMAN CONSEQUENCES OF THE BIO-PHYSICAL IMPACTS OF CLIMATE DISRUPTION

- *Rising Aggression, Abuses, Injuries, Deaths, and Violent Crime*: Relatively few studies have examined the aggression, abuse, injuries, deaths, and violent crime caused by climate disruption, primarily because it is difficult to assign a specific cause to any specific event. But this is beginning to change. Studies have found that above normal temperatures generate more violent assault, sexual violence, and homicides, as well as organized crime and civil unrest.[61] A 2019 study, for example, found that violent crime in Los Angeles increased by 5.7 percent on days that temperatures rose about 85 degrees Fahrenheit compared with cooler temperatures.[62] Another study predicted that warmer temperatures could lead to 9–40,000 additional suicides in the US and Mexico by 2050.[63] A report by the Overseas Development Institute and World Vision found that violence against children and climate disruption reinforce one another. The reason is that rising heat activates aggressive behaviors that can cause parents to adopt harmful coping mechanisms, including abusing their spouse, ignore or abuse their children, commit crimes, or abuse drugs or alcohol, all of which can traumatize their children.

- *Increasing Economic Damage*: The US has sustained 310 weather and climate disasters since 1980 that each caused overall damages/costs of $1 billion US or more. The NOAA National Centers for Environmental Information said the total cost of the 310 events exceeded $2.155 trillion. In 2021 alone, the US experienced 20 weather/climate disaster events with losses exceeding $1 billion each. In comparison, the 1980–2021 annual average was 7.4 disasters.[64] An assessment by the European Environmental Agency found that between 1980 and 2019 climate disruption-related extreme events caused economic damages totaling an estimated $530 billion US (EUR $446 billion) in EU countries.[65] The record number of hurricanes, wildfires, and floods that occurred globally that same year exacerbated by climate change cost the world $210 billion in damages, according to the reinsurance company Munich Re. Much more damage can be expected as temperatures rise.

- *Impacts on Businesses, Jobs, and Incomes*: The climate crisis will significantly impact local businesses, jobs, and incomes. Studies have documented how US economic output falls in hotter years compared with cooler ones by as much as 28 percent, with the primary reason being lost productivity.[66] In 2021, the non-profit CDP, which runs the global disclosure system used by investors, private companies, and local governments to manage their environmental impacts, projected $1.26 trillion in revenue losses for suppliers within the coming five years due to climate change, deforestation, and water insecurity. They also said that corporate buyers will experience an additional $120 billion in increased environmental costs by 2026.

- *Reduced Agricultural Output and Growing Food Insecurity*: Research indicates that in the next 30 years the net damage to food supply and food security due to the climate emergency will be significant and increase over time.[67] Plant growth, pollination, blooming, and fructification will all be affected by a disrupted climate system. As seen by the impacts on wheat of the record US Pacific Northwest heat wave in June 2021, extreme heat events can reduce or destroy crop production and nutritional value. Wildfire smoke also damages crops and taints food. More droughts increase the cost of, or make it impossible to grow crops. These and other impacts are already creating food insecurities in some parts of the world.[68] Adaptations might delay the effects, but when temperatures shoot close to or above the 2.7 degrees Fahrenheit (1.5 Celsius) extreme danger threshold, people in every nation are likely to experience rising prices and increasing food insecurities.

- *Water Shortages and Insecurity*: Increasing global temperatures are causing water to evaporate in larger amounts. The increased frequency and severity of droughts and the earlier melting of snow are combining with increased pollution and toxicity to cause water shortages and insecurity in many locations around the globe. For example, drought is already a serious problem in both the western US and in India, where the monsoon season is becoming more variable. Europe, China, and sub-Saharan Africa are also likely to experience increased drought. Approximately 74 percent of natural disasters that occurred worldwide between 2001 and 2018 were water-related, including droughts.[69] Droughts will continue to expand as global temperatures rise.

- *Increased Physical Illnesses and Diseases*: The global climate crisis directly affects the physical health of humans in many ways. The world is already seeing increasing respiratory and cardiovascular disease, injuries, and premature deaths related to extreme weather events, including heat waves, wind, rain, and snowstorms. Heat-related impacts such as heat stroke, heat exhaustion, respiratory failure, myocardial infraction, stoke, and death are also growing. Rising heat has also been found to cause declines in cognitive functioning.[70] Changing weather patterns are allowing infectious diseases such as diarrhea to occur in new areas. Researchers have found that accelerating wildfires produce smoke that includes fine particulate matter known as PM2.5 that damages human cells and organs, can trigger asthma attacks, generates stress due to the scent or sight of smoke, and in other ways erodes physical health.[71] Hotter temperatures are also increasing the production of pollen, and higher carbon dioxide levels are producing higher levels of allergens from plants. Climate disruption also produces indirect physical health impacts by affecting clean air, drinking water, food supplies, secure shelters, and other social and environmental determinants of health.

- *Mass Migration and Its Often-Harsh Push Back*: In 2017, 68.5 million people were displaced from Latin America, sub-Saharan Africa, and Southeast Asia, which is more than any previous time in world history. It is estimated that roughly a third of those people—between 22 and 24 million—were forced to migrate due to sudden extreme weather events including floods, wildfires, droughts, and more intense storms. The other two thirds migrated due to humanitarian crises. Slowly growing climate impacts such as desertification, sea-level rise, ocean acidification, and the destruction of ecosystems and loss of biodiversity are projected to activate many additional humanitarian crises, and cause millions more people to migrate.[72] Due to competition for jobs and resources, and the aversion some people have to newcomers with different racial, ethnic, cultural, or religious backgrounds, involuntary migration will often trigger harsh xenophobic reactions and social strife in areas where the migrants relocate. Forced migration will also generate significant stresses for the migrants.

- *Rising Costs for Mitigation, Adaptation, Food, Water, Health Care, Insurance, and More*: At least initially in some locations, the impacts of rising global temperatures can be reduced or decently managed using various technologies and physical preparedness and adaptation strategies. However, the size of the potential financial costs, just for the infrastructure required to protect coastal urban areas from flooding, for example, will often reach into the billions, which will make many investments difficult to make or sustain. In addition, the risks associated with failure will often be very high because it is difficult to predict with great accuracy the exact scale, location, and duration of specific impacts. Unexpected changes in weather and disaster patterns might also render expensive infrastructure obsolete much sooner than planned. These factors will often make some investments risky, which can scare off private and government funders.[73]

- *Accelerating Social and Health Inequities and Injustices*: The scale and scope of the impacts of climate overshoot will vary region to region worldwide, based on their location, geography, and ecology. But no matter where they are located, as previously stated, BIPOC and low-income groups, the elderly, those with preexisting mental health and physical health conditions, and other disadvantaged and marginalized populations will initially be most affected by the climate emergency. However, as temperatures rise close to and exceed the 2.7 degrees Fahrenheit (1.5 Celsius) extreme danger threshold, every human on earth will be impacted.

- *Chronic Toxic Stress Due to Constant Adjustments*: Any change can be stressful, and just as most people were stressed by the constant large and small adjustments they had to make in their lives during the COVID-19 pandemic, everyone will need to continually adjust to the relentless impacts of a disrupted climate system. People will, for example, need to be on high alert for the next major disaster and need to make changes in response to the impacts. Many others will need to be constantly aware of food or water shortages. And almost everyone will need to continually update their emergency escape plans so they can evacuate at a moment's notice, and in other ways make never-ending changes to prepare for, protect themselves from, and adapt to the relentless ecological, social, and economic impacts generated by the climate crisis. Relentless adaptations will also be necessary by the businesses and organizations where people work. The endless adjustments will, for many people, produce high levels of chronic toxic stress, which can be overwhelming and produce significant mental health and psycho-social-spiritual problems.[74]

- *Surprising Cascading Effects*: In addition to the direct impacts, as the information provided here describes, the many consequences of a disrupted climate system are certain to activate many previously unseen cascading effects to the ecological, social, and economic systems people rely on for their basic needs. These dynamics can already be observed, and when temperatures rise close to and overshoot the 2.7 degrees Fahrenheit (1.5 Celsius) danger threshold, they are certain to become frequent and extreme.

Figure 1.2 depicts the many forces that are interacting to produce the Traumacene. It illuminates the inherent interconnectedness of all things on planet earth.

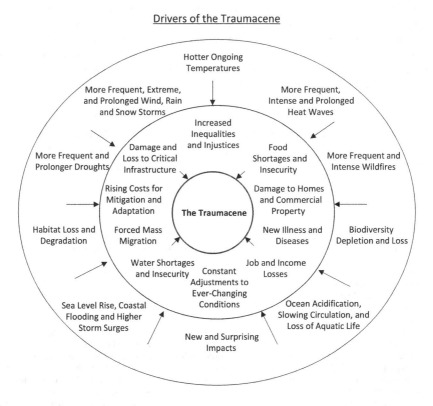

Figure 1.2 Drivers of the Traumacene

IN SUM: HUMANITY IS IN THE MIDST OF A CIVILIZATION-ALTERING MEGA-EMERGENCY

The point of describing these impacts in such detail is to underscore that, although life will go on, humanity is in the midst of climate-ecosystem-biodiversity mega-emergency that will profoundly alter every aspect of modern civilization. To bring this home, take a moment to answer the questions below and consider how the impacts will affect you:

- *Where do you live?* How will the climate emergency affect the nation, region, and community in which you live and your place of residence?
- *How do you make a living?* What type of job or other source of income do you have and how will the climate crisis affect it?
- *What do you love to do?* Whether it is hiking, gardening, traveling, or watching movies how will the climate emergency affect the things you love to do?
- *Who do you love?* How will the climate crisis affect your significant other, your children, relatives, friends and neighbors?
- *What do you believe in?* If you are a religious person, embrace spiritual principles, or hold strong economic or political beliefs, how will those principles be affected by the human-induced climate mega-emergency?

When answering these questions, I hope it becomes evident that humanity now faces two enormous interconnected challenges. Our activities are destroying the climatic and ecological conditions that allowed civilization to emerge and thrive. In doing so, we are also generating a wide range of new, wicked, and relentless physical, social, economic, and other impacts that will severely distress everyone and traumatize billions. Left unaddressed, the traumas will make it even more difficult to reduce the climate mega-emergency to manageable levels.

Unless new and expanded approaches are quickly adopted to prevent and heal them, a perfect storm of pervasive "wickedly" complex and intertwined psychological, emotional, and spiritual distresses and traumas will result that will produce the Traumacene.

The nature and consequences of the psychological, emotional, spiritual, and behavioral problems generated by during the Traumacene are the subject of the next chapter.

NOTES

1 *Washington Post.* (June 26, 2021). Historic, dangerous, prolonged and unprecedented' heat wave swells over Pacific Northwest. Obtained at https://www.washingtonpost.com/weather/2021/06/-25/pacific-northwest-heat-wave-seattle-portland/
2 Interview found at: https://www.msnbc.com/all-in/watch/gov-inslee-heat-wave-is-beginning-of-permanent-climate-emergency-115635781914
3 Lindsay B. and Dickson C. (June 2021). Village of Lytton, B.C., evacuated as mayor says 'the whole town is on fire.' *CBC News.* Obtained at: https://www.cbc.ca/news/canada/british-columbia/bc-wildfires-june-30-2021
4 World Weather Attribution. (July 2021). *Western North American Extreme Heat Virtually Impossible Without Human-Induced Climate Change.* Obtained at: https://www.worldweatherattribution.org/western-north-american-extreme-heat-virtually-impossible-without-human-caused-climate-change/
5 Berwyn B. (July 2021). A week after the pacific northwest heat wave, study shows it was 'almost impossible' without global warming. *Inside Climate News.* Obtained at: https://insideclimatenews.org/news/07072021/pacific-northwest-heat-wave-attribution-study-climate-change/
6 Arrhenius S. (1986). On the influence of carbonic acid in the air upon the temperature on the ground. *Philosophical Transactions*, 151, 237–276.

7 IPCC. (2014). *Climate Change 2014: Synthesis Report. Contribution of Working Groups I, II and III to the Fifth Assessment Report of the Intergovernmental Panel on Climate Change*. Geneva.
8 Myhre G. and Drew S. (2013). Anthropogenic and natural radiating forcing. *Climate Change 2013: The Physical Science Basis. Contribution of Working Group I to the Fifth Assessment Report of the Intergovernmental Panel on Climate Change*. Obtained at: http://www.climatechange2013.org/images/report/-WG1AR5_Chapter08_FINAL.pdf
9 Ibid.
10 Olsen L. M. et al. (2013). *NASA/Global Change Master Directory (GCMD) Earth Science*. Obtained at: https://earthdata.nasa.gov/earth-observation-data/find-data/idn/gcmd-keywords
11 National Oceanic and Atmospheric Administration. (March 15, 2021). *Climate Change: Global Temperature*. Obtained at: https://www.climate.gov/news-features/understanding-climate/climate-change-global-temperature
12 Plumer B. (January 10, 2022). U.S. greenhouse gas emissions bounced back sharply in 2021. *New York Times*. Obtained at: https://www.nytimes.com/2022/01/10/climate/emissions-pandemic-rebound.html
13 *International Energy Agency Global Energy and CO2 Status Report 2019*. Obtained at: https://www.iea.org/reports/global-energy-co2-status-report-2019
14 World Meteorological Association Greenhouse Gas Bulletin. (October 25, 2021). The State of Greenhouse Gasses in the Atmosphere based on Global Observations through 2020. Obtained at: https://library.wmo.int/docnum.php?explnumid=10838; and *NOAA Research News*. (April 2020). Despite pandemic shutdowns, carbon dioxide and methane surged in 2020: Carbon dioxide levels are now higher than any time in the past 3.6 million years. Obtained at: https://library.wmo.int/-doc_num.php?explnum_id=10838
15 Intergovernmental Panel on Climate Change. (2021). *Climate Change 2021: The Physical Science Basis. Summary for Policymakers*; and Raghuraman S. P. et al. (2021). Anthropogenic forcing and response yield observed positive trend in Earth's energy imbalance. *Nature Communications*, 12, 4577. Obtained at: https://www.nature.com/articles/s41467-021-24544- 4
16 Ghose T. (January 2015). Mesozoic era: Age of the dinosaur. *Live Science*. Obtained at: https://www.livescience.com/38596-mesozoic-era.html
17 US EPA. (May 2021). *Climate Change Indicators in the U.S.* Obtained at: https://www.epa.gov/-climate-indicators
18 Corpernicus Climate Change Services. (September 7, 2021). *Warmest Summer for Europe by Small Margin; August Globally Joint Third Warmest on Record*. Obtained at: https://climate.copernicus.eu/-copernicus-warmest-summer-europe-small-margin-august-globally-joint-third-warmest-record
19 Morris L. et al. (July 17, 2021). Death toll from European floods climbs to more than 150. *The Washington Post*. Obtained at: https://www.washingtonpost.com/world/2021/07/16/europe-flooding-deaths-germany-belgium/
20 World Weather Attribution. (August 2021). *Heavy Rainfall Which Led to Severe Flooding in Western Europe Made More Likely by Climate Change*. Obtained at: https://www.worldweatherattribution.org/heavy-rainfall-which-led-to-severe-flooding-in-western-europe-made-more-likely-by-climate-change/
21 NZ National Institute of Water and Atmospheric Research. (June 2021). *June Blows Hot and Cold – and Possibly Hottest of All*. Obtained at: https://niwa.co.nz/news/june-blows-hot-and-cold-%E2%80%93-and-possibly-hottest-of-al   l
22 *UN Climate Change News*. (October 27, 2020). Climate change is an increasing threat to Africa. United Nations. Obtained at: https://unfccc.int/news/climate-change-is-an-increasing-threat-to-africa
23 Intergovernmental Panel on Climate Change. (2022). *Climate Change 2022: Impacts, Adaptation, and Vulnerability*. Obtained at: https://www.ipcc.ch/report/ar6/wg2/
24 United Nations Intergovernmental Panel on Climate Change. (March 1, 2022). *Climate Change 2022: Impacts, Adaptation, and Vulnerability*. Obtained at: https://www.ipcc.ch/report/ar6/wg2/
25 Hausfather Z. (December 2017). Analysis: When might the world exceed 1.5C and 2C of global warming. *Carbon Brief*. Obtained at: https://www.weforum.org/agenda/2020/12/analysis-world-paris-agreement-climate-targets-change-emissions-global-warming/
26 Harvey F. (October 30, 2021) Climate experts warn world leaders 1.5C is 'real science', not just talking point. *The Guardian*. Obtained at: https://www.theguardian.com/environment/2021/oct/-30/climate-experts-warn-world-leaders-15c-is-real-science-not-just-talking-point
27 Jordans F. and Borenstein S. (April 4, 2022). UN warns Earth 'firmly on track toward an unlivable world.' *Associated Press*. Obtained at: https://apnews.com/article/climate-united-nations-paris-europe-berlin
28 *WMO Global Annual to Decadal Climate Update for 2021–2025*. Obtained at: https://hadleyserver.metoffice.gov.uk/wmolc/

29 World Meteorological Organization. (May 9, 2022). *WMO Update: 50:50 Chance of Global Temperatures Temporarily Reaching 1.5°C in Next Five Years.* Obtained at: https://public.wmo.int/en/media/press-release/wmo-update-5050-chance-of-global-temperature-temporarily-reaching-15%C2%B0c-threshold
30 Intergovernmental Panel on Climate Change. (2022). *Climate Change 2022: Impacts, Adaptation, and Vulnerability.* Obtained at: https://www.ipcc.ch/report/ar6/wg2/
31 Tong D. et al. (July 2019). Committed emissions from existing energy infrastructure jeopardize 1.5°C climate target. *Nature.* Obtained at: https://www.nature.com/articles/s41586-019-1364-3
32 Hausfather Z. (2017). *Analysis: Why US Carbon Emissions Have Fallen 14% Since 2005.* London: Carbon Brief.
33 Sterman J. and Booth Sweeney L. (2007). Understanding public complacency about climate change: adults' mental models of climate change violate conservation of matter. *Climatic Change* 80(3–4), 213–238.
34 Kaoru T. et al. (December 2019) Effects on the earth system after realizing a 1.5 C warming climate target after overshooting to the 2C level. *Environmental Research Letters.* Obtained at: https://-iopscience.iop.org/article/10.1088/1748-9326/ab5199
35 The National Academy of Sciences. (2009). Ecological impacts of climate change. Obtained at: https://www.nap.edu/catalog/12491/ecological-impacts-of-climate-change
36 Caballos G. et al. (July 25, 2017). Biological annihilation via the ongoing sixth mass extinction signaled by vertebrate population losses and declines. *Proceedings of the National Academy of Scientists.* (2017). Obtained at: https://pubmed.ncbi.nlm.nih.gov/28696295/
37 Trisos C. et al. (April 8, 2020). The projected timing of abrupt ecological disruption from climate change. *Nature.* Obtained at: https://www.nature.com/articles/s41586-020-2189-9
38 National Research Council. (2008). *Ecological Impacts of Climate Change.* Washington, DC: The National Academies Press. https://doi.org/10.17226/12491. Obtained at: https://nap.nation-alacademies.org/catalog/12491/ecological-impacts-of-climate-change
39 Gustin G. (April 27, 2022). UN report says humanity has altered 70 percent of the earth's lane, putting the planet on a 'crisis footing.' *Inside Climate News.* Obtained at: https://insideclimatenews.org/news/27042022/agriculture-land-report/
40 Buck H.J. (November 2021). *Ending Fossil Fuels: Why Net Zero Emissions Is Not Enough.* London UK and New York, NY: Verso Books.
41 Pidcock R. (2016). Half a degree makes a very big difference when judging how different parts of the world will feel the effects of climate change. *Carbon Brief.* Obtained at: https://www.carbon-brief.org/scientists-compare-climate-change-impacts-at-1-5c-and-2c
42 For more information, see The Global Footprint Network at: https://www.footprintnetwork.org/ (Full disclosure: I was one of the original board members of the GFN).
43 Fischer E.M. et al. (July 26, 2021). Increasing probability of record shattering climate extremes. *Nature Climate Change*, 11, 689–695. Obtained at: https://www.nature.com/articles/s41558-021-01092-9
44 IPCC Climate Change. (2021). *The Physical Science Basis. Contribution of Working Group I to the Sixth Assessment Report of the Intergovernmental Panel on Climate Change.*
45 National Interagency Fire Center. (2020). *Wildland Fire Summary and Statistics Annual Reports.* Obtained at: https://www.nifc.gov/fire-information/statistics
46 U.N. Environmental Agency. (February 23, 2022). Number of wildfires to rise by 50% by 2010 and governments are not prepared, experts warn. Obtained at: https://www.unep.org/news-and-stories/press-release/number-wildfires-rise-50-2100-and-governments-are-not-prepared
47 IPCC Climate Change. (2021). *The Physical Science Basis. Contribution of Working Group I to the Sixth Assessment Report of the Intergovernmental Panel on Climate Change.* Obtained at: https://www.ipcc.ch/report/ar6/wg1/
48 Ibid.
49 Ibid.
50 Park W. A. et al. (2022). Rapid intensification of the emerging southwestern North American megadrought in 2020–2021. *Nature Climate Change.* Obtained at: https://doi.org/10.1038/s41558-022-01290-z
51 Ibid.
52 IPCC Climate Change. (2021). *The Physical Science Basis. Contribution of Working Group I to the Sixth Assessment Report of the Intergovernmental Panel on Climate Change.*
53 Climate Central. (No date). Land projected to be below annual flood level in 2050. Obtained at: https://coastal.climatecentral.org/map/14/-8.4653/51.9061/?theme=sea_level_rise&map
54 Kulp S. and Strauss B. (October 29, 2019). *New Elevation Data Triple Estimates of Global Vulnerability to Sea-Level Rise and Coastal Flooding.* Obtained at: https://www.ncbi.nlm.nih.gov/pmc/articles/PMC6820795/

55 National Oceanic and Atmospheric Administration. (April 1, 2020). *Ocean Acidification*. Obtained at: https://www.noaa.gov/education/resource-collections/ocean-coasts/ocean-acidification

56 Boers N. (2021). Observation-based early-warning signals for a collapse of the Atlantic Meridional overturning circulation. *Natural Climate Change*. Obtained at: https://doi.org/10.1038/s41558-021-01097-4

57 Gustin G. (April 27, 2022). UN report says humanity has altered 70 percent of the earth's lane, putting the planet on a 'crisis footing.' *Inside Climate News*. Obtained at: https://insideclimatenews.org/news/27042022/agriculture-land-report/

58 Food and Agricultural Organization of the United Nations. (2020). *The State of the World's Forests*. Obtained at: http://www.fao.org/state-of-forests/en/

59 Almond R. E. A., Grooten M. and Petersen T. Eds. (2020). *Living Planet Report 2020 – Bending the Curve of Biodiversity Loss*. World Wildlife Fund. Obtained at: https://www.zsl.org/sites/default/files/LPR%202020%20Full%20report.pdf

60 Zhou X. et al. (August 2021). Excess of COVID-19 cases and deaths due to find particle matter exposure during the 2020 wildfires in the U.S. *Science Advances*, 7(33), Obtained at: eabi8789. https://doi.org/10.1126/sciadv.abi8789

61 Harper R. and Karnauskas K. (November 13, 2018). The influence of interannual climate variability on regional violent crime rates in the United States. *GeoHealth*. Obtained at: https://agupubs.onlinelibrary.wiley.com/doi/10.1029/2018GH000152; and Schinasi L. and Hamra G. (December 2017). A time series analysis of associations between daily temperature and crime events in Philadelphia, Pennsylvania. *Journal of Urban Health*. Obtained at: https://doi.org/10.1007/s11524-017-0181-y.
Otto F. (September 25, 2017). Violent crime increases during warmer weather, no matter the season.

62 Heilmann K. and Kahn M. (June 2019). *The Urban Crime and Heat Gradient in High and Low Poverty Areas*. National Bureau of Economic Research, Working Paper No. 25961. Obtained at: https://www.nber.org/system/files/working_papers/w25961/w25961.pdf

63 Burke M. et al. (July 2018). Higher temperatures increase suicide rates in the United States and Mexico. *Nature Climate Change*, 8, 723–729. Obtained at: https://doi.org/10.1038/s41558-018-0222-x

64 NOAA National Centers for Environmental Information. (April 8, 2022). *Billion Dollar Weather and Climate Disasters*. Obtained at: https://www.ncdc.noaa.gov/billions/

65 European Environmental Agency. *Economic Losses from Climate Related Extremes in Europe*. Obtained at: https://www.eea.europa.eu/data-and-maps/indicators/direct-losses-from-weather-disasters-4/assessment

66 Kiersz A. (July 19, 2019). This heat wave is going to make you — and the rest of America — less productive, by as much as 28%. *Insider*. Obtained at: https://www.businessinsider.com/heat-wave-effects-on-economic-productivity-2019-7

67 IPCC Climate Change. (2021). *The Physical Science Basis. Contribution of Working Group I to the Sixth Assessment Report of the Intergovernmental Panel on Climate Change*.

68 Yuanyu X. et al. (March 28, 2022). Tripling of western US particulate pollution from wildfires in a warming climate. *PNAS*, 119(13). Obtained at: https://www.pnas.org/

69 UNICEF. (May 18, 2021). *Water and Global Climate Crisis: 10 Things You Should Know*. Obtained at: https://www.unicef.org/stories/water-and-climate-change-10-things-you-should-know

70 Laurent J. et al. (July 10, 2018). Reduced cognitive function during a heat wave among residents of non-air-conditioned buildings: An observational study of young adults in the summer of 2016. *PLoS Medicine*, 15(7), e1002605. Obtained at: https://doi.org/10.1371/journal.pmed.1002605

71 Yuanyu X. et al. (March 28, 2022). Tripling of western US particulate pollution from wildfires in a warming climate. *PNAS*, 119(13). Obtained at: https://www.pnas.org/

72 Podesta J. (July 2019). The climate crisis, migration, and refugees. *Brookings Institute*. Obtained at: https://www.brookings.edu/research/the-climate-crisis-migration-and-refugees/

73 Amaro S. (April 21, 2021). How climate change could be a risk to your savings. *CNBC*. Obtained at: https://www.cnbc.com/2021/04/21/why-climate-change-is-a-risk-to-financial-markets.html

74 American Psychological Association. (October 2019). *Stress Won't Go Away? Maybe You Are Suffering from Chronic Stress*. Obtained at: https://www.apa.org/topics/stress/chronic

CHAPTER 2

The Causes and Consequences of Individual, Community, and Societal Traumas

It should be evident now that humanity faces a wide range of momentous interacting challenges. How should we respond? To help you think this through, I'd like to offer two different scenarios.

SCENARIO ONE: TWEAK BUSINESS-AS-USUAL

Imagine it is the year 2050. Other than additional funds that expanded individualized mental health treatment, direct human service, and disaster mental health programs, little has been done since the 2020s to prevent or heal the mental health and psycho-social-spiritual problems generated by climate overshoot. What would things look like?

Over the past 30-plus years, most nations implemented practices and policies that reduced greenhouse gas emissions and ramped up renewable energy. In some locations, efforts were also made to shift to carbon-farming to store more carbon in soils, and regenerate ecological systems and biodiversity. Nations with sufficient economic resources also hardened some of their physical infrastructure and took other steps to prepare for and adapted to the impacts of climate overshoot. But the fossil fuel industry, industrial agriculture, mining, timber, and other economic interests that benefited from the linear 'take it-make it-waste it' economic system, as well as the politicians they controlled, vehemently fought these changes so most ended up merely tweaking business-as-usual. The modifications that did occur primarily benefited wealthier nations and people. In addition, they were disconnected from efforts to prevent and heal the mental health and psycho-social-spiritual problems generated by relentless climate impacts.

The result was that, despite the commitments 131 nations made back in 2021 to reduce greenhouse gas emissions, average global surface temperatures still overshot the 2.7 Fahrenheit (1.5 Celsius) threshold that 30 years ago scientists determined would unleash unrelenting harmful impacts. In fact, temperatures in most regions of the world have now in 2050 increased by just over 3.6 degrees Fahrenheit (2 Celsius), and some areas are even hotter.[1]

As projected back in 2021, the impacts described in the previous chapter have all come to pass. Rising global heat has unleashed devastating compounding disruptions to the ecological, economic, and social systems people rely on for food, water, power, jobs, income, shelter, safety, health, and other necessities that severely stressed millions of people. Unrelenting extreme and prolonged wind, rain, and snowstorms, heat waves, wildfires, droughts, floods, and other disasters and resulting traumas are also now commonplace. Each year, the residences where millions of people live, and places where they work and recreate are damaged or destroyed, as are water, power, sewer, transportation, and other critical infrastructure systems leading to widespread injuries and deaths. Agricultural production has been depleted in many parts of the world, producing food and water shortages and insecurities. Job and income losses, physical health problems, and other traumatic stresses are now familiar occurrences.

Numerous oceanic islands and major coastal cities worldwide have been permanently or seasonally flooded, forcing millions of people to migrate elsewhere. That has both

DOI: 10.4324/9781003262442-4

traumatized the migrants and regularly triggered harsh reactions from residents living in the locations they entered. Many new and surprising harmful impacts have occurred as well.

Less wealthy nations, as well as lower-income groups, BIPOC residents, and older people in western nations have continually experienced the worst impacts. But not a single nation, community, or soul on earth has escaped the acute and chronic harmful impacts of climate overshoot.

The deeply held assumptions and beliefs billions of people once held that the world is a relatively fair, orderly, and manageable place have been shattered, leaving them in despair. The unwillingness of those with economic and political power to make the structural changes required to reduce the climate emergency to something manageable added to their distress and left them feeling hopeless. These reactions have not only undermined the mental health and psycho-social-spiritual well-being of individuals, but they also have generated widespread community and societal traumas.

Back in 2020, for example, 19 percent of adults in the US—over 47 million people— experienced a mental illness and another 4.55 percent experienced a severe mental illness.[2] Today, those numbers have more than doubled, with 40 percent of American adults experiencing some type of recognizable mental illness, including post-traumatic stress disorder, and 10 percent experience a severe mental illness. The remaining 50 percent of the population regularly experience depression, anxiety, grief, anger, loss of hope, and other psychological, emotional, or spiritual distresses. Extraordinary levels of distresses and traumas are now also present in all other nations.

Many people have tried to deal with their distress by using coping mechanisms that end up harming themselves or others. In 2020, for instance, 8 percent of Americans were diagnosed with drug abuse disorders. Now, 30 years later, more than 30 percent of the public has been diagnosed with the problem. In 2020, roughly 17 million Americans suffered from alcohol abuse, and today the number has more than tripled. In addition to creating significant physical health problems for the users such as hypertension, cancer, and lung, liver, and heart disease, the high level of substance abuse has undermined the health and safety of their families and entire communities.

A great number of people have also turned their distress outward toward their families, friends, and strangers, creating an epidemic of spousal and child abuse and neglect, poisonous 'us-versus-them' tribalism, rampant crime, interpersonal aggression, and violence. In addition, the stresses and traumas people experience have led to poor thinking and decision making. Many people, for example, have tried to protect themselves from the ongoing disruptions to the systems they rely on for basic needs and acute disasters in ways that aggravated the problem. Even in urban areas, forests have been cut down to protect people from wildfires. This released more carbon into the atmosphere, damaged soils, triggered flash floods that damaged residential and commercial property and critical infrastructure, and diminished the capacity of ecological systems to sequester carbon.

Back in the 2020s, the mental health systems of most nations were not very inclusive or effective. In the US, for example, less than 10 percent of the people who had a mental health disorder got effective treatment.[3] Today, 30 years later, this problem has been greatly magnified. Due to lack of trained professionals, where they are located, the high costs of services, and other issues, now less than 2 percent of those who experience mental health problems can obtain sufficient mental health treatment, and they are almost all wealthier people living in urban areas in wealthier nations. The rest of humanity is on its own. Clinical treatment and direct human services programs have essentially become nonfactors as ways to address today's widespread mental health and psycho-social-spiritual problems.

The combination of these impacts has fractured family and social relationships, produced unsafe and unhealthy social, economic, and political norms, generated widespread fear, and left billions of people feeling hopeless that anything meaningful can or will be done to minimize climate overshoot and the many wicked problems it has spawned.

A mammoth global pandemic of individual, community, and societal distresses and traumas now exists. The Traumacene is in full force, and it is not a pretty picture.

SCENARIO TWO: REGENERATIVE TRANSFORMATION AND RESILIENCE

Now, step back, take a few deep breaths, and imagine it is 2050 again. Only this time, envision that in the mid-2020s, people in many parts of the world realized the global climate emergency was a wicked problem that was very difficult to address because it resulted from numerous complex interconnected forces that defied standard solutions. They also recognized that it was no longer possible to prevent unyielding climate impacts. This led to the realization that the standard way mental health and psycho-social-spiritual problems were addressed was completely inadequate to prevent or heal the scale or scope of problems that lie ahead, and that entire communities needed to become involved. People also realized that the prevention and healing of psychological, emotional, and spiritual problems needed to be integrated into efforts to transform their economies by adopting a regenerative circular 'cradle-to-cradle' economic system.

So, across the world, people organized Resilience Coordinating Coalitions (RCCs) in their neighborhoods and communities. The RCCs brought together a wide and diverse group of local residents, groups, and organizations to jointly plan, implement, and continually improve measures that strengthened everyone's capacity for mental wellness and transformational resilience for relentless adversities. Actions to slash greenhouse gas emissions; restore ecological systems; prepare for climate impacts; and construct safe, healthy, just, and equitable climate-resilient local physical/built, economic, and ecological conditions were fully integrated into their efforts.

How would things look now, in 2050, and what would have happened in the previous 30-plus years to bring that about?

It took three to five years for most RCCs to mature to the point that they become effective because, as they scaled-up, the impacts of a disrupted climate system were also accelerating. The constant emergencies that occurred in their community often required RCCs to temporarily suspend their mental wellness and resilience-building activities to provide disaster mental health and other forms of assistance to impacted residents.

But by the late 2020s, RCCs were in full swing in many parts of the world. Their growth was spurred in part by the enactment of public policies that made the prevention and healing of distresses and traumas through community-based initiatives a top priority. To achieve that goal, the policies established technical assistance and Communities of Practice (CoPs) educational programs, as well as funding streams to support the community initiatives. Another factor that increased RCCs was that community members realized that anxiety, depression, grief, and other emotional states previously thought to be symptoms of pathology were now natural and common reactions to the state of the world. Rather than pathologizing people,

RCCs engaged community members in five interrelated foundational areas that helped them prevent debilitating levels of distress and trauma, heal those that occurred, and engage in solutions to the climate crisis.

In communities already severely traumatized, RCCs often began their efforts by engaging residents in trauma-healing gatherings. People shared their trauma stories with others in a safe and supportive environment and learned simple resilience skills that helped them begin to heal their suffering. In communities not yet overly distressed, RCCs started by engaging residents in discussions to determine what they cared about most and then showing them how those issues were connected to mental health and psycho-social-spiritual problems. The RCCs then helped residents map the local assets they felt could be used to address their concerns, and identify additional ones, that could enhance their capacity for mental wellness and transformational resilience during ongoing adversities.

Both approaches offered residents a pathway to heal the distresses and traumas they experienced and develop positive relationships with new people, which were two of the five core foundational areas RCCs focused on

To continue to build social connections, RCCs formed 'resilience innovation teams' that found ways to help different parts of the community host neighborhood block parties, organize Resilience Hubs, engage in work projects together, and carry out other activities that allowed residents to meet new people and overcome the social isolation that had previously dominated their area. These connections proved extremely important when disasters and emergencies occurred, as neighbors checked on and helped each other out, shared vital sources of information, and provided emotional support that prevented serious distresses and traumas. They also helped overcome the social and political polarization that had become dominant in recent years.

Because the issues residents voiced the greatest concern about frequently related to local social, physical/built, economic, or ecological conditions, RCCs also formed resilience innovation teams that organized ways for community members to address these factors. Groups of respected residents, religious, and community leaders, for example, came together to widely promote social norms that advanced safe, healthy, just, equitable, and resilient thinking and actions, and rebuke behaviors that violated these standards. Resilience innovation teams were also organized to construct safe, healthy, just, and equitable climate-resilient transportation systems, housing, public spaces, and locally owned and operated businesses. Other resilience innovation teams engaged residents in cleaning up polluted areas, regenerating forests, waterways, grasslands, and other ecological systems, and reviving biodiversity.

Because the RCCs knew their community had to do its part to reduce the climate emergency to manageable levels, all the innovation teams prioritized eliminating fossil fuels, shifting to clean renewable energy, and using ecologically regenerative designs, materials, and practices, to transition their economies to circular cradle-to-cradle systems. Their work was also designed to prevent serious damage from, and adapt to, the impacts of a disrupted climate system.

As residents began to develop greater social connections and work together to build supportive local conditions, they became interested in learning other things. So, RCCs organized resilience innovation teams that found ways to help all adults and youth become literate about what mental wellness and transformational resilience involve and how they can be cared for. This meant that everyone learned how traumas and toxic stresses can activate instinctive fight-flight-freeze reactions that, when unreleased, can cause them to harm themselves through the use of maladaptive coping mechanisms such as misusing drugs or alcohol, or harm others through neglect, aggression, or violence. Residents then learned simple 'Presencing' skills they could use to regulate and calm their body, mind, and emotions in any situation, as well as 'Purposing' skills that enabled them to find new meaning, direction, and hope amid adversities. The knowledge and skills built enormous confidence and peace of mind because people felt they could remain healthy and resilient in any situation.

At the same time, RCCs helped residents engage in specific practices that helped them remain mentally well and resilient during difficult times. This included practicing forgiveness, finding simple joys, laughing often, being grateful, continual learning, and caring for their physical health.

Ongoing engagement in these activities helped many residents prevent serious distresses and traumas, and heal themselves when they did occur. However, some community members were still severely traumatized by the relentless impacts of the climate emergency. This led RCCs to establish innovation teams that organized peer-led healing circles, therapeutic movement, art, theater, dance, journaling, meditation, and many other age and culturally accountable curative methods. Religious and spiritual healing were also emphasized in many communities. In addition, regular memorial events and ceremonies were held that helped residents grieve those who were lost and reaffirm the community's continuity, vigor, and resilience.

The strategies of the many different resilience innovation teams were carefully integrated with each other, and they and other RCC members met as a group at least monthly to share what they were doing and coordinate their efforts.

Mental health and direct human service professionals participated in all of these activities, but devoted most of their time to assisting people who were still so traumatized that they could not function or were at risk of harming themselves or others.

Strengthening these protective factors acted much like a vaccine. In this case, they enhanced the social connections, knowledge, and other resources that were needed to build a local culture that prevented and healed distress and trauma as residents engaged in climate solutions.[4]

A powerful sense of shared destiny and collective efficacy emerged that, among other benefits, motivated residents to quickly respond to injustices, violence, and other problems, and reestablish safe, healthy, just, and equitable conditions. Local entrepreneurs were also inspired to create innovative ways to power their communities with solar, wind, and other forms of clean renewable energy, produce ecologically regenerative goods and services, and restore local ecological systems. Their innovations led to all types of new businesses and meaningful living-wage jobs.

By mid-century these efforts had combined to prevent average global surface temperatures from rising more than 3.6 degrees Fahrenheit (2 Celsius) above preindustrial levels, and offered the potential that they might soon begin to cool back down. At the same time, everyone knew the dangers posed by climate overshoot were not going away. Yet, they also believed that by working together they could help everyone manage their distress, and heal when they were traumatized, as they did what was needed to reduce the climate crisis to manageable levels. Faith in the future was reestablished, and new and exciting opportunities continually blossomed.

WHICH SCENARIO WILL WE CHOOSE?

I've just offered a worse and best-case version of how the climate mega-emergency and the Traumacene it will generate can play out. We can choose which path to take. A major global initiative that mobilizes communities to enhance their entire population's capacity for mental wellness and transformational resilience as they engage in solutions to the climate emergency can prevent widespread distresses and traumas, heal those that occur, and motivate people to invent all sorts of previously unimaginable ways to address the crisis.

LEFT UNADDRESSED, THE CLIMATE EMERGENCY WILL GENERATE VAST INDIVIDUAL DISTRESSES AND TRAUMAS

To help you understand the need to aggressively pursue the best-case scenario, let's dive into the causes and consequences of widespread mental health and psycho-social-spiritual problems.

Even before the Covid-19 pandemic, millions of Americans and billions of people worldwide were severely stressed or traumatized due to childhood or family problems, toxic social isolation, job and income struggles, poverty, racism, sexism, and other systemic oppressions, fears of violence, and other adversities. The pandemic significantly increased these conditions. "We are seeing anxiety and depression, helplessness, and hopelessness everywhere we work," Joe Chrastil told me during an interview. He is the Director of the Industrial Areas Foundation Northwest and supports its 12 affiliates in the Northwest US, western Canada, New Zealand, and Australia that help people find hope and gain personal agency by building collective power to change conditions that adversely impact their lives.[5]

As described in the previous chapter, both the direct and indirect impacts of the climate emergency will generate even more distress. This can be thought of as a state of emotional suffering associated with stressors or demands that are difficult to cope with in daily life, that result from witnessing the harmful situation of others, or that are produced by fantasizing about impacts on the self or others that have not yet occurred.[6]

Eco-anxiety—the fear of being harmed by climate impacts and what the future holds—is an example of this type of distress. My wife and I experience this regularly as we live in a forested area that, due to the combination of a historic drought that has parched the Pacific Northwest and rising heat is now at great risk of wildfires and smoke emergencies every summer and fall. We previously cherished that time of year. We now fear it.

Millions of people will experience similar troubling emotions during the long climate emergency. As with my wife and I, most will be able to manage their distress in ways that allow them to go on with life without harming themselves, other people, or the natural environment.

Many individuals, however, are certain to experience more than distress: they will be traumatized. There are slightly different ways to define individual trauma. I find one of the best is that it results "from an event, series of events, or set of circumstances that are experienced by an individual as physically or emotionally harmful or life threatening, and that has lasting adverse effects on the individual's functioning and mental, physical, social, emotional, or spiritual well-being."[7] The events can range from a dramatic single-event or ongoing human-caused abuse, violence, racism, long-term unemployment, poverty, living in a deprived neighborhood, and/or being discriminated against. The traumas can also result from one-time or persistent ecologically generated events such as intense earthquakes, wind, rain, snowstorms, wildfires, floods, droughts, and other disasters and emergencies that people perceive as serious or life-threatening.

Some people can be more biochemically vulnerable to stressful experiences, and the likelihood of this increases if they experienced significant adversities during early childhood. However, major disasters and persistent overwhelming—or toxic—stresses are powerful forces that can cause anyone to experience significant distress or traumas because they often can overwhelm the brain's natural coping capacity.

In addition, an individual can be traumatized by the loss of their surrounding environment due to a wildfire, flood, drought, or other impacts. This can occur when people no longer have access to a landscape that "gave them spiritual solace, recreational activities, opportunities to meet with family and socialize, sometimes even gather the food they eat through hunting or fishing," according to Dr. David Eisenman, director of the Center for Public Health and Disasters at the University of California, Los Angeles.[8]

HUMANS CAN GET FROZEN OUTSIDE THEIR 'RESILIENT GROWTH ZONE'

Most people have what one of my organization's founding partners, The Trauma Resource Institute, calls a 'Resilience Zone.' This refers to an area in which our body, mind, and emotions are in a state of wellness. People naturally move up and down within their Resilience Zone during the day in response to different situations, but the ups and downs do not prevent them from feeling good, functioning well, and making decent decisions about how to respond to adversities.

However, when people experience a one-time or series of events perceived to be threatening, which can be called a trigger, they can get pushed out of their Resilience Zone into a high or low zone that prevents good decision-making and responses. This occurs because when we humans perceive a threat, our brain automatically releases the neurochemicals cortisol and adrenaline into the body to prepare us to fight back or flee the scene. If the rush of these 'stress hormones' is overwhelming, we can freeze or dissociate from what is occurring.

These are built-in survival reactions that enable our resilience for adversities. You *should* feel stressed when facing threatening situations because the 'fear and alarm center' of your brain (the amygdala) has revved up the sympathetic nervous system in your body—and sidelined your thinking mind—to concentrate all your energy on physically defending yourself.

Most people can release the fight-flight-freeze reactions generated by this natural survival response after the threat ends, or they find ways to deal with it, or they determine it was a false alarm. When this occurs, they return to their Resilience Zone, or what I call the 'Resilient Growth Zone,' to emphasize that when people are in this space, they can feel good and function well *and* use adversities as transformational catalysts to learn, grow, and find positive new sources of meaning, purpose, and healthy hope in life.[9]

But the unrelenting mix of cascading disruptions to the systems people rely on for basic necessities, and more frequent, extreme, and prolonged disasters generated during the long climate emergency, will produce traumas or relentless stresses that cause many people to remain stuck in constant fight, flight, or freeze reactions. This will impede their wellness and resilience because it will leave them frozen outside their Resilience Growth Zone in a 'high zone' where they are constantly wound up, manically worried about the past or future, edgy, agitated, or angry. Conversely, they can become frozen in a 'low zone' where they are always sad, depressed, numb, confused, or disconnected from reality.[10] In both cases, the traumatic reaction they experience will remain embedded in their nervous system, hidden from view, and unaddressed.

If the fear-based reaction people experience is not surfaced, processed, and released, the trauma can cause the brain to record separate fragments of the events. This can take the form of images, sounds, or physical sensations that lack a context. When individuals re-experience these sensations they can be reminded of past events, which activates fear and danger reactions to ongoing and future situations. This can lead them to unconsciously rehearse and reenact their traumatic experiences over and over again in their mind, and often in the physical world, as a means to find their way beyond it. This can produce actual biological changes to their nervous system that can keep them frozen in an unhealthy high or low state outside their Resilience Growth Zone.[11]

Without major efforts to prevent and heal them, the traumas generated during the long climate emergency will cause many people to be continually frozen outside the Resilient Growth Zone leading to unprecedented levels of individual anxiety, depression, post-traumatic stress disorder, complicated grief, increased suicidal ideation, and other individual mental health problems.[12] Being stuck in a high or low zone will also cause people to adopt maladaptive coping mechanisms such as misusing or abusing alcohol and/or other substances, or reacting aggressively or violently to anyone who seems threatening, including those who disagree with them or look, speak, or act differently. This will lead to even more spousal and child abuse and neglect, crime, interpersonal violence, and other psycho-social-spiritual problems that adversely affect the safety, health, and well-being of others.[13]

Figure 2.1 describes our Resilient Growth Zone.

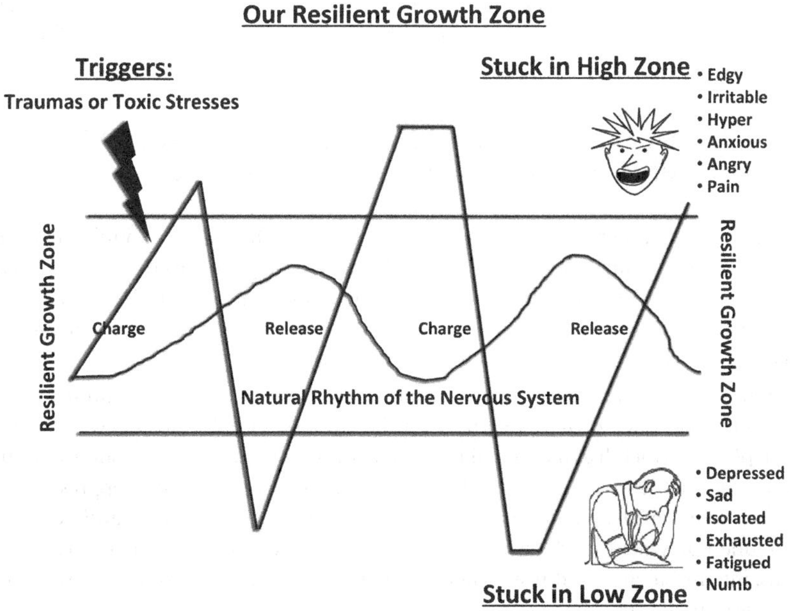

Figure 2.1 The Resilient Growth Zone
Source: Adopted from slide by Elaine Miller Karas, Executive Director of the Trauma Resource Institute.

HOPELESSNESS IS ONE OF THE GREATEST IMPACTS OF THE CLIMATE EMERGENCY

As the climate emergency intensifies, multitudes of people will come to believe they no longer have a safe place to retreat to within or outside themselves, and there is nothing they can do to stop the destructive impacts. These feelings of vulnerability will shatter the deeply held assumptions they hold that the world is a relatively safe, secure, and manageable place. For many, this will lead to a crisis of faith, where they feel abandoned by their God or Creator. Many others will experience a crisis of spirit, where they feel disconnected from the spiritual powers of nature, their ancestors, or other forces that leave them in a deep-seated state of meaninglessness and hopelessness. The result will be the destruction of telos, or the end goal, meaning, and purpose of their lives. Their conception of what happiness involves and how to live a good life will no longer make sense. With this loss, their sense of what constitutes proper behavior and the significance of one's acts will be lost.

Meaning and hope are interconnected; unless people find some healthy hope during the climate emergency they will find no meaning or purpose in life, but without meaning they will not discover healthy hope.[14] The loss of either can be debilitating. The belief that nothing matters and there is no hope for a better future will often be the most powerful cause of mental health and psycho-social-spiritual problems. The lack of healthy hope can cause people to harm themselves, harm others, or damage the natural environment, all of which circles back to produce more meaninglessness and hopelessness. As you have already read, I use the term 'psycho-social-spiritual' to describe the full range of harmful personal and interpersonal impacts generated by the climate mega-emergency and how they impact others.

In sum, unless expanded methods are quickly established to prevent and heal the traumas individuals experience during the climate emergency, they will often become the gravest threat to their ability to feel good, function well, and live a meaningful and fulfilling life.

LEFT UNADDRESSED, THE CLIMATE EMERGENCY WILL GENERATE PERVASIVE COMMUNITY TRAUMAS

While a growing number of people have a basic grasp of the nature of individual trauma, community and societal traumas are not well understood. This needs to quickly change because—in the absence of initiatives that enhance universal capacity for mental wellness and transformational resilience—the climate-ecosystem-biodiversity mega-emergency will produce far-reaching community and societal traumas.

Community trauma can be defined as an event, series of events, or chronic structural conditions that produce mental health or psycho-social-spiritual problems within an entire group of people. Much like individual trauma, community trauma can result from human-caused events such as widespread violence, systemic racism and other oppressions, large populations living in dilapidated neighborhoods, extensive homelessness and poverty, high levels of unemployment, and/or food shortages. Ecological disasters such as earthquakes, tsunamis, intense storms, heat waves, floods, wildfires, droughts, and other catastrophes and emergencies can also traumatize an entire community.

A poignant example of community trauma is the November 2018 wildfire that incinerated about 95 percent of the town of Paradise in the Sierra Nevada foothills of California. The Camp Fire was the deadliest wildfire in US history, killing at least 85 people and destroying nearly 19,000 homes, businesses, and other buildings. Research released in 2021 found that residents in and around the Paradise area experienced measurable increases in PTSD, depression, and anxiety disorders. These problems were worsened by previous adverse experiences involving childhood trauma.[15]

As the climate crisis escalates, these types of community traumas will become more frequent.

Another form of community trauma has been identified by Dr. Howard Pinderhughes, from the University of California San Francisco, and Prevention Institute. They define community trauma as an "aggregate of trauma experienced by community members or an event that impacts a few people but has structural and social traumatic consequences" for an entire community.[16] By community, they are referring to people residing in a specific geographical area such as a neighborhood or city. (However, as previously noted, a community can also mean people who affiliate with a group with the same identity such as an online network, a religious or spiritual community, or a group of refugees.)

Pinderhughes and Prevention Institute said "structural traumas" are "harm that individuals, families, and communities experience from the economic and social structure, social institutions, and social relations of power, privilege, and inequities and inequalities that may harm communities by preventing people from meeting their basic needs."[17] In other words, just as a particular event like a wildfire or series of ecological disasters and emergencies can cause community trauma, so can trauma be transmitted throughout an entire community due to a lack of sufficient resources and harmful social, economic, political, and ecological conditions and policies.[18]

The manifestations, or symptoms, of structural trauma appear in the social-cultural, economic, physical/build, and natural environments of a community. In the social-cultural environment, the symptoms can include fractured social relationships, disrupted social support networks, the prevalence of harmful social norms, and a low degree of cooperation and social efficacy.

Symptoms of structural trauma in the economic environment can include high levels of poverty, low availability of living-wage jobs, lack of access to educational and job training opportunities, and minimum private and public sector investments.

Symptoms of structural trauma in the physical/built environment can include harmful, inadequate, or deteriorating transportation infrastructure, residential housing and commercial buildings, and lack of green spaces and open areas where people can meet and recreate in safe and healthy ways. Signs of structural trauma in the natural environment often include high levels of pollution, toxicity, or the destruction or degradation of local wetlands, waterways, forests, and other ecological systems.

These symptoms often feed on each other to produce even more structural traumas in communities.[19] Following a pattern that mirrors individual trauma, high levels of community trauma can unravel the deeply held assumptions members hold about the fairness, safety, and manageability of the world and their role in it. This can lead to loss of meaning, purpose, and healthy hope in life, which produces high levels of community trauma.

When community trauma remains hidden from view, unspoken, and unaddressed, members can often unconsciously reconstruct and reenact the traumatic events to make sense of them. When these patterns occur, people often try to dull their pain by adopting coping mechanisms that can produce self-harm such as misusing alcohol and/or other drugs, or turn their distress outward and become aggressive or violent toward others, which creates more traumatic impacts on the community as a whole and its individual members.

As the climate emergency accelerates, the absence of methods to prevent and heal community trauma will often cause them to become widespread.

LEFT UNADDRESSED, THE CLIMATE CRISIS WILL ALSO GENERATE PERVASIVE SOCIETAL TRAUMAS

While community trauma affects people in a specific geographical area or a group with shared affiliation, societal trauma (also called collective trauma) refers to the impact of a calamitous event or series of events that disrupt the fabric of entire nations, cultures, or humanity as a whole.

Situations that can generate societal trauma include high-profile terrorist attacks, wars, historical and intergenerational racism, and other forms of oppression or genocide, global economic recessions, widespread famines or poverty, and other human-caused calamities. Ecologically generated events can also produce societal traumas, such as viral outbreaks, major earthquakes, tsunamis, and other large-scale emergencies and disasters.[20]

The physical damage and destruction, injuries, loss of life, and other consequences of these catastrophes can turn reality upside down for entire cultures and societies. Just as individual and community traumas can shatter the core assumptions and beliefs people hold about the world, societal trauma can destroy the sense of meaning held by entire populations about the nature of their culture and society, and their place in it. The fact that their lives are extremely fragile and vulnerable becomes ever-present, which can lead to deep-seated fear and shattered meaning, purpose, and hope.[21]

The despair, hopelessness, and unaddressed grief that results can produce what Thomas Hubl, in his book *Healing Collective Trauma*, describes as collective PTSD. The symptoms can include wholesale anxiety, depression, psychological and emotional numbing, low self-esteem, aggression, anger, and self-destructive behaviors such as alcohol and substance abuse and addiction, and suicidal ideation.[22]

Just like the fight-flight-freeze reactions experienced by an individual when they sense a threat, these reactions can initially be viewed as an adaptive survival strategy. They are society's attempt to cope with pervasive insidious fears. But if they continue and become fixed and dominant, they become socially dysfunctional and collectively destructive.

Societal PTSD can activate the search for a new source of collective meaning. For some people, this is found through adherence to, and identification with, a group that defines itself as special or unique to the point that it is honorable to suffer for, or even sacrifice one's life, or the lives of others, to defend. The (often romanticized) history of the group, and the (often glamorized) descriptions of the obstacles it overcame in the past espoused by group leaders provide members with a sense of meaning for their current struggles. This can lead to dangerous Groupthink, 'us vs. them' tribalism, political polarization, terrorism, wars, and other forms of violence.[23]

As seen by the societal trauma generated by American slavery, the World War II Holocaust, the September 11, 2001, terrorist attacks in the US and other genocides throughout history, the reactive thinking and behaviors that result from these devastating societal events can destroy the trust people have in others, what they accept as fact, and how they define truth. This often fractures relationships, produces unjust and harmful social norms, and leads to destructive private and public practices, policies, and institutions.[24] If societal traumas remain hidden and unaddressed, the symptoms can also be passed down from one generation to the next, producing historic and intergenerational trauma (more on this in a moment).

A poignant example of a societal trauma is the COVID-19 pandemic. Almost overnight, it brought entire nations to a screeching halt, caused the illness and death of millions of people, and created tremendous fear among others about contracting the disease. Massive numbers of people lost their jobs and incomes, most were forced to isolate themselves from others, and in other ways almost every aspect of society was profoundly impacted. Racism and other forms of oppression, as well as religious and political divides, intensified. The COVID-19 pandemic has shown how societal traumas can profoundly affect perceptions, beliefs, behaviors, and relationships at all levels of society.[25] And the impacts are certainly modest compared to what the rapidly accelerating global climate emergency will produce if we do not get prepared.

Ecological disasters can be a source of societal traumas. However, this typically refers to large-scale, but not global, catastrophes that eventually end and then give people time to recover. In contrast, as should be clear by now, the climate mega-emergency will produce a mixture of relentless disruptions to essential systems and acute disasters that will continue for decades or more and affect every individual, family, community, and nation on earth. Unless methods are established to strengthen the entire population's capacity to prevent distresses and traumas, and heal them when they do occur, the ongoing crisis will leave billions of people with little or no time to recover, at least in the way we now think of it.

Left unaddressed, another worrisome outcome of the global climate emergency is that people worldwide will eventually realize that humans, not natural forces, caused the calamity. Sociologist Kai Erickson said that a core element of societal (or what he called collective) trauma is the way those who are responsible for a human-caused catastrophe often deny responsibility and withdraw from the victims without an expression of regret, apology, or reparations. The betrayal of social trust that results makes people furious.[26]

Some nations, especially the US and other wealthier countries that are historically the largest producers of greenhouse gases, as well as certain industries, including fossil fuel producers, mining, logging, and industrialized agriculture corporations, are likely to be seen as the primary perpetrators. For decades their executives knew their practices and products were destabilizing the earth's climate and destroying vital ecological systems and species. But they deliberately bamboozled the public about these realities anyway. The politicians, financiers, and media pundits who defended them also hold significant responsibility for our current dire state. Growing awareness of their culpability could generate tremendous anger that triggers other human causes of societal trauma such as violence, terrorism, or wars.

Unless exceptional efforts are swiftly made to establish methods that can prevent and heal societal traumas, the long climate crisis will seriously damage or completely unravel entire nations, cultures, and global society.

HISTORIC AND INTERGENERATIONAL TRAUMA CONTRIBUTE TO THE CLIMATE CRISIS

Often embedded within individual, community, and societal traumas are historic and intergenerational trauma. As with the other forms of trauma, these terms have been defined in different ways. For our purposes, when trauma is experienced over time across generations by a group of people who share the same identity or affiliation, it can be called historic trauma.[27]

An example of human-caused historical trauma is that experienced by Native Americans. Generations of indigenous people have been exposed to repeated violence, colonization, forced assimilation, family separation, and personal and cultural loss. These historical traumas have altered traditional ways of child rearing, disrupted family structure, and splintered relationships. The reactions to these traumatic experiences show up as over-all poor physical and psychological health, including depression, substance abuse, and high rates of suicide. The historical trauma has also produced a completely understandable mis-trust of outsiders and government agencies. These forces have, for generations, disrupted the sense of community and culture within Native American tribes.[28]

Closely linked with historic trauma is intergenerational trauma (sometimes called trans-generational trauma), which can be defined as trauma that is transmitted exclusively within generations of family members, not different social groups.[29]

Intergenerational trauma can result from human-caused events such as the slavery that took place in the US, internment at refugee camps, the Holocaust, and other genocides. These traumas cause the victim to pass on their psychological and emotional distresses to their children, who in turn pass the suffering on to their children. It can also be produced when a child experiences parental neglect, abuse, divorce, alcohol or drug misuse, domestic violence, incarceration, or other adversities that cause them to adopt their own unhealthy emotional and behavioral reactions, which they then repeat when they become adults and pass on to their children.

Historic and intergenerational traumas are transmitted to future generations in a couple of ways. As mentioned, when the trauma experienced by an individual remains hidden and unresolved, it becomes embedded in their nervous system. When large groups of people experience this type of unhealthy traumatic reaction, it can cause those around them to adopt self-protective defense mechanisms that emulate the harmful patterns of those who were originally traumatized, and the pattern can then be repeated, again and again, over time.

This means historic and intergeneration trauma can be passed down to future gener-ations through parenting styles, storytelling, or when the fear of stigmatization or desire to forget the past and move on with life cause the original victims to stay silent about their experience. Unless the lived experience of traumatized people is made explicit, and the complex web of structural factors such as poverty, racism, and other forms of injustices are illuminated, future generations will remain unaware of what occurred and unable to learn from past events. This can lead them to adopt defense mechanisms that repeat the same traumatic reactions as their forbearers.

Both forms of trauma have contributed to the climate emergency.

Researchers on racial trauma, for example, have described how the origins of the white supremacy and racism seen in the US today began as far back as the 1400s in Europe. During that time, the idea of European blood purity and the use of race as a social construct—both of which are patently false concepts—were used to justify the colonization and seizure of land not inhabited by white Christians. Among other impacts, this led to the genocide of indigenous people and the enslavement of Africans in multiple locations, including in what we now call the US. Underneath the spiritual, legal, and political rhetoric that justifies white supremacy has always been the goal of creating and maintaining wealth, power, and priv-ilege. For many white people, race is often just a smokescreen that obfuscates and diverts attention away from these goals.[30]

From 1619 to 1865 slavery was legal in the US, and it then took another 100 years to end legal segregation. And the consequences are still very much alive today. Slavery is a profound historic trauma. It has also created deep-seated intergenerational traumas as the consequences have affected generation after generation of African Americans. White supremacy remains a powerful force in the US, and the traumas it produces continue to affect people of color today.

Racial trauma can take a serious toll on the mental and physical health of people of color. In some individuals, the effects are so profound that they develop symptoms similar to post-traumatic stress disorder. Racial trauma can also have a cumulative effect. In her book *So You Want to Talk About Race*, Ijeoma Oluo says racism is much like an abusive relationship, only in this case it is the equivalent of being in an abusive relationship with all of society.[31] The abuse occurs through different types of micro assaults, insults, and invalidations, as well as overt abuse, violence, and systemic inequities, injustices, and violence embedded within policing, the justice system, health care, housing, transportation, economic, educational, voting, and many other policies and structures.

Few people realize it, but the impacts of racism also harm the oppressors. The specious ideas some white Americans carry about their genetic superiority and their fears about losing money, power, and status lead them to deny or dissociate from the causes of and solutions to both their own suffering and the suffering their actions cause within others.

When they feel anxious or depressed, for example, many attempt to anesthetize themselves with mindless material consumption, social media, video games, food abuse, alcohol and drug misuse, or other diversions and distractions. When these approaches fail, they often lash out at their families, friends, or people who think, look, or act differently. In addition, many believe that laziness or moral ineptitude are the causes of poverty and other problems BIPOC populations struggle with, while refusing to acknowledge the effects of the 400 years of traumas passed down by their predecessors or the continual social, economic, and structural inequalities and injustices they deal with daily today.

The unwillingness of many white people to see and deal with reality, and the suffering they and their predecessors caused, also appears in the denial, apathy, and complacency they exhibit as the planet's climate and ecological systems collapse around them. Millions believe climate disruption is a hoax promoted by the politically liberal elite or scientists. They consequently oppose all efforts to acknowledge or address the problem. This could be thought of as the 'great dissociation' where many white Americans have completely disconnected from reality and exist in an almost delusional state.

Another example of how historic and intergenerational traumas contribute to the climate emergency is the Great Depression of the previous century. In the early part of the 1900s, industrial capacity rapidly increased to the point where it far exceeded demand. By the late 1920s, for example, just six months were required to produce all the cloth the US population needed each year, and just 14 percent of shoe factories could produce a full year's supply of footwear Americans needed. Industrialists such as John Edgerton, President of the National Association of Manufacturers, determined that to maintain profits, keep people employed, and avoid the social unrest he believed would result from too much leisure time, the public needed to be motivated to consume more and more goods. The marketing and advertising industries were created to convince people that their self-worth was determined by their level of material consumption and possessions. The goal of these industries was (and still is) to create dissatisfaction and persuade people that the solution to their poor self-image (that they deliberately helped create) was to keep buying more and more stuff. This was the origins of today's consumer culture.[32]

The belief that their self-worth was linked to material possessions caused millions of people to feel worthless when, in October 1929, the stock market crashed, and the Great

Depression began. In the following five years the economy shrank by 50 percent, a third of all banks failed, their customer's savings were eradicated, and unemployment rose to over 25 percent.[33]

The sudden shocking crash destroyed the nation's feeling of invincibility and left people feeling anxious, depressed, and fearful. Historian Harvey Green says that between 1929 and 1932, the suicide rate rose more than 30 percent. Family disputes over finances, food, and other basic needs often caused tensions to boil over, which frequently led to domestic violence and child abuse. Thousands of old and young people became so desperate that they ended up riding the rails as traveling hobos in search of work or some form of relief.[34]

The Great Depression is still seen as one of the defining historic and intergenerational traumas of the twentieth century. It left deep emotional scars that have been passed down to generation after generation of Americans. Some economists have concluded that the despair of the 1930s became so severe and lasted so long that millions of Americans came to believe that the 'American Dream,' which now included the right to continual material acquisition, had been unjustly taken away from them.[35]

One consequence is that whenever the economy experiences any type of significant downturn, many people are immediately gripped by fears of another Great Depression. Although it is by no means the only factor, these fears are an important force behind the demand for continued economic growth. The fears also contribute to the chorus of vehement objections that are always made to any public policy or regulation that reduces profitable economic activity.

In its current form, however, more economic growth requires more fossil fuels, resource extraction, and material consumption. The system generates more greenhouse gas emissions and other forms of waste, as well as increased ecological damage. These factors, of course, are the primary causes of the global climate-ecosystem-biodiversity mega-emergency. Continuing the fossil-fuel driven approach to economic growth is simply not possible on our ecologically finite planet without destroying the systems and structures that make life possible.

I'm not suggesting that the Great Depression is the only reason people want continued economic growth. I'm also not saying it is the only cause of the climate crisis. My point is that current conditions are always influenced by the past. The trauma produced by the Great Depression a century ago is still very much alive today, affecting the entire planet.

THE CLIMATE EMERGENCY IS THE ULTIMATE SYMPTOM OF UNRESOLVED TRAUMA

It should be clear by now that the distresses and traumas generated by the climate crisis are by no means caused by personal or family dynamics alone. It should also be evident that today's standard individualized approaches to mental health and direct human services cannot address the scale or scope of the wicked psychological, emotional, and spiritual distresses and traumas generated by wicked climate emergency. The complex interacting nature of these problems have, for the most part, gone unaddressed, resulting in growing distresses as well as individual, community, and societal traumas.

Severely stressed, numbed, and traumatized people often adopt denial or dissociation from reality as a means to cope with their distress, which is why they cannot comprehend or resolve complex problems like the climate crisis. The global mega-emergency can therefore be thought of as the ultimate symptom of unresolved trauma.

The Multisystemic Causes of the Traumacene

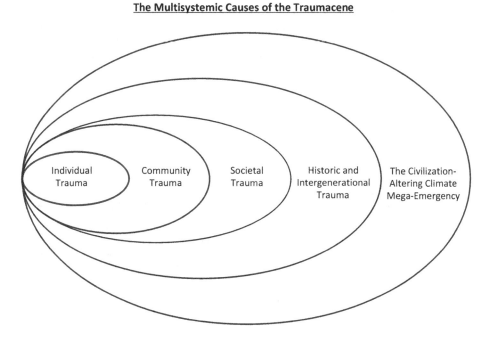

Figure 2.2 The Multisystemic Causes of the Traumacene

This illustrates that the past never ends. To understand what is happening today, look at the past. To get a glimpse of what the future will be like, look at what is happening now. This is why individual trauma must be viewed within the context of historic, intergenerational, community, and societal traumas. Each human is a complex bio-psycho-social-cultural-spiritual system in themselves. Each individual is embedded within a larger complex family system, which is embedded within an even larger complex system of neighbors, friends, and community, which is embedded within still larger systems of social norms and values, economic practices, and religious, financial, and political beliefs, power, and privilege. All these interlinked complex human systems are embedded within and shaped by the Earth's climate and ecological systems.

Figure 2.2 depicts how, if left unacknowledged and unaddressed, the global climate emergency will generate individual, community, and societal traumas that will interact to produce historic and intergeneration traumas that will accumulate and activate feedbacks that produce the global Traumacene.[36]

PREVENTION AND HEALING REQUIRE BUILDING POPULATION-LEVEL MENTAL WELLNESS AND TRANSFORMATIONAL RESILIENCE

Effective responses to the Traumacene will require entire communities to engage in efforts to enhance the capacity of all residents to prevent and heal distresses and traumas as they engage in actions that can reduce the climate crisis to manageable levels.[36] Just as almost everyone in the US, EU, and other wealthier nations today learns how to read and write, *the entire population* should now have the opportunity to learn how to strengthen their capacity for mental wellness and transformational resilience, and find powerful sources of meaning, purpose, and healthy hope for the future, as they also engage in actions that can reduce their contribution to the climate crisis.

New thinking, systems, structures, and policies will be needed to accomplish this, and a public health approach is required to guide the process. This is the focus of the next chapter.

NOTES

1 Schleussner C.-F. et al. (2016). *Differential Climate Impacts for Policy-Relevant Limits to Global Warming: The Case of 1.5 °C and 2 °C.* European Geosciences Union. Obtained at: https://esd.copernicus.org/articles/7/327/2016/
2 Mental Health America. *Prevalence of Mental Illness 2020.* Obtained at: https://mhanational.org/issues/2020/mental-health-america-prevalence-data
3 Leonhardt M. (May 10, 2021). What you need to know about the costs and accessibility of mental health care in America. *CNBC.* Obtained at: https://www.cnbc.com/2021/05/10/cost-and-accessibility-of-mental-health-care-in-america.html
4 This point was made by International Transformational Resilience Coalition steering committee Dr. David Pollack to describe the benefits of the "Resilience for All" policy proposal being developed by the ITRC.
5 Personal interview, January 6, 2022.
6 Davis M. H. (1983). The effects of dispositional empathy on emotional reactions and helping: a multidimensional approach. *Journal of Personality*, 51(2), 167–184.
7 SAMHSA. (2014). *SAMHSA's Concept of Trauma and Guidance for a Trauma-Informed Approach.* Rockville, MD: SAMHSA's Trauma and Justice Strategic Initiative.
8 Eisenman D. et al. (2015). An ecosystems and vulnerable populations perspective on solastalgia and psychological distress after a wildfire. *EcoHealth*, 12, 602–610. Obtained at: https://www.semanticscholar.org/paper/An-Ecosystems-and-Vulnerable-Populations-on-and-a-Eisenman-McCaffrey
9 See for example: Boss P. (2012). *Family Stress Management: A Contextual Approach.* Sage Books, Thousand Oaks, CA. Mariotti A. (2015). *The Effects of Chronic Stress on Health: New Insights Into the Molecular Mechanisms of Brain-Body Communications.* Future Science. Obtained at: https://www.ncbi.nlm.nih.gov/pmc/articles/PMC5137920/; and Hobfoll S. E. (1989). Conservation of resources: A new attempt at conceptualizing stress. *American Psychologist.* Obtained at: https://psycnet.apa.org/record/1989-29399-001
10 Trauma Resource Institute, Community Resilience Model. Obtained at: https://www.traumaresourceinstitute.com/home
11 SAMHSA. (2014). *Trauma-Informed Care in Behavioral Health Services. Chapter 3: Understanding the Impacts of Trauma.* Obtained at: https://www.ncbi.nlm.nih.gov/books/NBK207191/
12 Cianconi P. et al. (2020). The impacts of climate change on mental health: A systemic descriptive review. *Frontiers in Psychiatry.* Obtained at: https://www.frontiersin.org/articles/10.3389/fpsyt.2020.00074/full
13 See for example: Obradovich N. et al. (2018). Empirical evidence of mental health risks posed by climate change. *Proceedings of the National Academy of Sciences*; Clayton S. et al. (2017). *Mental Health and Our Changing Climate: Impacts, Implications, and Guidance.* American Psychological Association and ecoAmerica, Washington, DC: and other research on the mental health and psychosocial impacts of climate change in the ITRC Library: http://www.theresourceinnovationgroup.org/intl-tr-coalition
14 Boss P. (1999). *Ambiguous Loss: Learning to Live with Unresolved Grief.* Boston, MA: Harvard University Press.
15 Silveira S. et al. (2021). Chronic mental health sequelae of climate change extremes: A case study of the deadliest Californian wildfire. *International Journal of Environmental Research and Public Health*, 18(4), 1487. Obtained at: https://www.researchgate.net/publication/349046408_Chronic_Mental_Health_Sequelae_of_Climate_Change_Extremes_A_Case_Study_of_the_Deadliest_Californian_Wildfire

16 Pinderhughes H. et al. (2015). *Adverse Community Experiences and Resilience: A Framework for Addressing and Preventing Community Trauma*. Prevention Institute. Obtained at: https://www.preventioninstitute.org/publications/adverse-community-experiences-and-resilience-framework-addressing-and-preventing

17 Ibid.

18 Lehrner A. and Yehuda R. (2018). Trauma across generations and paths to adaptation and resilience. *Psychological Trauma: Theory, Research, Practice, and Policy*, 10(1), 22–29. Obtained at: https://www.researchgate.net/publication/322407819_Trauma_across_generations_and_paths_to_adaptation_and_resilience

19 Pinderhughes H. et al. (2015). *Adverse Community Experiences and Resilience: A Framework for Addressing and Preventing Community Trauma*. The Prevention Institute, Oakland, CA.

20 Ciano A. (August 2017). How to forget the unforgettable? On collective trauma, cultural identity, and mnemotechnologies. *Identity International Journal*. Obtained at: https://www.tandfonline.com/doi/full/10.1080/15283488.2017.1340160

21 Hirschberger G. (August 2018). Collective trauma and the social construction of meaning. *Frontiers in Psychology*. Obtained at: https://www.frontiersin.org/articles/10.3389/fpsyg.2018.01441/full; and Chang K. (2017). Living with vulnerability and resiliency: The psychological experience of collective trauma. *Acta Psychopathologica*. Obtained at: https://www.primescholars.com/articles/living-with-vulnerability-and-resiliency-the-psychological-experience-of-collective-trauma-104272.html

22 Hubl T. (2020). *Healing Collective Trauma*. Boulder, Colorado: Sounds True, Boulder, CO.

23 Hirschberger G. (August 2018). Collective trauma and the social construction of meaning. *Frontiers in Psychology*. Obtained at: https://www.frontiersin.org/articles/10.3389/fpsyg.2018.01441/full

24 Hubl T. (2020). *Healing Collective Trauma*. Boulder, Colorado: Sounds True.

25 Saul J. (2014). *Collective Trauma Collective Healing*. Routledge Publishing.

26 Erickson K. (1976). *Everything in its Path: Destruction of Community in the Buffalo Creek Flood*. New York, NY: Simon and Shuster.

27 Crawford A. (2013). "The trauma experienced by generations past having an effect in their descendants": Narrative and historical trauma among Inuit in Nunavut, Canada. *Transcultural Psychiatry*, 0(0), 1–31. Obtained at: https://pubmed.ncbi.nlm.nih.gov/23475452/

28 Brave Heart M. Y. H. et al. (2011). Historical trauma among Indigenous Peoples of the Americas: Concepts, research, and clinical considerations. *Journal of Psychoactive Drugs*, 43(4), 282–290. Obtained at: https://pubmed.ncbi.nlm.nih.gov/22400458/

29 DeAngelis T. (Feb. 2019). The Legacy of Trauma: An emerging line of research is exploring how historical and cultural traumas affect survivors' children for generations to come. *American Psychological Association*, 50(2). Obtained at: https://www.apa.org/monitor/2019/02/legacy-trauma

30 See for example: DeGury-Leary J. (2005). *Post Traumatic Slave Syndrome: America's Legacy of Enduring Injury and Healing*. Uptone Press; Fields K.E. and Fields J. F. (2012). *Racecraft: The Soul of Inequity in American Life*. Verso; and Menakem R. (2017). *My Grandmothers Hands: Racialized Trauma and the Pathway to Mending Our Hearts and Bodies*. Central Recovery Press.

31 Oluo I. (2018). *So You Want to Talk about Race*. New York, NY: Seal Press.

32 Kaplan J. (May/June 2008). The gospel of consumption: And the better future we left behind. *Orion*. Obtained at: https://orionmagazine.org/article/the-gospel-of-consumption/

33 Ibid.

34 Bernstein, Michael A. (1987). *The Great Depression: Delayed Recovery and Economic Change in America, 1929–1939*. Cambridge University Press, Cambridge, UK.

35 Amedeo K. (March 29, 2021). The 9 principle effects of the great depression: How this low point in American history still affects you today. *The Balance*. Obtained at: thebalance.com/effects-of-the-great-depression

36 Ibid.

CHAPTER 3

Elements of a Public Health Approach to Enhancing Mental Wellness and Transformational Resilience for the Long Climate Emergency

In the face of the pervasive distresses and traumas the long climate mega-emergency will generate the urgency of revamping the way the problems are prevented and healed cannot be overstated. The priority must shift from relying on mental health and human services professionals that assist individuals mostly one-at-a-time after they show symptoms of pathology, to empowering neighborhoods and communities to take responsibility for strengthening the entire population's capacity for mental wellness and transformational resilience as residents also engage in actions that reduce their contribution to the climate emergency.

The call for a more holistic approach is hardly new: It has been made for over three decades. The Ottawa Charter, a global agreement signed at the First International Conference on Health Promotion in November 1986 organized by the World Health Organization (WHO), promoted the principles of community participation and empowerment in promoting mental and physical health. Strengthening community action was one of the five key action areas described in the Ottawa Charter.[1]

The call for change was also made a decade ago by Dr. William Eaton, chair of the Department of Mental Health at the Johns Hopkins Bloomberg School of Public Health in his book *Public Mental Health*, when he said the field "must move beyond a narrow focus on clinical interventions to embrace the impact of community and population dynamics in promoting mental health, preventing mental illnesses, and fostering recovery."[2] Many other mental health professionals have also called for a public health approach to addressing mental health problems.[3] A brief history will explain why this came about.

The need for a more expansive approach emerged in response to the limitations of the biomedical model that dominated the field until the early 1990s (and still has considerable influence today). This model delivered significant advances in health; however, it almost exclusively focused on illness; emphasized genetic and biological causes; discounted the developmental, social, economic, and environmental determinants of mental health and psycho-social-spiritual well-being; and primarily promoted pharmaceutical and technological solutions.[4] Indeed, in many ways, the biomedical model matched the notion of individualism that grew so powerful in the late 20th century. It claimed that an individual's health and well-being can primarily be traced back to factors in their brain, which by necessity requires individualized treatment by highly trained professionals.

This model was challenged when the "rainbow model" was released.[5] It proclaimed that in addition to genetic and biological factors, social factors affected mental health, including the relationship between the individual and their lifestyle, community influences, living and working conditions, and overall societal conditions.

Although the rainbow model emphasized social determinants, it was eventually also deemed insufficient because it failed to highlight how crucial parental and family relationships are in shaping a child's brain in ways that can affect their mental health and well-being all the way through adulthood. It also failed to recognize how the complex interactions that occur between the social, cultural, economic, physical/built, and natural environments people live within can affect their psychological and emotional well-being, including the role

DOI: 10.4324/9781003262442-5

inequality, injustices, and powerlessness can play. And it did not address how an individual's belief system and sense of self-efficacy can affect their psychological, emotional, and spiritual well-being and resilience.[6]

The "Social-Ecological" model eventually emerged to address these missing elements. It recognizes that the experiences an individual has in their childhood and family life play an important role in shaping their attitudes, beliefs, and behaviors. But this is by no means the only factor that influences health and well-being. The connections people have with others; the norms and values that dominate the social networks they belong to; the way schools, businesses, faith-based, government, and other organizations perceive and treat them; how wealth and power are distributed; and the conditions of the physical/built and natural environment in which they live, work, and recreate all significantly influence mental and physical well-being and resilience. In addition, political circumstances and public policies can shape all of these factors (Figure 3.1).[7]

In short, numerous interacting factors influence the mental wellness and resilience of individuals, families, groups, organizations, communities, and entire societies. Accordingly, the social-ecological perspective recognizes that the possibility of influencing psychological

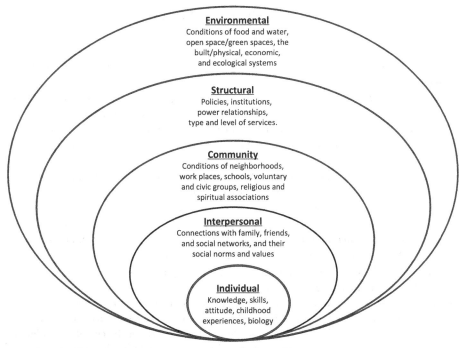

Each level interacts with the others to influence mental wellness and resilience.
Changes are required at all levels to prevent and heal climate distresses and traumas.

Figure 3.1 The Social Ecological Model
Source: Adapted from the UNICEF 5-Level Model. Poux S. (August 5, 2017). *Social Ecological Model Offers New Approach to Public Health*. The Borgen Project. Obtained at: https://borgenproject.org/social-ecological-model/

and emotional conditions in safe and healthy ways is best achieved when all of those factors are addressed.

The social-ecological model also emphasizes interdependency: the reality that psychological and emotional conditions are shaped by multiple interacting factors including personal and family dynamics, and the social, cultural, economic, physical/built, political, and ecological conditions in which people are born, grow, live, work, and play. This calls for expanding beyond individualized clinical treatment to approaches that simultaneously address all the interacting forces that affect the capacity for mental wellness and resilience.

The community is seen as having the greatest potential to accomplish this because it is the most common interface between these multiple interacting systems. The community is therefore the primary place of emphasis to prevent and heal individual, community, and societal distresses and traumas.

Despite the numerous calls for change, the crisis and illness-focused individualized clinical treatment and direct human service approaches continue to dominate the field. But the rapidly accelerating climate emergency makes the urgency of shifting to a holistic population-level approach crystal clear.

WHAT DOES IT MEAN TO ENHANCE MENTAL WELLNESS AND RESILIENCE?

Before diving into the details of a public health approach, let's clarify what it means to enhance mental wellness and resilience.

Mental wellness lies outside the medical model of health and thus cannot be officially defined or "diagnosed." It is therefore described in different ways. Some people characterize it as the absence of mental illness, which connects it with an individual's need for clinical treatment. Others see positive meaning in the term "health," but still associate it with mental illness.

The World Health Organization (WHO) emphasizes that individual mental health is "more than just the absence of mental disorders or disabilities." It defines it as "a state of well-being in which every individual realizes their own potential, can cope with the normal stresses of life, can work productively and fruitfully, and is able to make a contribution to their community."[8] Building on the WHO's definition, I use the term mental "wellness" rather than health to emphasize both "feeling good" and "functioning well."[9]

What then does "resilience" mean? Some psychologists define it as "bouncing back" from "adversity, trauma, tragedy, threats, or significant sources of stress."[10] This definition assumes adversities will end and give people time to bounce back to previous conditions. It also assumes that conditions will be similar after a major adversity to what they were beforehand. As discussed, however, this will often not be the case as the climate crisis intensifies. Returning to "normal" or previous conditions will simply not be possible because circumstances will continually change, often in harmful ways. In many locations, disasters and emergencies will occur relentlessly and provide less and less, or no time, for recovery. In addition, marginalized and impoverished populations, those who experience ongoing racism, sexism, and other systemic oppressions, and people who have been subjected to other forms of persistent toxic stresses or traumas don't want to return to previous conditions. They want to increase their sense of wellness substantially above pre-adversity levels. And in many cases, previous ways of living contributed to the climate emergency, so bouncing back to pre-crisis conditions can often make problems worse.

Suffering can either defeat or empower us. It can motivate us if we are able to find meaning in it and use the suffering for the benefit of others and the conditions around us. Rather than bouncing back, as I have already stated, enhancing resilience in the midst of the long climate emergency should therefore focus on helping people use adversities as catalysts to transform their situation into one that is *substantially more positive* than it was previously. In psychology, this is called "post-traumatic growth," "trauma-induced growth," or "adversity-based growth."[11]

Again, I call this "Transformational Resilience." It is the ability to transform the way we perceive and respond to distressing events by using self-chosen Presencing skills previously discussed to calm our body, mind, and emotions and then using self-selected Purposing skills previously discussed to use adversities as powerful catalysts to imagine and move toward a positive alternative future that provides new meaning, purpose, and healthy hope.[12]

TRANSFORMATIONAL RESILIENCE CAN OCCUR IN EACH OF THE SIX COMMON PHASES OF A DISASTER

Major disasters and emergencies typically have a number of common phases. I describe them as six phases and people can experience transformational resilience during any of them, although they engage in it most often during the last ones. As described in Figure 3.2 the phases are:

- *The Pre-Disaster Phase*: This often includes years or days of warnings about a potential disaster or emergency. For example, humanity has been warned for decades that the climate emergency will generate more frequent, extreme, and prolonged disasters and emergencies. Often, but not always, warnings are issued about a disaster such as a major storm or earthquake days or hours before it occurs. During the pre-disaster phase people can (but frequently do not) get physically, psychologically, and emotionally prepared for the event. To get psychologically and emotionally prepared, they can, for instance, intentionally learn Presencing (or self-regulation and co-regulation) skills to calm the body, mind, and emotions when they are distressed. They can also learn Purposing (or adversity-based growth) skills to enable them to use adversities as catalysts to learn about the world and themselves; grow as people; and find new sources of meaning, direction, and healthy hope. These skills will be described in greater depth in the chapters to come. When people get prepared in this way, they are much more likely to remain mentally well and resilient during a major disaster or emergency and use the event as an impetus to find ways to increase their own sense of well-being and often help others do so as well. The possibility of harmful consequences is much greater when people have not developed these capacities.

- *The Impact Phase*: This is the period when a major disaster or emergency occurs. During this phase, family members, strangers, or emergency responders will often put their lives on the line to save others. If people have enhanced their capacity for Presencing and Purposing before the disaster, they can remain mentally well and resilient and find new meaning and purpose in their lives by helping others who have been impacted by the event.

- *Community Cohesion Phase*: Also called the honeymoon phase, this occurs after the direct impacts of a disaster or emergency have ended and complete strangers often come together to provide food, water, shelter, and other forms of assistance as well as emotional support to others. Depending on the type and severity of the event, this phase can last for a few days or months. The use of Presencing skills, with a special emphasis

Six Phases Commonly Seen in Disasters

Figure 3.2 The Six Common Phases of a Disaster

Source: Adapted from: Hallock, D. (2010). *Understanding the Four Phases of Disaster Recovery.* Obtained at: https://duanehallock.com/2010/01/27/phases-of-disaster-recovery/; North Carolina Cooperative Extension Service (1999). *Common Stages of Disaster Recovery.* Obtained at: http://www.nj-ptc.org/training/materials/SHRP/FoodNutritionConf/DisasterRecovery.pdf; Joseph S. (2013). *What Doesn't Kill Us*; and Doppelt B. (2016). *Transformational Resilience*, Greenleaf Publishing.

on connecting with one's social support network, is very important during this phase to help people calm their body, mind, and emotions and prevent serious dysregulation. People with good Purposing skills can also find new meaning and direction in their lives by assisting others who are seriously impacted or traumatized. Although people can be distressed, the support and social cohesion generated during this phase allows most to remain mentally well and resilient. However, some people can develop post-traumatic stress disorder (PTSD) or other mental health problems.

- *The Disillusionment Phase*: The community cohesion phase eventually ends when people must go their own way to rebuild their lives. This is when most mental health and psycho-social-spiritual problems appear. Troubles can emerge when people struggle to deal with unresolved grief for the people, that were injured or died, or physical resources lost, when they grapple with the need to rebuild their residence or find a new place to live, cope with job and income losses, or deal with the many other issues involved with putting their lives back together. People without good Presencing and Purposing skills can experience severe anxiety, depression, PTSD, complicated grief, or other mental health problems during this phase. Others can try to anesthetize themselves from their pain by misusing alcohol or other drugs, or take their distress out on their family, friends, or strangers, leading to psycho-social-spiritual problems. Without effective skills and supports, these problems can continue for months and some people can remain dysregulated for years. However, the disillusionment phase can be avoided or be short-lived for people who have good Presencing and Purposing skills.

- *The Recovery Phase*: Most people will begin to recover a few weeks or months after a major disaster or emergency. During this phase people slowly recover their capacity to feel good and function well. Regression can occur, however, on the anniversary of the disaster, the day a loved one was lost, or other powerful reminders appear. Recovery can also be stalled, or completely halted, if another major disaster or emergency occurs, which unfortunately will be all too common as the global climate mega-emergency accelerates. Strengthening the capacity for both Presencing and Purposing will be crucial during this phase to help people continually move toward healing and recovery.

• *The Bounce Back and Transformational Resilience Phases*: If people are not continually set back by another major disaster, emergency, or anniversary events, weeks, months, or sometimes even years down the road, most are eventually able to return to some semblance of the psychological and emotional conditions they were in prior to the event. People with good Presencing and Purposing skills, however, are often able to use the adversity as a powerful catalyst to gain important new insights about the world and themselves, grow, and move toward a more positive future. The disaster activates their capacity for transformational resilience which enables them to find new meaning, purpose, and healthy hope in life, which very often includes helping others do the same. In fact, research has found that after a crisis, up to two-thirds of adults experience some type of increase in well-being.[13]

This illuminates that when people have sufficient capacity for Presencing and Purposing, they can experience transformational resilience in any or all of the six common phases of a disaster. However, as discussed in Chapter 2, it is very difficult for people to find new sources of meaning, purpose, and healthy hope if they are frozen in a fight, flight, or freeze reaction that pushes them outside their Resilient Growth Zone. As I will discuss throughout this book, the most potent way to prevent this is to form wide and diverse coalitions within neighborhoods and communities that engage the entire population in a range of activities that strengthen their capacity for Presencing and Purposing. When this occurs, residents will be able to connect with family, friends, and neighbors who can provide much needed emotional support and practical assistance, engage in specific practices that enhance their capacity for mental wellness and transformational resilience; use simple, self-administrable Presencing skills, and in other ways, enable people to safely release the trauma that is frozen in their nervous system; and return to their Resilient Growth Zone. When this occurs, it will then be possible for community members to utilize Purposing skills to turn toward and learn from adversities and use the lessons as powerful catalysts to find positive new sources of meaning, purpose, and healthy hope in life.[14]

The starting point of this process is to honestly acknowledge the bad that has happened or is happening. People can then decide what is truly important to them. This often involves clarifying the values they want to live by in the midst of adversities. This could include, for example, developing closer relationships with certain people, using their skills and strengths in some prosocial way, becoming more generous and kinder, or appreciating small things that remind of them of the precious gift they have of being alive. As people gain clarity about what they really care about, they set goals and begin to take small incremental steps to achieve them. The progress they make illuminates the reality that they can control how they respond during adversities. Achieving transformational resilience is a choice people make, not something that emerges magically on its own.[15]

Mental wellness and transformational resilience interact in positive ways. The ability to connect with others; calm the body, mind, and emotions when distressed; and use adversities to learn and grow are all resilient actions that affect mental wellness in positive ways. Further, the sense of self-efficacy that emerges when people know they can think and act in safe, healthy, and prosocial ways and find new meaning and healthy hope during adversities increases their subjective feelings of mental wellness.

Efforts to prevent and heal the distresses and traumas generated by the climate emergency should therefore address both mental wellness and transformational resilience because they are intimately linked.

WHAT IS HEALTHY HOPE?

Before going further, let me take a moment to clarify what I mean by "healthy hope." Hope can be thought of as a basic human survival mechanism. But the long-term nature of the climate emergency means hope must be harnessed in a healthy way. Healthy hope is not wishful thinking, such as believing a new technology will be developed that resolves the climate crisis or the impacts will not be as serious as scientist's project. This can produce unhealthy outcomes because it is something an individual desires but has no control over, and if it does not occur, they can become despondent.

Healthy hope is the conviction people hold that their future can be better and that they can play a key role in making it happen. It emerges when people: a) intentionally select meaningful personal goals; b) identify one or more pathways—or roadmaps—to follow to move toward those goals; and c) mobilize the willpower, that is, the mental energy and emotional commitment needed to keep moving down the pathway even when obstacles arise. In other words, healthy hope is "lived hope." It involves taking deliberate steps to improve the conditions of one's life through actions that one chooses, and it is best achieved with the support and involvement of others.[16]

Finding healthy hope will be essential to foster and maintain mental wellness and transformational resilience during ongoing climate adversities. It will also be vital to enable people to continually engage in activities that help slowly reduce the mega-emergency to acceptable levels. No single action can achieve this end, and people can become distressed even when they participate in a successful activity, such as decarbonizing a local hospital, but see no change in the level of global emissions.

The Rev. Paul Abernathy, CEO of the Neighborhood Resilient Project in Pittsburgh Pennsylvania, which you will learn more about in future chapters, underscored the need to help traumatized people find healthy hope when he told me, "If people do not have hope, when they believe trauma is the norm in their lives, they won't engage in anything new..." "To break through that is imperative—there needs to be a paradigm shift..." "This is why early wins are so important. People need to see the possibility of hope. Sustaining hope is also important. People have to be prepared for setbacks so they can continue to progress in the face of tragedy and trauma, remember the hope, and not fall back into despair."[17]

WHAT CONSTITUTES A MENTALLY WELL AND RESILIENT COMMUNITY?

The communities in which people live are one of the primary areas in which they play out their lives because it is where they interact with their families and friends and commonly work and recreate as well. Where people live therefore matters a great deal to the vast majority of them. Establishing and maintaining mentally well and resilient communities will thus be extremely important during the long climate crisis because they will be the primary arena in which individual, community, and societal distresses and traumas can be prevented and healed.

But what then does it mean for a community to be mentally well and resilient? Just as there is no single definition of individual mental health, there is no agreed upon definition of community wellness and resilience. However, I find one of the best is by Mindy Fullilove and Jack Saul who said, "Community resilience refers to the capacity of a community to overcome shared trauma or adversity via social cohesion, mutual support, hope, and the presence of communal narratives that give the experience meaning and purpose."[18]

Mentally well and resilient communities establish conditions that support the healthy development of children, adolescents, working-age adults, and older adults. The context allows members to successfully meet their own life challenges and provides the foundation that enables them to overcome significant adversities and fulfill their goals and potential.[19] These attributes are achieved when community members have positive social connections with others who have prosocial norms, good Presencing (self-regulation) skills as well as Purposing (adversity-based growth) skills, and engage in activities that promote individual and collective wellness and resilience. Having equitable access to quality educational opportunities; ample living-wage jobs; stable, safe, and healthy places to reside; numerous public spaces where people can safely meet and recreate; unpolluted air and water; and green areas where they can connect with nature are other key elements of mentally well and resilient communities.

These factors empower residents to minimize unhealthy and unsafe behaviors such as alcohol and drug misuse, crime, aggression, and violence. They can also motivate people to help their neighbors and other community members during times of distress. In addition, a mentally well and resilient community understands the harmful effects of and openly addresses racism, sexism, and other systemic oppressions, discriminations in housing, education, and job opportunities, as well as all types of stigma.[20]

These factors combine to produce the social cohesion and collective efficacy that can help residents overcome shared adversities; make needed changes in local conditions; and find constructive new sources of meaning, purpose, and healthy hope during ongoing adversities.

ELEMENTS OF A PUBLIC HEALTH APPROACH TO PROMOTING MENTAL WELLNESS AND TRANSFORMATIONAL RESILIENCE

How can a public health approach promote mental wellness and transformational resilience among individuals and communities? Just as efforts to prevent physical health problems such as heart disease, obesity, and diabetes involve making deliberate choices to change behaviors, a public health approach to mental wellness and resilience involves consistent systemic efforts to change norms, attitudes, habits, and behaviors to prevent problems before the onset of symptoms appear. Some fundamentals include:

- *Focus on the Entire Population*: As the social-ecological model describes, it is difficult to increase the mental wellness and transformational resilience of people in isolation from the condition of their environment. A public health approach therefore focuses on entire populations, not just individuals deemed to be at high risk or who show symptoms of psychopathology, although they must be given special attention, care, and added resources.
- *Prioritize Prevention*: This is important because if people understand how to alter their behaviors and practices to enhance their capacity for mental wellness and transformational resilience before the climate emergency worsens, they will have much greater capacity to safely overcome distressing experiences and find positive new sources of meaning, purpose, and healthy hope when they occur.

For example, if people have learned safe and healthy Presencing skills to calm their bodies, minds, and emotions, they will be able to see distressing situations more clearly, and make good decisions about how to respond. If they have developed close ties with family and friends, and have good connections with neighbors and others in their community, they will be able to obtain vital forms of emotional support and practical assistance when needed. Further, if they know the many benefits of Purposing skills that enable them to turn toward and use adversities as powerful catalysts to learn, grow, and find new sources of meaning, direction, and healthy hope, they are much more likely to engage in these prosocial actions.

To prepare people for the long climate emergency and the Traumacene it will produce, the top priority must therefore be to enhance their capacity to prevent debilitating levels of distress and trauma before they emerge. Methods to heal the traumas that do occur should be integrated into the prevention activities.

- *Think Systemically and Respond Holistically*: Because most mental health and psycho-social-spiritual problems result from the interplay between numerous personal, social, economic, built/physical, and ecological forces, a public health approach calls for multisystemic—also called multipronged—strategies to prevent and heal them. This means a comprehensive set of well-coordinated and integrated strategies that reach all the different populations and sectors in the community. This requires individuals, groups, and organizations to get out of their siloes, think systemically, and respond holistically. The strategies must start where people are at and recognize and build on community strengths, resources, and other protective factors. This requires that they be developed and delivered by a coalition of individuals, groups, and organizations that understand and are engaged with the many different populations and sectors of the community. As previously stated, individualized interventions and organizational programs focused on a specific issue or single population cannot build population-level wellness and transformational resilience.[21]

- *Emphasize Healing Through Group and Community-Minded Engagement, Not Clinical Treatment*: As stated, healing methods should be merged into prevention activities, but, the strategies must be non-clinical, meaning they should not prioritize direct mental health services such as psychotherapy and pharmacological therapies. This is important because the primary goal is not to treat symptoms of mental health and psycho-social-spiritual problems, but to prevent and heal them by enhancing everyone's capacity for mental wellness and transformational resilience. It is also important because many people will not participate if they perceive the initiative to be a mental health treatment program.[22] Further, as important as they are, disaster management and related mental health services should also not dominate. They can help alleviate some people's short-term suffering during a crisis. But this will not strengthen the entire population's capacity for mental wellness and transformational resilience for the relentless adversities generated during the long climate mega-emergency.

IDENTIFYING "PROTECTIVE" AND "RISK" FACTORS FORMS THE STARTING POINT

Using a public health approach to guide actions that can prevent and heal the widespread distresses and traumas generated during the long climate emergency begins by shifting the initial question that is typically asked in the clinical treatment field from "What disorders do individuals have and how do we treat them?" to the public health question of "What skills, strengths, and resources does the population have that can be utilized, and what additional ones can be established to strengthen everyone's capacity to prevent and heal distresses and traumas?"

The public health question leads to the identification of protective factors, or assets, that can buffer everyone from, and help them push back against, forces that undermine their capacity for mental wellness and transformational resilience.

After the protective factors are identified, the factors that can undermine the community's capacity for mental wellness and transformational resilience can be ascertained. These are called "risk factors," and they include characteristics, variables, or hazards that increase the likelihood that people will experience mental health or psycho-social-spiritual problems.[23] Risk factors should be identified only after protective factors are surfaced because it is easy for people to become fixated on all the things that are wrong or missing in their community and fail to see skills, strengths, and resources people have that enable residents to safely overcome adversities.

Another reason to identify protective factors before risks is because strengthening numerous protective factors at the same time has much greater potential for successful outcomes than trying to eliminate risks or fix deficits. That's because comorbidity (the simultaneous presence of two or more factors) is often the norm with mental health and psycho-social-spiritual problems, so multiple protective factors are most helpful in preventing problems. In addition, it is not always possible to measure the specific effect, or associate a specific risk factor, with any particular mental health or psycho-social-spiritual problem. Further, risk factors often interact in ways that limit the effectiveness of interventions focused on any single one.[24]

Both protective and risk factors often have a cumulative effect on the development or reduction of mental health and psycho-social-spiritual problems. People with multiple protective factors have much less probability of developing mental health problems, and those with multiple risk factors have a greater likelihood of doing so. At the same time, an individual who has several risk factors might still have greater capacity for mental wellness and transformational resilience than someone who is exposed to fewer risks because each individual perceives traumatic stresses in different ways.[25]

Again, the pervasive hardships that will be generated during the long climate emergency underscore that it is paramount to prioritize enhancing skills, strengths, social connections, and other assets that help people calm their body, mind, and emotions and find positive new sources of meaning, purpose, and healthy hope, rather than trying to reduce the factors that threaten that capacity. Strengthening assets has been shown to have much greater potential to empower people to build and maintain their capacity for mental wellness and resilience than striving to eliminate deficits or treat symptoms of pathology.[26]

That said, the identification of both protective factors and risk factors can provide the information needed to develop multisystemic strategies to increase the power of the protective factors and diminish the influence of the risk factors.

POPULATION-LEVEL PREVENTION COMBINES "PROPORTIONATE UNIVERSALISM" AND "LIFE-COURSE" APPROACHES

Strategies to enhance population-level capacity for mental wellness and transformational resilience focus on three interrelated forms of prevention.

- "*Universal*" (also called primary) prevention focuses on thwarting mental health and psycho-social-spiritual problems before they appear within the entire population. Examples include teaching all adults and school-age children how things that seem threatening or overwhelming stress can activate instinctive fight, flight, or freeze reaction that can push them outside their Resilience Growth Zone (RGZ) and then teaching them Presencing and Purposing skills to release the trauma embedded within their nervous system, return to the RGZ, and find constructive new sources of meaning, purpose, and healthy hope in life.

- "*Targeted*" (also called selective) prevention focuses on people with characteristics that place them at high risk of mental health or psycho-social-spiritual problems. Examples include giving special attention to people who live in a high-risk area, or who are typically marginalized in the community, and establishing regular contacts with people who are socially isolated.

- "*Intensive*" (also called indicative) prevention helps people who are already experiencing serious mental health or psycho-social-spiritual problems control and reduce their symptoms. Examples include helping people who misuse drugs or alcohol learn how to prevent relapse, and teaching them skills to manage their symptoms. Indicative prevention supports but is not the same as mental health treatment, as it occurs in the community setting, not clinical facilities (Figure 3.3).[27]

The three forms of prevention should complement, not compete, with each other. They form the multipronged approach needed to build population-level capacity for mental wellness and resilience. This is called "proportionate universalism," which means prevention actions should be universal but on a scale that is proportionate to the level of risk and known problems.[28]

Unfortunately, this approach is not often used. Instead, due to their training, mental models, and funding streams that focus on crisis, illness, deficits, and pathology, many mental health and human services organizations believe their job is to treat individuals mostly one-at-a-time after they experience psychological and emotional problems, or focus on those deemed "most vulnerable" or "at risk" separately from others.

Despite their best intentions, when professionals classify people in this way, they can become defined by their perceived deficits—what they can't do or don't have. They become

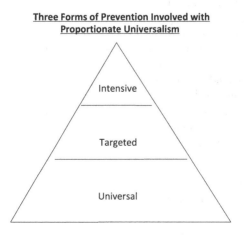

Three Forms of Prevention Involved with Proportionate Universalism

Intensive

Targeted

Universal

Figure 3.3 Three Forms of Prevention Involved with Proportionate Universalism

objects that should be treated or serviced. This type of thinking can tell people the problems they experience are solely their own doing and discount the family dysfunction, poverty, racism, ecological stressors or disasters, or other socio-ecological factors that contribute to them. It also ignores the skills, strengths, and other capacities they have that enable their resilience, while further isolating them from other people, rather than making them part of the larger whole.

Please don't misinterpret these comments. Special attention, care, and resources must be given to help people with physical or mental challenges, older residents, people living in high-risk zones, families and children who are at risk of ACEs, BIPOCs disadvantaged people to enhance their capacity for mental wellness and transformational resilience during the climate crisis. However, these groups will have much greater likelihood of doing so when they are meaningfully engaged in whole-community initiatives that help everyone enhance, reclaim, and sustain their capacity for psychological, emotional, and spiritual wellness and transformational resilience.[29] This will take time and skillful engagement. But it is essential to build universal capacity to prevent and heal distresses and traumas during the long climate emergency speeding our way.

A LIFE-COURSE APPROACH

In addition to simultaneously focusing on the three different types of prevention, to enhance population-level capacity for mental wellness and transformational resilience, the strategies developed by RCCs should employ a "life-course" approach. This means different approaches must be used with different age groups. This is important because people are typically exposed to different risk factors at different stages of their lives, so different protective factors should be emphasized for children, adolescents, working age, and older adults (Figure 3.4).[30]

Implementing proportionate universalism and life-course approaches in an integrated manner requires the development of multisystemic strategies that reach every population and sector, not a limited number of actions aimed solely at people who already have serious mental health problems or one specific group.

Developing and implementing this type of multipronged strategy requires a collaborative process that involves a wide and diverse range of local residents, civic groups, non-profit, private, and public organizations. The strength of this type of inter-organizational and inter-sectoral collaboration is that numerous stakeholders contribute to and facilitate the initiative by working together to achieve common goals.[31] This approach can engage community members, social networks, civic groups, and formal organizations in the development of innovative ways to address the complex challenges experienced by all of the populations and sectors in the community during the long climate emergency.

Figure 3.4 A Life Course Approach

The box below summarizes my perspective of the core principles of a public health approach to enhancing mental wellness and transformational resilience for the long climate crisis.[32]

Core Principles of a Public Health Approach for Building Population-Level Capacity for Mental Wellness and Transformational Resilience for the Long Climate Emergency

- *Think Systemically and Respond Holistically*: Use a social-ecological framework to assess and simultaneously address the many individual, family, social/cultural, physical/built, economic, and ecological factors that interact to affect people's capacity for mental wellness and transformational resilience.
- *Leave No One Behind*: View and respond to challenges through a population lens, not an individualized or single population one.
- *Prioritize Prevention*: Always emphasize community-based activities that enhance the capacity to prevent distresses and traumas, and integrate methods to heal traumas into the prevention strategies.
- *Strengthen Protective Factors*: Identify and build on existing skills, strengths, resources, and other protective factors and form new assets, while addressing risk factors, but emphasize protective factors.
- *Develop Multisystemic Strategies*: Develop multisystemic—or multipronged—strategies that integrate proportionate universalism with life-course approaches.
- *Utilize Best Science and Culturally Appropriate Methods*: Use data, best available science, evidence-based, evidence-informed, promising best, and traditional indigenous age and culturally accountable approaches to inform strategies, but think transculturally.
- *Build Unity and Equality*: Give special attention to individuals and groups that are typically underrepresented or marginalized, but do not isolate them from other community members or activities or establish siloed and fragmented approaches.
- *Ensure Just Approaches*: Always make sure that activities are designed and implemented in just and equitable ways and avoid exclusionary approaches.
- *Continually Assess Progress, Learn, and Improve*: Engage residents in regularly evaluating progress, learning what works and does not work, and use the findings to continually improve strategies and action plans.
- *Faith in Human Spirit*: Recognize that inherent within almost every individual, family, group, and community are the capacity to prevent mental health and psycho-social-spiritual problems and heal them when they occur.

COMMON PROTECTIVE FACTORS FOR INDIVIDUALS

A number of protective factors can help shield individuals from forces that can undermine their capacity for mental wellness and transformational resilience during the long climate emergency. Table 3.1 describes these factors.[33]

Table 3.1 Common Individual Mental Wellness and Resilience Protective Factors

- Robust connections with family, friends, and other community members.
- Psychological and emotional self-regulation skills.
- Ability to use adversities as catalysts to learn, grow, and find new sources of meaning, purpose, and healthy hope.
- Spirituality.
- Self-efficacy.
- Adherence to pro-social norms of behavior.
- Opportunities to engage in activities that are pro-social and in practices that enhance wellness and resilience.
- Sufficient and healthy food and water.
- Living in safe and healthy forms of shelter.
- Adequate income and living-wage job opportunities.
- Regular physical activity.

As I have already said and will soon discuss in greater detail, connections with other people is central to preventing and healing distresses and traumas especially during the long climate emergency, because relationships with family, friends, and neighbors provide the emotional support, safety, and practical assistance that are vital during adversities. Good relationships also allow people to share their distresses and traumas in a safe and supportive environment, which is a core element of the healing process.

I have already discussed the many benefits of Presencing (self-regulation) and Purposing (adversity-based growth) skills. Adhering to prosocial norms can help people feel good about themselves and increase their sense of self-efficacy because they are working toward the common good. Engaging in practices such as forgiveness, finding simple joys, laughing a lot, and continual learning enhances the capacity for both mental and physical wellness and resilience. Having safe and healthy places to reside and nourishing supplies of food and water allows people to devote their time and attention to matters beyond basic survival.

Because these protective factors help individuals push back against numerous types of risks at the same time, strengthening them will go a long way toward enhancing their capacity to sustain mental wellness and transformational resilience during the decades-long climate crisis.

COMMON RISK FACTORS FOR INDIVIDUALS

Table 3.2 describes a set of common risks factors that increase the possibility that an individual will experience mental health or psychosocial-spiritual problems.[34]

Without significant prevention efforts, the mix of compounding disruptions to the economic, social, and ecological systems people rely on for basic needs and acute disasters generated during the climate emergency will produce numerous traumatic stresses for individuals. This can occur, for example, when a loved one is injured or killed in a climate-intensified disaster, when people experience or witness crime or violence resulting from persistently high stress levels in the community, or when they constantly worry about what will happen next to them or their children.

The climate crisis is also certain to aggravate existing or directly produce many or all of the other risk factors described in Table 3.2. More frequent and intense heat waves and

Table 3.2 Common Individual Mental Health Risk Factors

- Persistent personal toxic stresses and traumas of any type.
- Adversities experienced at a young age including neglect, abuse, family conflict, violence, substance abuse, adult incarceration, and other ACEs.
- Lack of social connections, isolation, and loneliness.
- History of violent victimization and lack of sense of safety.
- Persistent poverty.
- Chronic unemployment and inadequate economic opportunity.
- Inadequate educational opportunities.
- Homelessness.
- Dilapidated, unhealthy, and unsafe housing and housing insecurity.
- Repeated history of racial, cultural, or sexual discrimination, inequality, or other injustices.
- Poor nutrition or food and water insecurity.
- Insufficient physical movement.

droughts, for example, can reduce agricultural production and the nutritional value of food, leading to water and food insecurity. The lost jobs and incomes caused by major wildfires or windstorms can lead to anger and low self-esteem among parents, who can attempt to self-medicate by misusing alcohol or other drugs, or take out their distress on their spouse or children, both of which can traumatize their young ones. Flooding caused by rising sea levels or higher storm surges can force people to migrate to different locations, leaving them without the social connections they count on for emotional support and practical assistance needed to address challenges.

When individuals experience many of these risk factors, which will often be the case as the climate crisis accelerates, the effects will multiply and generate significant distress as well as rampant psychological, emotional, and spiritual traumas.

COMMON COMMUNITY-LEVEL PROTECTIVE FACTORS

Just as a number of protective factors can play significant roles in helping an individual prevent and heal distresses and traumas, a set of community-level protective factors can buffer most, or all, of the population from threats and help them sustain their capacity for wellness and transformational resilience during the climate emergency. Table 3.3 describes several common community-level protective factors.[35]

When residents become engaged in positive activities that allow them to meet, work, or recreate with people with different backgrounds, they can develop connections that provide emotional support and practical assistance during climate adversities. When the social networks people belong to promote safe, healthy, just, and equitable social norms, they will be more inclined to act in ways that enhance, rather than undermine, mental wellness and transformational resilience, and oppose harmful actions when they occur. If an individual has equitable access to education and job training opportunities, and if living-wage jobs are available, their risk of poverty, homelessness, and the low self-esteem and shame that often are produced by the absence of these conditions will be minimized. When the physical/built and ecological conditions of a community provide safe and healthy places to live, work, interact, and recreate, people will feel confident that they can engage in social activities with others and go about their lives without fear.

Table 3.3 Common Community-Level Mental Wellness and Resilience Protective Factors

- Healthy social connections across racial, cultural, economic, and geographic boundaries in the community.
- Opportunities for positive social engagement.
- Promotion of healthy, safe, just, and equitable social norms.
- Community expectations and laws unfavorable toward alcohol and drug misuse, firearms, crime, aggression, and violence.
- Equitable economic opportunities and sufficient living-wage jobs.
- Healthy, safe, just and equitable physical/built conditions.
- Healthy and safe ecological conditions.
- Access to supportive associations such as school and after-school programs for youth, libraries, faith-based resources, social clubs, and other formal and informal networks, groups, and organizations.
- Plentiful safe and attractive open areas and green spaces where people can meet, interact, and recreate.
- Rituals and ceremonies that highlight wellness and resilience and build social connections and cohesion.
- Strong sense of collective efficacy.

COMMON COMMUNITY-LEVEL RISK FACTORS

As the social-ecological model depicts, the family, social, economic, physical/built, and eco-logical conditions people find themselves in can increase their chances of experiencing mental health or psycho-social-spiritual problems. These can be called "community-level" risk factors, and they have been associated with different types of problems. Table 3.4 describes a common set of community-level risk factors.[36]

As with individual risk factors, without widespread efforts to prevent them, the long climate emergency will directly produce toxic stresses and traumas that affect entire communities. A hurricane, for example, might flood or destroy an entire town or neighborhood and cause them to be abandoned, which will severely stress or traumatize all residents. A wildfire might burn down an entire town, leaving everyone homeless, without jobs and incomes, and in despair. Local business might close due to climate-generated disruptions to their supply chains, which reduces local tax revenues, and cause public agencies to disinvest in the maintenance of roads, power, and other critical infrastructure, particularly in neighborhoods dominated by BIPOC and low-income residents.

Left unaddressed, the long climate crisis will also aggravate many or all the other common community-level risk factors or produce altogether new ones. For instance, increased heat and drought-generated food or water shortages, or the in-migration of climate refugees can lead to dangerous us-vs-them divides in communities that heighten racial, ethnic, and economic inequities, and activate crime and violence. Widespread fear generated by constant climate adversities can produce social norms that promote unhealthy, unsafe, and unjust coping mechanisms.

To reemphasize, the fact that the climate emergency will aggravate both individual and community-level risk factors makes assessing them less important than identifying and strengthening protective factors that can simultaneously counter most or all of the risks and help individuals and communities defend themselves from the threats.[37]

Table 3.4 Common Community-Level Mental Health and Psycho-Social-Spiritual Risk Factors

- Community-wide toxic stresses and traumas.
- High levels of drug use, crime, delinquency, or violence.
- Lack of economic opportunity and high levels of poverty.
- Widespread family disruption in the community.
- Systemic inequalities and injustices in education, policing, and the criminal justice system.
- Low neighborhood and community attachment and bonds.
- Social norms favorable to unsafe, unhealthy, unjust, and inequitable behaviors, practices, and policies.
- Deteriorated local physical/build environment and polluted/degraded ecological systems.
- Lack of safe healthy green areas and open spaces where people can meet and interact.
- High social disorganization and low collective efficacy.

A FRAMEWORK FOR BUILDING UNIVERSAL CAPACITY FOR MENTAL WELLNESS AND TRANSFORMATIONAL RESILIENCE FOR THE CLIMATE EMERGENCY

It can be daunting to try to develop strategies that can strengthen each of the individual and community-level protective factors one-at-a-time and diminish the power of all the forces that can undermine those assets. The good news is that, as I briefly stated in the Introduction, I believe all of the protective factors can be strengthened by focusing on five interrelated foundational areas.[38] The five core areas include:

1. Build social connections across cultural, economic, and geographic boundaries in communities.

2. Ensure a just transition by creating safe, healthy, equitable, and supportive climate-resilient local physical/built, economic, and ecological conditions.

3. Cultivate universal literacy about what mental wellness and transformational resilience involve and how they can be cared for.

4. Engage residents in specific types of practices that help foster and sustain their mental wellness and transformational resilience.

5. Establish ongoing age and culturally accountable opportunities for residents to heal the traumas they experience.[39]

Part II of this book will describe how community-based mental wellness and transformational resilience building initiatives can get organized and develop goals, strategies, and action plans that engage residents in each of these five foundational areas.

NOTES

1 World Health Organization (1986). *The Ottawa Charter for Health Promotion.* Obtained at: https://www.who.int/teams/health-promotion/enhanced-wellbeing/first-global-conference
2 Eaton W.W. (2012). *Public Mental Health.* Oxford: Oxford University Press, p. 52.
3 See for example: Green L. and Kreuter M. (1991). *Health Promotion Planning: An Educational and Environmental Approach.* California: Mayfield Publishing Company; Barry M. and Jenkins R. (2007). *Implementing Mental Health Promotion.* London: Elsevier; Centers for Disease Control and Prevention. (2011). *Public Health Action Plan to Integrate Mental Health Promotion and Mental Illness Prevention with Chronic Disease Prevention;* Cohen N. and Galea S. (2011). *Population Mental Health: Evidence, Policy, and Public Health Practice.* Abingdon: Taylor & Francis; Jacka F.N. et al. (2012). Moving towards a population health approach to the primary prevention of common mental disorders. *BMC Medicine,* 10,

149; Cerdá M. et al. (2015). To treat or to prevent? Reducing the population burden of violence-related post-traumatic stress disorder. *Epidemiology*, 26, 681–689; Chen J. et al. (2018). Public health system-delivered mental health preventive care links to significant reduction of health care costs. *Population Health Management*; Sampson L. and Galea S. (2018). An argument for the foundations of population mental health. *Frontier Psychiatry*, 9, 600; and Inter-Agency Standing Committee. (2019). *Community-Based Approaches to MHPSS Programmes: A Guidance Note*. Obtained at: https:// interagencystandingcommittee.org/iasc-reference-group-mental-health-and-psychosocial-support-emergency-settings/iasc-community-based-approaches-mhpss-programmes-guidance-note

4   I am indebted to the Marguerite Regan, Dr. Iris Elliott, and Isabella Goldie for the history included in this section: Faculty of Public Health and Mental Health Foundation. (2016). Obtained at: https://www.mentalhealth.org.uk/publications/better-mental-health-all-public-health-approach-mental-health-improvement

5   Dahlgren G. and Whitehead M. (2006). *European Strategies for Tackling Social Inequities in Health*. World Health Organization Regional Office for Europe. Obtained at: https://www.euro.who.int/__ data/assets/pdf_file/0018/103824/E89384.pdf

6   See for example: Conway M. and O'Connor D. (2016). Social media, big data, and mental health: current advances and ethical implications. *Current Opinion Psychology*. Obtained at: https://pubmed. ncbi.nlm.nih.gov/27042689/; and Copeland W.E. et al. (2018). Association of childhood trauma exposure with adult psychiatric disorders and functional outcomes. *JAMA Network*. Obtained at: https://jamanetwork.com/journals/jamanetworkopen/fullarticle/2713038

7   See for example: Sallis J.F. et al. (2008). "Ecological models of health behavior" in *Health Behavior and Health Education: Theory, Research, and Practice*, ed. Glanz K., Rimer B.K., and Viswanath K. Jossey-Bass; and Centers for Disease Control and Prevention. *The Social-Ecological Model: A Frame-work for Prevention*. https://www.cdc.gov/violenceprevention/about/social-ecologicalmodel. html

8   World Health Organization. (2004). *Promoting Mental Health: Concepts, Emerging Evidence, Prac-tice* (Summary Report) Geneva: World Health Organization. Obtained at: https://apps.who. int/iris/handle/10665/42940

9   Mental Health Foundation, UK. (2013). *Building Resilient Communities*. Obtained at: https://www. mentalhealth.org.uk/publications/building-resilient-communities

10   American Psychological Association. (2020). *Building Your Resilience*. Obtained at: https://www.apa. org/topics/resilience

11   Calhoun L. G. and Tedeschi R. G. (2001). "Posttraumatic growth: the positive lessons of loss" in *Meaning Reconstruction & the Experience of Loss*, ed. R. A. Neimeyer, pp. 157–172. American Psycho-logical Association, Washington, DC.

12   As described in my book Doppelt B. (2016). *Transformational Resilience: How Building Human Resilience for Climate Disruption Can Safeguard Society and Increase Wellbeing*. Routledge Publishing, New York, NY.

13   Sansom G. T. et al. (2022). Compounding impacts of hazard exposures on mental health in Hous-ton, TX. *Natural Hazards*. Obtained at: https://doi.org/10.1007/s11069-021-05158-x

14   Schoon I. (2006). *Risk and Resilience. Adaptation in Changing Times*. Chapter 1. Cambridge University Press; Ungar M. (2013). Resilience, trauma, context, and culture. *Sage Journals*.

15   As described in my book Doppelt B. (2016). *Transformational Resilience: How Building Human Resilience for Climate Disruption Can Safeguard Society and Increase Wellbeing*. Routledge Publishing, New York, NY.

16   Gwinn S. and Hellman C. (2022). *Hope Rising: How the Science of Hope Can Change Your Life*. New York, NY: Morgan James Publishing.

17   Personal interview, November 5, 2021.

18   Fullilove M. T. and Saul J. (2006). "Rebuilding communities post-disaster in New York" in *9/11: Mental Health in the Wake of Terrorist Attacks*, ed. Neria Y., Gross R., Marshall R. D., Susser E. S., Cambridge University Press, pp. 164–177, Cambridge, UK.

19   Adapted from Canadian Population Health Initiative. (2008). *Mentally Healthy Communities: A Collec-tion of Papers*. Canadian Institute for Health Information, Ottawa, CA.

20   Adapted from: Davis R. et al. (2016). *Adverse Community Experiences and Resilience: A Framework for Addressing and Preventing Community Trauma*, The Prevention Institute; and Mental Health Commis-sion of New South Wales. *The Whole Community*. Obtained at: https://www.nswmentalhealthcom-mission.com.au/content/whole-community

21   Kania J., and Kramer M. (2011). Collective impact. *Stanford Social Innovation Review*, 9, 36–41. Obtained at: https://ssir.org/articles/entry/collective_impact

22   Purtle J. et al. (January 2020). Population-based approaches to mental health: history, strategies, and evidence. *Annual Review of Public Health* 41:201–21. Obtained at: https://www.annualreviews. org/doi/abs/10.1146/annurev-publhealth-040119-094247

23   SAMHSA. *Risks and Protective Factors*. Obtained at: https://www.samhsa.gov/sites/default/files/- 20190718-samhsa-risk-protective-factors.pdf

24 Ibid.
25 Ibid.
26 Wallerstein N. (2006). *What Is the Evidence on Effectiveness of Empowerment to Improve Health?* WHO Regional Office for Europe. Obtained at: https://www.euro.who.int/__data/assets/pdf_file/0010/74656/E88086.pdf
27 Kousoulis A. (2019). *Prevention and Mental Health: Understanding the Evidence So That We Can Address the Greatest Health Challenge of Our Times.* UK: Mental Health Foundation, pp. 18–20. Obtained at: https:// www.mentalhealth.org.uk/publications/prevention-and-mental-health-research-paper/read-online
28 Ibid., p. 21.
29 This last point was made by Gavin Atkins, Head of Communities at Mind in the UK during an interview on September 8, 2021.
30 For a number of reports on this issue see *Mental Health Disparities: Diverse Populations* on the American Psychiatric Association website: https://www.psychiatry.org/psychiatrists/cultural-competency/education/mental-health-facts
31 Hauf A. and Bond L. (2002). Community-based collaboration in prevention and mental health promotion: benefiting from and building resources of partnership. *International Journal of Mental Health Promotion*, 4(3). Obtained at: https://www.researchgate.net/publication/233643382_Community-Based_Collaboration_in_Prevention_and_Mental_Health_Promotion_Benefiting_from_and_Building_the_Resources_of_Partnership
32 Adapted from: Public Health Leadership Society (2002). *Principles of the Ethical Practice of Public Health.* Obtained at: https://www.apha.org/-/media/files/pdf/membergroups/ethics/ethics_brochure.ashx; Evans AC. and Bufka LF. (August 2020). Principles Guiding Population Health Framework for Behavioral Health at the American Psychological Association, *Prevention of Chronic Disease* 17, 200261. Obtained at: https://www.cdc.gov/pcd/issues/2020/20_0261.htm; and The National Prevention Science Coalition. (April 2019). *What is Prevention Science.* Obtained at: https://www.npscoalition.org/prevention-science
33 See, for example: Landau J. and Saul J. (2004). "Facilitating family and community resilience in response to major disaster" in *Living Beyond Loss: Death in the Family*, ed. Walsh F. and McGoldrick M. New York, NY: W W Norton & Co., pp. 285–309, New York, NY; Boss P. (1999). *Ambiguous Loss: Learning to Live with Unresolved Grief.* Boston, MA: Harvard University Press; and Saul J. (2014). *Collective Trauma Collective Healing.* Routledge Publishing, New York, NY.
34 See for example: Sax Institute. (2020). *Evidence Check: Mental Wellbeing Risk and Protective Factors.* VicHealth. Obtained at: https://www.vichealth.vic.gov.au/-/media/ResearchandEvidence/VicHealth; CDC, (March 2020). *Risk and Protective Factors for Violence Prevention.* Obtained at: https://www.cdc.gov/violenceprevention/youthviolence/riskprotectivefactors.html; and SAMHSA. *Risks and Protective Factors.* Obtained at: https://www.samhsa.gov/sites/default/files/20190718-samhsa-risk-protective-factors.pdf; The American Mental Wellness Association. *Risk and Protective Factors.* Obtained at: https://www.americanmentalwellness.org/prevention/risk-and-protective-factors/; Communities That Care. *Risk and Protective Factors.* Obtained at: https://www.communitiesthatcare.org.au/how-it-works/risk-and-protective-factors
35 Landau J. and Saul J. (2004). "Facilitating family and community resilience in response to major disaster," in *Living Beyond Loss: Death in the Family*, ed Walsh F. and McGoldrick M. New York, NY: W W Norton & Co., pp. 285–309; Boss P. (1999). *Ambiguous Loss: Learning to Live with Unresolved Grief.* Harvard University Press; and Saul J. (2014). *Collective Trauma Collective Healing.* Routledge Publishing.
36 Ibid.
37 Faculty of Public Health and Mental Health Foundation. (2016). *Better Mental Health for All: A Public Health Approach to Mental Health Improvement.* Mental Health Foundation UK, p. 28.
38 See for example: Huppert F. (2008). Psychological wellbeing: evidence regarding its causes and its consequences. *Journal of the International Association of Applied Psychology.* Obtained at: https://iaap-journals.onlinelibrary.wiley.com/doi/full/10.1111/j.1758-0854.2009.01008.x
39 This section is adapted from *Building Resilient Communities: Making Every Contact Count for Public Mental Health.* (2013). UK Mind for Better Mental Health and Mental Health Foundation, pp. 20–34. Obtained at: https://www.mentalhealth.org.uk/sites/default/files/building-resilient-communities.pdf

PART II

Organizing and Operating Community-Based Initiatives that Build Universal Capacity for Mental Wellness and Transformational Resilience

OVERVIEW

A number of common steps are involved with organizing and operating community-based initiatives that build universal capacity for mental wellness and transformational resilience for the climate emergency. Part II of this book will walk you through the steps.

The framework that is offered was developed through extensive research into population-level approaches to public health and mental health, as well as research and interviews with people involved with over 30 neighborhood and community-based initiatives in different parts of the US and other nations. My own personal education and experience also contributed to the framework.

Most of the neighborhood and community initiatives that were examined were organized by local community leaders in response to issues unique to their area, although a few were developed by state organizations, universities, or other external entities. Consequently, they all have different goals and operate in slightly different ways. Only a few describe their approach as a public health initiative although they use variations of the approach. And only a few directly address the impacts of the global climate emergency. Each addresses one or more of the five foundational areas that will be important to build the capacity for mental wellness and transformational resilience, but none focuses on all of them. I have tried to boil down the different emphases and approaches to the fundamentals.

My hope is that the framework and plan of action offered in this section will offer guidance on how neighborhoods and communities can create a local culture that prevents and heals climate-generated distresses and traumas, while engaging residents in actions that help reduce the climate crisis to manageable levels.

Before diving into the material, please remember that the focus is on how to empower communities to take ownership for building and sustaining everyone's capacity for mental wellness and transformational resilience for relentless adversities as they engage in climate solutions. As I have continually emphasized, this is very different from an expert-led approach where mental health and direct human service professionals strive to repair deficits seen in the community or treat individuals and families one at a time after they show symptoms of pathology. Because the global climate crisis will disrupt all levels of society, carefully coordinated multisystemic approaches will be needed to mobilize the capacity for mental wellness and transformational resilience among all individuals, families, groups, and organizations in communities.

The overall steps involved with organizing and operating initiatives in neighborhoods and communities that build universal capacity for mental wellness and transformational resilience include:

DOI: 10.4324/9781003262442-6

Step 1: Get Organized: The starting point is to organize a broad and diverse network of people representing the different neighborhoods, populations, social networks, groups, organizations, and institutions in the community into what can be called a Resilience Coordinating Coalition (RCC). RCC members develop a vision and mission statement and clarify the values and operating principles they will follow to achieve them.

Chapter 4 describes how this can be done.

Step 2: Begin Building Community Capacity

Option (A): Offer Trauma Healing Opportunities: If residents of a community are already appreciably traumatized, they will have little ability to focus on anything beyond meeting their basic needs. In these situations, one of the best ways for an RCC to begin its work is to engage residents in activities that help heal their trauma. As people begin to heal, they will often become more interested in other ways they can strengthen their capacity for mental wellness and resilience. Many will also consider participating in efforts to reduce their community's contribution to the climate emergency, especially if doing so addresses factors that contribute to their distress such as the poor housing, the lack of family wage jobs, or a polluted local environment.

Option (B): Engage Residents in Developing Community Resilience Portraits: Sometime after trauma healing events begin in distressed communities, or as a stand-alone starting point in others, RCCs can begin by actively engaging residents in discussions to determine what they care about most in their community, connecting those concerns to mental health and psycho-social-spiritual challenges, and then engaging them in mapping local protective factors, or assets, that can help them address the issues. This can lead to the development of a "Community Resilience Portrait." It can also begin to build the social connections needed to strengthen the capacity for mental wellness and transformational resilience and motivate people to engage in actions that help reduce their community's contribution to the climate crisis.

Chapter 5 explains how an RCC can engage in both of these options.

Step 3: Establish Vision, Goals, Strategy, and Action Plan: The information and insights generated through the RCCs initial activities should be used to craft a vision of success. To achieve that vision, specific goals, objectives, strategies, and action plans should then be developed. A number of semi-autonomous "Resilience Innovation Teams" composed of individuals, groups, and organizations that work with and are respected by different populations and sectors of the community should be formed to craft the strategies and implement the action plans.

Chapter 6 clarifies how an RCC can complete these steps.

Step 4: Implement the Strategy: RCCs should carefully coordinate the strategies developed by the different Resilience Innovation Teams to ensure that every population, geographic area, and sector of the community is engaged in equitable and just ways. Overlaps, gaps, fragmentation, and siloed activities should be identified and resolved.

Chapters 7 through 11 goes into detail about how an RCC can implement strategies that address each of the five foundational areas required to build universal capacity for mental wellness and transformational resilience for the long climate crisis.

Step 5: Continually Track Progress, Learn What Works, Innovate, and Improve: Throughout the entire process, the progress made by the different Resilience Innovation Teams in enhancing the capacity of residents for mental wellness and transformational

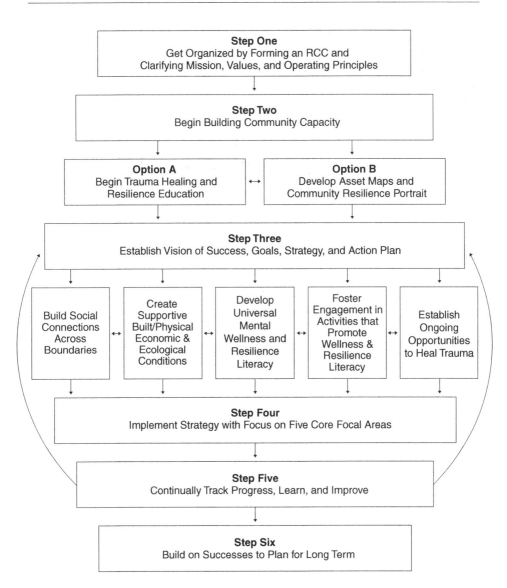

Figure PT02.1 Steps Involved with Organizing and Operating Community-Based Initiatives to Enhance Universal Capacity for Mental Wellness and Transformational Resilience

resilience should be assessed (Figure PT02.1). The information that emerges should be used to learn what works, what does not, and continually improve the strategies and action plans.

Step 6: Plan for the Long Term: Because the impacts of the climate emergency will continue for decades or longer, after a year or so of operation, an RCC should develop plans to sustain its activities over the long term. The plan should include: a) possible long-term sources of funding; b) methods to continue operations when staff and board changes occur; and c) how it can continue to offer its mental wellness and transformational resilience building activities when major emergencies occur and things are disrupted.

Chapter 12 discusses how an RCC can engage in Step 5 and Step 6.

Figure PT02.1 describes the interconnected nature of the six steps. Even though they will be described sequentially in the chapters to follow, the process is actually iterative, not linear. RCCs can emphasize some elements over others at different times and jump back and forth between various focuses depending on the issues that are most pressing in their community. In addition, information generated during one element should be used to adjust and improve many of the other focal areas.

Most important is to remember that, over time, if one or two of the steps have not been sufficiently addressed, the initiative could lose momentum and eventually ground to a halt. Implementing actions to continually fortify each of the steps will therefore be very important.

CHAPTER 4

Get Organized

For communities to build population-level capacity for mental wellness and transformational resilience for the global climate crisis, they must establish the social infrastructure that can support and sustain active involvement by local residents, groups, and organizations over the long term. The principle of active participation is central to this approach. It is based on the acknowledgment that positive change is more likely to occur when the people it affects are involved with the change process. Active participation by residents has the greatest chances of addressing local challenges and of establishing new pro-social norms and standards of behavior that are needed to prevent and heal distress and trauma. To achieve this requires organizing what can be called a Resilience Coordinating Coalition (RCC).

The purpose of an RCC is to bring together people who work with and are respected by every population, neighborhood, and sector of the community to co-create, implement, and continually improve age and culturally accountable actions that strengthen everyone's capacity for mental wellness and transformational resilience during constant adversities. In their own demographically and culturally tailored ways, these actions should focus on engaging all adults and youth in the five foundational areas involved with enhancing universal capacity to prevent and heal distresses and traumas.[1]

"The best way to structure this type of work is through a coalition that establishes the infrastructure that can support the kind of ongoing resilience building that is needed," Ruben Cantu, Associate Program Director for Community Trauma, Mental Health, and Violence Prevention at the Prevention Institute, told me. "That way, trusted messengers that community members know have their interests at heart are leading the effort."[2]

The three words included in the name Resilience Coordinating Coalition (RCC) are chosen for a specific purpose. The focus of the RCC is on enhancing the capacity for mental *wellness and resilience* for adversities, not fixing community deficits or treating symptoms of pathology. Achieving this requires well-constituted *coordination* among numerous individuals, informal and formal social networks, groups, and organizations that represent every population, geographic area, and sector of the community. And, the coordination must be done by a formally constituted *coalition* that meets regularly to plan, implement, evaluate, and continually improve actions, not an informal group that meets occasionally or advises other organizations. As long as these purposes are clearly understood, any name for this type of coalition can be used that makes sense to local residents (and few existing coalitions use this exact name for their group).

In large municipalities, RCCs can be organized in different neighborhoods. When this occurs, an umbrella RCC can also be established to link and coordinate the activities of the many different neighborhood RCCs. When an umbrella coalition is formed, great care must be taken to ensure that it does not divert attention, resources, or decision-making authority away from neighborhood RCCs, where most of the on-the-ground planning and implementation should take place.

In small and modest-sized communities, a single RCC can be established. In rural areas without large metro areas, a county-level or regional RCC can be established that coordinates the activities of different social networks, groups, and organizations spread across the region. Numerous RCCs exist throughout the US and in other nations, though as I said

DOI: 10.4324/9781003262442-7

only a few are explicitly focused on preparing people for the climate crisis. Here are some examples of different types of RCCs in the US and their sponsors. They are each focused on slightly different issues:

- The Whatcom Family & Community Network, located in Whatcom County, Washington, promotes the well-being of children, youth, and families by convening and supporting communities to build their capacity. The Whatcom Network coordinates two smaller coalitions located in different parts of the county, the Mt. Baker Community Coalition and the Whatcom Prevention Coalition.[3]
- The North Carolina Healthy and Resilient Community Initiative now has 46 county-level multi-sector coalitions operating, or in development, that are working to build community resilience for what they call the "Four ACEs": adverse childhood experiences, adverse community experiences, adverse climate experiences, and atrocious cultural experiences. The New Hanover County Resiliency Task Force, which you will learn about in this chapter, is one of the 46 coalitions.
- The Rhode Island Health Equity Zone Initiative supports 15 Health Equity Zone collaboratives in communities across the state. The initiatives are community-led, place-based approaches that promote healthy communities, eliminate unjust health disparities, and enhance the socioeconomic and environmental conditions of neighborhoods across the state.[4]

BENEFITS OF FORMING A RESILIENCE COORDINATING COALITION

Forming an RCC will offer neighborhoods, communities, and rural areas many benefits. A broad and diverse coalition can, for example:

- Bring together the wide range of perspectives, knowledge, experience, skills, and resources required to build whole-community capacity to respond effectively to the wicked mental health and psycho-social-spiritual problems generated by the climate crisis and its many related impacts.
- Enhance many more protective factors and achieve a much broader range of prevention and healing goals than any single profession, organization, or approach can do on their own.
- Engage a wide range of individuals and populations that are typically uninvolved or marginalized in community activities.
- Promote and reinforce social norms, practices, and policies that enhance mental wellness and resilience across numerous populations and sectors of the community.
- Avoid the stigmatization and negative labeling often associated with programs focused on specific individuals or populations, such as those with higher risk of mental health problems, or those deemed "disadvantaged" or determined to be "at risk" or "most vulnerable."
- Build the ongoing communications, trust, and collaboration needed among diverse partners to plan for and respond in just and equitable ways to climate-enhanced disasters and cascading disruptions to essential systems that produce all types of emergencies, food, water, housing, or power shortages, job struggles and income losses, and other challenges.

- Spot and prevent actions intended to reduce greenhouse gasses or prepare for climate impacts that unjustly harm BIPOC and low-income residents and other marginalized groups before they occur, and quickly reverse them when they do happen.
- Inspire and empower residents in ways that increase the likelihood that some will create innovative solutions to numerous challenges.
- Reduce squandered resources that often result from overlapping or siloed services, competition for funding, and tensions over ownership of models and programs.
- Greatly reduce the demands on mental health treatment and direct human service programs, which will enable them to focus their limited resources on individuals who cannot function or are at risk of harming themselves or others.
- Over time, reduce the need for government funding and support, including funding for mental health treatment, family support and other direct service programs, disaster mental health, and other services.

In many cases, the benefits of forming an RCC will also go far beyond preventing and healing climate-related distresses and traumas. An RCC can, for example:

- Engage the individuals, social networks, groups, and organizations needed to prevent and heal severe distresses and traumas resulting from human-caused emergencies such community violence, adverse childhood experiences (ACEs), and more. Prevent and heal distresses and traumas resulting from non-climate-related ecological emergencies such as viral outbreaks, earthquakes, and tsunamis.
- Bring people together to overcome the isolation, separation, and polarization that are undermining civility and blocking solutions to today's challenges that research has found result in large part from social and psychological conditions such as fear, anxiety, and lack of belonging, not political ideologies.[5]

The benefits of forming an RCC were stated very succinctly by Kristi Slette, Executive Director of the Whatcom Family & Community Network: "There is great power in our networks. And there is even more power in the network of networks in our community," she told me. "When we connect networks to networks, our efforts gain leverage and capacity to shift community mindset and increase support."[6]

Another perspective of the benefits of an RCC was shared with me by Robin Saenger, Founding Director of Peace4Tarpon in Tarpon Springs, Florida. It was the first grassroots initiative in the US focused on addressing the root causes of community violence and other problems, rather than merely treating symptoms. "Before we started our program there was lots of siloed stuff going on in our community".... But a wide and diverse set of between 15 and 30 people now attend each meeting and it has allowed many people and agencies to connect." Saenger concluded that "Community is the big deal. The human infrastructure is where the action is at."[7]

INITIAL STEPS IN ORGANIZING A RESILIENCE COORDINATING COALITION

There is no standard blueprint for organizing an RCC. Each coalition comes together in its own unique way. The Putnam County, New York, Community Resilience Coalition (CRC), for example, which enhanced child-focused community resilience for disasters, was organized by National Center for Disaster Preparedness at Columbia University, in partnership with local groups.[8] The CRC unfortunately ended when the original five years of project funding ran out and they were unable to raise additional funds because of the COVID-19 pandemic.[9]

Most RCCs, however, are formed by local community leaders who see the need and bring others together to discuss the possibility of forming a coalition. The Community Resilience Initiative (CRI) in Walla Walla, Washington, for example, was originated by one person: Teri Barila. She had been involved with local community relations work for 12 years and knew "a lot was already going on in the community." But she realized that "to make something bigger happen it had to be community wide." So she "interviewed about everyone in town" to see if they grasped the need for a community-wide focus. She then brought "direct frontline workers, policy makers, and public agencies together" into a coalition. The first word in the name was initially "Children's" but was eventually changed to "Community" to ensure that everyone understood that the CRI was focused on building resilience within the entire community, not just children and their families.[10]

No matter what their origins, a small group usually comes together to discuss forming an RCC.

The initial small group that formed the Putnam County CRC, for instance, consisted of personnel from the National Center for Disaster Preparedness at Columbia University, staff from the non-profit Save the Children, and Barbara Garbarino, a local community member with a background working with children and families.[11]

More than anything else, the initial meetings of the small group should emphasize establishing comradery and rapport, as few concrete goals can be accomplished unless these qualities exist. Getting to know each other personally, learning how each person sees things, and showing interest in issues they and their group or organizations are concerned about, all help generate good rapport.

As they get to know each other, the small group can share their ideas about what the vision of their RCC could be. This involves discussing the question "What do we want to create together?" Good visioning involves imagining new, positive, previously unthinkable conditions. The emphasis should be on what safe, healthy, just, equitable, and resilient responses to climate and other adversities would look and function like in say, five to ten years, and what the benefits would be for different populations, sectors, and the community as a whole.

After the small group develops their initial vision, they can compare it to how the community would look and function in five to ten years under a business-as-usual scenario. Discussions could then be held about different ways to achieve the vision, which can be turned into a mission statement (more about this in a moment).

The small group can then write up their initial vision, mission, and approach into a short document that can be shared with others. A social media presentation might also be developed if that is commonly used in the community to share information with others. Through this process, the originating group can become aware of the different ways each member sees local conditions and generate more rapport.

The small group can then take one more step and develop an "elevator speech," which is a short pithy talk describing why the neighborhood or community should form an RCC, and how it can be done. Answers to some of the possible questions people are likely to ask when they hear the elevator speech should also be crafted. After writing the elevator speech, members can practice giving it to each other. This will help everyone learn how to describe the need and benefits of forming an RCC to others, while also improving the elevator speech, and developing greater comradery.

It should be noted that the elevator speech developed by the initial small group will usually change as new awarenesses and ideas emerge. People involved with the start-up of the Walla Walla, CRI, for example, developed an elevator speech, but Teri Barila told me, "People get caught up in language and become better at the elevator speech when they share it.... It took us 2 years working with the full team to put together a really effective elevator speech."[12]

The small group that wants to form an RCC should then make a list of five to ten people who are involved with different neighborhoods, civic groups, or organizations they believe might be helpful to involve in the RCC. They can also identify who will contact and meet with people in each of the groups to give the elevator speech and learn about their possible interest. In addition to sharing the elevator speech, it will be helpful during the meetings with potential participants to ask for suggestions of other individuals, groups, and organizations to contact about possible involvement. This will grow the list of potential RCC participants beyond those that were initially identified.

After the originating small group speaks with a number of people and learns who might consider participating in the formation of an RCC, they can determine who to ask to become founding members.

The initial small planning team involved with the Putnam County CRC used this approach to organize their coalition. They developed an initial vision, mission statement, and goals and then transitioned to large monthly meetings. To expand their group, they contacted people in the local health department who agreed to distribute informational e-mails inviting other relevant community organizations to attend future meetings to discuss the formation of the CRC. Meeting space was provided in a Putnam County government facility, and seven to ten people attended the initial meetings, most of whom were from the local health department, schools, and a few day care centers.[13]

The way in which people are invited to become founding members of the RCC can be very important. When the originators extend invitations, they are establishing themselves as the people with the authority to do so, even if they do not yet have a formal role or title. This can begin to grow the community as invitees immediately feel a sense of welcome, importance, and belonging. When making an invitation, share why you feel the invitee will be an important member of the RCC and that their insights, talents, and capacities will be greatly valued. Even if they turn down the invitation, this can begin to build robust social connections in the community.

After 7–12 people involved with different neighborhoods, populations, and organizations agree to participate in forming an RCC, a meeting can be held to allow them to meet and strategize about the best way to move forward. As with the original small group, one of the primary goals of the first few meetings of the larger group should be to allow people to get to know each other and develop rapport. Time should be dedicated to allow each person to share who they are, what they do, what they care about, and why they are interested in participating in an RCC. Playful get-to-know-you exercises can be very helpful in the early stages of forming an RCC.

As the group develops rapport, a more detailed mission statement, vision of success, and approach for achieving it can be discussed. Engaging people in these dialogues will build ownership and increase interest in being involved. One outcome should be the development of a more refined and snappy elevator speech that participants can use to engage even more people in the RCC.

The seven to ten people who attended the initial meetings of the Putnam County CRC focused much of their time on developing a mission statement and goals and in doing so built connection and comradery.[14]

After these tasks are completed, a list of additional people to contact about becoming involved in the RCC can be developed, along with a plan outlining who will contact each person. The larger the number and more diverse the list of individuals, groups, and organizations that are contacted, the more likely it is that the RCC will represent a majority of the community.

It can take three to six months or so before 10–15 key individuals agree to participate in an RCC. When a sufficient number are committed, they can be asked to become founding members and form the initial RCC steering committee (or board of directors). If it makes sense, an interim three-to-five-person executive committee can be established as well.

As the group of seven to ten people that attended meetings of the Putnam County CRC clarified the CRC's mission statement and goals, more people started to attend the meetings. By the end of the first year, 20–25 people attended each meeting and they continued to participate through the entire process even though most had full time jobs and other responsibilities.[15] The CRC eventually grew to include public schools and a few private ones, summer camps, and child care organizations, the local Child Advocacy Center, numerous community action programs including food banks, disability groups, nursing homes, local hospitals, both the Girl Scouts and Boy Scouts, civilian patrol, local non-profit mental health organizations, bureau of energy services, numerous city, county, and state agencies, some law enforcement agencies, the Red Cross, and local town supervisors.[16]

It is very likely that some individuals and organizations, such as people involved with groups that are typically uninvolved or marginalized in community activities, a local school district, or government agency might be intrigued by the idea of participating in the RCC, but not be ready or able to formally commit. If asked, however, some might be able to offer in-kind support, such as free space for meetings as happened in Putnam County, or free copying, coffee/tea and snacks at meetings, or free promotion. Some individuals and organizations might also offer small financial donations or discretionary grants to help get the RCC off the ground.

ROLES OF RCC MEMBERS

When reaching out to community members about participating in the RCC, it will often be helpful to explain the different roles they can play. Each RCC member can take on different roles. Although they will differ in every RCC, in general the roles include:

- Helping to develop the RCC's mission, vision, goals, strategies, and action plans and ensuring that they are achieving their desired ends.
- Helping to recruit and engage additional individuals, groups, and organizations in RCC activities.
- Actively participating in one or more of the RCC's Resilience Innovation Teams that devise and implement strategies to foster mental wellness and transformational resilience within different neighborhoods, populations, and sectors of the community.
- Helping to recruit, hire, and/or supervise staff.
- Identifying and/or securing specialists to assist with RCC activities.
- Locating potential funders and/or assisting with the development of funding requests.
- Providing volunteer and/or paid staffing support to schedule, organize, and operate RCC events.
- Actively participating in as many RCC events as possible.

- Providing research, reviews, writing, and/or editorial assistance to produce RCC documents.
- Promoting the work of the RCC to local residents, public officials, the media, and others.

WORKING THROUGH EXISTING ORGANIZATIONS AND NETWORKS OR STARTING A NEW COALITION

Rather than starting an entirely new RCC, the original small group that seeks to form a coalition might consider approaching an existing human service, environmental, or other type of organization about serving as the host or anchor institution for the effort. This might make sense if the RCC organizers are seeking a known organization to facilitate the initiative, provide administrative support, and act as a fiscal sponsor to allow them to raise funds.

This approach will succeed, however, only if the existing organization is committed to expanding beyond its current mission and approach to support an initiative that builds universal capacity to prevent and heal distresses and traumas as people also reduce their community's contribution to the climate emergency. This can be difficult for many existing organizations. Some might initially voice interest in broadening their focus. But time constraints, the mental models that dominate the organization, or funding constraints might soon lead them to revert back to their previous focus.

If it becomes clear there is no existing organization that can serve as the anchor institution for the RCC, a local coalition of organizations can be considered. This might include, for example, a coalition focused on some aspect of the climate emergency, adverse childhood experiences, trauma-informed care, or other issues. Expanding an existing coalition of organizations can avoid the burnout people often feel when numerous networks exist in their community. As with individual organizations, however, this approach will succeed only if the existing coalition is committed to expanding its thinking, goals, strategies, and membership to help the entire population prevent and heal distresses and traumas, as they also reduce the community's contributions to the climate crisis.

One of the potential drawbacks of working through an existing coalition can be a lack of adaptability. RCCs must be willing to think differently, continually innovate, and support new approaches to prevent and heal the distresses and traumas generated during the long climate emergency. Making this shift will often be difficult for coalitions that have firmly established goals and procedures, and the social norms that dominate them might generate resistance to new ways of perceiving and addressing challenges.

For this reason, rather than working through an existing organization or coalition, the small group that seeks to organize an RCC will often need to form a new free-standing coalition. A non-profit or government organization that decides to participate in the RCC can then be asked to serve as its anchor organization and fiscal sponsor.

EXPANDING PARTICIPATION IN THE RCC

No matter what entity serves as the anchor institution and fiscal sponsor, an RCC should use a localized version of an "outside-in" approach to continually broaden participation in the coalition. This involves expanding beyond well-known individuals, organizations, or elected officials to ask residents to recommend people and groups that should become involved in the RCC. The coalition's initial focus should be people with[17]:

- *Influence*—the ability to make things happen in different neighborhoods and sectors;
- *Information*—about people and issues affecting the community;
- *Resources*—such as contacts, time, facilities, and money;
- *Expertise*—in working with the many different populations, sectors, and issues the RCC will engage with;
- *Lived Experience*—those already feeling the effects of different types of distresses and traumas.

Using these five criteria, people involved with the following groups and sectors should be asked to participate in the RCC steering committee/board of directors and/or on a Resilience Innovation Team:

- Grassroots leaders respected by individuals and groups that are typically marginalized or uninvolved in community activities;
- Neighborhood associations, community-based organizations, and underserved populations;
- Formal and informal social networks such as book clubs, hiking groups, sports clubs and others;
- Civic organizations such as the YWCA/YMCA, arts, theatre, heritage groups, and Rotary clubs;
- K-12, after-school, and summer youth programs;
- Adult education and job training programs, community colleges, and universities;
- Faith and spirituality groups;
- Elder care and others working with seniors;
- Non-profit, private, and public health care providers, including those representing nurses, doctors, and health care organizations;
- Non-profit, private, and public mental health and human services organizations, including social workers;
- Volunteer groups and professional organizations focused on climate mitigation and adaptation and ecological conservation and restoration;
- Social justice, climate, and environmental justice leaders;
- Disaster preparedness and response organizations and those that provide food/water/shelter/power/sanitation services during emergencies;
- A wide range of business associations and private firms;
- Police and others involved with community safety, security, and the justice system;
- Government officials involved with mental and physical health, economic development, the physical/built, and natural environments;
- Local funding organizations such as United Way and philanthropic foundations;
- Elected officials;
- Other voluntary, non-profit, private, and public sector networks, groups, and organizations.

As an example, the Resiliency Task Force in New Hanover County, North Carolina, is overseen by a Steering Committee that oversees eight subcommittees. Over 100 organizations have participated in the Resiliency Task Force meetings, seminars, and subcommittee tasks over the past three years.[18]

Mental health and direct service professionals should participate in the RCC as equals, or support it by serving as advisors or coaches. They should not, however, be the sole leads because if this happens, many people are likely to view it as a mental health treatment initiative and choose not to participate (more on this soon).

Some individuals, such as those working with BIPOC residents that might be skeptical of involvement, or organizations such as a local hospital, might voice interest in the RCC, but initially decline to participate due to lack of time or the desire to see how the RCC functions before becoming engaged. This is to be expected. The RCC should continually invite uninvolved individuals and organizations to observe how it functions. Successes should be continually highlighted in the local news and through social media and social support networks for everyone in the community to see. After seeing how the RCC operates, and observing its progress and what it offers residents, over time more individuals, groups, and organizations will join the coalition.

Making it easy for people to participate in RCC meetings and events will also encourage people to participate. This can include, for example, offering free bus passes or organizing ride sharing opportunities to allow people to attend. Providing food and beverages can also make it easier for people to participate. In addition, free gift cards usable at local businesses can be given to residents to encourage participation.

RCC MEMBERS SHOULD CONSTANTLY PRACTICE GOOD COMMUNICATIONS AND CONFLICT RESOLUTION SKILLS

Bringing people together who have not previously worked with each other will require an explicit effort to build trust, good communications, and effective conflict resolution skills. These qualities will be very important because in stressful conditions, the different perspectives and needs of neighborhoods, groups, and organizations can easily escalate into conflicts that diminish the effectiveness of the RCC. Dedicating time to allow people to get to know each other and develop good rapport, learn how to communicate in ways that builds respect and trust, and constructively resolve conflicts will be extremely important. Learning and practicing these skills will also offer an important role model that people throughout the community can follow to communicate effectively and resolve conflicts.

Effective communicators are able to explain their ideas in clear and simple terms, express their feelings in an open and non-threatening way, listen carefully to others, and ask questions to clarify their meaning. They are also willing to alter their beliefs if what they hear from others seems reasonable. In addition, good communicators are able to initiate dialogues about issues or tensions they sense could exist within the group. And, they are able to reflect on the interactions occurring within their group, consider how to improve their own responses, and encourage others to do so as well.

Developing these capacities requires openness to new ideas and respect for the varied perspectives of all of the different members of an RCC. The mutual trust needed to develop and implement strategies to prevent and heal climate distresses and traumas will emerge only when RCC members are willing to speak honestly and respectfully, support one another, and continually seek constructive feedback on ideas. This requires that members see each other as collaborators, not competitors, which is all too common when funding or different strategies are discussed.

It takes time to develop these capacities. It will therefore be important for an RCC to continually dedicate time to learn and practice good communications and conflict resolution skills. This can occur informally through ongoing discussion among RCC members. It can also be done through the use of role plays and conflict resolution games that allow people to practice skills in non-threatening situations.

In addition, when tensions arise in the process of developing goals and strategies, it will be very important for an RCC to openly acknowledge and honestly discuss what has occurred, and dedicate time to clarifying how to communicate and resolve conflicts better in the future.

CLARIFY THE RCC'S MISSION AND VISION

After a core group of founding members has been organized into an RCC, it should build on the mission statement developed by the original organizers and craft a mission statement that everyone supports. To develop a mission statement, the RCC should answer basic questions such as: "What are the top priorities of local residents?", "How do they relate to mental health and psycho-social-spiritual problems, and how can we address their needs in ways that strengthen their capacity for mental wellness and transformational resilience?", and "How will we operate to achieve these goals?" The answers to these questions should be written up into simple one-to-two sentence-long action-oriented assertions that describe the purpose and goals of the coalition, who it will engage, and how it will accomplish its goals. Developing a good mission statement requires thinking long-term in a big picture way. For example:

- The mission of the Whatcom Family & Community Network is to: "Promote the well-being of children, youth, and families by convening and supporting communities to build their capacity."
- The mission of the New Hanover County North Carolina Resiliency Task Force is: "To build our community's resiliency, we work to reduce and prevent ACEs (trauma), respond to existing trauma in children, adults and providers with knowledge, empathy, and compassion, and create opportunities for our community to form meaningful connections with one another."[19]
- The mission of the Walla Walla CRC is: "Inspiring healthier communities with science-based insights in order to promote and cultivate resilience."[20]

Again, none of these organizations, and only a few of the ones mentioned in this book, are explicitly focused on building resilience for climate distresses and traumas—though directly or indirectly they all address some aspects of the issues.

After the mission statement is developed, the RCC should clarify its vision of success. The vision should describe its dream for the future—the ideal way RCC members would like things to look and function in the community when it has built universal capacity for mental wellness and transformational resilience. A good vision statement should be written in the present moment, not future tense, but be forward looking. Like the mission statement, it should be written as a short powerful unequivocal description of the ideal conditions the RCC seeks to achieve. The vision should also be inspirational and create a vivid picture in people's minds of why the RCC's work is very important. At the same time, it should not be pie-in-the-sky, and not include metrics or be too specific.

- The vision of the Whatcom Family & Community Network is: "a thriving community built on equity, social connection, participation, and opportunities."
- The vision of the New Hanover County Resilience Task Force is: "New Hanover County is a compassionate and resilient community."[21]
- The vision of Climate Resilience Communities, which operates in the southern region of the San Francisco Bay area, is: "dedicated to serving the underrepresented through empowering community voices to implement climate solutions that bring about unity and resilience."[22]

RCC members should know that the specifics of their mission and vision will likely change over time as more information is generated, its activities mature, and the impacts of the climate emergency plays out. But the core elements will usually remain similar.

CLARIFY THE RCC'S CORE VALUES

From the accelerating distresses and traumas generated by climate adversities, to the staffing, funding, and other typical organizational struggles, an RCC is certain to face numerous challenges. To ensure continued wise and skillful decision-making during difficult times, after the RCC clarifies its mission and vision, it will be important to adopt a clear set of core values. The values adopted by the RCC will also help attract additional participation and motivate residents to engage in its activities.

- The values that the Whatcom Family & Community Network operates under include: Empowerment; Collective Action; Education; Connection; Inclusion; Love; Healing; and Equity.
- The core values of the CRI in Walla Walla include: Connection; Culture; Diversity; Knowledge; Resilience; Sustainability; and Well-being.[23]
- The Healthy and Resilient Community Initiative in North Carolina, which the New Hanover County Resilience Task Force is a member of, operates under six core values (adopted from SAMHSA—the US Substance Abuse and Mental Health Services Administration): Trust; Support; Collaboration; Safety; Empowerment; History; and Culture.[24]

It is important to remember that both explicit values such as those that are publicly stated above and implicit values, which are unstated but nevertheless powerful, will be important to the success of the RCC. If, for example, an RCC begins to value revenue over activities that build social connections, or if they locate most of their work in wealthier neighborhoods and ignore low-income or BIPOC areas, residents will come to believe that the coalition's explicitly stated value of equity is fake and that money and power are their actual implicit values. This will lead to a loss of faith and trust in the integrity of the RCC.

The difference between how the RCC addresses intrinsic and extrinsic values will also be important. Intrinsic values tend to focus on compassion, connection, and kindness toward everyone, including the natural environment and biodiversity. Extrinsic values tend to focus on a desire for status, wealth, power, or other forms of self-aggrandizement.

When asked what they really care about, most people will prioritize intrinsic values. Research has found, for example, that the vast majority of both children and adults tend to favor "benevolence" above all other values, which means enhancing the welfare of people around them. Yet, a small percentage of people will describe extrinsic values as most important to them. These individuals typically are not interested in connecting with others, nor are they concerned about their community. They also tend to have higher levels of stress, anxiety, anger, depression, and dissatisfaction than people who hold intrinsic values.[25]

The values people hold are not shaped by some mysterious force. They result from the norms and values promoted within their family, by people in their social networks, and by the religious or spiritual, economic, and political environments in which they live. If an RCC wants to enhance everyone's capacity to prevent and heal distresses and traumas as they help reduce the climate emergency to manageable levels, they will need to continually promote intrinsic values such as connectedness with others, empathy, and engagement in pro-social actions that help others and regenerate tattered ecological systems, and downplay extrinsic values.

CLARIFY THE RCC'S OPERATING PRINCIPLES

The values that the RCC chooses to guide its activities should be closely connected with a set of agreed upon operating principles. Operating principles describe the way the RCC will put its values into practice to achieve its vision. They help guide decision-making and allow things to get done quicker. The operating principles can also circle back to influence the RCC's mission, vision, and values.

The Whatcom Family & Community Network has three core operating principles:

- *Connection*: Relationships and collaboration are at the heart of all our work. We believe community "change happens at the speed of trust."
- *Resilience*: In the face of exposure to significant adversity (trauma), resilience is the capacity of individuals [and communities] to navigate their way to the all the resources needed to sustain well-being.
- *Prevention*: WFCN aims to build communities of healthy, happy children, adolescents, families, and neighbors. Health and well-being are the end result of all we do.

The North Carolina Healthy and Resilient Community Initiative has four overall guiding principles[26]:

1. *Responsive*: The initiative's processes and deliverables are guided by the experiences and expressed needs of local coalition members. The ongoing input of coalition members is integral in the planning and implementation of resilience-focused strategies.

2. *Data and Science Driven*: The science of adversity and resilience guides the NC Healthy and Resilient Communities work. Evidence and population data will inform desired outcomes.

3. *Asset and Trauma-Informed*: The initiative assumes that communities are more likely than not to have a history of trauma. By recognizing and uplifting individual and community assets, communities can be defined by their strengths as they work to become more trauma resilient.

4. *Racial Justice and Equity Focused*: This work is centered on identifying and reducing unfair differences in access to opportunity, power, and resources. It is only possible to develop strategies to address disparities by first acknowledging the connection between adversity and racism and the disproportionate health and well-being outcomes across race and ethnicity.

Building Resilient Neighborhoods in Victoria, British Columbia, which "brings citizens, groups, organizations, businesses, and local governments together to create more resilient communities together," has six core operating principles[27]:

1. *Working at multiple scales and across sectors.*
2. *Encouraging both the short- and long-term view.*
3. *Providing inspirational examples of change to create hope and motivate action.*
4. *Assessing local resilience to optimize limited resources.*
5. *Going beyond conventional planning.*
6. *Providing opportunities for people to engage in different ways.*

OTHER IMPORTANT OPERATING PRINCIPLES TO CONSIDER

The operating principles of the programs described above shine the light on a number of important principles RCCs should consider adopting. They include:

- *Servant and Participatory Leadership*: An RCC should be led by respected members of the community who prioritize serving others over their own interests. They should be able to communicate effectively with and serve as "links" between both community leaders and residents who are otherwise usually marginalized or uninvolved in community activities. The leaders should not be firmly committed to any specific theory or approach to building mental wellness and resilience, and thus be able to encourage RCC members to co-create innovative locally tailored, age and culturally accountable strategies.[28] Good leaders should also able to reframe discussions by asking powerful questions rather than providing their own answers and create feelings of safety that allow people to feel comfortable gathering together to discuss difficult issues. And the goal of a good leader should be to empower others to be the best they can be, not promote themselves.
- *Do No Harm—Protect Social Justice, Equity, and Human Rights*: Unequal and unjust norms, practices, and policies can create and aggravate mental health and psycho-social-spiritual problems for both the oppressed and oppressors. It is therefore essential for a RCC to explicitly state that social justice, equity, and human rights will guide all of its activities and that they are committed to not marginalizing or in other ways doing harm to any individual, neighborhood, or population.
- *Climate Science, Systems Thinking, Neuroscience, and Transformational Resilience*: RCCs should use credible scientific information grounded in the social-ecological model to design strategies to prevent and heal mental health and psycho-social-spiritual problems. They should also learn the basics of systems thinking to understand how the climate crisis will activate cascading disruptions in one ecological, economic, or

social system that feed back to activate problems in others, and conversely how positive changes in one high leverage area can produce a virtuous cycle that activates beneficial changes elsewhere. In addition, RCC members should utilize the principles of neuroscience to understand—and teach others—how traumas and toxic stresses can activate fight, flight, freeze reactions that affect people's body, mind, emotions, and behaviors and how, when unreleased, those reactions can affect individuals, families, communities, and entire societies. And, an RCC will benefit by utilizing the principles of Transformational Resilience, because a positive reinforcing cycle can be activated when many residents have enhanced their capacity for presencing (self-regulation) and purposing (adversity-based growth) that allows them to find new meaning, direction, and healthy hope during adversities.[29]

*   *Continual Learning, Innovation, and Improvement*: RCCs will frequently need to alter their goals and strategies as the climate emergency accelerates, new information emerges, and different challenges appear. This will require the willingness to recognize and alter deeply held assumptions and beliefs that previously seemed unassailable. Like peeling an onion, new insights will continually emerge as the RCC continues its activities. A commitment to become a "learning community" that constantly learns new things, revises its assumptions and beliefs, and subsequently alters their strategies and action plans should therefore be a core operating principle (I'll say more about this in the Conclusion of this book).

*   *Ground-Up Culturally Accountable Strategies*: The ability of an RCC to engage residents in activities that strengthen their capacity for mental wellness and transformational resilience will be determined by the extent to which they trust, support, and are willing to participate in the initiative. To achieve this, the initiative must focus on what is important to them, how those issues are related to mental health and psycho-social-spiritual issues, and the community must come to own it. The activities will therefore vary based on the demographics, cultural make-up, and history of trauma in the different neighborhoods, populations, and sectors of the community, and the resources that are available or can be obtained. The RCC should always design its activities from the ground-up to address local interests, concerns, and conditions.

*   *External Partnerships*: To continually learn, adjust, and improve its operations and strategies, the RCC should establish relationships with other community initiatives, and with state, regional, and national organizations engaged in one or more of the five foundational areas involved with building universal capacity for mental wellness and transformational resilience. Partnerships with universities, external funders, evaluators, and others that can offer guidance, training, research, resources, and other forms of assistance will also be very helpful.

IDENTIFY EFFECTIVE COMMUNITY LEADERS AND STAFF FOR THE RCC

An RCC will typically begin as a fairly informal entity, with the original group of organizers taking the lead to engage members in the creation of a mission, vision, core values, and operating principles, and others participating as their time allows. This approach makes sense in the start-up phase of the RCC because some of the people who initially participate are not necessarily the individuals that will be most active 6–12 months or more down the road. Some people will get involved out of enthusiasm that quickly wanes, others will become engaged out of duty and then drop out after they feel they have done their part, some will simply wear out due to too many commitments, and others will find they do not have the attributes required to work collaboratively with diverse coalitions. For this reason, the leadership of RCC should be kept as loose as possible for the first year or so, and responsibilities should be spread around to as wide a set of people as possible.

During this time, it will be important to continually search for individuals who can become effective leaders of the RCC. It will also be important to keep an eye out for people who can lead the many "Resilience Innovation Teams" that should be organized to develop mental wellness and transformational resilience strategies for all of the different populations and sectors in the community (more on this in a moment).

Finding good leaders can often be a difficult task that is full of uncertainty. A common mistake is to quickly decide that people who speak the most or the loudest, or already have the attention of major organizations, elected officials, or funders, can be effective leaders of the RCC. These people often seem like safe choices. But rushing to judgment will often backfire as many boisterous well-connected people are primarily interested in themselves, or their own organization's needs, not the welfare of the community as a whole. They might also skew the focus of the RCC to emphasize higher status socioeconomic neighborhoods, groups, or sectors which will make enhancing population-level capacity for mental wellness and transformational resilience difficult to achieve.

For these reasons, it will often be best to spend time getting to know everyone and watching how different people operate through the lens of the operating principle of Servant and Participatory Leadership just described. After a while, the attributes, skills, and commitment levels of different people will sort themselves out, and effective leaders can be identified.

A similar process should be used to find top quality staff. A 2018 national survey found that one of the bigger challenges faced by non-profits is attracting and retaining employees.[30] A primary reason is that most non-profits offer lower wages than can be obtained in the private sector, and they also have less long-term stability than public sector jobs. The ability to support and facilitate diverse groups, and work with residents that have different backgrounds, also requires a certain type of mindset and skills.

RCCs should take the time needed to find the right people for the job. One way to do this is to keep an eye on people who volunteer for RCC activities to see if someone has the right qualities. Local, or even regional and even national searches, can also be used. No matter what approach is used, to attract the right type of applicants, the RCC should emphasize the positive mission and social benefits of the job, as well as the values and operating principles that shape its working environment.[31]

In addition to finding people to lead and staff the RCC, during the first year or so of operation coalition members should be looking for effective grassroots and neighborhood leaders. They will not necessarily be particularly well-known or high-achieving people. Instead, they are often individuals with the innate ability to bring residents together, open doors, and inspire them to work together to address local challenges. This type of leader can usually be found throughout the community, and RCC members should try to identify and engage them in their efforts to enhance the entire population's capacity for mental wellness and transformational resilience and engage residents in climate solutions.[32]

OFFER EARLY BASIC EDUCATION AND
TRAINING FOR RCC MEMBERS

Early on in the development of the RCC, it will be very important for members to become apprised about what will be needed to implement its mission, vision, and operating principles. Members should also get up to speed on the basics of a public health approach to preventing and healing distresses and traumas, and on the fundamentals of the climate emergency. Educational events should also be held on servant leadership, group facilitation, asset mapping, trauma-informed responses, and the five foundational areas involved with building universal capacity for mental wellness and resilience for the climate emergency.

The sooner an RCC begins this type of basic training the better, as it can provide members with the understandings and skills they need to work effectively with community members. It is also important because the previous education and training of many coalition members is not likely to have addressed these issues. Guest speakers can be engaged, and educational opportunities can found online at little to no cost by partnering with a local university or other community coalitions that are seeking similar trainings.[33]

MENTAL HEALTH AND HUMAN SERVICE PROFESSIONALS
CAN PLAY IMPORTANT ROLES

Mental health and direct service professionals can play very important roles in an RCC. For example, if they have the right mindset, skills, and time, they can explain the neurobiology of trauma and toxic stress to members of the RCC (help everyone become "trauma-informed"). They can also help everyone increase their literacy about mental wellness and resilience by teaching them simple self-administrable Presencing (self-regulation) and Purposing (adversity-based growth) skills. In addition, they can train local residents in how to teach that information and skills to others in the community through peer-to-peer events. And, as previously stated, they can serve as advisors and coaches to an RCC. In these roles, they might, for example, connect the RCC to external organizations and experts or seek out potential government or philanthropic funds.

In addition, to emphasize again, the most important role mental health professionals can play is to provide mental health services to people who, even after engaging in community-based mental wellness and resilience building activities, still cannot function or are at risk of harming themselves or others. They should seek to reduce the impacts of debilitating mental health problems, prevent relapses and further complications, and support their recovery. Funding mechanisms used to pay for existing mental health treatment services can be used to support this work, which will remain very important as the climate crisis plays out.

SELECT AN APPROPRIATE
ORGANIZATIONAL STRUCTURE

Much like it approaches leadership development, in the first year or so, an RCC will typically operate with an informal organization structure. However, when a sufficient number of individuals, groups, and organizations decide to participate in the RCC, it will usually benefit by developing a more formal structure.

The RCC steering committee/board should continue to serve as the overall decision-making body of the coalition. However, because no single group or organization can assist all of the different populations of a community, "Resilience Innovation Teams" composed of individuals, groups, and organizations that work with and are respected by different neighborhoods, populations, and sectors should be formed to plan and engage these groups in activities that strengthen their capacity for mental wellness and transformational resilience as they reduce their contribution to the climate crisis. This will require a good deal of well-coordinated decentralization.

This wording might seem like a contradiction. But a "Ring Team" or "Hub and Spoke" structure can be a useful way to coordinate the efforts of numerous semi-independent Resilience Innovation Teams. Different Resilience Innovation Teams can be formed, for example, to work with specific neighborhoods, K-12 schools, working age adults, seniors, higher educational institutions, volunteer and civic groups, recreational clubs, private businesses, healthcare providers, public agencies, and other populations and sectors (Figure 4.1).

On a regular basis, each of the Resilience Innovation Teams should continually share the strategies they develop and the activities they propose to implement with the RCC executive committee and all other Resilience Innovation Teams to ensure that everyone knows

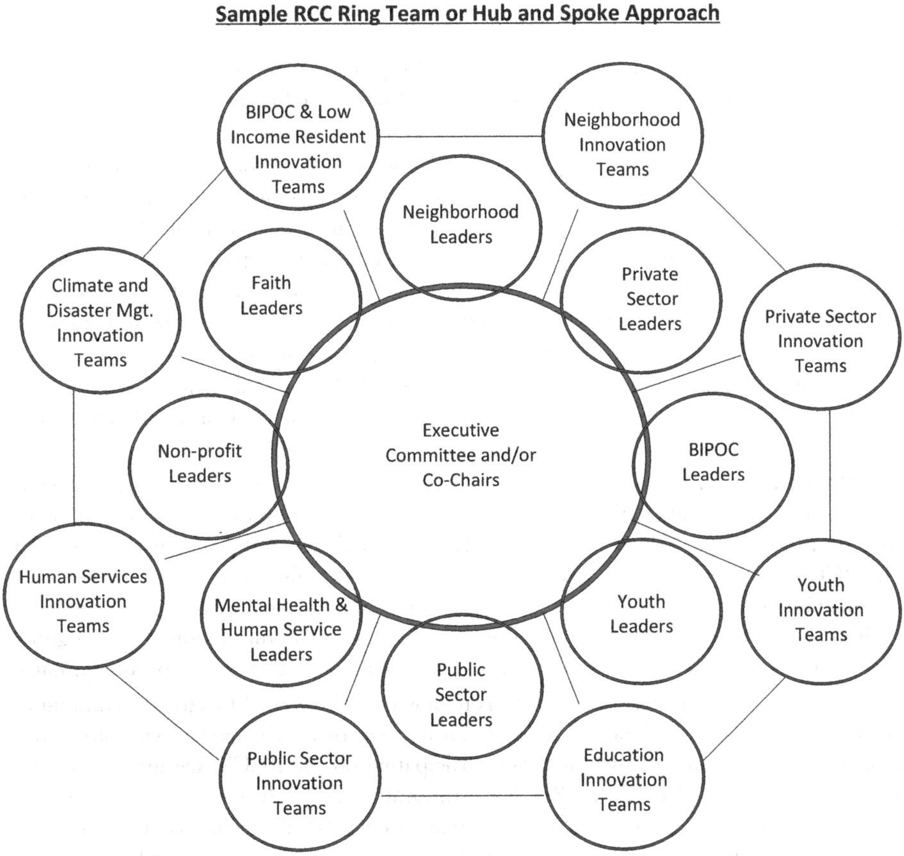

Sample RCC Ring Team or Hub and Spoke Approach

Figure 4.1 Sample RCC Ring Team or Hub and Spoke Approach

what is happening, identify overlaps and gaps, obtain feedback, and in other ways integrate and coordinate their efforts.

For example, a K-12 school Resilience Innovation Team might focus on children in public schools. When they share their strategies with the larger RCC and other Resilience Innovation Teams, someone might point out that children in private schools, or that are being homeschooled, should also have the opportunity to be engaged. This can spur efforts to contact people who operate private schools and work with the parents of homeschooled children to ask if they would like to participate in the RCC's mental wellness and transformational resilience building activities.

In addition, when organizations involved with different Resilience Innovation Teams find they are planning to submit grant proposals to the same funder, discussions can occur to clarify how to distinguish the proposals, or possibly merger them.

The Resiliency Task Force in New Hanover County, North Carolina, uses a ring team organizational structure. Their eight subcommittees function fairly independently and report back to a steering committee on a monthly basis, which oversees their work and helps to guide the work of the entire Task Force.[34]

FUNDING AN RCC

Some community-based initiatives, such as Peace4Tapron in Tarpon Springs, Florida, begin without funding and operate for years without it. "Not having funding served us very well," founder Robin Saenger told me. "We were not beholden to anyone."[35]

Most community-based initiatives, however, will, in fairly short-order, need to secure funding to cover administrative costs and hire staff. Without funding, the efforts by volunteers run the risk of petering out and the RCC's efforts can stall or terminate. Raising funds, however, can be challenging because it is often difficult for start-ups to do so. In addition, most resources for mental health work currently go to government agencies or professional organizations for clinical treatment, not community-based mental wellness and resilience building initiatives. However, a carefully developed approach can achieve success.

One of the best ways to raise start-up funds is to ask RCC members to consider making personal donations, and to ask them to also request donations from their friends, colleagues, and others they know in the community.

The RCC can also use crowdfunding platforms such as GoFundMe to raise start-up funds. This approach allows the RCC to share their work and request large and small donations from potentially millions of individuals and organizations that might want to help. The RCC can create a website that describes its vision and mission that can be linked with its crowdfunding page. It can also set a fundraising goal and track donations so people can see how the campaign is going. In addition, creating a page on the website that recognizes people who contribute funds can be helpful (though some donations might be anonymous).

Another way to raise both start-up and ongoing funds is for the RCC to hold community fundraisers. This can be done by the RCC on its own, or in partnership with other well-known local organizations, such as those participating on the RCC's steering committee/board, or that are involved with a Resilience Innovation Team. It often helps to organize a fundraising committee to develop the campaign strategy. Small donations of $15 to $100 (US) can be solicited. Strategies can also be developed to approach residents who are known to have the potential to make larger donations.

After the RCC has achieved some success, it can approach local, state, or even national philanthropic foundations for funding. National and state/provincial governments should also enact policies that fund community-based initiatives.

It might take a number of years before foundations will fund the RCC because most, especially large ones, avoid start-ups and prefer to support established non-profits with proven track records. However, a local United Way agency or small philanthropic foundation might be willing to invest early on if they see progress. Or, the RCC can approach an existing non-profit that receives grants from external foundations to see if they can be included in a grant proposal the organization is submitting. Over time, as the RCC becomes established and develops a track record, it can approach a larger foundation on its own for funding.

A number of community-based initiatives in the US focused on adverse childhood experiences and drug and alcohol problems currently obtain funding from local, state, or federal government sources. They often need to shape their programs to meet the criteria of the government grants, which can reduce their ability to continually innovate, change directions, and improve their offerings. But this is currently the only way they can obtain public funds.

In the Conclusion of this book, I'll discuss the need for all levels of government to establish grant programs that provide long-term funding for community-based mental wellness and resilience building initiatives.

NOT ALL RCCS NEED TO TAKE THIS APPROACH

Even though this chapter has discussed the steps involved with organizing an RCC, not all community-based coalitions need, or will be able, to go this route. Some neighborhood or community coalitions will simply not have the ability and resources required to complete all of the steps. Others will avoid them out of concern that they will make the RCC another top-down bureaucratic organization that decides on its own what is best for residents. And, depending on the size of the community, the scale of the traumas residents experience, and resources that are available, sometimes the best approach will be for neighborhood associations and other informal groups to do the work without organizing a formal RCC. This can succeed as long as the people involved continually take the time to clarify what they are striving to achieve and why, evaluate their core assumptions and beliefs, and constantly evaluate their progress, learn, and improve.

The ultimate goal of all community members committed to enhancing universal capacity in their community to prevent and heal distresses and traumas and engaging residents in solutions to the climate emergency should be to empower them to innovate and create new and inspiring safe, healthy, just, and equitable local conditions. If that goal remains clear, the type of organizational structure they use will not be all that important.

A CHECKLIST CAN HELP

The checklist offered at the end of this chapter can be used if you desire to organize an RCC and want to determine the extent to which the elements involved with getting it up and running have been addressed.

The first public actions an RCC can take after it has gotten organized are discussed in the next chapter.

CHECKLISTS FOR ORGANIZING AN RCC

Answering the questions in the charts below will help you assess the degree to which your group is ready to function as a broad and diverse Resilience Coordinating Coalition (RCC). You don't need to answer "Yes" to every question. But the more you answer "Yes" the greater the likelihood that an RCC is ready to get up and running.

I. Getting Organized	Yes	No	Comments
Did the small group that desired to form the RCC develop an initial mission, vision of success, and approach for achieving it?			
Did the initial group make a list of people to share their mission, vision, an approach with, and ask to participate?			
Did the initial group create and practice an "elevator speech" to explain the RCC in simple compelling terms to others?			
Do you now have at least 7–15 respected people from different neighborhoods, social networks, groups, and organizations in the community interested in an RCC?			
Has the team of 7–15 discussed what its mission, vision of success, values, and operating principles will be?			
Has the team of 7–15 selected an interim executive committee/board and/or co-chairs to make daily decisions for the RCC?			
Has the initial team of 7–15 discussed how the RCC will communicate with each other and resolve conflicts?			
Does the initial team of 7–15 have a plan to invite additional individuals, groups, and organizations to participate in the RCC?			

II. Membership: Who is Involved?	Yes	No	Comments
Individuals who work with grassroots groups and people typically uninvolved or marginalized in the community?			
Neighborhood leaders?			

II. Membership: Who is Involved?	Yes	No	Comments
Civic and voluntary organizations (e.g., YWCA/YMCA, Rotary)?			
K-12 educational organizations?			
Youth after-school and summer programs?			
Elder support and care organizations?			
Volunteer and non-profit environmental, conservation, and climate organizations?			
Community colleges and universities?			
Private businesses and business associations?			
Adult job training organizations?			
Religious and spirituality leaders?			
Organizations that provide food/water/ power/shelter/sanitation during disasters and emergency situations?			
Climate adaptation and mitigation professionals, groups, and organizations?			
Public health professionals?			
Doctors, nurses, and other physical health professionals and institutions?			
Disaster response professionals?			
Justice system representatives (e.g., police, courts)?			
Mental health professionals and institutions?			
Non-profit, private, and public direct human service professionals and organizations?			
Local funders?			
Local government agencies focused on infrastructure, open spaces, parks, economic development, the natural environment, and climate change?			
Local elected officials?			
Does the initial RCC now represent all of the populations, neighborhoods, and sectors in the community? If not, who is missing?	Yes	No	Others to Involve

III. Organizational Planning	Yes	No	Comments
Has the RCC developed a plan to educate and train its steering committee/board and members in core information and skills?			
Has the RCC developed a plan to identify and recruit effective leaders and staff?			
Has the RCC organized "Resilience Innovation Teams" to design and implement strategies to enhance mental wellness and resilience among different populations and sectors of the community?			
Has the RCC discussed a "ring team" or similar organizational structure to coordinate strategies by different semi-independent Resilience Innovation Teams?			
Has the RCC developed a fundraising plan?			

NOTES

1 For more on the importance of organizing coalitions of local residents, civic groups, and organizations to plan and implement activities that foster and sustain mental wellness and resilience see, for example: Butterfoss P.G. et al. (1993). Community coalitions for prevention and health promotion. *Health Education Research*, 8, 315–330; Foster-Fishman P.G. et al. (2007). Building an active citizenry: the role of neighborhood problems, readiness, and capacity for change. *American Journal of Community Psychiatry*, 39, 91–106; Kania J. and Kramer M. (2011). Collective impact. *Stanford Social Innovations Review*, 9, 36–41; and Hawkins J.D. et al. (1992). Promoting science-based prevention in communities. *Addictive Behaviors*, 27, 951–976.
2 Personal interview, December 3, 2021.
3 Website: https://wfcn.org/about/vision-and-values/partners/
4 Rhode Island Health Equity Zones: https://health.ri.gov/programs/detail.php?pgm_id=110[8]
5 Harwood R. (2022). *Civic Virus: Why Polarization is a Misdiagnosis*. The Harwood Institute. Obtained at: https://theharwoodinstitute.org/civic-virus-report
6 Personal interview, September 30, 2021.
7 Personal interview, September 21, 2021.
8 Personal interview, October 28, 2021.
9 Website: https://www.putnamcountyny.com/health/community-resilience-coalition/
10 Personal interview, September 20, 2021.
11 Personal interview, October 28, 2021.
12 Personal interview, September 20, 2021.
13 Personal interview, October 28, 2021.
14 Personal interview, October 26, 2021.
15 Personal interview, October 28, 2021.
16 Ibid.
17 This list is a slight adaptation of: Block P. (2018). *Community: The Structure of Belonging*. Oakland, CA: Berrett-Kohler, p. 123.
18 New Hannover County Resiliency Task Force: https://www.nhcbouncesback.org/who-we-are-1
19 Ibid.
20 Community Resilience Initiative: https://criresilient.org/who-we-are/
21 New Hanover County Resilience Task Force: https://www.nhcbouncesback.org/
22 Climate Resilient Communities: https://www.climatecommunities.org/
23 Community Resilience Initiative: https://criresilient.org/who-we-are/
24 Smart Start: https://www.smartstart.org/smart-start-releases-building-healthy-resilient-communities-across-north-carolina-report/

25 Bilsku W. et al. (June 2013). Assessment of children's value structures and value preferences. *Swiss Journal of Psychology*, 72. Obtained at: https://www.researchgate.net/publication/263909096_Assessment_of_Children's_Value_Structures_and_Value_Preferences; and Schwarz S. and Barni A. (May 2001). Value hierarchies across cultures: taking a similarities perspective. *Journal of Cross-Cultural Psychology*, 32, 3. Obtained at: https://pure.royalholloway.ac.uk/portal/files/1893335/schwartz_bardi_2001_value_hierarchies_across_cultures.pdf

26 Smart Start: https://www.smartstart.org/smart-start-releases-building-healthy-resilient-communities-across-north-carolina-report/

27 Building Resilient Neighbourhoods: https://www.resilientneighbourhoods.ca/communities/

28 Landau J. (October 2007). Enhancing resilience: families and communities as agents for change. *Family Process*, 46. Obtained at: https://www.researchgate.net/publication/5944602_Enhancing_Resilience_Families_and_Communities_as_Agents_for_Change

29 Information about Transformational Resilience can be found on the ITRC website: http://www.itrcoalition.org ; Also see: Doppelt B. (2016). *Transformational Resilience: How Building Human Resilience to Climate Disruption Can Safeguard Society and Increase Wellbeing*. Routledge Publishing, New York, NY.

30 WIPFLI CPAs and Consulting. (2018). *Challenges and Priorities for Nonprofit Organizations: 2018 Outlook Survey Report*. Obtained at: https://www.wipfli.com/-/media/wipfli/downloadable-files/np-2018-outlook-survey-report.pdf

31 Preston E. (1989). The non-profit worker in a for-profit world. *Journal of Labor Economics*, 7(4), 438–463. Obtained at: https://www.jstor.org/stable/2535137; and Emanuele R. and Higgins S. (March 2000). Corporate culture in the nonprofit sector: a comparison of fringe benefits with the for-profit sector. *Journal of Business Ethics*, 24(1), 87–93. Obtained at: https://link.springer.com/article/10.1023/A:1006215031400

32 Harwood R. (2021). *Unleashed: A Proven Way Communities Can Spread Change and Make Real Hope for All*. Kettering Foundation Press, p. 75, Dayton, OH. Obtained at: https://www.kettering.org/catalog/product/unleashed

33 This point was made by Kristi Slette, Executive Director of the Whatcom County, Washington, Family and Community Network during a personal interview on September 30, 2021. In different forms it was also made by many other people involved with community-based initiatives that I interviewed for this book.

34 Personal interview with Tina Pearson, Director, and J'vanete Skiva, Assistant Director for Equity, Education, and Engagement on May 9, 2022.

35 Personal interview, September 21, 2021.

CHAPTER 5

Begin Building Community Capacity for Mental Wellness and Transformational Resilience

After the founding members of the resilience coordinating coalition (RCC) steering committee/board or directors have clarified their mission, core values, and operating principles and in other ways become organized, they can begin to engage residents in activities that strengthen their capacity for mental wellness and transformational resilience and implement local solutions to the climate crisis. Two approaches can be considered.

OPTION 1: BEGIN WITH TRAUMA HEALING GATHERINGS

In communities where many residents are traumatized, a good way for an RCC to start is to organize trauma-healing gatherings. These events should allow people to share their distresses and trauma in a safe and supportive environment, hear from other residents who are experiencing something similar, and then learn simple resilience skills that help them begin to heal. This is important because if people are severely traumatized, they will have little interest in, or ability, to attend to anything beyond their basic needs. After participants learn that the suffering they experience is the result of natural psychobiological fight–flight–freeze reactions, and learn simple self-administrable Presencing resilience skills that help release their trauma frozen in their nervous system, they will begin to feel and function better. This starts the healing process that can open the door to engagement in other issues. They can then learn simple self-administrable Purposing skills that help them engage in pro-social actions that help them find new sources of meaning, direction, and healthy hope for the future.

Ruben Cantu, with the Prevention Institute, emphasized the need to start this way during an interview. "Healing is the first thing many communities need before they can act on anything else. If people are traumatized it's hard for them to work on strategies to prevent more harm. So healing is often the starting point."[1]

One-way RCCs can begin to heal the community is by organizing Healing Circles (sometimes called Listening Circles). These events can involve 5–100 people or more in discussions and exercises that activate healing. The RCC can ask residents with expertise in these areas to facilitate the gatherings. If local expertise does not exist, the RCC can bring in external professionals or organizations to facilitate the gatherings.

For example, the Trauma Resources Institute (TRI) has offered trauma-healing workshops in numerous communities throughout the US using their Community Resilience Model (CRM). They also offered CRM training in Rwanda, Ivory Coast and other locations in Africa; India and Nepal in Asia; Guatemala and Mexico; Northern Ireland; Turkey; and other locations in Europe.[2] In addition, they offered online CRM sessions for people in Ukraine during the attack by Russia.

After the Camp Fire burned parts of Northern California in November 2018, the Trauma Resource Institute ran a workshop for local providers. "When CRM was offered I jumped on board," Norma Servin-Lacy told me. She is Program Manager of Outreach Prevention & Education Programs at Northern Valley Catholic Social Services in Redding, California. She now hosts support groups that teach CRM skills to help adults and children

DOI: 10.4324/9781003262442-8

learn to track their own nervous system in order to bring the body, mind, and spirit into balance, as well as meditation, self-affirmation, and other resilience skills to numerous people. "They give people daily tools for self-regulation," she told me.

To engage Latinos who are often very nervous about being stigmatized if they acknowledge struggling with mental health issues, her organization partners with low-income housing complexes and farm and labor groups to host support groups. "We pick a day and hold a session late in the day when people can come," said Servin-Lacy. "We make sure there is food and snacks—that's important." As a result, the topic of mental health and trauma is becoming more normalized. Before it was "what's wrong with you" and it's now shifted to "what's going on with you" and we are now teaching from the min-shift of 'what is working within you' and work to build from that aspect.[3]

Resources for Resilience (R4R), which is based in Ashville, North Carolina, and offers strength-based somatic resilience programs, facilitated Listening Circles for crisis workers who worked in stressful conditions after Hurricane Florence hit the coast of North Carolina in the U.S. in the fall of 2018.

The Center for Mind-Body Medicine (CMBM) has offered community-wide trauma-healing programs in post-Katrina New Orleans, and in Sonoma County, California, after major wildfires traumatized residents. They also ran similar programs in Broward County, Florida, after the shooting at Marjory Stoneman Douglas High School. In addition, they led the largest population-wide trauma-healing program ever offered in Gaza, which was attended by more than 280,000 children and adults, and led a parallel program in Israel. As part of its work, the CMBM offers train-the-trainer programs that train people who learn healing skills on how to teach them to others.

"We begin by teaching community leaders how to use mind-body medicine techniques such as meditation, yoga, guided imagery, and movement to deal with their stress and trauma," Dr. James Gordon, Founder and CEO told me. "We then teach them how to teach the CMBM model to the people they work with, and we provide them support."[4]

No matter what approach is used, the healing events should help residents increase their understanding of how their body, mind, emotions, and consequently their behaviors are affected by traumas and toxic stresses, and how to use simple age and culturally accountable Presencing resilience skills to release the trauma and begin to heal. This begins to enhance literacy about mental wellness and resilience within the community (more on this type of literacy in Chapter 9). Equally important, as previously noted, when residents see and hear from others who experience similar distresses and trauma, they will realize they are not broken or defective: they are experiencing a natural survival reaction designed to protect them from harm.

The healing gatherings should also allow residents to meet and interact with people they do not know. This can begin to build new social connections that will be vital to sustaining mental wellness and resilience as the climate emergency accelerates. There is no way for people to heal from trauma when they are isolated from each other. And no amount of individualized curative work or clinical therapy, on their own, is powerful enough to allow a person to heal from the combination of climate-generated relentless disruptions to the systems they rely on for basic needs and acute disasters. Robust connections with others who are engaged in the process of healing will be needed to foster widespread mental wellness and transformational resilience.

Over time, the positive feelings people experience after they begin to heal will lead many to become more interested in engaging in the other foundational areas the RCC emphasizes that help enhance their capacity for mental wellness and transformational resilience during persistent climate adversities.

As many of the organizations just mentioned do, after participants have engaged in the initial healing gatherings, those that are interested can be trained to teach the healing and resilience information and skills to other residents. People who have been traumatized and learned how to heal are often in the best position to help others heal. This can begin to build a cadre of local residents who can lead peer-to-peer healing gatherings. And, learning how to teach healing and resilience skills to others can be a powerful way for someone to further integrate the information and methods into their own life.

Throughout engagement in healing activities, RCC members can learn about the risk factors that are producing mental health and psycho-social-spiritual problems within different populations and sectors of their community. They can also learn about the protective factors that help different groups push back against those stressors and maintain their psychological, emotional, and spiritual wellness and resilience. This information will prove very valuable when the RCC decides to develop the Community Resilience Profile discussed below.

A SLIGHTLY MODIFIED APPROACH

In communities that are distressed but still functioning sufficiently, an RCC can begin its activities by holding a conference keynoted by a well-known speaker who can offer a vision of how the community can begin to address its challenges.

The Resilience Network of the Gorge, which was launched in the rural community of The Dalles, Oregon, started this way. A major conference keynoted by Dr. Sandra Bloom helped to kick off the initiative. Dr. Bloom shared the Sanctuary Model she co-developed, which is a trauma-informed approach that promotes safety and recovery from adversity.[5] The event was followed by the formation of a steering committee to guide the community resilience building and healing efforts. The Resilience Network went on to help individuals and organizations in rural Hood River, Wasco, and Sherman counties become trauma-informed. It also offered resilience training to many groups.[6]

The Walla Walla, Washington, Community Resilience Initiative (CRI) also launched its efforts in this way. Founder Teri Barila invited Dr. Rob Anda, who is one of the principal investigators of the original study on Adverse Childhood Experiences (ACEs), to give a talk to community members. This helped people understand some of the problems they were seeing in the community and motivated many to participate in efforts to prevent and heal them.[7] The CRI now focuses on all types of local traumas and toxic stresses experienced by community members.

In Chapter 10, more details are offered about how RCCs can organize trauma-healing gatherings.

OPTION 2: BEGIN BY ENGAGING RESIDENTS IN DISCUSSIONS ABOUT THEIR ISSUES OF GREATEST CONCERN, ASSET MAPPING, AND THE CREATION OF A COMMUNITY RESILIENCE PORTRAIT

In communities not seriously traumatized, or as a follow-up in distressed communities after trauma-healing has been underway for a while, the RCC can launch its initiative by actively engaging residents in discussions to identify the issues they care about most. The discussions should focus on what community members see as vital for their health, wellness, and resilience, and avoid venting about gripes and pet peeves.

After identifying what they care about, the discussion should shift to helping residents see how those issues are often linked to their capacity to remain psychologically, emotionally, and spiritually well and resilient. Discussions can focus on how the forces that create the issues they are concerned about are produced by unacknowledged and unaddressed fight, flight, or freeze reactions that produce mental health and psycho-social-spiritual problems. They can then discuss how the way the community responds to those issues often reinforces existing or creates altogether new distresses and traumas for residents. This type of discussion can help residents realize that the issues they are concerned about result from systemic structural factors that require whole-community solutions.

After these discussions are completed, residents can begin to map the local protective factors, or assets, that can be used to address their concerns and enhance their capacity for mental wellness and transformational resilience. This approach engages residents through a strength-based wellness and resilience lens, not a deficit or problem-solving perspective.

Identifying the interests of residents and their views of local assets is best done before the RCC develops its specific goals, objectives, and strategies because the information that emerges will shed important light on how the five foundational areas involved with building universal capacity for mental wellness and transformational resilience can be enhanced. It will also help residents understand which local protective factors they can strengthen, risk factors they can minimize, and those they have little influence on. For example, there are many ways residents can connect those who are isolated with neighbors or nearby, civic, or faith-based groups. However, residents alone will have little sway over federal or state minimum wage laws that affect local poverty rates.

The Walla Walla Community Resilience Initiative used a variation of this approach to develop its strategy. "If you want to work in a neighborhood you don't go in with what you think they need. You listened to what they want" Teri Barila told me.[8] Almost all of the other community-based initiatives I looked at, and practitioners I interviewed, also use variations of this approach as a starting point to engage residents in developing a portrait of their town's capacity for wellness and resilience.

HOW TO DEVELOP A "COMMUNITY RESILIENCE PORTRAIT"

The following describes an overall approach RCCs can use to engage residents in a process that identifies their chief concerns, links them with mental health and psycho-social-spiritual problems, and then maps the assets that can be used to address them. One outcome can be a comprehensive "Community Resilience Portrait" that identifies the strengths, resources, and other protective factors that can be used to help residents respond to adversities in safe, healthy, equitable, and resilient ways. However, the production of a written document is not essential. More important is that the entire process should bring residents together in dialogues that begin to build the social connections needed to prevent and heal distresses and traumas and motivate people to reduce their contribution to the climate emergency.[9]

There is no one-size-fits-all approach to this work. Each community should use a method that fits its local demographics, conditions, and resources.

Clarify Geographic Boundaries

A first step is for the RCC to clearly define the geographic boundaries of the area that will be assessed. This is important because residents often do not think of their neighborhood or community by the legally defined boundaries that exist. The RCC should work with residents to decide what geographic areas to focus on when discussing issues, with specific street names or landmarks to identify borders if possible, and what regions should be defined as outside the focal area.

Once the geographic area is clarified, its demographics should be identified. This includes the number of people who reside in the area, and their make-up including age, gender, ethnicity, disabilities, income levels, and more.

Decide on What Information to Collect

After gathering that information, the RCC's next step is to determine the type of protective factors, or assets, and possibly the risk factors, which will be examined. To the extent that it exists, for example, information can focus on assets such as[10]:

- Citizen associations ranging from tenants' associations, charitable groups, elderly groups, fitness groups, book clubs, animal care groups, and more through which people come together to pursue common goals;
- Institutions such as schools, universities, hospitals, libraries, museums, human service organizations, and local government agencies that offer helpful services and/or safe locations for people to meet and engage with each other;
- Supportive physical/built assets such as roads, walking and bike trails, parks and open space, and other public spaces that are part of the community's infrastructure;
- Supportive aspects of the local economy such as for private and non-profit businesses, food providers, community gardens, credit unions, and business associations that provide living-wage jobs and strive to reduce their ecological impacts;
- Ecological assets such as local forests, waterways, wetlands, and open spaces;
- Older, middle age, and younger individuals including activists, entrepreneurs, artists, and others with unique and helpful skills and capacities;
- Supportive social narratives or stories that are repeated in different parts of the community about the resilience past and current residents have shown during adversities, and those that promote intrinsic values such as caring for others and conserving nature;
- The level of literacy about mental health and resilience that exists in the community;
- Opportunities for people to participate in practices that help them sustain wellness and resilience, and where they are located, such as practicing forgiveness, finding simple joys, laughing often, being grateful, continual learning, and caring for physical health;
- Rituals and memorial events that highlight the strength and resilience of residents;
- Other assets serve as protective factors for different neighborhoods, populations, sectors, or the entire community, including pro-social norms that exist.

For each of the assets, the RCC should identify their location, services they provide, number and type of people served (and who is excluded), hours of operation, cost of engagement (user fees etc.), influence in the community, and other similar factors.

After the assets are identified, it can sometimes—but not always—be helpful to identify risk factors that can undermine these protective factors. Assessing risk factors should not be the first or a primary focus because it can easily lead residents down a rabbit hole into discussions about all the deficits and problems that exist in their community. If the RCC decides to focus on risks, it should be made clear to everyone that the goal is simply to illustrate factors that could work against their efforts to strengthen the community's assets. It should also be continually emphasized that, especially as it pertains to the long climate mega-emergency, efforts to fortify the assets and establish additional ones are much more important to enhancing community wellness and transformational resilience than trying to eliminate or diminish risk factors.

Risk factors that can be examined can include types, levels, and locations of:

- Socially isolated individuals and populations
- Alcohol and other drug abuse and addiction
- Poverty levels and locations
- Types of violence and their primary locations
- Types of crime and their primary locations
- Racism and other forms of oppressions
- Poorly built, dangerous, or socially disruptive physical infrastructure such as roads highways, and water and power systems
- Dilapidated, unsafe, and unhealthy residential housing and commercial buildings
- Toxic pollution and the areas and populations most affected
- Areas that lack trees, vegetation, and other green spaces
- Other risk factors, including harmful social norms, practices, and policies.

The information available on both the protective and risk factors will vary community-to-community, though in most, more information will be available on risk factors than protective factors, as that is what most researchers and government agencies tend to focus on.

Some communities will have access to ample information produced by the national, state/provincial governments, counties, municipalities, or universities. Local newspapers, TV and radio stations, libraries, neighborhood and business directories, and other resources might also offer important information. Other communities will have limited data and information. Do an internet search, talk to people in different public and non-profit organizations and universities, and in other ways look around to see what data is available.

Engage Residents in Discussions about What They Care about and Then in Asset Mapping

The RCC can organize the initial information that is gathered into a short, easy-to-read draft "Resilience Snapshot." When possible, the RCC can also locate the individuals, organizations, institutions, services, and other assets that are identified in the draft snapshot on a physical map of the area. The draft asset maps can make it easy for people to visualize and make sense of the information.

The purpose of the draft Resilience Snapshot should be made very clear to residents: it is designed merely to kick off conversations among residents about the assets that exist in their area that help foster mental wellness and resilience. Make sure everyone knows that significant deletions, additions, and improvements are expected in both the document and maps by the time a final "Community Resilience Portrait" is completed.

This is important because sometimes facts and figures found in research studies are limited in time, only address a narrow set of issues, or examine specific populations researchers were mandated to assess or could find funds to analyze. In addition, quantitative studies usually do not reflect the perspectives of residents about the past and current protective and risk factors that exist in their community. Information obtained from community members will clarify the factual data and identify important assets and issues that the quantitative data the RCC gathered did not address or has misconstrued. In addition, the broader the perspectives offered by community members, the more credible and helpful the final Community Resilience Profile will be.

There are several ways to obtain the perspective of residents about the issues they care most about and the assets that can be used to address their concerns.

- *Written Resilience Surveys*: One of the simplest ways to understand the concerns of residents and how they view local assets (and possibly risk factors) is to develop a series of questions revolving around the key points highlighted in the initial draft Resilience Snapshot and asset maps. The questions can be organized into a written and/or electronic survey. The questions included in the survey can also provide the format used during the personal interviews and group discussions described below. To obtain feedback from people in specific neighborhoods or sectors, the survey can be emailed to individuals using email lists provided by community organizations involved with the RCC. The surveys can also be sent out by regular postal mail, although this requires the use of paper and can be more expensive and time consuming than electronic surveys. In addition, telephone surveys can be used. RCC member organizations and other organizations in the community can also be asked to post a link to the questionnaire on their websites, and to promote them through social media and other venues. For more randomized feedback, local newspapers can be asked to publish an article about the questionnaire and include a link to where it can be found. Local radio and TV stations can also be asked to do the same.

  There are pros and cons to using surveys. The upside is that with enough time and promotion, the RCC can obtain many responses. The downsides are that residents might not respond to the questionnaire if they are unfamiliar with the sponsoring organization, are concerned they will somehow be exposed to unwanted attention, or don't want to give their email address to others. In addition, some people won't take the time because they believe nothing will come of it, or they are not tech-savvy and cannot easily access an online questionnaire. Each RCC will need to decide if surveys are worth it and, if so, what approach makes sense to use.

- *Carefully Selected Personal Interviews*: In addition to a survey, or as a free-standing option, targeted interviews can be completed with 10–20 key community members to gather their views about the draft Resilience Snapshot and asset maps. For the best results, try to interview a diverse set of community members either through in-person or telephone interviews. The list could include, for example, people involved with neighborhood associations and grassroots groups of various kinds, K-12 school educators, non-profits leaders, private company executives, the chief of police, social and environmental justice leaders, health care providers, emergency responders, as well as elected officials and government officers. Using the same questions included in the survey described above, the interviewees should be asked to describe their primary concerns, and what they believe constitute their neighborhood or community's assets that can be used to address them. Open-ended questions can also be asked to allow the interviewees to offer their views about issues that the pre-determined questions did not address. In addition to gathering information that might shed more light on the community's assets and risk factors than is reflected in the draft initial Resilience Snapshot, the interviews might surface new sources of data and completely different perspectives on local issues.

- *Focus Groups*: Focus groups can be another good way to gather information about the primary concerns of community members, as well as their views about the information presented in the initial Resilience Snapshot and asset maps. Focus groups typically involve eight to ten people in 60–90 minute sessions. The facilitator poses specific questions, and then listens to the group discuss the issues. This often surfaces a great deal of information about their beliefs, attitudes, and perceptions. In this way, focus groups often provide more diverse types of information than interviews with individuals and questionnaires. However, the information that is generated will often be less detailed than can be obtained through other means. In addition, focus groups require skilled facilitation. Without this, the discussions can get sidetracked into unrelated topics (working with universities can frequently be helpful to obtain good facilitation). Focus groups with diverse people are most helpful. For example, focus groups composed of youth, people of color, parents, faith leaders, social service providers, and others can provide a good cross-section of information that can help improve, and refine, the draft initial Resilience Snapshot and asset maps.

- *Town Hall Resilience Meetings*: If the RCC has the capacity to organize large town hall meetings, and local residents respond well to this type of event, they can also provide important sources of information. However, they can be more difficult to organize and facilitate than the other options. When holding a town hall, it will be important to publicize the event long in advance through multiple sources. A special emphasis should be placed on encouraging attendance by people who do not normally attend these types of public events. Otherwise, you are likely to only attract people who typically speak at public meetings, which will provide skewed perspectives. If a large number of people show up, it will again be best to organize them into small groups of five to eight people so everyone has the opportunity to speak. As with focus groups, a standard set of questions should guide the discussion. An individual in each small group should be asked to take good notes, and someone else should be asked to write the highlights on large flip charts for everyone to see. To keep the groups on task, the facilitator(s) will need to give participants a specific timeline to complete discussions of each question.

- *The Most Helpful Approach: Neighborhood Resilience Dialogues and Asset Mapping*: By far the best way to truly understand what residents care about, and how they view their community's protective factors, is to actively engage them in personal group discussions. This can be done as an addition to the options above, or as the stand-alone sole approach. A two to three-hour meeting can be held in which 10–100 or more residents come together to share their top concerns, connect those issues with mental health and psycho-social-spiritual problems in the community, and then discuss the assets they believe exist that can be used to address the issues. If a draft Resilience Snapshot and asset map have been developed, they can serve as the starting points for the discussions. Or the discussions can begin without any previously developed information. The more diverse the people that participate the better, and a standard set of questions should again guide the discussions. If a small group attends, everyone can be engaged in a discussion. As with the other options, if a large number of people show up, small groups of five to eight people can be formed and each group should be asked to identify someone to take detailed notes, someone else to handle the asset mapping process, and another person to write the key points in large letters on a flip chart so everyone can easily see them.

Developing Asset Maps

Asset maps allow residents to see, in visual terms, the strengths, resources, and other protective factors that exist in their community. When people identify assets and see their location on a map, they often have greater ability to determine how they can be used to address their concerns. The maps also help people think about how additional assets can be formed and how the local capacity for mental wellness and transformational resilience can be enhanced. In addition, engaging local residents in the development of asset maps can establish a powerful sense of ownership of the issues and motivate them to actively engage in efforts to strengthen and expand the assets.

The overall process of creating an asset map includes[11]:

- Obtain a physical map that contains the geographic areas that were identified by the RCC, and draw lines on it to clearly show the boundaries of the area that is being mapped. This might require enlarging the map.
- If a draft Resilience Snapshot has been developed, locate the assets that were identified on the map, and mark the actual street locations of each of them, along with the type of services, supports, who they serve, and other supports they provide people in the area.
- Then, actively engage residents in discussions about the draft asset maps and have them use dot stickers to amend and improve them. This involves identifying and mapping assets such as those previously described.
- It is usually helpful to create a legend on the side of the map to clarify what each of the colors represents. Use different colors for different types of resources and assets. Some assets—and thus stickers—might overlap on the map. All this information will provide a visual representation of the assets people believe exist in their area, and where they are physically located.
- Make sure the asset map is visually appealing and clearly highlights the assets, including where resources are clustered, and gaps in geographic areas or populations being served.
- When the mapping has been completed, a facilitator should summarize the key points depicted on the map for all to hear. Further discussions should then take place focused on questions such as: "How do these assets help individuals, neighborhoods, and groups sustain their capacity for mental wellness and transformational resilience during adversities?," "What assets are underused?," "Where are the most obvious gaps or weaknesses in our assets and resources?" and most importantly, "How might we be able to strengthen the existing assets, and form additional ones, to enhance everyone's capacity for mental wellness and transformational resilience during adversities?" Questions about the community's awareness of the serious nature of the climate emergency and if and how they believe they can help reduce local emissions and prepare for and adapt to climate impacts can also be addressed.

- After engaging people in these dialogues, residents should be asked to discuss next steps. This can include what they are willing to personally do to strengthen existing assets or form new ones, and how they can personally engage in climate solutions. It can also include what should be done with the asset maps. The next steps could include, for example, holding meetings, or going door-to-door in different blocks and neighborhoods, to share the asset maps and engage residents in discussions about ways to strengthen them and establish additional ones. Other options could include sharing the maps with the organizations that were identified as assets to gather their views about how their services could be linked with others or in other ways expanded. In addition, the maps could be shared with local policy makers, and discussions could begin about revamping their programs or policies to strengthen the assets, establish additional ones, and reduce the influence of the risk factors that undermine mental wellness and transformational resilience.

Engaging residents in discussions to identify their top concerns, linking them to mental health and psycho-social-spiritual problems, and then mapping the assets available to address them is often extremely enlightening for everyone involved. However, as previously stated, even more important is the social connections that can be established through the process. The trust and comradery that often emerges will be extremely important to build the community's capacity to prevent and heal distresses and traumas during the long climate emergency. The relationships will also help build the collective efficacy that will be necessary to motivate people to engage in local climate solutions.

Figure 5.1 offers an example of what a community asset map can include.

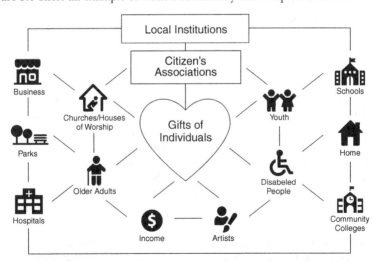

Community Assets (physical, social capital, economy)

- Recognize your physical assets and economic ones
- Look with new eyes
- Look at the assets of the economy of the community-businesses, etc.
- Build partnerships
- Keep evolving

Figure 5.1 Sample Community Asset Map
Source: With permission from the Asset-based Community Development Institute at DePaul University.

Integrate the Information and Asset Maps into a Draft "Community Resilience Profile"

If a draft Resilience Snapshot was developed, the information included should be combined with the material generated during the surveys, interviews, meetings with residents, and asset mapping processes to produce a thorough profile of the community's capacity for mental wellness and transformational resilience. The Community Resilience Profile should, to the extent possible, provide a comprehensive picture of the strengths, resources, characteristics, and other protective factors that are available to help residents enhance their capacity for mental wellness and transformational resilience during ongoing adversities (and possibly factors that can undermine that ability as well) and engage in climate solutions.

When stating the conclusions, the Community Resilience Profile should openly declare any important limitations that exist. This can include, for example, whether enough relevant data was found, or if the information is somewhat outdated, limited in scope, or narrowly focused on specific issues, populations, or sectors. The opinion should also state whether the perspectives of residents who participated represent the entire community, or whether they might only reflect certain neighborhoods or sectors, and which areas, populations, or sectors are not well represented in the feedback. In addition, the opinion should clarify that the profile merely represents the point in time during which the information was gathered and the conversations occurred, and that it can look very different in the future. This type of statement can clarify that the capacity for mental wellness and transformational resilience of local residents is fluid and can significantly improve if specific actions are taken.

Reengage Residents in Discussions to Finalize the Community Resilience Profile and Identify Paths Forward

After the Community Resilience Profile is completed, residents should again be actively engaged in discussions that build on their previous dialogues and focus on how to strengthen existing assets, establish additional ones, and enhance the capacity of all adults and youth to prevent and heal distresses and traumas. If it has not been previously addressed, this is when the need for the community to reduce its contribution to the climate emergency, and prepare for climate impacts, can be added to the discussion to identify possible paths forward. The information that results should be used by an RCC to form its goals, strategy, and action plan for building universal capacity for mental wellness and transformational resilience.

The Community Resilience Profile and assets maps will often prove to be valuable sources of information long after they are created, so decisions about where they will be housed after the process ends will be important. For example, if they are located on the website of a public agency or non-profit organization, many residents will not know about or make the effort to find them. A good approach will therefore often be for the entity that houses the document to send out a web link to their members, social networks, and numerous groups and organizations in the community with a request to post it on their websites. People will be more likely to see the link and access it when it is posted on websites they regularly visit.[12]

UNIVERSITY STUDENTS CAN OFTEN ASSIST

When a university exists nearby, or the RCC can contact one, it may be possible to obtain free or low-cost assistance from students, supervised by their professors, to complete the process. Professors are often looking for interesting projects that give their students an opportunity to learn skills and complete credit hours. Check around and see who might be interested. If it goes well, university students are also likely to want to obtain additional credits by assisting the RCC with other projects.

The San Francisco Neighborhood Enhancement Network (NEN), which is a "cohort of government, non-profit, academic, faith-based, private sector, philanthropic and civic agencies and institutions" focused on "empowering communities to achieve their self-identified resilience goals" uses this approach. As you will learn about in Chapter 7, the NEN engages residents from different neighborhoods in asset mapping to prepare for disasters, much of the research, and many other tasks are completed by local university students.

Peace4Tarpon in Tarpon Springs, Florida has also successfully used university students to complete some of its work. They developed a close relationship with the Western Florida University School of Public Health had 30 students each semester for two terms generating documents based on a public health approach to problems in the community.

THE ABUNDANT COMMUNITY EDMONTON APPROACH TO ASSET MAPPING

A different way to map the assets of a community is the approach used by Abundant Community Edmonton (ACE) in Canada. This is "a grassroots initiative fostering neighbour- to-neighbour relationships. The goal — to cultivate a culture of care and connection, increase the sense of belonging and inclusion, and ultimately create a healthier and livable city — one block at a time."[13]

The vision of ACE is: Neighbours connected at the block level and in the neighbourhood. Together we form a strong, caring and supportive blocks and neighbourhoods where we look out for one another, share our talents, skills and resources with one another, recreate together, and collectively create the neighbourhoods we desire. The village is reinvigorated in our imaginations and in our city neighbourhoods.[14]

To achieve this vision, ACE trains "Block Connectors," who are people that live on each block, to go door-to-door to speak with residents and identify each person's skills, gifts, interests, and passions. These assets are put into a database that allows people with similar talents, hobbies, and passions to connect and engage in activities together.

The outcomes include greater awareness and activation of the diverse needs, skills, and experiences of residents, more people contributing to neighborhood life according to their interests and abilities, and greater capacity for neighbors to watch out for each other. It has also created a safer and healthier village for children to grow and play, as well as people looking in on seniors and others who can use additional care. The overall outcome has been "better overall mental and physical health through new opportunities for relationships and recreation."[15]

"Our work starts by identifying individual assets," coordinator Howard Lawrence told me. "The process connects people at the neighborhood level so it is a rising tide that floats all boats."[16]

THE RURAL OPPORTUNITIES INSTITUTE'S SYSTEMS MAPPING APPROACH TO TRAUMA

The use of systems maps is still another way to engage residents in mapping their community's protective and risk factors. The Rural Opportunity Institute (ROI), located in Edgecombe County, North Carolina in the US used this approach. In 2017–2018, ROI engaged more than 860 local residents in a systems mapping engagement process to diagram and understand the forces driving stress, trauma, and Adverse Childhood experiences (ACEs) in their community. The outcome was a working map that allowed residents to visually see and understand the systemic patterns that are creating the harmful outcomes they were experiencing, and how different actions could activate healing and begin to restore health, wellness, and resilience in the community.

The power of the mapping process came from its ability to bring together people of diverse backgrounds to document their stories and transfer their thinking and belief systems out of their heads and onto paper. The results were represented visually by drawing feedback loops that showed how one factor affected others. ROI felt that people can often keep only a limited set of relationships or ideas in their head at a time, so a key benefit of this process is its ability to create visual representations that show many different complex relationships, and how those relationships are interconnected and affect each other to influence mental health. The end goal is to use the map to identify "leverage points," residents can focus on, which are changes made in one or two places that can activate positive changes throughout the entire system.

The systems map in Figure 5.2 resulted from the process.

Participating in the system mapping process helped many community members recognize the systemic and cyclical nature of the traumas that resulted from the prevalence of punishment and isolation of children who failed to behave in acceptable ways, and how this resulted in more stress and trauma for the children and for the community. Residents said their goal was to shift away from punishment and toward healing, while equipping those who had experienced trauma to be positioned and capable of providing support and healing to others. Involvement in the systems mapping process also empowered participants to begin to learn how to heal themselves, and enabled their healing by connecting them with people they did not know.

In addition, participants said the diversity of people involved with the systems mapping process contributed to its success. The different experiences and knowledge each person brought allowed everyone to hear different perspectives and created a shared understanding of trauma and resilience.

RCCs should consider using a similar systems-mapping approach to help local residents understand how climate-generated toxic stresses and trauma can activate vicious cycles that produce more trauma, and how changes in one or more aspects of their community's existing systems can activate a virtuous cycle that heals individual and community traumas and fosters universal capacity for mental wellness and resilience.

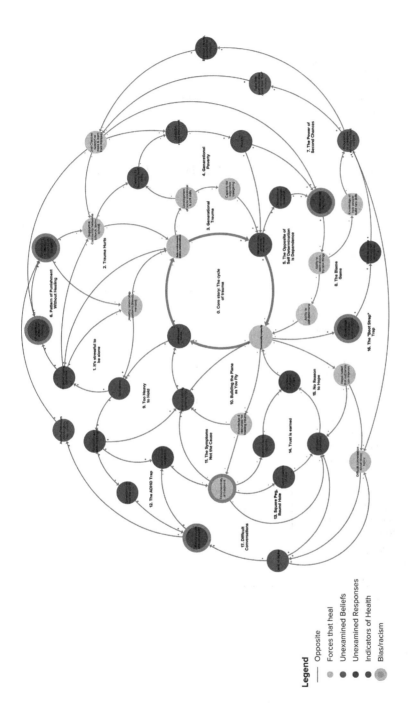

Legend

Opposite
Forces that heal
Unexamined Beliefs
Unexamined Responses
Indicators of Health
Bias/racism

Figure 5.2 Rural Opportunities Institute Systems Map

CONCLUSION

The checklist at the end of this chapter can help the RCC determine the extent to which it has addressed the key elements involved with launching efforts to strengthen the capacity of all residents for mental wellness and transformational resilience.

No matter what approach is used to begin, the information that results should be used by the RCC to develop its goals, strategy, and action plan. The steps involved in completing these actions are discussed in the next chapter.

CHECKLIST FOR BEGINNING TO BUILD COMMUNITY CAPACITY

I. Getting Organized	Yes	No	Comments
Did the RCC begin its efforts by offering residents opportunities to begin to heal their distress and trauma?			
Did the RCC begin its efforts by offering workshops or conferences with keynote speakers who offered a vision of a resilient community?			
Did the RCC begin its efforts by engaging residents in discussions about the issues they care about most in their community?			
Did the RCC help residents see the connections between the issues they care about and mental health and psycho-social-spiritual problems?			
Following from above, did discussions about issues residents care about most lead to their engagement in mapping the local assets that can help them address their concerns?			
Did the RCC develop a draft Resilience Snapshot of the neighborhood or community?			
Did the RCC actively engage residents in discussions about the draft Resilience Snapshot and asset mapping and produce a more comprehensive Community Resilience Portrait?			

I. Getting Organized	Yes	No	Comments
Did the RCC actively engage residents in discussions about the Community Resilience Portrait and gather their views on pathways forward?			

NOTES

1 Personal interview, December 3, 2021.
2 For more information about The Trauma Resource Institute go to: https://www.traumaresourceinstitute.com/
3 Personal interview, November 4, 2021.
4 Personal interview, November 17, 2021.
5 For more information about Dr. Sandra Bloom's work go to: https://sandrabloom.com/book-series/the-sanctuary-model/
6 For information about The Resilience Network of the Gorge go to the MARC program website: https://marc.healthfederation.org/communities/oregon-columbia-river-gorge-region
7 Personal interview, September 20, 2021.
8 Ibid.
9 The information presented in this section is derived from a combination of a number of sources including: UCLA Center for Health Policy Research. *Asset Mapping.* Obtained at: http://healthpolicy.ucla.edu/programs/health-data/trainings/documents/tw_cba20.pdf; The Canadian Centre for Community Renewal. (2000). *The Community Resilience Manual: A Resource for Rural Community Recovery and Renewal.* Obtained at: https://communityrenewal.ca/sites/all/files/resource/P200_0.pdf; and Digital Promise. *Asset Mapping: A Guide for Education Innovation Clusters.* Obtained at: https://digitalpromise.org/wp-content/uploads/2018/09/asset-mapping.pdf
10 For more information, see: Kretzmann J. and McKnight J.L. (1993). *Building Communities from the Inside Out: A Path toward Finding and Mobilizing a Community's Assets.* ACTA Publications, Chicago, Illinois.
11 Ibid.
12 This point was made to me by Howard Lawrence the Coordinator of Abundant Community Edmonton during a conversation in late December 2021. Information about his program can be found here: https://www.edmonton.ca/programs_services/for_communities/abundant-community-edmonton
13 Abundant Community Edmonton. Found at: https://www.edmonton.ca/programs_services/for_communities/abundant-community-edmonton
14 Ibid.
15 Abundant Community Edmonton. (January 2021). *Resource Guide to Neighborhood Leadership and Neighborhood Connectors.* Obtained at: https://www.edmonton.ca/sites/default/files/public-files/documents/ACE-ResourceGuideNeighbourhoodLeadership.pdf
16 Personal interview, December 30, 2021.

CHAPTER 6

Establish RCC Goals, Objectives, Strategies, and Action Plans

After people begin to engage in trauma-healing gatherings, and/or following the development of the Community Resilience Profile, the RCC should use the information that was generated to establish specific goals, objectives, strategies, and action plans to strengthen the entire population's capacity for mental wellness and transformational resilience and engage residents in climate solutions. As with the previous steps, these actions should be developed through a deep and broad participatory process because the interests and desires of residents should form the basis for the RCC's purpose and approach.

DETERMINE THE RCC'S GOALS

Goals are the broad primary outcomes the RCC wants to achieve. Setting goals provides a sound basis for planning, implementing, and evaluating the RCC's activities. RCC members and local residents might sometimes have a general idea of what is needed to enhance their community's capacity for mental wellness and transformational resilience and engage in climate solutions, but not a clear vision. When goals are agreed upon, however, everyone can more easily understand what the RCC will seek to achieve.

In addition, the goals set by the RCC should highlight the community's potential, not its deficits and problems. This can spur creativity that produces new ideas about how to enhance the capacity of residents for mental wellness and transformational resilience as they engage in activities that reduce their contribution to the climate emergency and prepare for and adapt to its impacts.

SOME EXAMPLES OF GOALS

Here are some examples of the goals community-based resilience-building initiatives have adopted:

The goals of Peace4Tarpon in Tarpon Springs Florida, which looks through a "trauma-informed lens" to address the root causes of challenges are as follows[1]:

- *Connect* residents and service providers to available resources;
- *Inform* citizens and professionals on research that shows direct causes and outcomes of adverse childhood and adult experiences (trauma);
- *Transform* communal and personal attitudes toward health, renewal, resolution, resilience, and compassion;
- *Heal* people, systems, and communities through trauma-informed prevention practices and resolution methods.

The goals of the North Carolina Healthy and Resilient Communities Initiative are to[2]:

DOI: 10.4324/9781003262442-9

- reduce multiple forms of childhood adversity, including negative social and environmental drivers of health.

- increase protective factors and positive childhood experiences (PCEs) for children, families, and communities.

- promote systems change, through community infrastructure and cross-sector collaborations, for preventing, responding to, and learning from exposure to toxic stress and trauma.

The goal of Abundant Community Edmonton in Alberta, Canada, is as follows:

- To cultivate a culture of care and connection, increase the sense of belonging and inclusion, and ultimately create a more healthy and livable city—one block at a time.

Making rapid progress on one or more of the goals an RCC adopts will be very important because it shows residents the coalition is serious about its mission and not a waste of time and resources. Otherwise, as Father Paul Abernathy, CEO of the Neighborhood Resilience Project in Pittsburg, Pennsylvania, told me, "Our efforts can undermine the community unless people can see progress."[3]

CLARIFY THE RCC'S OBJECTIVES

After determining goals, the next step is to clarify the RCC's objectives. These are the specific measurable results the RCC wants to achieve within a specific time period to meet the goals. Objectives should be achievable yet challenging and be directly connected with the RCC's vision and goals. They should also include specific timelines. Each of the Resilience Innovation Teams might develop different objectives for the various neighborhoods, populations, and sectors they engage with.

For example, following from the previous example, an objective of the goal of building social connections might be to

Increase by 20 percent within one year and by 50 percent within five years the number of seniors and other isolated people that are in daily contact with someone who will spend time with them and assist with their physical needs.

In its early years, the Community Resilience Initiative in Walla Walla adopted the objectives (Figure 6.1).

DEVELOP THE RCC'S STRATEGIES

The strategies developed by the RCC are the approaches that will be used to implement their objectives and achieve their goals. When developing strategies, it is essential to involve local residents so that it is culturally appropriate and supported. "The community itself needs to decide what the strategy will look like," Ruben Cantu with the Prevention Institute told me during an interview.[4]

As with objectives, if the RCC has organized a number of Resilience Innovation Teams, they will each need to develop strategies that make sense for the neighborhoods, populations, and sectors they are engaged with.

a. By 2010, increase awareness of the ACE study and its implications for our Valley's children and adult health. This will be measured by (1). seating the CRI team. (2) having an action plan improved, (3) creating a parent team, and (4). developing other significant infrastructure components, such as a financial plan. These indicate a commitment at the community level.

b. By 2010 increase selected WWSD staff awareness of ACEs by 50% as reflected in the pre and post staff surveys and increase support for addressing ACE-related behaviors in selected classrooms by 75%.

c. By 2010-2011 school year, increase knowledge of ACEs and resilience by 50% in parents of Lincoln High School as a surrogate population—as measured by pre- and post-surveys.

d. By 2011, increase the knowledge of the impact of ACEs and benefits of resilience among community members by 25% as measured by pre- and post-surveys.

e. By the end of 2010-2011 school year, improve knowledge and behavior of community members involved in working with high ACE students (specifically Lincoln and JJC staff) by 75% with the use of Complex trauma training process.

f. By 2011, increase priority constituent partners' use of ACE-related tools by 100% as shown by pre- and post-surveys.

g. By 2011, in at least three priority constituent partners, improve the attitude of staff toward parents/youth of high ACE background by 50%.

h. By 2011, improve delivery service performance by having at least one agency demonstrate a positive change in outcomes based on the new model/framework "through the lens of ACEs."

Figure 6.1 Walla Walla CRI Objectives

It will be important for the RCC to build its strategies in a logical manner. Each activity should connect to and build on others. A logic model can be used to develop this type of strategy. This is a systematic and visual way to develop and present the RCC's strategy to local residents, groups, organizations, funders, and others. Words and pictures are used to describe the RCC's perspective on how a sequence of activities will build on each other to achieve its vision and goals. Mapping the synergy between proposed activities will help the RCC's members think through, in a logical way, what their actions will achieve, how they will interact, and what the outcomes will be.

As RCC members work through the logic map, adjustments can be made that help avoid mistakes and prevent dead ends. This can be a challenging and time-consuming process. But taking the time to complete a logic map can create an approach that can successfully foster universal capacity for mental wellness and transformational resilience in the community as residents engage in climate solutions.

There are a number of different logic models. Each RCC will need to decide which one makes sense to use.[5] Three of the most commonly used models are:

1. *A Theory of Change* approach, which describes how specific actions will build on each other to produce the desired outcomes. It can be helpful for grant writing and fundraising purposes.

2. *An Activities-based* approach, which focuses on the specifics of the implementation process, including the steps an organization will take to achieve its desired goals.
3. *An Outcome-based* approach, which seeks to connect resources and activities with desired results and impacts over, for example, a one-to-three year and a four-to-six year timetable.

Figure 6.2 describes a sample outcome-based logic model.[6]

In this sample model:

1   *Resources* are the human, financial, neighborhood, organizational, and community resources the RCC will use to execute its activities.
2   *Activities* are what the RCC will do with the resources, such as the events it will organize, tools it will create or use, and actions that will be taken to implement its activities.
3   *Outputs* are the specific products of the activities the RCC engages in, such as number of neighborhood meetings held and number of people involved.
4   *Outcomes* are the changes in attitude, understanding, skills, social connections, activities, practices, and level of mental wellness and transformational resilience seen in the neighborhood and community as a result of the RCC's efforts.
5   *Impact* is the fundamental changes that will occur in individuals, neighborhoods, social networks, groups, organizations, and the community as a whole as a result of the outcomes. It will likely take a number of years to see the impacts, and they are likely to shift over time.

An RCC's mid- and long-term outcomes and overall impacts should describe changes in the five foundational areas that need to be emphasized to strengthen universal capacity for mental wellness and transformational resilience for the climate emergency. For example, the long-term impact of building robust social support networks could be that "A majority of residents now have family, friends, or neighbors residing somewhere in the community they can turn to for practical assistance and emotional support during both acute disasters and ongoing adversities."

Medium-term outcomes show changes in thinking, practices, and behaviors that result from the actions the RCC has taken to help produce the impact. A medium-term outcome for the foundational area of building robust social support networks could be, "More residents feel confident in their ability to respond constructively to adversities due to the increased social connections they developed."

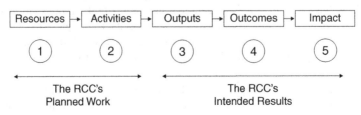

Figure 6.2 Sample Logic Model

Short-term outcomes are the immediate results the RCC wants to achieve. They will be the primary focus of the RCC's work. Short-term outcomes can include increased awareness, knowledge, skills, or motivation. To follow up on the previous example, a short-term outcome for building social support networks could include, "More residents are taking part in neighborhood activities."

Developing a Logic Model

An eight-step process can be used to develop the RCC's logic model.

Step 1: Identify the RCC's vision and goals.

Step 2: Identify the populations and sectors the RCC wants to engage with. Make sure they are inclusive of everyone in the community.

Step 3: Select the long-term impacts that best meet the RCC's vision and goals.

Step 4: Select the medium-term outcomes that would best achieve the RCC's long-term impacts.

Step 5: Select the short-term outcomes that would have the best chance of producing the medium-term outcomes.

Step 6: Identify the activities the RCC will use to achieve its short-term outcomes.

Step 7: Identify the resources (or inputs) the RCC will employ to implement the activities that are listed in Step 6.

Step 8: Identify the indicators that will be used to measure success or failure in achieving the RCC's short- and medium-term outcomes and long-term impacts.

Completing these steps will help the RCC develop a logic model that describes the work it will do in the near-term, and how it will contribute to the medium-term outcomes and overall changes that create a culture of mental wellness and transformational resilience in the community.

THE PROS AND CONS OF EVIDENCE-BASED APPROACHES

Let me take a moment now to discuss why it is important to focus on more than "evidence-based" approaches when developing strategies. Evidence-based approaches are strategies or techniques that research has validated as effective. Using these approaches can be very beneficial. At the same time, they come with numerous limitations.[7]

One shortcoming is that evidence-based approaches emerge only after researchers decide a strategy or intervention is worth researching, and they can secure funding to support their investigation. This can be difficult and takes time. It also requires a considerable investment of time to determine the outcome of any specific technique, which again limits the number of researchers and funders willing to participate. All of this significantly limits the number of approaches that have been examined and found to meet "evidence-based" criteria.

In addition, most of the approaches deemed evidence-based apply to individual mental health treatments. Researching how interventions can prevent and heal widespread mental health and psycho-social-spiritual problems generated by the interactions between personal, family, social, economic, physical/built, and ecological factors is much more difficult, and consequently few approaches have been studied or deemed to be evidence-based.

Further, as most of the community-based initiatives I examined have experienced, effective approaches to preventing and healing persistent mental health and psycho-social-spiritual problems felt by large populations typically emerge through the ongoing development and testing of different approaches, not predetermined interventions. So if RCCs use only evidence-based approaches, rather than continuing to test out and develop new ways to prevent and heal the "wicked" mental health and psycho-social-spiritual problems that emerge during the long climate emergency, innovation could grind to a halt. As conditions change, many evidence-based approaches are likely to become outdated or even counterproductive, leaving RCCs without the tools they need to proceed. This is simply untenable given the nature of the civilization-altering period of history we are now entering.

Another important limitation of evidence-based approaches is that they often discount or ignore the methods that Indigenous Peoples have, for centuries, used to prevent and heal psychological, emotional, and spiritual problems. Yet, there is a tremendous amount to learn from indigenous communities worldwide about how to build individual and collective capacity for mental wellness and transformational resilience and heal distresses and traumas when they occur.

All this is to say that it can be helpful to use evidence-based approaches—when they exist for the specific issues and time period in which they apply. At the same time, there are many evidence-informed and promising best practices, as well as culturally appropriate approaches that can be used, including methods long used by Indigenous Peoples.

Communities can also develop their own approaches to building universal capacity for mental wellness and transformational resilience that are based on solid evidence but not officially deemed evidence-based. The key is to keep the underlying evidence-based goals front and center. For example, there is overwhelming evidence that having robust connections with others is vital to sustaining good mental wellness and resilience, particularly during adversities. However, there is no one-size-fits-all approach to build social connections. Communities should develop their own age and culturally accountable strategies to bring people together to build them. Thus, the specific strategies an RCC uses might not be evidence-based, but the goal of their work is based on unequivocal evidence.

One of the best ways to know if an approach is beneficial is to simply ask people how they feel after participating. This was affirmed by Ann DuPre Rodgers, Executive Director of Resources for Resilience in Asheville, North Carolina, during an interview. "The resilience approaches we teach are not evidence-based yet," she told me. "But when people go through our training they always feel better, and that's all they need to know it is effective."[8] When this type of feedback is received and monitored over the long term, it is evident you are on the right track.

SELECTING INDICATORS

The indicators adopted by the RCC should seek to show how short-term outcomes combine to produce the mid-term outcomes and make a long-term difference. Objective indicators are fairly straightforward and measure facts about the community that can be obtained from government statistics and various research reports, such as those used in the Community

Resilience Profile. This type of indicator often does not, however, assess the status of, or changes in, perceptions, attitudes, and values found in a community. The RCC should therefore also select indicators that are good proxies of these attributes and that, taken together, can provide a decent appraisal of whether those characteristics or outcomes are present and/or to what degree they have changed. Information about these types of indicators is gathered through interviews, focus groups, and other approaches that were used to develop the Community Resilience Profile.

An example of an indicator that can determine if more residents are taking part in neighborhood activities could be "the number of people who attend neighborhood meetings or events." This indicator can be tracked by monitoring how many people attend different meetings or activities.

EXAMPLES

The Community Resilience Initiative in Walla Walla used a logic model with indicators to map out their strategy, which at that time focused on reducing adverse childhood experiences and increasing parental resilience.[9] Figure 6.3 describes their approach.

Another way to describe a logic model, which was also offered by the Community Resilience Initiative of Walla Walla is shown in Figure 6.4.

Parent Outreach
Connecting Activities, Outcomes and Indicators

Goal 1: Community conversant in ACEs and Resilience

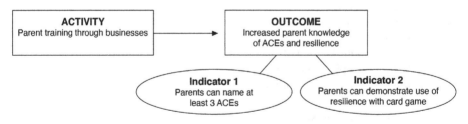

Goal 2: Community capacity development to sustain CRI goals

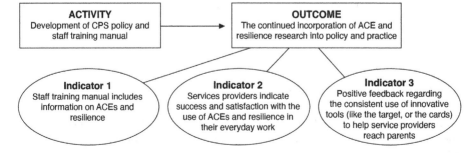

Figure 6.3 Community Resilience Initiative Logic Model

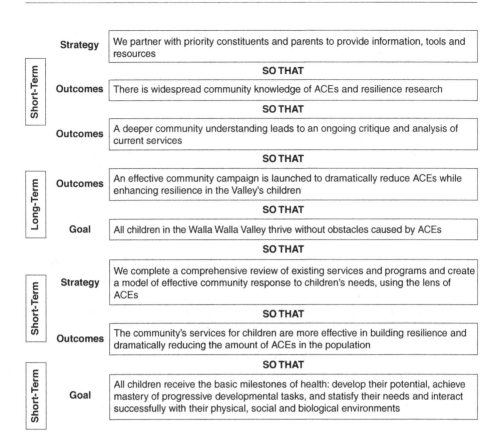

Figure 6.4 Another Way the Community Resilience Initiative Described Its Logic Model

EACH RCC RESILIENCE INNOVATION TEAM SHOULD USE A LOGIC MODEL TO DEVELOP ITS STRATEGY

Logic models should be developed by the RCC as a whole and/or by each of the RCC's Resilience Innovation Teams to think through and describe how they will help the neighborhoods, populations, and sectors they are working with engage in the five foundational areas involved with building universal capacity for mental wellness and transformational resilience.

- An excellent reference for developing a logic model focused on establishing robust social support networks is *Social Capital, Health, and Wellbeing: A Planning and Evaluation Toolkit* by the Health Inequalities Standing Group of Edinburgh, Scotland.[10]

- A helpful reference for developing logic models on psychological and emotional resilience-building efforts with children and families was developed by the U.S. Department of Health and Human Services titled *Using Logic Models Grounded in Theory of Change to Support Trauma-Informed Initiatives to Build Resilience in Children and Families.*[11]

- Another sample logical model that can be used to design resilience-building initiatives for children and families is the Oregon MCH Tile IV *Trauma, ACEs and Resilience* diagram.[12]

- A logic model for building supportive physical/built and economic conditions is the U.S. Economic Development Administration's *Economic Development Logic Model*.[13]
- Logic models for promoting overall wellness and resilience literacy can be found on the *Listing Logic Models on Health Education* site.[14]
- The National Ecosystem Services Partnership developed a document on creating logic models for ecological restoration titled *Building and Using Conceptual Diagrams*.[15]
- *Metrics for Healthy Communities* offers sample logic models for numerous issues ranging from Affordable and Supportive Housing, to Access to Healthy Food, Transit Development, increasing Physical Activity, Worksite Wellness, Elementary and Secondary Schools, and more.[16]

DEVELOP ACTION PLANS

After the RCC develops its strategy, it can craft an action plan. This describes the RCC's day-to-day activities and tactics, with timelines, and individual, group, and organizational responsibilities, which will be used to implement the strategy.

When the action plan is finalized, implementation can begin. This does not mean the planning process is over. An action plan should never be considered a final static document. It will need to continually evolve due to new information and insights that emerge and changes that occur in the community as the climate emergency intensifies.

For this reason, it will be essential for the RCC to embrace a nimble, flexible, iterative approach to planning and implementation. New information should be continually used to adjust and improve the approach. This will allow for continual course correction and improvements.

TRACKING AND EVALUATING PROGRESS

RCCs will need to continually track and evaluate the progress of their strategy and action plan. This is important to learn what works, what does not, and constantly improve. It is also important to highlight successes for residents to see, and to secure continued funding.

As previously discussed, indicators and measures to evaluate progress should be established before the RCC begins to implement its strategy, not after it is underway, as the way progress is tracked can influence the way the strategy and action plan are implemented.

As the strategy and action plan are developed, on its own, or in partnership with academic institutions, other organizations, or consultants the RCC needs to decide what indicators it will measure, and how and when evaluations will take place.

In addition to completing periodic formal assessments, each of the Resilience Innovation Teams involved with the RCC should regularly report their progress, and the changes they have seen, to the larger RCC steering committee/board and all of the other Resilience Innovation Teams. When obstacles appear, or activities do not produce the outcomes that were desired, the Resilience Innovation Teams should inform the entire RCC how they will examine their assumptions and beliefs, alter their approach, and in other ways get their strategy back on track.

The evaluation should also be used by the RCC to identify additional resources that are needed to strengthen and expand its efforts. With this information in hand, RCC members can join with other organizations to advocate for needed resources to civic, non-profit, private, and government entities. The RCC should also advocate to local non-profit and private organizations as well as government agencies and elected officials to ensure that marginalized populations receive the same level and type of services and resources during disasters and emergencies as other groups do.

USE THE CHECKLIST TO DETERMINE PROGRESS

The checklist offered at the end of this chapter can be used by RCCs to determine whether it has addressed each of the core steps involved with developing goals, objectives, strategies, and action plans to achieve those ends.

The strategies developed by an RCC to prevent and heal distresses and traumas should, both directly and indirectly, help residents engage in the five foundational areas required to strengthen universal capacity for mental wellness and transformational resilience for the long climate emergency. Part III of this book will go into detail about what each of the five foundational areas involves and how they can be enhanced.

CHECKLIST FOR DEVELOPING RCC GOALS, OBJECTIVES, STRATEGIES, AND ACTION PLANS

	Yes	No	Comments
Did the RCC use the information obtained from residents during the initial healing gatherings and/or asset mapping and the creation of a Community Resilience Profile to establish clear goals?			
Did the RCC develop specific objectives to achieve its goals?			
Did the RCC use a logic model to develop strategies for achieving its goals and objectives and engage every population and sector of the community in building mental wellness and transformational resilience?			
Did the RCC craft an action plan complete with timetables and responsibilities to implement its strategy?			
Did the RCC carefully coordinate and integrate the strategies and action plans developed by the different Resilience Innovation Teams?			

NOTES

1 Peace4Tarpon: https://www.peace4tarpon.org/sample-page/vision-mission/
2 Smart-Start. *NC Building Healthy and Resilient Communities Study* (July 2021). Obtained at: https://www.smartstart.org/smart-start-releases-building-healthy-resilient-communities-across-north-carolina-report/
3 Personal interview, November 5, 2021.
4 Personal interview, December 3, 2021.
5 Center on KTDRR, American Institute for Research. *Types of Logic Models.* Obtained at: https://ktdrr.org/ktlibrary/articles_pubs/logicmodels/types.html
6 This material was adapted from the W.K. Kellogg Foundation's (2017) *Step-By-Step Guide to Evaluation.* Obtained at: https://www.betterevaluation.org/sites/default/files/WKKF_StepByStepGuideToEvaluation_smaller.pdf
7 The information included in this section was adapted from: Cook S., Schwartz A., and Kaslow N. (July 2017). Evidence-based psychotherapy: advantages and challenges. *Journal of Neurotherapeutics.* Obtained at: https://www.ncbi.nlm.nih.gov/pmc/articles/PMC5509639/; and Berg H. (October 2019). Evidence-based practice in psychology fails to be tripartite: a conceptual critique of the scientocentrism of evidence-based practice in psychology. *Frontiers in Psychology.* Obtained at: https://www.frontiersin.org/articles/10.3389/fpsyg.2019.02253/full
8 Personal interview, January 20, 2022.
9 With permission from Teri Barila and the Community Resilience Initiative.
10 Health Inequalities Standing Group of Edinburgh. *Social Capital, Health, and Wellbeing: A Planning and Evaluation Toolkit.* Obtained at: https://www.communityscot.org.uk/content/social-capital-health-and-wellbeing-a-planning-and-evaluation-toolkit
11 Ingoldsby E. et al. (August 2020). *Using Logic Models Grounded in Theory of Change to Support Trauma-Informed Initiatives Trauma-Informed Approaches: Connecting Research, Policy, and Practice to Build Resilience in Children and Families.* U.S. Department of Health and Human Services. Obtained at: https://aspe.hhs.gov/sites/default/files/private/pdf/262051/trauma-informed-logic-models.pdf
12 Oregon MCH Tile IV. (2018). *Trauma, ACEs and Resilience.* Oregon Health Authority. Obtained at: https://www.oregon.gov/oha/PH/HEALTHYPEOPLEFAMILIES/DATAREPORTS/MCHTITLEV/Documents/Trauma%20and%20resilience_logic%20model_Jan2018.pdf
13 U.S. Economic Development Administration, *Economic Development Logic Model.* Obtained at: https://www.eda.gov/files/performance/ED-Logic-Model.pdf
14 Listing Websites about Health Education Logic Models. Obtained at: https://find-study-now.com/health-education-logic-model/
15 Olander L. et al. (No date available). *Building and Using Conceptual Diagrams.* National Ecosystem Services Partnership. Federal Resource management and Ecosystem Services Guidebook. Obtained at: https://nespguidebook.com/assessment-framework/conceptual-diagrams/
16 *Metrics for Health Communities.* (No date available). Wilder Research and the Federal Reserve Bank of Minnesota. Obtained at: http://metricsforhealthycommunities.org/logic-models/about-logic-models

PART III

The Five Foundational Areas RCCs Must Emphasize to Enhance Universal Mental Wellness and Transformational Resilience for the Climate Emergency

Enhancing the entire population's capacity to prevent and heal the distresses and traumas generated during the climate-ecosystem-biodiversity mega-emergency, while engaging in solutions to the crisis, will require focusing on five interrelated foundational areas. Figure PT03.1 describes the five focal areas.

As with other aspects of working with neighborhoods and communities, there is no one-size-fits-all approach to addressing the five foundational areas. The sequence in which they are addressed is not that important. The strategies the Resilience Coordinating Coalition (RCC) and its Resilience Innovation Teams develop to address them must be built upon the interests and concerns of local citizens, the protective factors that exist locally, and additional ones that can be formed.

This means each RCC is likely to emphasis different foundational areas at different times. Some will be more difficult to address than others, especially if the community is already traumatized by violence, poverty, income struggles, racism, inequalities, and other systemic oppressions, or by significant climate impacts. But it will important for the RCC to always keep the five foundational areas in mind because they are all essential.

Further, when residents engage in any one of the five foundational areas, a virtuous cycle can be activated that enhances their understanding of, and interest in, participating in some or all of the others. By keeping all five front and center, for example, efforts to build robust social connections can be enhanced by bringing residents together to create supportive local physical/built, economic, and ecological conditions. As they engage in those activities, residents can also increase their literacy about mental wellness and resilience and learn how to engage in certain practices that can greatly enhance those capacities. As collective cohesion grows, and people increase their literacy about mental wellness and transformational resilience, they will be less concerned about being stigmatized if they participate in trauma healing gatherings. They will also be less likely to stigmatize others who exhibit symptoms of mental health struggles. This will increase the community's ability to heal suffering and trauma.

Even though I will describe the foundational areas one chapter at a time, please remember that RCCs can start by emphasizing any of them, but do so in ways that feedback to address other areas. In addition, remember that major transformations usually happen only after long periods of small achievements. RCCs will need to stay focused, prioritize achieving incremental but visible progress, while not expecting swift large-scale changes, as this is likely to undermine progress. If RCC members stay at it, the small successes will build on themselves and eventually produce surprising types of fundamental changes.

DOI: 10.4324/9781003262442-10

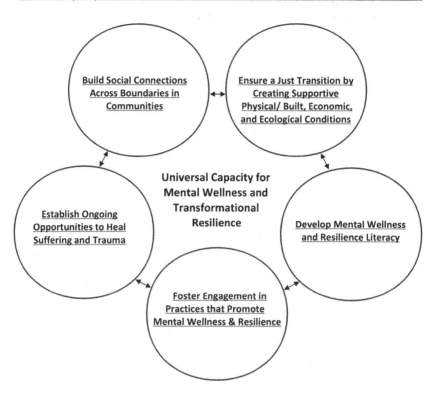

Figure PT03.1 The Five Foundational Areas Involved with Building Universal Capacity for Mental Wellness and Resilience for the Climate Crisis

CHAPTER 7

Build Social Connections across Boundaries in the Community

The historic heat wave that baked the Pacific Northwest in June 2021 led to more than 90 heat-related deaths in Washington State, and more than 80 in Oregon. Most of the people who died lived alone and were elderly. Social isolation clearly increased the risk of death.

Research on other heatwaves offers additional information about who is at risk during these events. In general, people who are 65 and older, live alone, and those with chronic diseases have disproportionately higher risks. That's because they have less mobility and therefore cannot move to cooler places and have no one to check on and assist them in emergencies. At the same time, women typically do better than men because they tend to have more robust ties with family and friends.[1]

These findings apply to much more than heatwaves. The lack of social connections is a key driver of many types of mental health problems including anxiety, depression, post-traumatic stress disorder (PTSD), and increased suicidality, as well as physical health problems such as drug and alcohol abuse and family abuse that can result from emergencies. One meta-analysis of research studies found that isolation and lack of social connections are twice as harmful to mental and physical health as obesity, and significantly increase the risk of premature mortality.[2]

THE IMPORTANCE OF BUILDING SOCIAL CONNECTIONS

This information underscores that establishing and maintaining robust connections with family, friends, and other residents in the community will, without a doubt, be the most important way to "future-proof" individual and collective mental wellness and transformational resilience during the long climate emergency. This is often called building "social capital," and in this chapter, I will describe it as its own free-standing focus.[3] However, building robust social connections across boundaries in a community should also be a core focus of each of the other foundational areas that are essential to build and sustain universal capacity for mental wellness and transformational resilience.[4]

As the social-ecological model describes, a substantial amount of research has found that anywhere between 40 percent and more than 80 percent of an individual's health and wellness can be directly or indirectly attributed to social factors.[5] In many ways, the relationships people have with others form the cornerstone of their lives. Research indicates that both the availability and perception of close family and friends who provide unconditional emotional support, practical assistance, and a sense of safety, which is often called "strong ties,"[6] or "bonding" social relationships,[7] help people function well, feel good, and respond constructively to adversities.

Having robust bonds with family and friends has been shown to reduce the rates of anxiety and depression, produce higher self-esteem, generate greater empathy, and lead to more trusting and cooperative relationships.[8] Strong bonding relationships can also strengthen the immune system, help people recover from physical injury and disease, and lead to a longer

DOI: 10.4324/9781003262442-11

life. Conversely, a lack of bonding relationships has significant harmful consequences for both mental health and physical health.[9]

In addition to helping people build strong bonds with family and friends, to enhance the entire population's capacity for mental wellness and transformational resilience during the long climate crisis, it will be equally important to build what are often called "weak ties" or "bridging" and "linking" social connections.

Bridging social support networks are connections between one's bonding network and other bonding networks in the community. They "bridge" the divides that typically separate people, such as race, class, religion, and geography, and help community members develop a sense of common destiny and build cohesion and collective efficacy.[10] Healthy bridging connections with people outside your bonding network can also activate a positive feedback loop, whereby those you interact with want to spend more time with you, which increases your connections with others, which enhances your capacity for mental wellness and transformational resilience.[11]

Further, connecting your personal bonding network with other bonding networks in the community is important because research has found that in the first five days of a major disaster, survival depends largely on family and friends, not emergency responders.[12] The people who died in the historic June 2021 Pacific Northwest heatwave, for instance, would have likely had a much greater chance of survival if they were part of bonding or bridging social support networks.[13]

Bridging social support networks often emerge through the informal associations people have with others. This means the groups of two to six people who meet for coffee or exercise together, and the bowling, knitting, woodwork, photography, bird watching, and many other types of groups people belong to. Most of these associations do not have a name. Yet, they are how people often meet others and develop relationships.[14] Bridging social support networks can also be developed through deliberate efforts by an RCC to bring together people from different locations in the community to engage in block parties, civic projects, celebrate events, and participate in other group activities.

These are called "weak ties" because people don't live with or share intimate details about their lives with people in their bridging network (if they did they would be part of their bonding network). However, these connections distribute vital information throughout the community, help people share and release the stress and trauma they experience, and in other ways help enhance their capacity for mental wellness and transformational resilience (Figure 7.1).

The importance of bridging social support networks was made clear to Dr. Daniel Aldrich, the Director of the Security and Resilience Studies Program at Northeastern University, and one of the top researchers in the field after he studied who survived and who did not after a tsunami hit India and an earthquake occurred in Japan. In India, he found that the people who fared best weren't those with the most money or the most power. They were people who knew lots of other people—that is, the most socially connected individuals. He found the same pattern in Japan. "Really, at the end of the day, the people who will save you, and the people who will help you," said Aldrich, "they're usually neighbors."[15]

Equally important to bonding and bridging networks during the long climate emergency will be the development of vast numbers of "Linking" social support networks in communities. These are links between bonding and bridging networks and individuals and organizations with important resources such as food, water, shelter, and energy, or that hold significant economic or political power or official authority in the community.

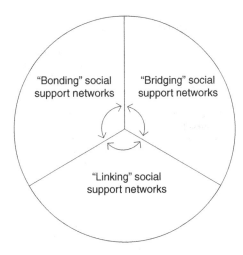

Figure 7.1 Three Interrelated Types of Social Support Networks Needed for the Climate Emergency

An example is a relationship between a neighborhood member and staff from a local charity that can provide food and shelter during a wildfire or storm that damages residences. When the individual learns where these resources can be found, they share the news with their bonding and bridging networks, which quickly spread it throughout the community.

Another example is a relationship between a community member and an elected official that allows the individual to gain access and convince the official to stop a local utility from turning off the electricity in a low-income neighborhood in favor of a wealthier one during a storm-generated power outage. After the meeting, the community member tells their bonding and bridging networks about the discussion and urges everyone to contact the official to show their support. The social support networks then quickly spread the word and the official receives significant pressure to act.[16]

As with bridging social support networks, linking networks are often called "weak ties" because they are usually not people one regularly interacts with or shares intimate details of their lives. However, this does not mean they are any less important than "strong ties." As vital as close ties are with family and friends, relationships with people outside one's bonding and bridging networks expand the psychological, emotional, and spiritual safety net that protects people from the negative effects of stressful events (Figure 7.2).[17]

This emphasizes the importance of building robust bonding, bridging, and linking social support networks. "We need all three types of those ties during a shock," said Dr. Aldrich. "Without them, things go really badly."[18]

The fear, anxiety, lack of empathy, and polarization seen in many communities today can give the impression that most residents no longer have the capacity to develop relationships with others who look, act, or think differently. This is not accurate. When people take the time to listen to others they do not know, identify practical issues they are all concerned about, and talk about ways to address them, positive connections can occur. Creating a welcoming environment, practicing co-regulation skills, and providing a strong sense of safety and support are key elements of the process (more information about this will be provided in Chapter 9).

```
┌─────────────────────────────────────────────┐
│          Core Elements of Social Capital      │
│                                               │
│  Bonding: "Strong" ties with family members   │
│  and/or a circle of friends who provide       │
│  emotional support and practical assistance   │
│  when needed.                                 │
│                                               │
│  Bridging: "Weaker" but important ties that   │
│  connect people across cultural, economic,    │
│  and geographic boundaries and provide        │
│  access to important ideas, information,      │
│  resources, and support in the community.     │
│                                               │
│  Linking: "Weaker" but important              │
│  connections between people with resources,   │
│  authority, or power in the community that    │
│  provide access to essential goods and        │
│  services or can affect changes in practices, │
│  policies, and outcomes.                      │
└─────────────────────────────────────────────┘
```

Figure 7.2 Core Elements of Social Capital

THE IMPORTANCE OF BUILDING SOCIAL CONNECTIONS AMONG YOUTH, BIPOC RESIDENTS, AND OTHER POPULATIONS—BUT DON'T SEPARATE OR ISOLATE THEM

RCCs should give a number of groups special attention when designing and implementing strategies to enhance mental wellness and transformational resilience by building robust social connections. Young people are one.

A global study completed in 2021 found that 59 percent of the 10,000 young people surveyed in 10 countries reported feeling very or extremely worried about the climate crisis, and 84 percent were at least moderately worried. Moreover, youth also reported feeling afraid, angry, powerless, guilty, ashamed, despairing, hurt, grief, and depressed by climate disruption, making comments such as "humanity is doomed" and "people have failed to care for the planet." Most of those surveyed said the anxiety and distress were affecting their daily life and ability to function. Three-quarters of respondents aged 16–25 felt the "future is frightening."[19]

The U.S. Surgeon General issued a report in November of that same year that highlighted the urgent need to address the nation's youth mental health crisis, and the report identified the climate crisis as a factor that shapes the mental health of young people.[20]

In addition to fears about the climate crisis, many young people feel isolated today. A study by Harvard University in 2021 found that 61 percent of young adults in the U.S. felt "serious loneliness." In addition, 43 percent of young adults reported increases in loneliness after the COVID-19 pandemic began. Almost 50 percent of those young adults reported that no one in the past few weeks had "taken more than just a few minutes" to ask how they are doing in a way that made them feel like the person "genuinely cared."[21]

A study in the UK completed during the early stages of the pandemic found similar results. Thirty-five percent of young people said they felt lonely often, or most of the time, despite spending three hours a day on social media.[22]

As with all other community members, to enhance the capacity of youth to prevent and heal climate-generated distresses and traumas, it will be essential to help them personally connect with others, learn simple Presencing resilience skills to calm their body, mind, and emotions, and engage in Purposing resilience skills to find new sources of meaning, direction, and healthy hope for and faith in the future.

My experience is that most young people want to make a difference and help others. This desire can be enhanced by bringing youth together and helping them engage in activities that matter to them and make a difference in the lives of others or the condition of their community or local environment. When given the opportunity, the natural creativity of youth can be activated and all sorts of positive changes can result in their personal lives, schools, neighborhoods, or community. Engaging with others in these activities can help each youth realize they matter as people. When they see signs of progress, they will also realize that every day, they can do something that helps others or helps reduce the climate crisis to manageable levels. This can be very empowering and help build healthy hope.

An outstanding organization doing this type of work is the Mycelium Youth Network. It works in the San Francisco Bay area to "bridge the gap between the increasing incidents of climate-related disasters and the ability of young people, who will inherit the world, to respond to those challenges with creativity, courage, resilience, hope, and real-world practical skills and training." They focus on building ancestrally-grounded climate resilience and their work is free or offered at low cost to low-income youth in the area.

"Kids are always pushing against boundaries and looking for new ways to look at things that adults often don't want to do," Founder and Executive Director Lil Milagro Henriquez told me. "It is very important to think big. We need new ideas on climate change. So we need to help youth think big.... If you are building out work for young people, tie it to the climate plan of their city or state. This pushes policy makers to change."[23]

As they build social connections and engage in meaningful activities, youth can also learn what mental wellness and transformational resilience involve and how they can enhance these qualities within themselves and help others do so as well. They can also learn how to engage in the simple practices that can enhance their capacity for wellness and resilience, which will be discussed in Chapter 10. And when young people are severely distressed or traumatized, they can participate in the age-appropriate healing activities that are discussed in Chapter 11.

In addition to youth, special emphasis should be placed on the populations that, at least initially, are most vulnerable to the mental health and psycho-social-spiritual impacts of the climate crisis. They include communities that have experienced historical and current disinvestment, oppression, and marginalization, such as BIPOC residents, older adults who live alone, immigrants, and rural and low-income communities. It also includes communities located in high-risk zones such as on low-lying areas at risk of flooding. People with pre-existing mental health illnesses or mental health conditions are also at higher risk of climate-generated mental health or psycho-social-spiritual problems.[24]

However, great care must be given to avoid focusing on youth separately from adults, or on high-risk or vulnerable populations in isolation from others in the community because this approach comes with significant risks. In a pattern seen time and again throughout history, when certain populations are defined as "vulnerable" or "at risk" people who are not members of those groups will discount their importance or show little concern about their plight. At the turn of the 19th century, for example, industrialized cities became incubators of diseases such as cholera and yellow fever, and the poor were the most at risk so little was done to address the problems. It was only when the diseases infected and killed the middle class and wealthier populations that the problems were fixed. The long climate emergency will impact everyone and only when people realize this will meaningful change occur.

In addition, focusing on one subgroup or population separately from others can easily revert back to the fragmented and siloed approaches that dominate in many communities today. This could end up increasing the segregation and social isolation these populations already experience, and end up pitting them against other groups for attention, funding, and other resources.

To avoid these pitfalls, efforts to build the capacity for mental wellness and transformational resilience among different subgroups should be integrated into a holistic population-level approach. To achieve this end, it will be essential to make youth, BIPOC and low-income residents, migrants, seniors, and other vulnerable populations equal partners in the RCC steering committee/board and on Resilience Innovation Teams that develop and implement strategies. Throughout all of these activities, it will be essential to increase everyone's connection with others, sense of belonging, and healthy hope.

EFFECTIVE STORYTELLING CAN MOTIVATE SOCIAL NETWORKS TO PROMOTE SAFE, HEALTHY, JUST, AND EQUITABLE NORMS

Building robust bonding, bridging, and linking social support networks throughout a community are also key to countering harmful social norms because they can transmit stories that promote safe, healthy, just, equitable, and ecologically regenerative thinking and behaviors.

The widely accepted and expected ways of thinking and acting that dominate some families, groups, and communities can lead people to believe that drinking excessive amounts of alcohol or misusing other drugs is a right of passage for adolescents or an acceptable way for adults to handle stress. Parents might believe that social norms endorse threatening or striking their children or using excessive physical restraints when they fail to follow their directives. Or social norms might make racism, sexism, and other forms of oppression acceptable, or even expected. These types of unhealthy, unsafe, unjust, and inequitable norms harm the people that promote them and those affected by them. In addition, the norms that dominate certain populations and communities can ignore the importance of, or even oppose, the need to conserve and regenerate the planet's climate system, ecosystems, and biodiversity.

To address these types of harmful norms, bonding, bridging, and linking networks can continually convey stories that promote healthy, safe, just, equitable, and ecologically regenerative standards of behavior.[25]

The stories that people repeatedly hear greatly influence how they think about the world and the way they act. For example, the major religions of the world are all based on stories that have shaped almost every aspect of human history. Storytelling that describes right ways of living has also been part of indigenous cultures for thousands of years.

More recently, research has recognized the power of storytelling to educate and influence people's thinking and behavior.[26] Digital storytelling with the elderly, for instance, was recently found to be associated with improved brain health, memory, and social engagement.[27]

Similar findings have been observed for young children as well.[28] In addition, research has found that good storytelling can help people make meaning out of suffering and enhance healing from family violence, physical illness, disasters, and ecologically generated traumas.[29]

In short, good storytelling is vital to prevent and heal problems in almost every community and culture worldwide.

To strengthen the capacity for mental wellness and transformational resilience and motivate people to engage in solutions to the climate emergency, social support networks can transmit stories that emphasize intrinsic rather than extrinsic values. This means values such as gratitude toward others, social justice, and caring for the climate, ecological systems, and biodiversity that make our lives possible. These messages can counter the extrinsic values that have come to dominate many populations today that emphasize external approval or rewards such as power over others, wealth, and social status.

To accomplish this, stories must connect with the mental "frames" people hold—their internal psychological structures—that determine how they see the world and that shape their thinking and behavior. Most people hold some type of intrinsic values as part of their cognitive frame, though those values can often be forgotten or ignored when they are frozen in a high or low space outside their resilience growth zone. The key is to connect with people, learn how they see the world, and then share stories that tap into the intrinsic values they hold that are part of their mental frame.[30]

Influential storytelling combines information with metaphors, symbols, images, and personal examples people can relate to that paint a picture in their mind of important ideas or messages. Facts and figures are important, but usually influence thinking and behaviors only when they are included in stories that speak to the personal experiences people have had and create empathy for others.

Good storytelling captures people's attention and makes it easier for them to process information when they are consumed by other tasks. Good storytelling also allows people to put themselves in the same situation, which reduces defensiveness and helps them learn complicated concepts that can alter behavior and lead to positive change. In addition, good storytelling can expand adherence to pro-social norms by showing people that if others can do it so can they.

Effective stories often include short phrases or images that symbolize an issue. The #MeToo movement, for example, quickly went global because a simple phrase told a story of sexual harassment or violence that many women related to, which empowered them to speak out about their own experience and demand change. The simple two-word phrase activated numerous changes. As the movement grew, for instance, several states passed laws prohibiting the use of nondisclosure agreements in sexual misconduct cases, a number of survivors of sexual abuse got financial restitution, and people who had never thought about sexual harassment before realized how much it had affected women they knew.[31] Many additional changes are likely in the future.

Powerful storytelling is also needed to paint a clear picture of important issues that are often obscured by powerful interests. This point was made to me by Jacqui Patterson during an interview. She is the founder and executive director of the Chisholm Legacy Project. Her organization is doing leading-edge work helping BIPOC residents, and black women in particular, working on the frontlines of climate justice obtain the resources they need to ensure a just and equitable transition from an "extractive to a living economy centered in caring for the earth, equity, and justice." Patterson told me, "Big money uses narratives like 'natural gas' to make their product sound good when it is actually mostly methane that is harmful to people and the environment.... We need narratives that clarify what is positive and what is negative."[32]

This underscores the importance of who tells the stories that dominate public attention. When the narratives are shaped by those with economic power they can often make people believe half-truths or outright falsehoods that fortify their domination. When those in power control the social narratives they can also prevent any other story from even being considered. This includes how people can live a meaningful life without the goods and services they provide, or the social, economic, religious, or political ideologies they promote that aggravate the climate crisis.

This is why it will be vital for RCC members to come together to continuously convey stories through their community's social support networks that help residents understand what appropriate prosocial behavior involves, and describes a real-world picture of how they can live a meaningful life in the midst of the long climate emergency.

Good storytelling on its own, of course, cannot generate the changes needed to motivate people to enhance their capacity to prevent and heal distresses and traumas or engage in climate solutions. But effective storytelling is essential to produce these outcomes. For these reasons, it will be very important for RCC members to learn how to continually communicate stories that promote safe, healthy, just, equitable, and ecologically regenerative ways of thinking and acting. *The Framework Institute* offers resources RCCs can use to learn how to craft and tell powerful stories for social change.[33] *Storytelling For Good* also offers helpful resources.[34] *The National Storytelling Network* includes links to storytelling resources for youth, educators, and other populations.[35]

BUILDING SOCIAL CONNECTIONS CAN ENHANCE COLLECTIVE EFFICACY

Using good storytelling to build robust social capital is a central element in creating "collective efficacy." This means that when numerous people share the belief that through their unified efforts they can overcome challenges and achieve important outcomes, they become more effective and increase the likelihood of achieving their goals.[36] For example, in communities where neighbors share the belief that they can band together to prevent crime, research has found significantly less of it.[37] Strong collective efficacy can also bring community members together to prevent social, economic, health, and other forms of inequity and injustice.[38] And collective efficacy will be vital to empower residents to build universal capacity for mental wellness and transformational resilience as they engage in actions that help reduce the climate emergency to manageable levels.

It is important to realize that robust social capital and the collective efficacy it can create are difficult to measure because they are not concrete things like financial capital. They involve an ever-shifting network of relationships that must be continually nurtured. But the existence of hearty social capital and collective efficacy can be observed when neighbors assist each other, and when community members with different racial, cultural, economic, spiritual, or political affiliations join together to press for change and address important issues.

BUILDING ROBUST SOCIAL CONNECTIONS CAN HELP OVERCOME TODAY'S POLARIZATION

Building robust social connections and telling stories that alter harmful social norms and enhance collective efficacy can be difficult today. Numerous factors are causing many communities worldwide to become more divided and fragmented. In many locations, the social capital required to address today's complex challenges seems to have dissipated. Social media and smartphones, for all the benefits they provide, have in many ways aggravated the problems because they do not provide protection from irresponsible communications or ways for people to interact and thoughtfully discuss issues face-to-face.

Only personal interaction can overcome the disconnection, isolation, and polarization that permeate today. As you will read about in a moment, holding neighborhood block parties, linking residents with similar interests, and engaging community members in addressing "kitchen table" issues they care about are constructive ways to develop personal connections.

COMMUNICATING WITH PEOPLE WHO HOLD DIFFERENT PSYCHOLOGICAL FRAMES

Taking the time to get to know your neighbors and understand their psychological frames is an essential part of this process. The starting point is to take the time to brainstorm what you might have in common with people who you believe hold different beliefs and perspectives from your own. This could be a value you share, such as caring for your children, saving money, or living in a safe place. It could also be things you might both enjoy such as gardening or being outdoors.

The next step is to prepare for the conversation by thinking through how to link the issues you might have in common with mental health and psycho-social-spiritual issues and the benefits of reducing your community's contributions to the climate emergency. For example, you could talk about how your child is now constantly distressed and worried about what the future holds given the accelerating disasters they see on TV and social media. Another example could be to talk about how hotter temperatures, heat waves, and droughts are making it difficult for you to enjoy the outdoors, or reducing the number and type of vegetables you can grow in your garden, while driving up the costs of water to irrigate them.

When these links become clear, the next step is to connect them with possible solutions that speak to the things you have might in common with the person. To follow on the previous example, you might mention that you have decided to help your child find healthy hope by installing LED energy-efficient lighting throughout your house to reduce your electrical consumption and save money, or that you are purchasing an electric vehicle to eliminate the high costs of and impacts of gasoline. Or you could share that you are going to plant more trees in your yard to cool it during heatwaves or install a drip-irrigation system in your garden to ensure sufficient water for the growing season and save money.

After preparing in this way, be ready to listen closely to the people you interact with. Good listening involves dropping any assumptions you have about who the people are, making them feel safe and welcome, and trying to truly understand what they are saying. Keep listening for things you agree on. When you find something you have in common, actively engage in discussions with respect and empathy and avoid any hint of dismissiveness, even if their perspective seems factually incorrect, biased, or just plain wacky.

A personal experience helped me grasp this point. A few years back, I was involved in an effort to enact a resilience policy in the State of Oregon legislature. The bill had to be passed by the Senate Preparedness Committee in order to be heard by the full Senate. Two members of the committee were hardcore climate deniers. I spent time with one of them and found that he was distressed by the historic wildfires that were occurring throughout the state. He had also seen debilitating mental health problems in people he worked with in the military and supported addressing post-traumatic stress disorder and other mental health issues. But his psychological frame and associated political affiliation made acknowledging the climate emergency a hot-button issue that he vehemently opposed. So the legislation we crafted focused on building resilience for the mental health problems generated by wildfires, droughts, and other disasters, and never included climate change. We also never mentioned climate change during the senate hearing that was held on the bill, and the committee unanimously passed it. (Unfortunately, the legislation never became law because it got stalled in the appropriations process, and the Republican delegation then walked out of the legislative session to oppose a different climate bill, which ended the entire session.)

This encounter taught me an important lesson: Even in these extremely polarized times, by taking the time to connect with people and understand how they see the world, it is possible to identify common interests and work together to achieve them. Taking this approach can both build social connections and increase personal and collective efficacy.

EXAMPLES OF HOW RCCS CAN INTENTIONALLY BUILD STRONG AND WEAK SOCIAL CONNECTIONS

Abundant Community Edmonton, operated by the city of Edmonton, Canada, is one of the best programs I've seen explicitly focused on building social connections. "In the same way that physical nutrients are so important for our health, so are three relational nutrients important to our physical and mental health," Howard Laurence, coordinator of Abundant Community Edmonton told me. "They are family, friends, and neighbors."[39]

As discussed in Chapter 5, Abundant Community Edmonton develops these relational nutrients by having a local volunteer—a block connector—go door-to-door interviewing people on their block (which includes about 20 households) to ask about their skills, gifts, interests, and ideas for the neighborhood. They also ask if they are willing to share their interests with others in the neighborhood. The information is inserted into an online database that is shared with all the neighbors. This allows residents to learn who in their area has similar interests, and helps them connect with them to share their skills or passions. For example, people who like to do woodworking, knitting, or take early morning walks can meet and engage in these activities with others with similar interests. The block connectors also keep residents informed about upcoming neighborhood parties and other local events. Two-thirds of the 173 neighborhoods in Edmonton now have a block connector, and they help residents connect at the block level, host block socials, form local groups, and in other ways build social capital.

To support the block connector program, the city's Abundant Community Edmonton program developed a Resource Guide that describes the role of the connectors and how they can engage with their neighbors. In addition, it developed a Guide describing the entire program and the different roles residents can play in building social connections. And during the COVID-19 pandemic, they distributed "Connected Neighbours" cards that were filled out by individuals who wanted to help people who were isolated, quarantined, or in other ways experiencing challenges. The knowledge of who was interested in helping others assisted many residents. All of these resources can be found on their website.[40]

An assessment completed in 2020 found that 84.2 percent of Block Connectors felt a lot more or moderately more connected to their block (immediate neighbors) and 61.5 percent felt a lot more or moderately connected to their neighborhood. The majority of Block Connectors also reported additional benefits including a "strengthened sense of connection, enhanced existing relationships, and increased overall wellbeing being the largest." In addition, "66.7 percent had neighbours that joined existing groups because of their connecting work, and 45.2 percent had created new groups to socialize, share, and learn from each other."

The 2020 assessment also found the majority of neighborhoods involved with the program are addressing two or more of the seven responsibilities of a neighborhood defined by John McKnight.[41] Thirty-two percent were enabling the health of residents; 75 percent were assuring safety and security; 31 percent were stewarding the environment; 16 percent were nurturing and shaping the local economy; 40 percent were contributing to local food production; 20 percent were assisting with raising children; and 44 percent were providing community care. Only 0.04 percent said they were not engaged in addressing any of these responsibilities.[42]

These findings indicate that Abundant Community Edmonton is establishing social connections that produce significant benefits for resident and nature.

The Neighborhood Empowerment Network (NEN) in San Francisco, California, is another outstanding initiative focused on building the social capital required to enhance community resilience to climate and other adversities. Hosted by the San Francisco Department of Emergency Management, the NEN is comprised of non-profits, government agencies, foundations, faith-based and academic institutions, and civic networks that are committed to establishing and maintaining local cross-sector networks at the neighborhood level that work year-round to advance a community's resilience at the individual, organizational, and community levels.

The NEN's goal is to establish a cohort of neighborhood stakeholders that may be called upon to activate during a disaster by convening them together in advance to strengthen their capacity to protect the community's most vulnerable residents. Cohort members are identified by local civic leaders using an asset-mapping exercise that flags local stakeholder organizations that either manage essential resources or serve vulnerable populations. Once identified, the stakeholders are convened in a strategic planning workshop that features a tabletop exercise that challenges participants to respond to an earthquake for 72 hours with no meaningful support from the government and use only the resources that are in the community at the time of the disaster.

The goals of the exercise are the following:

- map the assets and resources available in the community;
- increase awareness and interoperability among local agencies of the crucial role they will play in the response to the disaster and related challenges;
- increase the level of interoperability and trust between the community and the government's first response agencies; and
- identify any gaps that the community will face in meeting the care and shelter needs of their most vulnerable residents.

The identified gaps are converted into goals and objectives that are included in a resilience action plan (RAP) that guides the investments of the community as they advance their resilience goals. The RAP also hosts a risk/hazard assessment that leverages local knowledge of their neighborhood's risks as well as a governance framework that provides a flexible platform for local leadership to make decisions before, during, and after emergencies. The

RAP is a dynamic asset and is updated annually to accommodate social, cultural, and economic changes.

Over the course of the last decade, the NEN has created a suite of programs in concert with its partner communities that are housed in the NEN's Empowered Communities Program. The programs include:

- The HUB, which is the name for the local cross-sector network of stakeholder organizations that are actively participating in the community's resilience-development work before, during, and after a disaster. At the center of the HUB is an anchor institution that has the political capital to establish and maintain the network and coordinate the implementation of its RAP.

- The Neighborfest Program, which uses the fun of the traditional block party to advance the disaster resilience of a block by increasing the readiness of residents to meet the care and shelter needs of their most vulnerable neighbors as they shelter in place during times of stress. By leveraging the Neighborfest Host Playbook, Host Committees acquire the relationships, skills, and resources to be there for their neighbors when they need help the most.

- Resilient Leadership Academies for adults and youth that empower them to become stakeholders in advancing their community's resilience goals in the face of stressors such as climate change and earthquakes.

The NEN has found that engaging residents in these types of ground-up planning processes build a "soft" culture of trust and reciprocity and a "hard" list of goals and objectives. Residents not only develop connections with people they previously did not know, they also develop trust in first responder organizations and city agencies that are important during disasters and emergencies. All this builds the social efficacy required to enhance and sustain individual and collective resilience during stressful situations.

An assessment completed in 2020 of the Neighborfest Program's contribution to the ability of participants to support their neighbors while they sheltered in place (SIP) during the COVID-19 lockdown found remarkable results[43]:

- 81 percent of hosts believed that the Neighborfest significantly elevated the level of social cohesion within their communities.

- 100 percent of hosts believed that the relationship-building component of Neighborfest made it easier to identify neighbors that either needed help or could help those around them while they sheltered in place during COVID-19.

- 86 percent of hosts felt that Neighborfest enhanced their community's preparedness for the COVID-19 SIP orders.

Although the study focused on the COVID-19 lockdown, it demonstrates the effectiveness of the approach for many types of adversities.

"No one organization or agency can save a community," Daniel Homsey, director of the NEN told me. "We need ground-up resilience based on relationships and trust between residents, non-profits, the Red Cross, faith organizations, the private sector, academic organizations, and others."[44]

Building Resilient Neighbourhoods in British Columbia, Canada is another initiative that understands the importance of enhancing social capital to build resilience. Its goal is to help neighborhoods and communities build resilience for "major social, environmental, and economic challenges and threats" including climate change, resource depletion, and financial instability. To achieve this goal, they convene residents and community leaders to develop a "Resilience Assessment" that helps identify their neighborhood's strengths and vulnerabilities based on a "Characteristics of Resilience" framework that is provided. They then convene groups to review the findings of the assessment and use it to identify resilience priorities for the neighborhood. This forms the basis for the development of a community-wide strategy. Through the process of assessing and planning, social connections are made and collective efficacy grows.[45]

One outcome of their work is the establishment of a "Resilience Hub." In this case, the Hub is an actual physical bench located in the neighborhood with solar plugs people can use to charge their phones when the electrical system is out of service. Underneath the bench is a locked box that includes a clipboard with a list of everyone's name, address, and information such as if they live alone or with others. The box also includes supplies that can be used during an emergency.

When residents come together to construct the bench they get to know each other. When a bench is finalized a major celebration is held with food, music, and more. This often leads to many other neighborhood activities, such as picnics. In addition to enhancing resilience to disasters, the process builds social capital.

"We look at our work through a resilience lens, not an emergency preparedness lens," Michelle Colussi told me. She is a manager at the Canadian Centre for Community Renewal which operates the Resilient Neighbourhoods program. "We know resilience is about building relationships and values and being a good neighbour."[46]

RCCs can use these initiatives as models to develop their own unique age and culturally appropriate ways to build social capital in their neighborhood or community.

OTHER WAYS RCCS CAN BUILD ROBUST SOCIAL CONNECTIONS ACROSS BOUNDARIES

- *Model the Importance of Building Social Connections During All RCC Meetings and Events*: RCCs should prioritize building social connections in all of its meetings and in every activity it sponsors. This can be done, for example, by taking time to allow RCC steering committee/board and Resilience Innovation Team members to connect and share what is on their minds, and also offering ways for observers at events to meet and engage with each other. The key point RCC members should always keep front-and-center is that building social connections is as or more important than any specific physical deliverables they produce.

- *Organize a Social Capital Resilience Innovation Team*: RCCs should organize an innovation team composed of people from different neighborhoods, civic, non-profit, private, and public organizations who jointly plan and implement ways for neighbors and different populations and sectors to continually interact with and create social connections with people they don't know. This can include block parties, clean-up events, tree plantings, community gardening, and other types of civic activities. Free busing, ride shares, biking, walking, and other forms of transportation should be organized to help people travel to the events, and whenever possible food and beverages should also be provided. Here are some examples of ways that Social Capital

Resilience Innovation Teams can build social support networks across boundaries in their community:

- *Organize Resilience Hubs Across the Community*: The examples described in this chapter offer different ways to form Neighborhood Resilience Hubs. It should be a top priority to organize them throughout the community. In addition to helping residents prepare for and respond effectively to disasters and emergencies, the relationships they build will be extremely important to enhance and sustain the capacity for mental wellness and transformational resilience during the long climate emergency. Vashon Island in Washington State has over 200 hubs, all run by volunteers. In addition to building social connections, they provide emergency radios and TVs that allow people to find out what is happening, and other resources for emergencies.[47] Climate Crew works across the U.S. with libraries, churches, schools, non-profits, and other community organizations to establish Climate Resilience Hubs that help residents respond to extreme weather events.[48]

- *Organize "Making Connections" Events*: To address social isolation among San Diego's East African refugee population, the Prevention Institute and United Women of East Africa Support Team launched the Making Connections Initiative. Participants co-developed a "culturally- and community-rooted space" in which to gather, connect, and support each other. Having this safe space helped them experience a sense of belonging and to grow their collective capacity to identify and advocate for solutions to challenges such as the lack of affordable housing, and educational and employment opportunities. Prevention Institute has facilitated similar projects in many U.S. cities, and RCCs can work with them, or establish their own unique Making Connections initiative.

- *Organize "Meet Me" Events*: RCCs can use the "Meet Me Downtown" program developed in Phoenix, Arizona as a model to get diverse residents together. These are after-work mixer and fitness events held weekly that get people out on the streets and into local bars and restaurants. A variety of walking and running routes direct people to different neighborhoods and businesses that offer deals for those who make it there.[49]

- *Close Streets to Show Movies or Plays Outdoors*: RCCs can work with neighborhoods and local governments to close off a street or find a location where movies or plays produced by local actors can be shown to any resident who wants to attend. Taking It To the Streets offers an example RCCs can follow.[50]

- *Make a "Table" for Neighborhood Conversations*: Much like the San Francisco NEN, RCCs can help community members organize ice cream parties or hold potlucks that bring diverse residents together to meet, eat, and talk. The Longest Table, organized in Tallahassee, Florida, offers an example.[51]

- *Set up "Nextdoor" Social Media Sites*: RCCs can encourage the use of Nextdoor or other social media platforms that allow neighbors and local organizations to connect electronically and share information. It is being used throughout the U.S. and in many parts of the European Union. My wife and I are members of a Neighborhood Association that uses Nextdoor to communicate.

- *Utilize Resources Available from Key Organizations in the Field*: The Coalition to End Social Isolation and Loneliness, and its sister organizations the Foundation for

Social Connection and Global Initiative on Loneliness and Connection, have numerous studies, methods, and tools RCCs can use to build robust social connections in their community.[52]

You get the idea. There are numerous ways RCCs can bring residents together to get to know each other and develop social capital. RCCs should actively engage local residents in discussions about how to build social connections. The RCC's ultimate goal should be to make the creation of robust social connections and personal and collective efficacy a community expectation and norm.

The chart provided at the end of this chapter can be used by RCC members to determine the extent to which they have addressed the key elements of building robust social support networks in the community.

Engaging residents in actions that create supportive local physical/built, economic, and ecological conditions in the community is one of the best ways to build robust social support networks. This is the topic of the next chapter.

CHECKLIST

To what extent is the RCC building robust social support networks across boundaries in the community?

	Yes	No	Comments
Do RCC steering committee/board and Resilience Innovation Team members have a good grasp of the importance of building robust social connections in their community?			
Does the RCC have a strategy to build robust bonding relationships in the community?			
Does the RCC have a strategy to build robust bridging relationships in the community?			
Does the RCC have a strategy to build robust linking relationships in the community?			
Does the RCC have a strategy to encourage local bonding, bridging, and linking social support networks to share stories that promote safe, healthy, just, equitable, and resilient norms of behavior?			
Does the RCC have a way to determine the extent to which social capital is being enhanced in the community?			

NOTES

1 Many articles. See for example: Suh C. (2019). Beating the heat: save lives by being a good neighbour. *Samuel Centre for Social Connectedness*. Obtained at: https://www.socialconnectedness.org/beating-the-heat-save-lives-by-being-a-good-neighbour/; and Losee J. et al. (February 2022). Social network connections and increased preparation intentions for a disaster. *Journal of Environmental Psychology*. Obtained at: https://www.sciencedirect.com/science/article/abs/pii/S0272494421001791
2 Holt-Lundstad J. (March 2015). Loneliness and social isolation as risk factors for mortality: a meta analytic review. *Sage Journals*. Obtained at: https://journals.sagepub.com/doi/10.1177/1745691614568352
3 Aldrich D. (2012). *Building Resilience: Social Capital in Post-Disaster Recovery*. University of Chicago Press, Chicago, IL.
4 UK Mind for Better Mental Health and Mental Health Foundation. (August 2013). *Building Resilient Communities: Making Every Contact Count for Public Mental Health*, p. 21. Obtained at: https://www.mentalhealth.org.uk/sites/default/files/building-resilient-communities.pdf
5 Holt-Lunstad J. (December 2022). Social connection as a public health issue: the evidence and a systemic framework for the prioritizing the "Social" in social determinants of health. *Annual Review of Public Health*. Obtained at: http://doi.org/10.11.1146/annurev-publhealth-052020–110732
6 Breines J. (March 2014). Are some social ties better than others? *Greater Good Magazine*. Obtained at: https://greatergood.berkeley.edu/article/item/are_some_ties_better_than_others
7 Aldrich D. (2012). *Building Resilience: Social Capital in Post-Disaster Recovery*. University of Chicago Press.
8 Claridge T. (2018). *What Is the Difference Between Bonding and Bridging Social Capital?* Social Capital Research. Obtained at: https://www.socialcapitalresearch.com/difference-bonding-bridging-social-capital/
9 Holt-Lunstad J. (December 2022). Social connection as a public health issue: the evidence and a systemic framework for the prioritizing the "social" in social determinants of health. *Annual Review of Public Health*. Obtained at: http://doi.org/10.11.1146/annurev-publhealth-052020–110732.
10 Claridge T. (2018). *What Is Bridging Social Capital?* Social Capital Research. Obtained at: https://www.socialcapitalresearch.com/what-is-bridging-social-capital/
11 See for example: Yang C. Y. et al. (2016). Social relationships and physiological determinants of longevity across the human life span. *Proceedings of the National Academy of Sciences*. Obtained at: https://pubmed.ncbi.nlm.nih.gov/26729882/; Teo A.R. et al. (2013). Social relationships and depression: ten year follow-up from a nationally representative study. *PLoS One*, 8(4). Obtained at: https://pubmed.ncbi.nlm.nih.gov/23646128/; and Honn Qualls S. (2014, March 6). What social relationships can do for health. *ASA Generations*. Obtained at: https://www.asaging.org/
12 Schoch-Spana M. et al., (2007). Community engagement: leadership tools for catastrophic health events. *Biosecurity and Bioterrorism: Biodefense Strategy, Practice, and Science*, 5(1), 10–11. Obtained at: https://pubmed.ncbi.nlm.nih.gov/17437348/
13 Wolf J. et al. (2010). *Social Capital, Individual Responses to Heat Waves and Climate Change Adaptation: An Empirical Study of Two UK Cities*. Elsevier Global Environmental Change. Obtained at: www.elsevier.com/locate/gloenvcha
14 This point was made very clearly to me by Peter Block during a personal interview on December 20, 2021.
15 Vedantan S. (July 2011). The key to disaster survival? Friends and neighbors. *All Things Considered, National Public Radio*. Obtained at: https://www.npr.org/2011/07/04/137526401/the-key-to-disaster-survival-friends-and-neighbors
16 See for example: Yang C. Y. et al. (2016). Social relationships and physiological determinants of longevity across the human life span. *Proceedings of the National Academy of Sciences*; Teo A.R. et al. (2013). Social relationships and depression: ten year follow-up from a nationally representative study. *PLoS One*, 8(4); and Honn Qualls S. (2014, March 6). What social relationships can do for health. *ASA Generations*.
17 Granovetter M. (1973). The strength of weak ties. *The American Journal of Sociology*, 78(6), 2360–2380. Obtained at: https://snap.stanford.edu/class/cs224w-readings/granovetter73weakties.pdf
18 Botkin-Kowacki E. (July 14, 2021). How to rebound from disasters: resilience starts in the neighborhood. *News@Northwesten*. Obtained at: https://news.northeastern.edu/2021/07/14/how-to-rebound-from-disasters-resilience-starts-in-the-neighborhood/
19 Hickman C. et al. (December 2021). Climate anxiety in children and young people and their beliefs about government responses to climate change: A global survey. *The Lancet Planetary Health*, 5(12). Obtained at: https://www.thelancet.com/journals/lanplh/article/PIIS2542–5196(21)00278-3/fulltext

20 Office of the Surgeon General (December 6, 2021). *Protecting Youth Mental Health: The U.S. Surgeon General's Advisory*. Obtained at: https://www.hhs.gov/sites/default/files/surgeon-general-youth-mental-health-advisory.pdf

21 Weissbourd R. et al. (February 2021). *Loneliness in America: How the Pandemic Has Deepened an Epidemic of Loneliness and What We Can Do About It*. Making Caring Common, Harvard Graduate Institute School of Education. Obtained at: https://mcc.gse.harvard.edu/reports/loneliness-in-america

22 YoungMinds (2020). *Coronavirus: Impact on Young People with Mental Health Needs*. Obtained at: https://www.youngminds.org.uk/media/xq2dnc0d/youngminds-coronavirus-report-march2020.pdf

23 Personal interview, September 29, 2021.

24 Lawrance E. et al. (May 2021). *The Impact of Climate Change on Mental Health and Emotional Wellbeing: Current Evidence and Implications for Policy and Practice*. Grantham Institute, Briefing Paper No. 36. Obtained at: https://www.imperial.ac.uk/grantham/publications/all-publications/the-impact-of-climate-change-on-mental-health-and-emotional-wellbeing-current-evidence-and-implications-for-policy-and-practice.php

25 Plastrik P. et al. (2014). *Connecting to Change the Works: Harnessing the Power of Networks for Social Impact*, Washington D.C.: Island Press.

26 Falk E. (June, 2021). Op-Ed: why storytelling is an important tool for social change. *Los Angeles Times*. Obtained at: https://www.latimes.com/opinion/story/2021-06-27/stories-brain-science-memory-social-change

27 Staggart J. et al. (December 2019). Implementing digital storytelling for digital health-related outcomes in older adults: protocol for a systemic review. *JMIR Research Protocols*. Obtained at: https://www.ncbi.nlm.nih.gov/pmc/articles/PMC6942188/

28 Brockington G. et al. (May 2021). Storytelling increases oxytocin and positive emotions and decreases cortisol and pain in hospitalized children. *PNAS*, 118(22). Obtained at: https://www.pnas.org/doi/10.1073/pnas.2018409118

29 Henyon H. (2021). *Storytelling as a Therapy Tool: Using Story to Heal Trauma and Abuse*. Las Vegas, NV: Lifestyle Entrepreneurs Press.

30 Lakoff G. (2014). *The All New Don't Think Like an Elephant*. White River Junction, VT: Chelsea Green Publishing.

31 North A. (October 2019). 7 positive changes that have come from the #MeToo movement. *Vox*. Obtained at: https://www.vox.com/identities/2019/10/4/20852639/me-too-movement-sexual-harassment-law-2019

32 Personal interview, April 6, 2022.

33 The Framework Institute: https://www.frameworksinstitute.org/

34 Storytelling for Good: https://storytelling.comnetwork.org/

35 National Storytelling Network: https://storynet.org/about-nsn/

36 Goddard R. D. et al. (2004). Collective efficacy beliefs: theoretical developments, empirical evidence, and future directions. *Educational Researcher*, 33(3), 3–13.

37 Sampson R. et al. (1997). Neighborhoods and violent crime: a multilevel study of collective efficacy. *Science*, 277(5328), 918–924.

38 Many studies. See, for example: Butel J. and Braun K. (2019). The role of collective efficacy in reducing health disparities: a systematic review. *Family Community Health*, 42(1). Obtained at: https://pubmed.ncbi.nlm.nih.gov/30431465/; Higgins B. R. and Hunt J. (2016). *Collective Efficacy: Taking Action to Improve Neighborhoods*. National Institute of Justice, Washington, DC. Obtained at: https://www.ojp.gov/pdffiles1/nij/249823.pdf; Anderson E. (1999). *Code of the Street*. Norton Books, New York, NY; and Sampson R.J. et al. (1997). Neighborhoods and violent crime: a multilevel study of collective efficacy. *Science*, 277, 918–924. Obtained at: https://www.science.org/doi/10.1126/science.277.5328.918

39 Personal interview, December 30, 2021.

40 Abundant Community Edmonton: https://www.edmonton.ca/programs_services/for_communities/abundant-community-edmonton

41 McKnight J. (Undated). *Neighborhood Necessities: Seven Functions that Only Effectively Organized Neighborhoods Can Provide*. ABCD Institute, DePaul University, Chicago, IL. Obtained at: https://resources.depaul.edu/abcd-institute/publications/Documents/2013_NeighborhoodNecessities.pdf

42 Abundant Community Edmonton. Neighborhood Services. *2020 Impact Report*. Obtained at: https://www.edmonton.ca/programs_services/for_communities/abundant-community-edmonton

43 McCall S.J, et al. (2020). *NEN Neighborfest Program Performance Report: 2020 COVID19 Pandemic*. Obtained at: https://www.empowersf.org/wp-content/uploads/2021/12/Neighborfest-Perf.-COVID19-Report-Version-1.pdf

44 Personal interview, September 21, 2021.

45 For more information, go to: https://www.resilientneighbourhoods.ca/communities/
46 Personal interview, November 18, 2021.
47 I was told about the Vashon Island resilience hubs by Jim Diers during an interview on January 21, 2022. For more information, go to: https://www.vashonresilience.org/vite
48 Climate Crew: https://www.climatecrew.org/resilience_hubs
49 Meet Me Downtown, Phoenix: http://meetmedowntownphx.com/
50 DeJesus A. (July 23, 2021). 'Taking It To The Streets' free film series: bringing community together one movie at a time. *silive.com*. Obtained at: https://www.silive.com/news/2021/07/taking-it-to-the-streets-free-film-series-bringing-community-together-one-movie-at-a-time.html
51 The Longest Table: https://tlh.villagesquare.us/event/the-longest-table/
52 Coalition to End Social Isolation and Loneliness: https://www.endsocialisolation.org/who-we-are

CHAPTER 8

Ensure a Just Transition by Creating Healthy, Safe, Just, and Equitable Climate-Resilient Local Physical/Built, Economic, and Ecological Conditions

The Living Cully coalition, located in Northeast Portland, Oregon, is a long-term collaboration between four non-profit organizations that seeks to improve the quality of life for BIPOC and low-income residents of the Cully neighborhood. It is a diverse low-income community that has long suffered from underinvestment, lack of access to environmental amenities and infrastructure, and high levels of pollution. Led by the non-profit organization Verde, which helps communities by building environmental wealth through social enterprise, the Living Cully coalition uses sustainability to combat poverty and displacement in the community. The other partners include Habitat for Humanity Portland Region, Hacienda Community Development Corporation, and the Native American Youth and Family Center.

Part of the Living Cully coalition's strategy includes building, rehabilitating, and preserving a large number of affordable housing units. In addition to building new single family residences, for example, Habitat for Humanity agreed to invest in weatherization for low-income homes. The coalition also developed a community energy plan focused on climate justice for local residents. It has increased the rate of local business development and living-wage job creation and assists low-income families to achieve economic self-sufficiency through job creation, job training, and a variety of incentive programs. In addition, they have invested in parkland, open space, community gardens, and natural areas.[1]

Following a long decline, the US coal industry crashed a decade ago when methane (aka natural gas) greatly reduced the demand for coal. The decline has hit Appalachia particularly hard and produced massive job losses because much of the economy has been built on coal. The collapse exposed the paradoxes generated by coal mining and coal-fired power generation for local communities. They provide jobs and boost local tax revenues. But they also pollute the air, threaten the health of everyone working at and living near a facility, and disrupt the global climate system which puts everyone now and in the future at risk.

Community leaders across the region have developed innovative plans to diversify the local economy by establishing environmentally friendly alternatives to coal. Refresh Appalachia and its partner Reclaiming Appalachia Coalition, for example, are putting people back to work cleaning up discarded coalfields and transitioning those sites to farmlands and forestry enterprises. They are also promoting tourism and outdoor recreation by turning old railroad tracks into a network of trails, creating better access to rivers with nature trails and kayak ramps, and other means. Job retraining and educational opportunities have also been launched to help former coal workers develop the skills needed in new industries, including an emerging Appalachian renewable energy sector.[2]

These examples show how community groups can come together to ensure a just transition for residents by helping them create healthy, safe, just, and equitable climate-resilient local conditions.

The need for a just transition applies to local physical/built conditions, including transportation, housing, and public spaces. It is also urgently needed to address the conditions of the local economy, jobs, and incomes. And a just transition is necessary to conserve and regenerate local ecological systems and species in ways that benefit everyone equally.

DOI: 10.4324/9781003262442-12

Figure 8.1 Key Elements of Supportive Local Conditions

One reason a just transition is needed is that unhealthy and unsafe transportation infra-structure, dilapidated housing, insufficient green spaces, and polluted or degraded ecological conditions are powerful risk factors that can generate widespread anxiety, depression, hope-lessness, and other mental health problems. They can also lead to psycho-social-spiritual problems such as alcohol and drug misuse, crime, and violence in communities. These prob-lems emerge in part because unhealthy and unsafe local conditions can create fear, aversion, and shame within the population that constrain human interaction and dampen engage-ment in pro-social activities (Figure 8.1).[3]

In addition, people who lack living-wage jobs, or experience long-term unemployment, have a three times greater chance of experiencing severe anxiety, depression, loss of self-esteem, and low self-confidence, even compared with those who have low-paid employment. Unemployed people can be less psychologically and emotionally resilient than those who have jobs. The lack of a job can often activate a vicious cycle, because mental wellness is an important influence on an individual's employability and their capacity to secure and retain a job, so the lack of employment can make further employment difficult or impossible. Being unemployed, or lacking a living-wage job, also produces toxic stress that can have long-term impacts on physical health.[4]

Residents experience the impacts of poor local conditions, which is why they often point to some aspect of local physical/built, economic, or ecological conditions as their top con-cerns when asked what they care about most in their community. These kitchen sink issues are at the top of most people's concerns. Unless significant efforts are made to prepare these systems for and adapt them to the many impacts of a disrupted climate system in just and equitable ways, all these problems will be greatly aggravated.

On the other hand, building healthy, safe, just, and equitable climate-resilient local physical/built, economic, and ecological conditions can increase the health and safety of residents, which helps expand their interactions with others, builds social connections, and in other ways strengthens their capacity to prevent and heal mental health and psycho-social-spiritual problems. Focusing on these practical issues can also help communities overcome the toxic isolation and disconnection so many people experience today that often leads to social and political divisiveness. And these actions are essential to reduce the community's contribution to the climate crisis and prepare for and adapt to its impacts.

This is why, even though it might be novel for people in the mental health and social service fields, RCCs need to make building supportive local physical/built, economic, and ecological conditions one of the five foundational focuses of their efforts to build universal capacity for mental wellness and transformational resilience and engage residents in climate solutions. All this work must be done in ways that ensure a just transition, which you will learn about throughout this chapter. As residents engage in these activities and see progress, new meaning, purpose, and healthy hope for the future will grow.

BUILD HEALTHY, SAFE, JUST, AND EQUITABLE CLIMATE-RESILIENT LOCAL PHYSICAL/BUILT CONDITIONS

The conditions of the places where people live, play, recreate, learn, and age greatly influence their capacity for mental wellness and transformational resilience, as well as their physical health.[5] The practices and policies found in many communities today, however, often promote just the opposite. There are numerous examples of transportation, housing, parks, and open spaces, and other systems that are intentionally designed to create isolation and disconnection, or oppress low-income or BIPOC residents. Not only can this lead to numerous types of mental health and psycho-social-spiritual problems, it can also produce profound distrust in government, big business, and many professional organizations.

Further, without explicit preventative mechanisms, efforts to slash local greenhouse gas emissions, regenerate ecosystems and biodiversity, and prepare for and adapt to the impacts of the climate emergency can set-in-stone existing, or increase the unsafe, unhealthy, unjust, and inequitable systems and produce widespread mental health and psycho-social-spiritual problems.

This must quickly change, and RCCs can lead the way by placing an explicit focus on creating safe, healthy, just, equitable, and climate-resilient physical/built conditions in their neighborhood and community.

Healthy Places by Design is one of the leading organizations involved with these issues. Although they acknowledge other areas should be addressed, they place a primary focus on three: transportation infrastructure, housing, and public spaces. Following their lead, I am going to focus on these areas here.[6]

Healthy, Safe, Just, and Equitable Climate-Resilient Transportation Infrastructure

Safe, accessible, affordable, and equitable transportation options, including walking, biking, buses, trains, and vehicles, are essential to connect people to places they need and want to go. However, in many industrialized nations, and the US in particular, transportation systems prioritize travel in personal vehicles that promote isolation and separation. When vehicles, trains, and planes run on gas, diesel, or kerosene, they also pollute neighborhoods, generate climate-damaging greenhouse gases, and essentially subsidize the fossil fuel industry. In addition, research has found that the type of transportation available to people can affect their mental health by diminishing their physical movement, keeping them isolated, and producing high stress due to long commutes.[7]

In addition, in many cities, major roads and highways dislocate and separate communities of color and low-income populations, resulting in a pattern of disrupted social networks, concentrated pollution, and difficulty in using safe, clean, low emission transportation options such as walking, biking, and public transportation.[8]

RCCs can address these issues by actively engaging local residents, governments, and businesses in rebuilding transportation systems, and constructing new ones, that establish equitable access for all ages and populations to safe and healthy zero-emissions public transportation as well as safe walking and biking routes. The systems should include accessory supports such as secure crosswalks for walking and reduced traffic speeds. The use of electric vehicles powered by clean renewable energy, recharging stations located in numerous neighborhoods, vehicle sharing, and other low- or no-emission approaches should also be top priorities.

All of these options should be designed with justice and equity as a centerpiece. This means everyone should benefit and the risks generated by the activities should spread equally throughout the community. They must also all be constructed using the cradle-to-cradle approach, which involves using ecologically regenerative designs, materials, processes, and practices, all powered by clean renewable energy (more about this in a moment). In addition, they should be located in areas and constructed in ways that can prevent serious harm from the impacts of a disrupted climate system and enable them to be rapidly rebuilt after a serious impact has occurred. Further, local residents should be trained, employed, and paid living wages to complete all of the work.

Healthy, Safe, Just, and Equitable Climate-Resilient Housing

Housing and mental wellness are closely related. Research has found that having poor housing undermines mental wellness. The UN World Health Organization (WHO), for example, found that living in housing with structural defects and poor maintenance is directly linked to greater psychological distress and poor development in both adults and children.[9] Conversely, living in safe, healthy, affordable, and stable housing enhances it.[10] Without significant prevention efforts, the availability of housing with these positive qualities will deteriorate in many communities as the impacts of the climate emergency unfold.

People who live in unsafe housing can often feel stressed, anxious, and depressed. The stress can lead to sleep problems that affect their mental wellness. Poor housing can also make it difficult to eat well. Mold, dampness, and polluted air quality can affect physical health, which circles back to affect mental health. The stress generated by poor housing can lead to relationship difficulties with significant others, family members, and friends. Relationship breakdowns, in turn, can lead to further housing problems.[11]

As Healthy Places by Design points out, the housing system in most communities is complex, and collaboration among many interests is needed to address the multiple goals of safety, health, affordability, equity, quality, stability, and cultural sensitivity. This is why the involvement of a broad and diverse RCC is essential.[12]

RCCs can address these concerns by working with local residents and public, private, and non-profit development organizations to refurbish existing and construct new climate-resilient housing. As much as possible, the focus should be on mixed-use development that promotes safety, health, and equity, provides easy access to healthy foods and places of employment, and enhances connections between neighbors.[13] Affordable housing should be integrated into every neighborhood in the community.

Harsher weather extremes generated by the climate emergency also underscore the importance of establishing policies and other mechanisms to help residents refurbish existing residents, and construct additional housing that provides good protection from major storms, extreme cold, heat waves, and other dangerous conditions. Shifting to a decentralized power grid by providing financial assistance and technical support to help residents install solar panels on homes, or creating community solar gardens that provide energy to groups of neighbors, can prevent power outages during disasters, reduce the costs of energy, and help residents slash their ecological footprint. In addition, as described below, numerous types of public spaces should be spread throughout neighborhoods.

Just like with transportation, the design, construction, and maintenance of housing should follow the cradle-to-cradle model, and be designed to withstand likely climate impacts. In addition, local residents should be trained, employed, and paid living wages to complete the work.

Healthy, Safe, Just, and Equitable Climate-Resilient Public Spaces

Public spaces such as parks, green spaces, libraries, community centers, playgrounds, dog parks, community gardens, greenways, waterfronts, sidewalks, public schoolyards, and public plazas play important roles in communities. One of the most significant is that their location, design, and how they are managed says a lot about who is valued and who it not, and whether health and wellness are more important than profit and power.

When public spaces are located, designed, and operated in ways that promote safe ongoing interactions between different cultural and socioeconomic groups, they provide residents with healthy places to meet, recreate, access nature, and increase their sense of belonging.[14] These opportunities help build the social connections that will be vital during the long climate crisis to promote mental wellness and transformational resilience. When public spaces are located or designed in ways that make them inaccessible to some people, or when they are allowed to become unsafe, run down, or polluted, they promote isolation, disconnection, and other unhealthy conditions.

RCCs can address these issues by engaging local residents, government agencies, and other organizations in planning, designing, and constructing healthy, safe and inclusive public spaces. The spaces should welcome diverse community members who live nearby, as well as those from other locations. Equity and inclusion should, from the start, drive location, design, and maintenance decisions. The spaces should be deliberately designed to promote physical and psychological safety and allow people to interact with others.

Designing public spaces that promote intergenerational engagement will also be important as these types of connections are a powerful way to connect different age groups, races, and cultures. For example, parks and playgrounds can be located next to senior centers.[15]

The design, construction, and maintenance of public spaces should be done equitably to prevent injustices such as the exclusion of BIPOC and low-income residents, and to prevent gentrification. As with housing, all the efforts should follow the cradle-to-cradle model. And again, local residents should be trained, employed, and paid living wages to complete this work.

THE NEED FOR COMMUNITY-LED SOLUTIONS

As with the other foundational areas involved with strengthening universal capacity for mental wellness and transformational resilience, entire communities must be involved in creating safe, healthy, just, and equitable climate-resilient local transportation, housing, and open spaces. Residents should be actively engaged and lead these efforts because the conditions directly affect their lives.[16]

"This work requires a collaborative approach," said Risa Wilkerson, Executive Director of Healthy Places by Design. "We have found that when you promote local capacity and leadership for collaboration, the work can build momentum for longer-term results." Wilkerson went on to tell me, "This requires that professionals take a step back and support local efforts.... Social connection is a virtuous cycle. It builds on itself and leads to move civic engagement."[17]

Examples of How RCCs Can Build Local Healthy, Safe, Just, and Equitable Climate-Resilient Physical/Built Conditions

Climate-Resilient Communities (CRC), which operates in the southern peninsula of the San Francisco Bay area, builds alliances between local residents, schools, local governments, and community-based organizations to help under-resourced communities build physical resilience from climate-related impacts such as sea level rise and economic instability. CRC's climate-based Adaptation program works with and manages the North Fair Oaks Climate Ready Team and the East Palo Alto Climate Change Community Team that respond to community priorities by establishing programs to help them prepare for and adapt to sea level rise and other climate impacts. Executive Director Violet Wulf-Saena told me that even when government funding exists to prepare homes for climate impacts, such as the State of California now provides, most low-income households don't know about it, don't know how to apply, or find the application process too complicated. So, CRC created the Resilient Home program that helps families in the East Palo Alto and Belle Haven areas access funds to install new roofing, solar panels, and in other ways prepare for climate impacts.

"My experience has been that solutions identified by communities actually do work in protecting people and helping them survive," said Wulf-Saena. "It is not what government prioritizes, it is what communities prioritize that is key."

The Alliance for Community Transit-Los Angeles (ACR-LA) is a broad-based coalition of 37 organizations that is building a grassroots movement for more equitable public transportation systems. In partnership with the Community Power Collective and Koreatown Immigrant Workers Alliance, ACR-LA is growing a movement that empowers low-income residents to shape policies and funding decisions. This is accomplished by organizing parents and residents in East LA and Koreatown and helping them develop skills to become effective leaders and spokespeople in transit justice campaigns.

The New York City Learning Collaborative for Multifamily Affordable Housing Resilience was launched as part of the city's Hurricane Sandy Recovery and Rebuilding Program after about 20 percent of the city's public housing stock was flooded by the event in 2012. The interdisciplinary Collaborative was formed to help member organizations improve the resiliency of their affordable housing properties and safeguard them from future disasters. The Collaborative has served approximately 14,500 low- and moderate-income households so far and continues to strengthen disaster preparedness skills, improve the physical resilience of their properties and work collaboratively to identify best practices for resilience in the multifamily affordable housing field.[18]

RCCs can use these initiatives as examples to create their own unique approaches to creating supportive local physical/built conditions.

Other Ways RCCs Can Build Safe, Healthy, Just and Equitable Local Climate-Resilient Physical/Built Conditions

- *Model Healthy, Safe, Just, and Equitable Physical/Built Conditions during RCC Meetings and Events*: RCC members can demonstrate their commitment to creating supportive local physical/built conditions by, for example, urging members to use zero or low emission transportation options to attend meetings, and whenever possible using healthy and safe facilities powered by clean renewable energy for events. (To show people how poor facilities can affect wellness, RCCs can also hold a meeting in locations that are unhealthy or unsafe and afterwards ask participants what they experienced).

- *Organize Physical/Built Resilience Innovation Teams*: RCCs can organize Resilience Innovation Teams that develop strategies to rebuild existing and construct new healthy, safe, just equitable, and climate-resilient transportation, housing, and public spaces. When doing so, they can help residents understand how the activities enhance their capacity for mental wellness and transformational resilience and reduce their contribution to the climate emergency. Some examples of what the innovation teams can engage in include:

  - *Form Walking- and Bicycle-Friendly Districts*: In 2019, 62 percent of the residents in Copenhagen, Denmark, used a bike to travel to work or school. Residents biked a total of 894,000 miles every day. More than $45 (US) had been invested per capita in bicycle infrastructure.[19] Many other cities are also establishing walking- and bicycle-friendly districts. RCCs can use the Bicycle Friendly Community Program, developed by the League of American Bicyclists, to encourage cyclists and show that people on bikes were good for small businesses. They can also use the approach developed by Walker Friendly Communities to establish walker- and pedestrian-friendly neighborhoods.[20]

  - *Organize Car-Free Days*: Cities in many nations worldwide now participate on global Car-Free day held on or around September 22 every year. RCCs can join the World Car-free Network to establish their own car-free days.[21]

  - *Create Undrivers Licenses*: Residents of Seattle's Ballard neighborhood, working with the organization Sustainable Ballard, started issuing official-looking "undriver licenses" to residents who pledged to use alternative transportation. RCCs can replicate this type of undrivers license, which entitles the bearer free access to board the shufflebus, a foot-powered, Fred Flintstone type vehicle that gets observers thinking about what they can do to reduce their carbon footprint.[22]

  - *Turn Alleys into Gathering Places*: RCCs can use the "More Awesome Now" program in Vancouver, Canada as an example to turns alleys (or laneways as they are called in Canada) that were formerly dark forbidding places into vibrant accessible places that allow people to meet, network, exercise, and play together. Some of the alleys can stretch for blocks and include basket-ball courts, cafes, and foosball tables, and other things that facilitate social engagement.[23]

○ *Install Community Solar Gardens*: Solar gardens are being installed in many locations around the world. They create accessible access to clean renewable energy for groups of people that don't own a home, don't have good solar access, or can't afford to install a system on their own. They also reduce greenhouse gas emissions and offer residents a great learning opportunity. When they are specifically designed for BIPOC and low-income residents they also contribute to a just transition away from fossil fuels. RCCs can find information about community solar gardens from the Solar Energy Industries Association and many other resources.[24]

○ *Refurbish Local Parks and Create New Ones*: Worn-out equipment in parks and playgrounds can deter its use. RCCs can use the guide created by the Center for Urban Pedagogy to press for changes that make parks and play areas more useable and attractive.[25] When people use healthy attractive parks, their capacity for mental wellness and resilience improves, and many are likely to become more committed to conserving and restoring nature.

These ideas are offered merely to demonstrate that there are many ways RCCs can pursue building supportive local physical/built conditions. RCCs should get creative and explore many possibilities that make sense in their community.

BUILD HEALTHY, SAFE, JUST, AND EQUITABLE CLIMATE-RESILIENT LOCAL ECONOMIC CONDITIONS

A robust local economy is a foundation of a resilient community. However, high-tech automation has eliminated thousands of jobs, globalization has shifted others to low-income nations, and other factors have caused many communities to struggle to secure living-wage jobs. In addition, BIPOC residents are often discriminated against in business development and job creation. The impacts of the long climate-ecosystem-biodiversity mega-emergency will often intensify these struggles and create altogether new ones. Without effective training, technical assistance, and transitional funding, the need to eliminate the local use of fossil fuels, dramatically slash greenhouse gas emissions, regenerate ecological systems, and prepare for and adapt to climate impacts are also likely to create financial and other impacts on local businesses, jobs, and wages.

To address these challenges, RCCs can craft strategies to transform their local economies into just and equitable climate-resilient zero-carbon ecologically regenerative systems. Community-based regeneration, not corporate or government driven growth strategies, must form the basis of the new approach. Protecting and regenerating the climate and ecological systems must always take priority over the generation of profits and wealth. RCCs can support this transition by paying careful attention to the core functions of their local economy to support locally owned and operated businesses that generate living-wage jobs for residents with all types of background and skills, not just those trained in high-tech or who have college degrees.

Even though huge corporations employ many people, it is small, locally owned businesses that have the most positive economic impact on communities. Small, locally owned businesses typically generate higher incomes for people in a community than large, non-local firms, which can depress local wages and economies.[26] Small locally owned businesses also keep a larger share of their economic output within the community than businesses with outside ownership, and invest it in local schools, public safety, roads, parks, affordable housing, and other essential public services.

One of the biggest challenges facing communities today, however, is how to assist local entrepreneurs to create new local businesses and sustain them during difficult times. Access to capital is often a major constraint. Another is to find ways to avoid the harmful effects that massive corporations like Amazon and big box stores like Walmart can have on local businesses and living-wage jobs.

In addition to supporting the start-up of locally owned businesses, RCCs will need to develop strategies to help local firms shift away from fossil fuels and slash the greenhouse gas emissions and ecological impacts produced throughout their entire value chains, from resource extraction all the way through the production, sales, use, and disposal of their goods. This will require a transition to a cradle-to-cradle economic model.

RCCS CAN HELP LOCAL BUSINESSES QUICKLY TRANSITION TO A CRADLE-TO-CRADLE ECONOMIC SYSTEM

The industrial revolution was initially powered by coal and eventually by petroleum and methane (natural gas) as well. The increased energy available to humans led to all types of technological innovations that made life easier and dramatically increased life expectancy. From the start, the burning of fossil fuels added greenhouse gas emissions to the earth's climate and many of the new technologies degraded ecological systems and harmed biodiversity. However, their scale was small compared with the size of the earth's resources, the number of people using them was petite, and the benefits to humans were huge, so few people were concerned about the impacts.

Today, the use of fossil fuels, ever-expanding technologies, and the population growth and immense material consumption of industrial nations have produced a degenerative linear "take it-make it-waste it" economic system that threatens all life on earth. Massive amounts of raw materials, water, and fossil fuels are extracted from the earth, processed, and used to produce vast quantities of goods for mass consumption. The entire value chain is primarily powered by fossil fuels and generates gigantic amounts of climate-damaging greenhouse gas emissions, toxic substances, solid waste, and ecological damage. Just like the initial beneficiaries of the industrial revolution, most people today give little thought to how the economic system is degrading the earth's ecological systems and structures that make their lives possible, or how the corporations that control the system use science and psychology to deliberately addict people to products that can produce a vast array of mental health and psycho-social-spiritual problems.

The industrial revolution led to an entirely new economic system. It is now time once again to fundamentally revamp the economy by establishing a regenerative "cradle-to-cradle" system. This is a circular framework that, in its purest form, produces goods made exclusively of sustainably extracted and manufactured materials and non-toxic substances and uses regenerative processes throughout the value chain. At the end of their useful life, the products are disassembled and recycled and used as materials for new products, or safely returned to the soil as non-contaminating biological nutrients. The entire process should produce little to no waste or greenhouse gases, and be powered by solar, wind, or other forms of clean renewable energy.[27] As much as possible, a transition to regional and local value chains will also be important.[28] Products and processes that can knowingly produce psychological, emotional, and spiritual distress should be prohibited.

To make these changes, RCCs can support local firms that produce goods residents actually need and can continually use (rather than products used once or twice and then discarded), and businesses that offer important non-resource intensive services for residents. In addition, RCCs can support local solar, wind, and other businesses producing clean renewable energy, and those in the energy and water efficiency, green building, agroecological farming (also called carbon farming), non-toxic 100 percent recyclable packaging, battery-powered vehicle manufacturing, and numerous other regenerative sectors.

Shifting to a safe and healthy regenerative cradle-to-cradle economic system must also be done in ways that prepares local businesses and their value chains to withstand the forceful impacts of a disrupted climate system. This can involve, for instance, (re)locating them in areas that are relatively safe from wildfires, floods, and other extreme events. As with residential buildings, their facilities must also be designed and constructed to prevent damage from destructive weather events. Good insulation and other forms of weatherization, as well as air cooling systems and other mechanisms, will be important to protect them from extreme cold and heat events. These changes must be completed in ways to ensure that everyone benefits equally and BIPOC residents, low-income, and other marginalized groups are not unjustly impacted.

RCCS CAN HELP INDIVIDUALS AND HOUSEHOLDS CUT THEIR ECOLOGICAL FOOTPRINTS

RCCs can also assist individuals and households to use these principles and practices to slash their ecological footprints. In addition to reducing the community's impacts on the environment, this will help local businesses reduce their ecological footprint by creating demand for ecologically regenerative goods and services.

One focus should be to establish technical assistance and funding programs to help residents improve the energy efficiency of their homes. As discussed, another emphasis should be to help all homes with good solar access install solar panels to generate their own electricity. Residents who do not own homes and dwellings without good solar access can join a community solar garden.[29]

Eliminating food waste, eating lower in the food chain—in particular reducing the consumption of meat produced by industrial fossil fuel-dependent agricultural processes—buying less material intensive stuff, and walking and biking more often are just a few of the multitudes of other ways individuals and households can reduce their ecological footprints. RCCs can find numerous resources on the Internet to guide their efforts to help residents reduce their ecological footprints.

As they engage in this work, RCCs should always keep in mind that, as important as they are, changes by individual, households, and local businesses alone cannot reduce the climate crisis to manageable levels. The mega-emergency is caused by faulty energy and economic systems, structures, and policies. These systemic problems make it very difficult for many businesses, households, and individuals to significantly reduce their ecological footprints on their own. For this reasons, as I will discuss in a moment, RCCs will need to support residents and organizations to advocate for systemic changes.

The collective resolve that can result when local businesses and residents come together to focus on these goals will often motivate people to become entrepreneurs and create exciting new business opportunities that generate living-wage jobs, lift many out of poverty, and give community members a powerful new sense of meaning, purpose, and healthy hope for the future.

Examples of How RCCs Can Help Build Healthy, Safe, Just, and Equitable Climate-Resilient Local Economic Conditions

- *Greensburg Kansas Built Back Green after a Record Tornado*: On the night of May 4, 2007, Greensburg, Kansas, was hit by an EF-5 tornado that had wind speeds of more than 200 mph. The tornado killed more than ten people and destroyed or severely damaged 90 percent of the community. Like many other small farming towns, prior to that day Greenburg was declining but remained a close-knit community with a population of about 1,400. After discussions among survivors to determine their community's future, they decided to become the greenest little town in the US. A city council resolution required that all large public buildings in Greensburg with a footprint larger than 4,000 square feet must meet the LEED platinum standards of the US Green Building Council and utilize renewable energy sources. The new City Hall, hospital, and K-12 school were all built to LEED platinum standards. Private businesses joined in and rebuilt to high green standards. Today, the city boasts of having the most LEED Certified buildings per capital in the world. Some people consider the recovery a mixed success, but most of their struggles are related to issues many other small towns face today. The green recovery remains a key factor in building hope and bringing the town back from near destruction.[30]

- *Spartanburg South Carolina Implements Model Economic Revitalization and Environmental Justice Project*: Residents of Spartanburg, working through the community-based non-profit ReGenesis, partnered with local and federal agencies, academia, private companies, and other non-profits to successfully clean up and revitalize the blighted and struggling Arkwright and Forest Park communities. The initiative now stands as an international model of environmental justice success. Two Superfund sites and six Brownfield sites that contributed to higher-than-normal incidents of disease and death among local residents were cleaned up. This led to extensive redevelopment of the blighted areas including the creation of new housing and parks, health clinics, improved transportation access, better emergency preparedness, and the elimination of food deserts. New businesses and employment opportunities emerged as public health increased and crime and illegal activities declined, which has improved the quality of life and safety of residents. Harold Mitchell, Executive Director of ReGenesis, said the project, "...explains the significant additional benefits that have improved community infrastructure, built safer neighborhoods, and created community empowerment through education, job training, and job creation."[31]

  RCCs can use the examples provided by Greensburg and Spartanburg to craft their own innovative strategies to build local just and equitable climate-resilient economic systems that improve health, safety, job, and ecological conditions.

Other Ways RCCs Can Build Healthy, Safe, Just, and Equitable Climate-Resilient Local Economic Conditions

- *Model Regenerative Economic Conditions During RCC Meetings and Events*: RCCs can show their commitment to building a just and equitable climate-resilient local economy by purchasing goods and services for events from local owned and operated companies that pay their employees living wages, even if they are more expensive than huge chain stores can provide. They can also utilize products that are generated with cradle-to-cradle materials, processes, and practices throughout their value chain and have a tiny ecological footprint.

- *Organize a Regenerative Economy Resilience Innovation Team*: RCCs can strengthen local economic conditions and create living-wage jobs by forming a Resilience Innovation Team composed of local residents and public, private, and non-profit economic development, education, job training, and other organizations. The teams should jointly plan and implement actions that spur the growth of locally owned and operated small businesses that use cradle-to-cradle practices and produce ecologically regenerative goods and services. As they do so, the capacity for mental wellness and transformational resilience of everyone involved will be enhanced. Here are examples of actions that RCCs can consider:

  ○ *Adopt a Community Bill of Rights*: To ensure a just transition to a socially, economically, and ecologically healthy and equitable restorative economy, RCCs can push for the adoption of a local Community Bill of Rights (CBR). A CBR moves decision-making away from the top-down centralized government and corporate decision-making that dominates many communities to one that empowers residents to make just and equitable decisions on issues that affect their community and their lives. The issues that can be included in the CBR are environmental rights, including the right to clean air and water, a livable climate, and safety rights, workers-rights, indigenous sovereignty, the rights of nature, and more.[32]

  ○ *Follow the Institute for Local-Self-Reliance's (ILSR) 12 Recommendations*: The ILSR issued a report in January 2022, describing 12 ideas RCCs can use to make small business development the driving force in their local economic development strategies. They include: (1) Build a strong infrastructure to cultivate, grow, and support small businesses; (2) Close the racial entrepreneurial gap; (3) Develop grocery stores in underdeveloped communities; (4) Cultivate small-scale manufacturing and local and regional supply chains; (5) Improve small business procurement policies and practices; (6) Buy commercial property and place it in a community land trust; (7) Create local delivery services; (8) Promote small businesses and shopping small; (9) Capitalize a publicly owned bank; (10) Support employee business ownership; (11) Improve broadband access for small businesses; and (12) Invest in commercial district improvements that help small businesses. An RCC's Regenerative Economy Resilience Innovation Team should investigate how these recommendations can be applied in their community.[33]

  ○ *Educate and Train the Adult Workforce*: Workforce development and job readiness programs will need to focus on enhancing the knowledge, skills, and capacities of working-age people to engage in cradle-to-cradle business development and jobs. Education should not train people for jobs that automation is likely to soon eliminate. Instead, it should emphasize learning how to be creative and develop advanced skills such as critical thinking, problem-solving, social skills, leadership, and teamwork because these are attributes new technologies cannot replace. Special attention should be given to individuals and groups with high risk of joblessness such as BIPOC and low-income populations, school dropouts, and formerly incarcerated community members.[34]

○   *Form Perpetual Purpose Trusts*: This is a new type of corporate structure that confers shares in a company not to individual owners but to a mission. Under this structure, the company works toward upholding principles, not maximizing profits. This means profits say in the business and company executives will be committed to fair compensation and robust benefits. Five states in the US have trust laws that allow Perpetual Purpose Trusts to be established: Oregon, Delaware, New Hampshire, Wyoming, and Maine. RCCs in these states can promote the use of this corporate structure, and those in other states and nations can join with other organizations and businesses to establish a similar approach.[35]

○   *Organize Economic Regeneration Consulting Services*: BRING is a non-profit organization in Springfield, Oregon, that offers a wide range of services that help local businesses shift to a cradle-to-cradle economic model.[36] Their Rethink program provides free hands-on advice to local firms on how to reduce waste, recycle more, and use electricity, water, and materials efficiently. Businesses that meet certain benchmarks receive a Rethink Recognition Award and publicity for their efforts. BRING's consulting services offer fee-based greenhouse gas inventorying, waste studies, and other technical services to local firms. Their Construction Materials Recovery and Reuse Program promotes sustainability in the local building community. RCCs can work with local non-profits to establish similar types of services.

○   *Provide Innovative New Sources of Capital*: Access to capital is often a major barrier to starting a business. In Seattle, some business owners have bypassed traditional lenders and used crowdfunding to bankrolling aspiring firms. As part of Washington state's Fund Local Program, dozens of businesses turned to a hybrid form of crowdfunding developed by Community Sources Capital for the funds to open or expand their operations.[37] RCCs should consider establishing their own unique sources of local capital.

○   *Grow Community Farms*: Fresh vegetables provide both economic and health benefits for everyone, especially BIPOC and low-income residents who live in food deserts. To ensure that residents have healthy foods, RCCs can support food systems grounded in justice and equity by mirroring the approach developed by Soul Fire Farm, an Afro-Indigenous centered community farm located in New York "committed to uprooting racism and seeding sovereignty in the food system." The farm trains "the next generation of activist-farmers and strengthening the movements for food sovereignty and community self-determination." Their food sovereignty programs "reach over 160,000 people each year, including farmer training for Black and Brown growers, reparations and land return initiatives for northeast farmers, food justice workshops for urban youth, home gardens for city dwellers living under food apartheid, doorstep harvest delivery for food insecure households, and systems and policy education for public decision-makers."[38] RCCs can find innovative ways to replicate this type of community farm in their area.

•   *Create Menus to Help Households Reduce Their Carbon Footprint*: Sustainable Ballard[39] and its sister organization, Groundswell Northwest,[40] an all-volunteer organization in Seattle, Washington created a menu of actions households can take to reduce their carbon footprint. Each action was assigned a specific number of points. If a household could reach a specific total, it was awarded a Green Household yard sign. Many people engaged.[41] RCCs can use a similar approach to help households reduce their ecological footprint.

Again, these examples are offered merely to demonstrate that there are many ways RCCs can engage residents in building supportive local economic conditions. RCC members should innovate and develop strategies that resonate with community members.

Create Local Healthy, Safe, Just, and Equitable Climate-Resilient Ecological Conditions

This book has documented how a disrupted climate system generates significant individual, community, and societal distresses and traumas. The health of local air and water and vitality of ecological systems and biodiversity also affects local mental health and psycho-social-spiritual well-being.

A study completed in the UK, for instance, found that exposure to even small levels of air pollution was linked to increased mental health problems.[42] Research also identified a link between certain air pollutants and mental health problems such as depression, dementia, anxiety and suicide. The risk of poor health outcomes was found to be particularly high among young people living in urban areas, with children being three to four times more likely to have depression at age 18 if they have been exposed to polluted air at age 12.[43] Another study found a link between high traffic-related air pollution and childhood anxiety levels.[44] Research in Toronto, Canada, validated this by finding that increases in ozone, nitrogen dioxide, and other pollutants were all associated with increased visits to the hospital emergency room, sometimes up to five days after the initial exposure.[45]

Separation from nature can also produce mental health problems. One study found that people living more than two thirds of a mile (one kilometer) away from a green space have a nearly 50 percent higher likelihood of experiencing severe stress than those living less than 300 yards (roughly 300 meters) from a green space. Researchers in the Netherlands found that people living in residential areas with the least green spaces had a 44 percent higher rate of diagnosed anxiety disorders than people who lived in the greenest residential areas.[46]

In contrast, research found that people report less mental distress and higher life satisfaction when they live in areas dominated by greenery. Having access to even small green spaces can reduce symptoms of depression for people who live near them, especially in low-income neighborhoods.[47] Evidence also suggests that physical activity in green spaces has stronger mental health benefits than physical activity in non-green spaces.[48]

Efforts to regenerate local ecological systems will help communities in other ways as well. For example, healthier soils are rich in organic matter and microbial activity, which allows them to sequester more carbon, absorb more water to prevent erosion and topsoil loss during flooding, and improve crop yields.

At the same time, ecological protection and regenerative initiatives can help communities conserve the open spaces they value, protect clean air and water, and enhance human health.[49] Planting trees throughout the community, for example, provides shade that cools off areas during heat waves, offers habitat for birds and other forms of biodiversity, increases local carbon sequestration, and creates more opportunities for people to connect with nature. Cleaning up and restoring local waterways can reduce the risk of damaging floods, enhance habitat for riparian and aquatic species, and provide residents with safe places to swim, fish, and recreate. All of these benefits can help strengthen local economies and build healthy hope for the future.

Examples of How RCCs Can Build Healthy, Safe, Just, and Equitable Climate-Resilient Local Ecological Conditions

- *Taomi Rebuilds as an Eco-Village*: The small rural village of Taomi, located in the mountains of central Taiwan, has experienced an incredible community-led ecological transformation that also enhanced the local economy. For years, the town had been economically distressed and young people left because they saw no future. Then, in 1999, a major earthquake devastated the community. Many people lost their lives, and almost half of the houses in the village and numerous other structures were destroyed. After the devastation, Liao Chia-chan, the visionary president of the community's New Homeland Foundation, engaged the community in mapping its assets. With the assistance of biologists, they discovered that Taomi was home to 23 of the 29 species of frogs found in Taiwan. There were also abundant dragonflies, butterflies, fireflies, and birds. Community leaders decided to build on these assets by turning Taomi into an eco-village. Residents worked to restore the natural environment. They removed concrete walls that lined the river. They built ponds to reduce flooding and attract wildlife. Volunteers of all ages reforested the area with native plants and trees. Forty-five local residents were certified as naturalists to lead tours for visitors. Residents also established 32 bed and breakfasts to house visitors. Others learned how to use local ingredients to make meals for restaurants they established. Still others started organic gardens to grow food for the restaurants and feed themselves. Some of the gardens are cultivated by young students and elders with dementia. Taomi has become a center for the arts as well, with sculptures and murals of frogs, caterpillars, butterflies, and other environmental themes now common. Young people are returning for the jobs and wonderful lifestyle Taomi now offers, which in 2021 was visited by a half-million tourists.[50]

- *Residents and Faith Leaders in Louisiana Are Playing an Active Role in Restoring the Coastline*: Every day Helen Rose engages community leaders in vulnerable areas like Plaquemines Parish, south of New Orleans, in coastal restoration. For decades, the land in their area has been disappearing at alarming rates due to rising sea levels and the channelization of the Mississippi River. Rose does most of her work, however, with faith leaders in greater New Orleans who care about environmental issues, "but lacked opportunities to engage in ways that felt meaningful." During field trips to freshwater diversion sites, bayou boat rides, and flights over the coast, faith leaders can see firsthand the impact of coastal land loss. But they also see the potential of large-scale restoration projects that can rebuild the coast and protect their communities and culture. "For faith leaders, there's something very appealing about the fact that we are building land," said Rose. "Faith communities often bear the brunt of taking care of people after natural disasters. There's an appetite to be part of the solution that prevents or addresses the causes of natural disasters."[51]

RCCs can use the examples offered by both communities to engage residents in restoring ecological systems in ways that enhance the local economy and culture.

Other Ways RCCs Can Build Healthy, Safe, Just, and Equitable Climate-Resilient Local Ecological Conditions

- *Model Ecologically Regenerative Practices During RCC Meetings and Events*: RCCs can demonstrate their commitment to regenerating both local and global ecological systems by using 100 percent recycled paper, non-toxic writing instruments, cups and dishes that can be reused, and other ecologically sound materials at all meetings and events. When they are available, the RCC can hold events in facilities powered by solar energy or other clean renewable sources of energy. RCC members can also calculate their own personal and household ecological footprints and share how they are reducing them with others. And, they can calculate and continually reduce the ecological footprints of events it holds and tell residents about it.

- *Organize Local Ecological Regeneration Innovation Teams*: The teams can actively engage residents, as well as many types of civic, non-profit, private, and public organizations, in crafting and implementing strategies that help local organizations eliminate pollution and other forms of ecological harm. Like the two examples above, the Innovation Teams can also engage residents in regenerating local forests, grasslands, waterways, wetlands, and biodiversity throughout their community. Here are some examples of what the Innovation Team can do:

  ○ *Organize Habitat Regeneration Teams*: Every year Save the Bay, an NGO in the San Francisco area, engages thousands of volunteers to plant upward of 20,000 native plants across the Bay Area to restore wetland transition zone habitat for wildlife. The number of plants and species that have been planted at a restoration site, the pounds of invasive species that have been removed, and other benefits have been enormous.[52] RCCs can follow this approach and engage volunteers of all ages in restoring local ecological systems and species. They can also engage K-12 schools, higher education institutions, civic organizations like the YMCA and Rotary, and many other groups and institutions in ongoing ecological regeneration efforts.

  ○ *Form Local Watershed Councils*: When watersheds (river basins) have multiple land owners, the actions of any of them, as well as the many users, can undermine the health of vegetation, soils, riparian areas, ground and surface water, and avian, terrestrial, and aquatic species. Accordingly, all land owners and managers, as well as regular users, must be engaged in efforts to conserve and restore a basin. RCCs can organize Watershed Councils to achieve this. These are voluntary, community-based, non-regulatory groups that come together on a regular basis to analyze the health of their watershed and plan and implement projects to conserve and restore them. Most watershed councils work with government agencies and private landowners, and many, but not all, have paid staff. In the mid-1990s, an organization I directed, the Pacific Rivers Council, helped establish the watershed council program in Oregon that grew to become a core element of the State of Oregon Watershed Enhancement Board. There are now over 40 watershed councils that cover most of the large basins in the state. Oregon is one of the few states with this type of community-based model for conserving and restoring land

and water "ridgetop-to-ridgetop."[53] RCCs can use this model to establish their own approach to collaborative watershed regeneration. They can also advocate for state/provincial and national policies to authorize, support, and fund these types of initiative.[54]

○ *Organize Neighborhood Tree Planting and Park Development Events*: Hundreds of residents in Seattle Ballard Neighborhood, organized block by block, have planted 1,200 street trees in one day. Its sister organization Groundswell Northwest has created 20 parks during the past 20 years, including areas reforested with native plants and creating a salmon estuary. RCCs can engage the Neighborhood Resilience Hubs they help organize and many other neighborhood groups in similar activities.

○ *Promote Rewilding*: Rewilding restores an area to its original uncultivated condition. It shifts management away from the centuries-long practices aimed at providing only for human needs and incorporates indigenous practices with new landscape designs to allow wildness to reclaim an area. Many rewilding efforts take place in wild areas and include, for example, reintroducing biodiversity high up in the food chain to stabilize other species. The reintroduction of wolves in Yellowstone National Park in 1995 is an example. But cities ranging from New York to Tokyo are beginning to rewild as well by reintroducing native species, creating parks in empty lots, and allowing nature to reclaim open spaces. RCCs can connect with the Global Rewilding Alliance and other organizations for information about how they can engage in wilding.[55]

As before, these ideas are offered merely to spur the creativity of RCC members. There are many other ways the coalition can engage community members in protecting and regenerating local ecological systems. The key is to keep thinking outside-the-box.

SUPPORTING RESIDENTS INVOLVED WITH ACTIVISM

Residents engaged in creating supportive physical/built, economic, and ecological conditions will often become motivated to advocate for new practices and policies. Little meaningful change occurs without strong persistent advocacy. But the advocacy should focus as much on community-based changes as it does on new state/provincial, national, and global policies because a growing body of research has found that local initiatives can make a difference.[56] Not only can changes in local conditions help reduce a community's greenhouse gases, regenerate ecological systems and biodiversity, and create new businesses and jobs, they can build the collective efficacy needed to produce bottom-up pressure for change at the state/provincial, national, and international levels.

Effective advocacy involves several important ingredients. One is that all new proposals or policies that activists push for should be thoroughly researched, and residents should be asked for their input to ensure it meets their needs. Media campaigns are also essential to generate sufficient pressure on business executives and elected officials to adopt a new practice or policy, and the campaigns often need to begin long before the specifics of new policy proposals are made public.

At the same time, advocates should be prepared for opposition—even from family, friends, and neighbors—when they push for anything that challenges the status quo. They need to know going in there is going to be disapproval, conflict, and even spectacle. The opposition typically starts with dismissal or ridicule that can leave advocates feeling ignored. However, when they begin to show even small signs of success, strong resistance can emerge. For example, people might claim it is impossible and harmful to eliminate fossil fuels. Or, they could attack the formation of an RCC as "too big a lift" or "not evidence-based" or use much harsher language to condemn an idea.[57] This is to be expected. Even those you think will be on your side can end up opposing change if it challenges their mental frame, norms, or in some way threatens their lifestyle. Sometimes the most vocal opponents are people with little to no previous experience in the issues being challenged. They often get engaged because they are angry at the world, the proposed changes threaten their religious, economic, or political ideologies, or they want to feel part of a cohort. Strong opposition can also occur from people you previously thought would support the change. This can occur, for example, when colleagues fear their job or entire profession might be threatened, or the changes seem to require a good deal of extra work or money. Advocates should be prepared for all of this.

Also, remember that some residents will find advocacy uncomfortable, especially if conflict or confrontation are involved. This will limit the number of people who are willing to be involved. Creating change takes time, and before they achieve success, the people who choose to become activists are likely to experience defeat and frustration. Even when they are successful, advocates can sometimes become disillusioned after they realize their achievements did little to address the global climate crisis. For example, even when walking and biking become a dominant form of transportation in a community, global carbon emissions might still rise, causing people to question the value of their efforts.

It will therefore be vital for RCCs to help people involved with advocacy learn and continually practice both Presencing and Purposing resilience skills because they will help them calm their body, mind, and emotions as they engage in the work, and use setbacks as catalysts to find new meaning, purpose, and healthy hope. Activists will also need to devote time to develop the camaraderie and trust needed among their group to ensure that they support each other in stressful times and avoid "eating their young." Using the principles and methods involved with finding healthy hope discussed in Chapter 3 will be very important as well.

Above all, advocates should remember that to some people any call for major change often seems unnecessary or extreme. But when positive changes occur new approaches often suddenly appear reasonable, long overdue, and welcomed. If advocates continually support each other, keep innovating, and remain relentless, history shows *they can succeed!*

A JUST TRANSITION IS ESSENTIAL

All of the work described in this chapter must be done in ways that ensure a "just transition." This term acknowledges three realities. First, that both the impacts of, and responses to, the climate mega-emergency will often generate unavoidable social, economic, and ecological impacts. Second, without explicit strategies and policies to prevent them, those changes will often unduly impact BIPOC and low-income residents and communities throughout industrialized nations and worldwide. Third, as different economic sectors, governments, and communities decide how to respond to the challenges, they have an ethical and moral responsibility to ensure an equitable distribution of both the benefits and downsides associated with the choices they make.

Just transition initiatives must include three ingredients[58]. The first is the active *participation* of affected communities in planning and advancing solutions. The second is the *anticipation* of negative impacts through impact assessments that help foresee and address harmful consequences. The third is significant ongoing *support* through targeted financial programs and capacity building that prioritizes the vulnerable populations and communities.

In other words, just as no one should be left behind when building the capacity for mental wellness and transformational resilience, a just transition requires that no one should be left behind in the shift away from today's ecologically degenerative linear economic system to a circular regenerative approach. This means the transition must recognize and address the historic harm done to BIPOC and low-income residents. It also means practices and policies must be adopted to prevent unjust and unequal impacts from actions that reduce greenhouse gas emissions and prepare for and adapt to climate impacts. In addition, it means every community, neighborhood, and population—not just wealthier people living in safer locations—must benefit equally from the transition to ecologically regenerative climate-resilient systems.

These changes require that decisions about how and where to refurbish existing and construct new supportive physical/built, economic, and ecological conditions must be made with the active involvement of community members—especially BIPOC and low-income residents—not government agencies or corporate interests on their own because the decisions about what occurs will affect their lives. As they have throughout history, women can play a very important leadership role in a just transition.[59]

Jacqui Patterson, founder and executive director of the Chisholm Legacy Project succinctly summarized the need for a just transition when she told me, "This is vital in a time of persistent racism. Even people who have the best intentions, who think they are not racist, often don't recognize the racism embedded in decisions they make that affect the community."[60] Indeed, a just transition is essential to build safe, healthy, just, and equitable climate-resilient local conditions.

A CHECKLIST

The checklist provided at the end of this chapter is offered as a way for RCCs to ensure they have covered the important elements involved with building healthy, safe, just, and equitable climate-resilient local physical/built, economic, and ecological conditions.

Keep in mind that the social connections residents make with others as they engage in these activities will be as important as any specific external physical or policy changes that are achieved. The more people develop relationships with others, the greater the likelihood they will be able to feel good and function well during the long climate emergency. This can also motivate them to become interested in other ways they can enhance their mental wellness and resilience. Engaging in specific practices to accomplish this is the focus of the next chapter.

CHECKLIST

For ensuring a just transition by creating safe, healthy, just, and equitable climate-resilient local physical/built, economic, and ecological conditions.

	Yes	No	Comments
Did the RCC develop and implement strategies to build safe, healthy, just, and equitable climate-resilient local transportation systems?			
Did the RCC develop and implement strategies to build safe, healthy, just, and equitable climate-resilient housing?			
Did the RCC develop and implement strategies to build safe, healthy, just, and equitable climate-resilient public spaces?			
Did the RCC develop and implement strategies to support local entrepreneurs to maintain existing and create new locally owned businesses that use cradle-to-cradle practices and provide living-wage jobs?			
Did the RCC develop and implement strategies to help local businesses eliminate ecological impacts throughout the value chain of their products and services?			
Did the RCC develop and implement safe, healthy, just and equitable climate-resilient strategies to support conserve and regenerative local ecosystems and biodiversity?			
Has the RCC taken steps to support activists that decide to become involved with pushing for new practices, regulations, and policies?			
Has the RCC taken explicit steps to ensure that all its efforts to create supportive local physical/built, economic, and ecological conditions are done in ways that ensure a just transition?			

NOTES

1   Living Cully: https://www.livingcully.org/; and Enelow N. and Hesselgrave T. (2015). *Verde and Living Cully: A Venture in Placemaking.* Ecotrust and Economics for Equity and Environmental Network. Obtained at: https://ecodistricts.org/information-exchange/verde-living-cully-venture-placemaking/
2   Refresh Appalachia: https://coalfield-development.org/refresh-appalachia/; and Reclaiming Appalachia Coalition: https://reclaimingappalachia.org/
3   Pinderhughes H. et al. (2015). *Adverse Community Experiences and Resilience: A Framework for Addressing and Preventing Community Trauma.* The Prevention Institute. Obtained at: https://www.prevention-institute.org/publications/adverse-community-experiences-and-resilience-framework-addressing-and-preventing
4   Wilson H. and Finch D. (April 16, 2021). Unemployment and mental health. *The Health Foundation UK.* Obtained at: https://www.health.org.uk/publications/long-reads/unemployment-and-mental-health; and Rooney K. (Jan 28, 2021). This is why mental health should be a political priority. *World Economic Forum.* Obtained at: https://www.weforum.org/agenda/2021/01/poverty-mental-health-covid-intervention/
5   See for example: Suarez G. et al. (April 2022). The impact of neighborhood disadvantage on amygdala reactivity: pathways through neighborhood social progress. *Developmental Cognitive Neuroscience,* 54. Obtained at: http://doi.org/10.1016/j.dns.2022.101061
6   Healthy Places by Design and Social Isolation Learning Network. (2021). *Socially Connected Communities. Solutions for Social Isolation.* Obtained at: https://healthyplacesbydesign.org/socially-connected-communities-solutions-for-social-isolation/
7   Cooper E. et al. (November 2019). Transport, health, and wellbeing: an evidence review for the Department for Transport. *NatCen Social Research.* Obtained at: https://assets.publishing.service.gov.uk/government/uploads/system/uploads/attachment_data/file/847884/Transport__health_and_wellbeing.pdf
8   Ibid.
9   World Health Organization. (2018). *WHO Housing and Health Guidelines.* Obtained at: http://apps.who.int/iris/bitstream/handle/10665/276001/9789241550376-eng.pdf?ua=1
10 Mental Health Foundation. (Sept 2021). *Housing and Mental Health.* Obtained at: https://www.mentalhealth.org.uk/a-to-z/h/housing-and-mental-health
11 Ibid.
12 Healthy Places by Design and Social Isolation Learning Network. (2021). *Socially Connected Communities. Solutions for Social Isolation.* Obtained at: https://healthyplacesbydesign.org/socially-connected-communities-solutions-for-social-isolation/
13 Ibid.
14 American Planning Association. (June 2019). Planning for Equity Policy Guide. Obtained at: https://planning.org/publications/document/9178541/
15 Healthy Places by Design and Social Isolation Learning Network. (2021). Socially Connected Communities. Solutions for Social Isolation. *International Institute for Sustainable Development.* Obtained at: https://healthyplacesbydesign.org/socially-connected-communities-solutions-for-social-isolation/
16 Healthy Places by Design. (2021). *Socially Connected Communities: Action Guide for Local Government and Community Leaders.* Obtained at: https://healthyplacesbydesign.org/wp-content/uploads/2021/03/Socially-Connected-Communities_Action-Guide-for-Local-Government-and-Community-Leaders.pdf
17 Personal interview, February 15, 2022.
18 Adaptation Clearing House. *Learning Collaborative for Multifamily Housing, New York City, New York.* Obtained at: https://www.adaptationclearinghouse.org/resources/learning-collaborative-for-multifamily-housing-resilience-new-york-city-new-york.html
19 *Wired Magazine* (June 2019). The 20 most bike-friendly cities on the planet, ranked. Obtained at: https://www.wired.com/story/most-bike-friendly-cities-2019-copenhagenize-design-index/
20 Walker Friendly Communities: https://www.walkfriendly.org/
21 World Carefree Network: https://www.worldcarfree.net/
22 This example was provided to me by Jim Diers, who was the first director of the City of Seattle's Department of Neighborhoods in 1988, after an interview on January 21, 2022.
23 More Awesome Now, Laneway Activations: https://hcma.ca/project/more-awesome-now/
24 Solar Energy Industries Association: https://www.seia.org/initiatives/community-solar
25 Center for Urban Pedagogy: Center for Urban Pedagogy.

26 Business News Daily Editor. (February 26, 2020). Small business is good for local economies: big business is not, researchers say. *Business News Daily*. Obtained at: https://www.businessnewsdaily.com/1298-small-business-good-for-economy.htm

27 McDonough W. (2022). *Cradle to Cradle*. Obtained at: https://mcdonough.com/cradle-to-cradle/

28 See, for example: International Labour Office. (Feb. 2007). *An Operational Guide to Local Value Chain Development*. Obtained at: https://www.ilo.org/wcmsp5/groups/public/---ed_emp/documents/publication/wcms_165367.pdf; and Guerra K. et al. (Nov, 2021). Local value chain models of healthy food access: a quantitative study of two approaches. *Nutrients*. Obtained at: https://www.ncbi.nlm.nih.gov/pmc/articles/PMC8624271/

29 Community solar gardens, also called shared solar. For more information, see for example: https://www.communitysolaraccess.org/

30 See the City of Greensburg, Kansas: https://www.greensburgks.org/residents/recovery-planning/long-term-community-recovery-plan/view; and *Associated Press*. (Nov. 25, 2019). Greensburg green rebuild is considered a mixed success. Obtained at: https://www.kansas.com/news/state/article237731654.html

31 *PR Newswire*. (March 31, 2021). Project called international model for environmental justice and revitalization: new report outlines how cleanup of contamination saved lives and a community. Obtained at: https://www.prnewswire.com/news-releases/project-called-international-model-for-environmental-justice-and-revitalization-301259605.html

32 Community Environmental Legal Defense Fund. (2022). Community Bill of Rights. Obtained at: https://celdf.org/community-rights/

33 Smith K. (January 24, 2022). *New Report: Small Businesses Big Moment*. The Institute for Local Self-Resilience. Obtained at: https://ilsr.org/

34 Gary S. (March 2020). The Oregon stewardship trust: a new type of purpose trust that enables steward-ownership of a business. *University of Cincinnati Law Review*, 88(3). Article 4. Obtained at: https://scholarship.law.uc.edu/uclr/vol88/iss3/4/

35 Gary S. (March 2020). The Oregon stewardship trust: a new type of purpose trust that enables steward-ownership of a business. *University of Cincinnati Law Review*, 88(3). Article 4. Obtained at: https://scholarship.law.uc.edu/cgi/viewcontent.cgi?article=1352&context=uclr

36 BRING Recycling: https://bringrecycling.org/

37 Community Sources Capital: https://community-wealth.org/content/community-sourced-capital

38 Soul Fire Farm: https://www.soulfirefarm.org/

39 Sustainable Ballard: https://www.sustainableballard.org/

40 Groundswell Northwest: https://www.groundswellnw.org/

41 This example was provided to me by Jim Diers after an interview on January 21, 2022.

42 Carrington D. (August 27, 2021). Air pollution linked to more mental illness. *The Guardian*. Obtained at: https://www.theguardian.com/environment/2021/aug/27/air-pollution-linked-to-more-severe-mental-illness-study

43 Roberts S. et al. (February 2019). Exploration of NO_2 and $PM_{2.5}$ air pollution and mental health problems using high-resolution data in London-based children from a UK longitudinal cohort study. *Psychiatric Research*. Obtained at: https://www.sciencedirect.com/science/article/pii/S016517811830800X

44 Nickerson S. (September 2019). Even small spikes in air pollution can threaten children's mental health, research suggests. *EcoWatch*. Obtained at: https://www.ecowatch.com/air-pollution-childrens-mental-health-2640650546.html

45 IQ*Air* (July 2021). *Is there a Link between Air Pollution and Mental Health?* Obtained at: https://www.iqair.com/us/blog/air-quality/air-pollution-and-mental-health

46 Healthy Places by Design and Social Isolation Learning Network (2021). *Socially Connected Communities. Solutions for Social Isolation*. Obtained at: https://healthyplacesbydesign.org/socially-connected-communities-solutions-for-social-isolation/

47 South E., Hohl B. and Kondo M. (July 2018). Effect on greening vacant land on mental health of community-dwelling adults: a cluster randomized. *Jama Network*. Obtained at: https://jamanetwork.com/journals/jamanetworkopen/fullarticle/2688343

48 Ibid.

49 Center for American Progress. (January 8, 2020). *Building a 100 Percent Clean Future Can Drive an Additional $8 Billion a Year to Rural Communities*. Obtained at: https://www.americanprogress.org/article/building-100-percent-clean-future-can-drive-additional-8-billion-year-rural-communities/

50 This story was sent to me by Jim Diers, who was the first director of the City of Seattle's Department of Neighborhoods in 1988, after an interview on January 21, 2022. Jim had recently returned from a visit to Tamoi.

51 Walton Family Foundation. (August 25, 2020). *Engaging Local Communities to Restore a Vulnerable Coastline.* Obtained at: https://www.waltonfamilyfoundation.org/stories/environment/engaging-local-communities-to-restore-a-vulnerable-coastline
52 Rangel K. (January 26, 2022). Vegetation monitoring. *Save the Bay.* Obtained at: https://savesfbay.org/vegetation-monitoring
53 My experience developing the watershed council movement is what led me to investigate whether community-based approaches could also prevent and heal the mental health and psycho-social-spiritual problems generated by the climate crisis and engage residents in climate solutions.
54 For more information, see the Network of Oregon Watershed Councils at https://www.oregon-watersheds.org/who-we-are/oregon-watershed-councils/; and Oregon's Watershed Council Program at: https://www.dfw.state.or.us/fish/STEP/docs/SS14_Resources.pdf
55 Global Rewilding Alliance: https://www.rewild.org/wild-about/global-rewilding-alliance
56 Celata F. et al. (2019). Sustainability transitions to low carbon-societies: insights from European community-based initiatives. *Springer Nature.* Obtained at: https://link.springer.com/content/pdf/10.1007%2Fs10113-019-01488-6.pdf
57 The phrase "too big a lift" is a direct quote made by a county public health department staff member in my hometown during a discussion about forming an RCC. Her comment dissuaded some people from engaging.
58 Bouyé M. et al. (August 6, 2019). Tackling inequality through climate action. *World Resources Institute.* Obtained at: https://www.wri.org/insights/growing-momentum-just-transition-5-success-stories-and-new-commitments-tackle-inequality
59 For more information, see: Climate Justice Alliance at: https://climatejusticealliance.org/just-transition/; and the Chisholm Legacy Project at: https://thechisholmlegacyproject.org/about-us/
60 Personal interview April 4, 2022.

CHAPTER 9

Cultivate Universal Literacy about Mental Wellness and Resilience

Twelve years after Hurricane Katrina hammered New Orleans in the U.S., Brandi Wagner remained disabled and unable to work because of the depression and anxiety she developed after the 2005 historic storm. As told to Politico, she was also in treatment for opioid addiction that developed after she started taking prescription painkillers and drinking heavily to anesthetize herself from the distress she experienced as she tried to recover after the hurricane. Wagner's experience is not unusual.[1]

During the "disillusionment phase" of a major disaster discussed in Chapter 4 that follows the community cohesion phase, mental health and psycho-social-spiritual problems can build for months or years and end up being far more severe than the physical injuries or psychological problems that appear during and immediately after the impact phase. Persistent toxic stresses, such as those generated by climate-generated compounding disruptions to the ecological, social, and economic systems that provide people with food, water, jobs, incomes, and other basic needs, can also build for years and produce long-standing mental health and psycho-social-spiritual problems.

This underscores that another foundational area that will be essential for RCCs to focus on during the long climate emergency is to help everyone understand what mental wellness and resilience involve and how to care for them.[2] This can be called mental wellness and resilience literacy, and it flows from the concept of health literacy, which is the "degree to which individuals have the capacity to obtain, process, and understand basic health information needed to make appropriate health decisions."[3]

It should be noted that although health literacy campaigns have become common over the years, they often shortchange the mental health aspects of health. This illustrates that even many healthcare professionals do not have a good grasp of mental health and resilience literacy. They fail to grasp that there is no physical health without mental health.[4]

Mental wellness and resilience literacy includes, but goes beyond merely helping human services providers and community leaders become "trauma-informed," which primarily focuses on teaching them the neurobiology of trauma and toxic stress so they avoid further traumatizing people they work with. This involves asking "what happened to them" rather than "what's wrong with them." Building universal literacy involves enabling all adults and youth to understand what is involved with mental wellness and transformational resilience and teaching them simple self-administrable skills they can use to enhance those qualities.[5] RCCs can help residents learn the information and skills through stand-alone activities. Building mental wellness and resilience literacy should also be integrated into the RCC's efforts to engage people in the other four foundational areas involved with enhancing universal capacity to prevent and heal mental health and psycho-social-spiritual problems (Figure 9.1).

In specific, mental wellness and resilience literacy involve building the entire population's understanding of[6]

a   how traumas and toxic stresses can activate fight-flight-freeze reactions that, when unacknowledged and unreleased, can undermine their mental wellness and resilience;

DOI: 10.4324/9781003262442-13

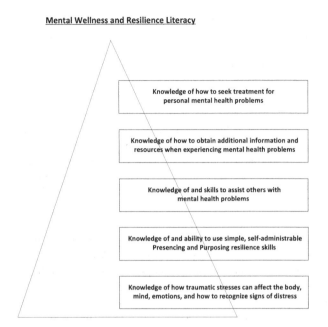

Mental Wellness and Resilience Literacy

Knowledge of how to seek treatment for personal mental health problems

Knowledge of how to obtain additional information and resources when experiencing mental health problems

Knowledge of and skills to assist others with mental health problems

Knowledge of and ability to use simple, self-administrable Presencing and Purposing resilience skills

Knowledge of how traumatic stresses can affect the body, mind, emotions, and how to recognize signs of distress

Figure 9.1 Key Elements of Mental Wellness and Resilience Literacy

b   simple, self-administrable "Presencing" skills and methods they can use to recognize signs of problems and deliberately calm their body, mind, emotions, and behaviors when distressed;

c   simple, self-administrable "Purposing" skills and methods they can use to turn toward and learn from adversities and find new meaning, direction, and healthy hope in the midst of adversities;

d   knowledge and skills that enable them to assist and support others who experience show symptoms of mental health or psycho-social-spiritual problems;

e   knowledge of when and how to seek personal assistance and treatment for uncontrollable problems.

Enhancing each of these capacities will be extremely important during the constant toxic stresses and acute disasters and emergencies generated during the long climate emergency.

To assess mental health literacy in the United States, researchers analyzed a national survey of people who were asked to describe what was wrong with a person who exhibited certain symptoms that were provided to them in a document. Overall, 54 percent of the participants were unable to identify signs of anxiety, 31 percent were unable to recognize signs of depression, 37 percent were unable to identify signs of alcohol abuse, and 32 percent were unable to recognize symptoms of prescription drug misuse. Of the people who did recognize the symptoms of these problems, few knew what to do about it. This indicates a low level of mental health literacy in the US.[7]

A 2018 inventory of United States West Coast resilience building programs by my organization, the International Transformational Resilience Coalition, came to similar conclusions. It found that, at best, 5 percent of the public had access to opportunities that enhanced their knowledge about mental wellness and resilience.[8] This is likely the case throughout most of the US as well. Studies completed in Europe found similar low levels of mental health literacy.[9]

The degree of mental wellness and resilience literacy is closely associated with positive and negative mental health conditions. The lack of such literacy, for instance, indicates limited ability to recognize personal signs of distress and minimal capacity to identify signs of problems within others. These limitations lead to poor mental—and physical—health, higher mortality rates, and greater use of healthcare services.[10] They can also lead to stigmatization and discrimination against people who experience mental health problems.[11]

People with good mental wellness and resilience literacy, in contrast, have greater capacity to maintain their ability to feel good, function well, and find constructive sources of meaning, purpose, and healthy hope during adversities. When people understand how mental health problems can occur, and how wellness and resilience can be enhanced and sustained, they are also more likely to avoid stigmatizing others who exhibit signs of problems and instead find ways to assist them. In addition, improved mental wellness and resilience literacy can reduce the many health inequities that exist, and reduce demands on mental health, social services, and physical healthcare providers.

As I have repeatedly stated in regard to the other four foundational areas that are important to foster population-level mental wellness and transformational resilience, just as most people in industrialized nation's learn how to read and write, *everyone* should now become literate about what mental wellness and resilience involve and how to enhance and sustain the knowledge and skills so they are prepared for the impacts of climate crisis.

Dr. James Gordon, Founder and Executive Director of the Center for Mind Body Medicine, made this point when he told me, "We need true community mental health now, led by people who are concerned about their community, where everyone understands how they can remain healthy and what to do when problems appear." He went on to say, "The time to start is now. These are foundational tools to live in satisfying ways and it should be done in all aspects of communities."[12]

The Neighborhood Resilience Project in Pittsburg, Pennsylvania, places a major emphasis on building mental wellness literacy. "We have a community orientation educational process to help people understand what is happening to them," CEO Rev. Paul Abernathy told me. "We have content developed by behavioral health members and then community members are trained in how to present it to others in culturally appropriate ways and relate it to their own experiences."[13]

As underscored by the Neighborhood Resilience Project, universal mental wellness and resilience literacy cannot be developed by holding a few workshops for social service and community leaders. Literacy building must be ongoing, led by residents who connect it to their own personal experiences, and reach the entire community.

To accomplish this, RCCs will need to examine different types of community-wide mental wellness and resilience literacy campaigns, and then craft well-coordinated multipronged strategies to implement them. The strategies should emphasis three interrelated types of knowledge and skills.

HELP ALL ADULTS AND YOUTH BECOME "TRAUMA-INFORMED"

Dealing with distressing experiences generated by climate-driven cascading disruptions to essential systems and acute disasters will often feel overwhelming—as though all the pressures of the world are upon us. A critical first step in building mental wellness and resilience literacy will therefore be to help everyone—all adults and youth—become "trauma-informed." This involves using simple age and culturally accountable methods to help people understand why they feel good and can function well when they remain within their "Resilient Growth Zone" (RGZ as described in Chapter 2), and why they can feel bad and function poorly when their instinctive fight-flight-freeze reactions are activated and they are pushed out of their RGZ and become frozen in a "high" or "low" condition. People can then be taught simple ways to notice physical sensations in their body that signify they are stuck in a high or low zone, such as muscle tension and headaches, as well as psychological signs such as constant ruminating about past or future problems, automatic fear-based reactions to noises or words, and other symptoms of problems.

This information can help residents understand that what they are experiencing is not the result of some internal flaw or deficiency. It is the outcome of built-in survival instincts. Their body is doing what it is designed to do to protect them from threats. It is when their reactions to real or perceived threats remain frozen in their nervous system that unhealthy consequences appear. But what they are experiencing is perfectly natural. There is nothing wrong with them. This can create a new story about the self that relieves blame, guilt, and shame.

It will also be essential to help every resident understand how the reactions of groups that experience persistent traumatic stresses can mirror the reactions of individuals who are frozen outside their RGZ. The natural fight-flight reactions group members experience can feed off each other and produce collective survival reactions that, when left unaddressed, cause members to harm themselves with maladaptive coping mechanisms such as misusing alcohol or other drugs, or turn their distress outward and become aggressive or violent toward others, including their family or people considered different or outsiders.

HELP EVERYONE LEARN SIMPLE SELF-ADMINISTRABLE PRESENCING (OR SELF-REGULATION AND CO-REGULATION) RESILIENCE SKILLS

As people become trauma-informed, the next step is to teach them simple self-administrable skills and methods to calm their body, mind, and emotions so they can move out of the high or low zone they are stuck in back into their RGZ. Experiencing this type of internal relief helps people understand how trauma and toxic stress is affecting them. It also begins to build self-confidence that they can manage their distress in any situation, which increases self-efficacy and creates great peace of mind.

These are often called self-regulation skills. As you have read throughout this book, I call them Presencing skills because they involve taking deliberate steps to bring oneself back to the present moment rather than being consumed by images or reminders of the past or fears about the future. Presencing skills help people manage disruptive emotions and impulses rather than allowing them to control how one thinks, feels, and acts.

Enhancing the capacity for Presencing can be achieved by helping everyone build robust bonding social connections with others. As I will discuss in Chapter 11, it can also happen by learning simple, self-administrable, age and culturally appropriate breath-based, body-based (somatic), thought-based, or movement-based resilience skills. In addition, therapeutic dancing, art, theatre, writing, and other expressive techniques as well as caring for animals, connecting with nature, religious or spiritual devotion, and other methods can help people become more Present. All these activities can stimulate the parasympathetic nervous system, which calms the sympathetic nervous system that activates during fight-flight-freeze reactions.

Another important Presencing skill is to remember, or rediscover, and utilize the skills, strengths, and resources one has to deal with stressful situations. I call this tapping into your "Circles of Support"[14] and the Trauma Resource Institute calls it "Resourcing."[15] Both approaches help people remember and utilize the skills, strengths, and resources they used in the past to overcome adversities and apply them to their present situation. It can also lead to the development of new skills and resources. Learning how to recognize and manage "thinking distortions" such as catastrophizing and blaming others for the distress one experiences is another important Presencing skill.[16]

The ability to remain Present by using self-regulation skills can be easily disrupted when we interact with people who are psychologically and emotionally dysregulated. This is why learning co-regulation Presencing skills is also important. Co-regulation involves interacting with other people in ways that help both parties manage their in-the-moment thoughts and emotions. This can include, for example, speaking with others in a warm, calming tone of voice, verbally acknowledging their distress, and using words, body language, and behaviors that help moderate everyone's psychological and emotional conditions. When one person calms their nervous system, it can help another calm theirs as well.[17]

The importance of teaching resilience skills to address the distresses generated by the climate emergency was shared with me by J'vanete Skiva, Assistant Director for Equity, Education, and Engagement with the New Hanover County Resiliency Task Force. "Our area's climate makes us prone to natural disasters; specifically hurricanes. People of color tend to be hit the hardest. We are training community providers in resilience skills so they take care of and do not re-traumatize people they are serving. We use a racial equity lens for everything we do, even our training". Skiva went on to say, "We are living in slow motion disasters. These adverse community and climate experiences disproportionately affect people of color."[18]

HELP EVERYONE LEARN SIMPLE SELF-ADMINISTRABLE PURPOSING (OR ADVERSITY-BASED GROWTH) RESILIENCE SKILLS

Enhanced capacity for Presencing will be essential but not sufficient during the long climate emergency. That is because, as previously discussed, the mixture of cascading disruptions to essential systems and acute disasters will often cause people to lose meaning, spirit, and hope for the future. Purposing, which is my term for what in psychology is often called adversity-based growth, is the third element of good mental wellness and resilience literacy. It can help people overcome despair by discovering new sources of meaning, direction, and healthy hope during adversities.

The starting point of enhancing the capacity for Purposing is to teach all adults and youth how to turn toward and learn about the world and self during adversities and make some sense of them.[19] This can be achieved by continually asking "what can I learn?" from a distressing experience. Learning can be difficult because people frequently want to deny what happened or dissociate from adversities. This can be a helpful short-term response to cope with distressing experiences. However, when it continues, numerous problems can emerge. In contrast, when people have made the effort to calm their body, mind, and emotions, and turn toward and learn from a difficult situation, they often find powerful new forms of meaning in their experiences.

Clarifying and living out one's most important values during adversities is another essential aspect of Purposing because it puts us in a better place to deal with adversities.[20] Values are life concepts or principles that clarify what is important to us and guide our behavior. They help us decide how to treat others—and the natural world as well. When we live in accordance with our most cherished values we have a compass to shape our decisions about how to act in stressful situations. This can enhance our self-esteem, build self-confidence, and provide us with a sense of meaning and purpose that can reduce feelings of being overwhelmed by climate adversities. Clarifying what one stands for and living by those values will be extremely important to sustain mental wellness and transformational resilience during the long climate crisis.[21]

Living out values that lead people to engage in pro-social activities is a powerful way to find meaning, purpose, and healthy hope during adversities. Engaging in pro-social actions becomes more likely when they are not so overly challenging or complex that they produce immobility. Doing simple things to help other people, whether it be a friend or stranger, can have a profound effect on a person's life.[22] Research has found that this type of action can improve the functioning of the immune system and stimulate the production of serotonin in both the recipient of the kindness and the person extending the kindness. Brain research has also found that giving to others can stimulate the reward areas in the brain and create positive feelings. In addition, assisting others can increase feelings of self-worth, strengthen existing relationships, and build new social connections. And, to repeat, having robust connections with others will be the most important protective factor involved with enhancing and sustaining mental wellness and transformational resilience during the long climate crisis.[23]

Further, engaging in activities that help reduce the climate emergency to manageable levels, such as eliminating the use of fossil fuels and unnecessary household consumption, or regenerating local forests, is another important way to live out one's core values. Studies have found that many aspects of well-being are higher in those who engage in volunteering projects, compared with those who do not.

In sum, finding a purpose that helps other people or the natural environment will be a profoundly meaningful way to help oneself during the long climate mega-emergency.

ALL THREE ASPECTS OF MENTAL HEALTH LITERACY HELP PEOPLE RECOGNIZE WHEN TO SEEK HELP

Helping everyone become trauma-informed and learning both Presencing and Purposing skills are cornerstones of building universal mental wellness and resilience literacy. It will be crucial for everyone to obtain this information and learn these skills and capacities before the climate emergency intensifies so they can utilize them during persistent adversities.

As the top element of Figure 9.1 at the beginning of this chapter illustrates, when people have a basic understanding of what is happening within them when they are distressed, but cannot find ways to moderate their reactions, they will also have more capacity to grasp the need to obtain additional information about what they are experiencing. If additional, information is not sufficient to help them feel and function better, they will also understand the need to seek mental health assistance from a trained professional.

MENTAL WELLNESS AND RESILIENCE LITERACY CAN REDUCE STIGMATIZATION

When people understand how traumatic and stressful situations can activate natural fight-flight-freeze reactions that are intended to protect them from harm, but become problematic when they go unreleased, they tend to become less inclined to stigmatize others with mental health problems. People will even sympathize with those who exhibit troublesome behaviors, because they now realize that the individual is likely experiencing something similar to what they themselves might have once gone through. Rather than denigrating struggling people or looking away, residents will often reach out and find ways to help. This might include explaining how the distress they are experiencing likely results from an instinctive reaction to perceived threats, and how simple Presencing or Purposing skills might help them release the survival reactions and allow them to feel and function better. If this information is not sufficient to help the person, they can be connected with a mental health professional.

EVERYONE WILL BENEFIT BY INCREASING MENTAL WELLNESS AND RESILIENCE LITERACY

Mental wellness and resilience literacy is often low among civic, nonprofit, private, and public human service workers such as doctors, nurses, emergency response staff and volunteers, law enforcement professionals, and people who provide food/water/shelter/power/sanitation and other essential services in disasters.

Many of these people are unclear about what is happening within them when they are distressed, and unsure about how to care for themselves. They also do not understand what might be occurring to people around them who think and behave poorly, and they are unsure about how to help without stigmatizing them or further traumatizing them.

I often see this firsthand in transformational resilience workshops I facilitate for healthcare providers. Doctors and nurses consistently say they know that 50 percent or more of the physical health problems people come in with are related to mental health problems. But they are not trained in mental health literacy, so all they can do is prescribe medication. They know this only addresses symptoms, not the root causes of health problems, which often leaves them disheartened by their inability to provide effective care. These feelings, combined with the strains resulting from working in the dysfunctional healthcare system, leave many feeling overwhelmed and depressed.

Time and again I have seen that, after healthcare providers learn that the worries and tensions they experience are due to natural fight-flight-freeze survival reactions in their nervous system, and then use simple Presencing skills to calm their body, mind, and emotions, they invariably begin to feel and function better. When they take a step further and employ simple Purposing skills to use difficulties as learning opportunities to find new meaning in their work, they almost always report feeling even better and performing their job more effectively with greater purpose and healthy hope.

I have also found mental wellness and resilience to be low among people in the climate, environmental, social justice, and related fields. I have personally seen this time and again when working with climate scientists, environmental professionals, and activists. Their work can be very stressful and frustrating because little change results. Some of these people end up turning their anger and irritation inward on themselves and become hyperactive, or misuse drugs or alcohol. Others turn their distress outward and criticize or undermine their fellow workers or activists. Increasing mental wellness and resilience literacy among everyone involved in these fields will be very important as the crisis intensifies.

Examples of How RCCs Can Build Universal Mental Wellness and Resilience Literacy

* *Trainings by the New Hanover County, North Carolina, Resiliency Task Force*: The Task Force has trained over 400 people in the Community Resilience Model (CRM) developed by the Trauma Resource Institute. CRM educates participants about all three focuses involved with mental wellness and resilience literacy. The Resilience Task Force also offers trainings in Reconnect for Resilience (R4R) developed by Resources for Resilience, as well as Connections Matter, Mental Health First Aid, and Be the Bridge, a faith-based curriculum that assists people traumatized by racism and systemic injustices. In addition, they offer films about resiliency and other resources.[24]

* *Trainings Offered by the Putnam County Community Resilience Coalition (CRC)*: The CRC offered two train-the-trainer programs that focused on mental health literacy. They started by helping people understand how traumas and toxic stresses can affect the body, mind, and emotions. They then taught healthy breathing and other self-regulation skills. The people who participated in the initial trainings went back to their organizations and trained others in the information and skills. However, as previously mentioned, when their funding ran out, they were not able to follow up on this initiative.[25] Connected to the CRC's efforts, the nonprofit organization Save the Children offered "Journey of Hope" trainings at schools/camps/girl scouts and childcare centers. This is "an age-specific curriculum designed to help children and their caregivers understand, process and express their feelings and emotions. The program builds healthy coping skills through structured games, stories and positive behaviors in a safe, small group setting."[26]

  CRC Coordinator Barbara Garbarino told me, "One of the Town Supervisors repeated on many occasions how he felt this training "saved lives" when their after-school program was hit by a tornado in May 2018. He said staff and children knew how to stay calm, take shelter, and stay safe. It was one of the many things we did that I feel left a very positive impact on some lives."[27]

* *Purposing Demonstrated by the Bearded Fisherman Project:* This a powerful example of how people who experience suffering can engage in Purposing and help others as a way to help themselves. Before they met, two big burly men, Rick Roberts and Mick Leyland, had both attempted suicide, and Roberts had experienced homelessness. Roberts and Leyland became friends when the former moved to Gainsborough, England, and Roberts joined a fishing group in which Leyland participated. "We both suffer from depression and anxiety, and so fishing was a release for us," Roberts told the New York Times. "We used to sit there just chatting about things that

we won't chat to anyone else about." They soon realized the same kind of bonding connections could help other men in difficulty. So, they started a weekly community group. The group members would meet at a local community center, where they would drink tea and open up to each other about their problems. This led to the Bearded Fishermen project.

The COVID-19 pandemic required the project to shift its approach but not its goals. They moved their meetings online and set up a call center. Eventually, they started a suicide-prevention Night Watch, which monitors "known suicide hot spots" in the community. In groups of four with GPS, flashlights, radios, and first aid kits, residents now walk around areas where numerous suicides have occurred to spot troubled people. They also offer to help families whose members suddenly disappear. "There are a lot of people here who have been out of work for a while, who desperately want work," Leland told the New York Times. "They get to that point where they think, "I'm better off not being here.""

Out of their own suffering, both Roberts and Leyland found a purpose that propelled them to help others. Together, they help people develop vital social connections, learn how to prevent serious mental health problems, and are making the world a better place. In doing so, they are also greatly benefiting themselves.[28]

RCCs can use the examples provided by these groups to identify innovative ways to enhance the community's mental wellness and resilience literacy.

Other Ways RCCs Can Build Universal Mental Wellness and Resilience Literacy

*   *Build Mental Wellness and Resilience Literacy Among All RCC Members*: One of the first steps an RCC can take is to build mental wellness and resilience literacy among the people involved with the steering committee/board and Resilience Innovation Teams. After RCC members have a good grasp of the information, they will be better equipped to educate their family, friends, colleagues, and community members.
*   *Organize a Mental Wellness and Resilience Literacy Innovation Team*: The team should develop strategies that ensure that all adults and youth in the community have the opportunity to enhance their literacy about mental wellness and resilience. Handbooks and other materials can be distributed to provide instructions on how to teach these issues. The strategies can include the following:
    *   *Supporting Existing Adult Mental Wellness and Resilience Literacy Programs*: An RCC can survey the community to identify and support mental wellness and resilience literacy programs for adults that exist in the community. They might be found in educational institutions, community centers, libraries, YMCAs/YWCAs, faith and spirituality centers, workplaces, business associations, government agencies, adult services offered by humanitarian aid organizations, and other adult-oriented organizations.[29] Support might include finding volunteers to help at events, securing free meeting space, doing free promotion, connecting them with potential funders, and other actions.
    *   *Supporting Existing Youth Mental Wellness and Resilience Literacy Programs*: An RCC can also identify and support existing youth mental wellness and resilience literacy programs. They might be found in preschool and K-12 schools, 4H

programs, community centers, YMCAs/YWCAs, youth groups, youth-focused spirituality and faith programs, youth sports programs and camps, college preparatory and job apprenticeship programs, summer school and high school transition programs, and other youth-oriented organizations. Again, support might range from recruiting volunteers to help at programs, finding free meeting spaces in different areas of the community, promoting the program, locating potential funders, and other actions.

○ *Educating Community and Grassroots Leaders*: Mental wellness and resilience literacy education programs should also be offered to leaders of civic, nonprofit, faith, neighborhood, private, and public organizations. A special emphasis should be given to leaders of grassroots groups and those that are typically uninvolved in community activities or marginalized, which can be followed by train-the-trainer events.[30]

○ *Educating Police, Fire, Emergency Responders, and Health Care Professionals*: All police, fire, emergency responders, healthcare, and other frontline workers should develop exemplary mental wellness and resilience literacy. They will benefit from learning information and skills that enable them to care for themselves in distressing situations. They will also benefit by learning how to see signs of psychological and emotional distress in others, and knowing how to assist them without stigmatizing or in other ways harming them.[31]

○ *Educating K-12 Education, Community College, and University Faculty, Staff, and Students*: Public, nonprofit, and private educational institutions of all types, sizes, and locations in the community should be engaged in programs that build mental wellness and resilience literacy among their faculty, staff, and students.

○ *Educating the General Public*: A constant stream of educational materials and training workshops should be offered to the general public to increase their literacy about mental wellness and resilience. Public education can include talks to local groups, webinars, workshops, and conferences presented by outside experts, TV and radio events, publications in local newspapers, community-cafes, social media postings, websites, fliers, promotion through social networks, and other web-based mediums.[32]

Helping every resident in the community increase their mental wellness and resilience literacy will allow many to grasp that when they are continually distressed, they are likely frozen outside their Resilience Growth Zone. Rather than believing they are weak or flawed, they will realize that their body is trying to protect them from a threatening situation. This awareness can lead them to use their own self-selected Presencing skills to calm their body, mind, and emotions, and move back into the RGZ. They can then also use their own self-chosen Purposing skills to find new sources of meaning, purpose, and healthy hope.

Having this type of information and using these skills will provide a powerful antidote to the traumatic stresses that are generated during the long climate mega-emergency, and greatly reduce the possibility that people will harm themselves or others. In addition, when residents know how constant stress can affect someone, they will no longer stigmatize people who are struggling with mental health issues and instead find ways to assist them. Further, when people understand how acute traumas and chronic toxic stresses can affect the thinking and actions of groups, they will have greater capacity to help people engaged with those parties cool down and make wiser and more skillful decisions about how to respond to distressing situations.

The checklist found at the end of this chapter provides a way for RCC members to know if they have covered the basics of building mental wellness and resilience literacy in the community.

After community members develop a basic understanding of mental wellness and resilience literacy, they will often become more interested in engaging in specific practices that can enhance this capacity. These activities are the focus of the next chapter.

CHECKLIST

For Building Exemplary Mental Wellness and Resilience Literacy in the Community

	Yes	No	Comments
Did the RCC take steps to ensure that everyone in the community became trauma-informed?			
Did the RCC take steps to ensure that everyone in the community learned simple self-administrative "Presencing" skills?			
Did the RCC take steps to ensure that everyone in the community learned simple self-administrative "Purposing" skills?			
Did the RCC scan the community to identify and support existing adult-focused mental wellness and resilience literacy programs?			
Did the RCC scan the community to identify and support existing youth-focused mental wellness and resilience literacy programs?			
Did the RCC investigate and help organize many other age and culturally appropriate methods to build universal literacy about mental wellness and resilience?			

NOTES

1 Vestal C. (October 2017). 'Katrina Brain': the invisible long-term toll of megastorms. Long after a big hurricane blows through, its effects hammer the mental health system. *Politico*. Obtained at: https://www.politico.com/agenda/story/2017/10/12/psychological-toll-natural-disasters-000547/
2 Kutcher S. et al. (2016). Mental health literacy: past, present and future. *The Canadian Journal of Psychiatry*, 61(3), 154–158. Obtained at: https://pubmed.ncbi.nlm.nih.gov/27254090/

3   U.S. Health Resources and Services Administration. (2019). *Health Literacy*. Obtained at: https://www.hrsa.gov/about/organization/bureaus/ohe/health-literacy/index.html

4   Dr. Brock Chisholm, the first Director-General of the World Health Organization (WHO), coined the phase "without mental health there can be no true physical health."

5   Jorm A. (2012). Mental health literacy: empowering the community to take action for better mental health. *American Psychologist*, 67, 231–243. Obtained at: https://psycnet.apa.org/doiLanding?doi=1 0.1037%2Fa0025957

6   Barry M. M. and Jenkins R. (2007). *Implementing Mental Health Promotion*. London, UK: Churchill Livingston/Elsevier Publishers.

7   Skidmore M. (2017). Mental health illiteracy, sigma more common in men, young adults, higher incomes. *Healio Psychiatry*. Obtained at: https://www.healio.com/news/psychiatry/20170504/-mental-health-illiteracy-stigma-more-common-in-men-younger-adults-higher-incomes

8   *Preparing People on the West Coast for Climate Change: Recommendations for Making Psychological & Psycho-Social-Spiritual Resilience Education and Skills Training for Climate Adversities Universal in California and the Pacific Northwest* (2019). International Transformational Resilience Coalition: http://www.theresourceinnovationgroup.org/preparing-cc-west-coast-report/

9   Van der Heide I. et al. (2016). Health literacy in Europe: the development and validation of health literacy prediction models. *European Journal of Public Health*, 26(6), 906–911. Obtained at: https://pubmed.ncbi.nlm.nih.gov/27312257/

10 Ibid.

11 Jorm A. F. et al. (2006). Research on mental health literacy: what we know and what we still need to know. *NZ Journal of Psychiatry*, 40(1), 3–5. Obtained at: https://pubmed.ncbi.nlm.nih.gov/16403031/

12 Personal interview, November 17, 2021.

13 Personal interview, November 5, 2021.

14 Doppelt B. (2016). *Transformational Resilience*. Routledge Publishing, New York, NY.

15 Trauma Resource Institute. *The Community Resilience Model*. Obtained at: https://www.traumaresourceinstitute.com/crm

16 Doppelt B. (2016). *Transformational Resilience*. Routledge Publishing, New York, NY.

17 Alexander P. et al. (September 2017). *Handbook of Self-Regulation of Learning and Performance*. Routledge.

18 Personal interview May 9, 2022.

19 See for example: Park C. (2010). Making sense of the meaning literature: an integrative review of meaning making and its effects on adjustment to stressful life events. *Psychological Bulletin*, 136(2), 257–301. Obtained at: https://pubmed.ncbi.nlm.nih.gov/20192563/; and Doppelt B. (2016). *Transformational Resilience*. Routledge Publishing, New York, NY.

20 Schaefer S.M. et al. (2013). Purpose in life predicts better emotional recovery from negative stimuli. *PLoS One*, 8(11). Obtained at: https://journals.plos.org/plosone/article?id=10.1371/journal.pone.0080329

21 See for example: Moynihan D. et al. (2019). A life worth living: evidence on the relationship between prosocial values and happiness. *American Review of Public Administration*. Obtained at: https://www.ncbi.nlm.nih.gov/pmc/articles/PMC6588195/; and Cresswell D. et al. (2013). Self-affirmation improves problem-solving under stress. *PloS One*, 8(5). Obtained at: https://journals.plos.org/plosone/article?id=10.1371/journal.pone.0062593; and Martela F. and Steger M. (2016). The three meanings of meaning in life: distinguishing coherence, purpose, and significance. *The Journal of Positive Psychology*, 11(5), 531–545.

22 See for example: Ledoux J. and Gorman J. (2001). A call to action: overcoming anxiety through active coping. *The American Journal of Psychiatry*. Obtained at: https://pubmed.ncbi.nlm.nih.gov/11729007/; and Calhoun L. G. and Tedeschi R. G. (2001). "Posttraumatic growth: the positive lessons of loss" in *Meaning Reconstruction & the Experience of Loss*, ed. R. A. Neimeyer, pp. 157–172. American Psychological Association. Obtained at: https://psycnet.apa.org/record/2001-00141-008

23 Lawton. R. N. et al. (March 2020). Does volunteering make us happier, or are happier people more likely to volunteer? Addressing the problem of reverse causality when estimating the wellbeing impacts of volunteering. *Journal of Happiness Studies*. Obtained at: https://link.springer.com/article/10.1007/s10902-020-00242-8; and Health Essentials. (October 2020). *Why Giving Is Good for Your Health*. Cleveland Clinic. Obtained at: https://health.clevelandclinic.org/why-giving-is-good-for-your-health/

24 New Hanover County Resiliency Task Force: https://www.nhcbouncesback.org/

25 Personal interview, October 26, 2021.

26 Personal email, October 27, 2021.

27 Ibid.

28 I heard about the Bearded Fisherman Project during a personal interview with Dr. Antonis Kou-soulis, who is with the Mental Health Foundation in the UK on October 28, 2021. The information provided in the story is excerpted from: Specia M. (Dec 6 2020). As pandemic threatens Britain's mental health these 'Fisherman' fight back. *New York Times*. Obtained at: https://www.nytimes.com/2020/12/06/world/europe/uk-mental-health-suicide-coronavirus.html

29 Public Health England. (2015). *Local Actions on Health Inequities: Improving Health Literacy to Reduce Health Inequities*. UCL Institute of Health Inequities, London, UK. Obtained at: https://www.instituteofhealthequity.org/resources-reports/local-action-on-health-inequalities-health-literacy-to-reduce-health-inequalities

30 For examples, see the manuals that were developed for the Community Partners in Care project in Los Angeles: https://communitypartnersincare.org/resources-for-services/

31 Public Health England. (2015). *Local Actions on Health Inequities: Improving Health Literacy to Reduce Health Inequities*. UCL Institute of Health Inequities, London, UK. Obtained at: https://www.instituteofhealthequity.org/resources-reports/local-action-on-health-inequalities-health-literacy-to-reduce-health-inequalities/health-literacy-improving-health-literacy-to-reduce-health-inequalities-full.pdf

32 Ibid.

CHAPTER 10

Foster Engagement in Specific Practices that Support Mental Wellness and Resilience

An article on the Upworthy website in 2019 speaks to the heart of the issues discussed in this chapter. It recounts a story of a mother named Mary Katherine Backstrom who posted a story on her blog about how her daughter taught her the power of forgiveness in a few short words.

My daughter and I just had a knock-down, drag-out bedtime hour. Finally, about ten minutes ago, I put her to bed and through clinched teeth, said 'I love you Holland, but not another word tonight. You are going to sleep now. I'm done fussing over stuffed animals.

"Mommy?" she said. I paused on the way out the door, literally biting my tongue I was so frustrated. "What is it, Holland?" "I DO have one more thing to say." Of course she did. She was standing on the bed with her hands on her hips, too. Her hair was wild, and she was using her arm to wipe her tears and snot away from her face.

"Mommy," my three-year old said, staring me down with venom in her tiny voice… "I FORGIVE YOU!!!" Then she laid down and cried and honest to goodness, for a hot minute, I didn't know what to do. The way she said "I forgive you," made it sound like cuss words. I walked over to the bedside and leaned over. "Baby girl, do you know what forgiveness means?" She was still sniffling, her face shoved deep into her Little Mermaid pillow. "Yes," she muttered. I really had to hear this. "It means you were wrong, and I'm tired of being mad, and now I'm going to sleep and my heart won't have a tummy ache." So there you have it, folks.

Tonight, I was taught a lesson in forgiveness by a three-year old. It was a gut punch, too. And you're dang right, I climbed in that bed and loved on her. Because to be honest, MY heart had a bit of a tummy ache. I was reminded by my toddler to never go to bed in anger. Because when you do, your heart will have a tummy ache. And you know what? I've been alive for thirty-five years, and I've got to give it to her: She's not wrong.[1]

If a three-year old can grasp the benefits of forgiveness, then we all can. Indeed, encouraging community members to regularly practice forgiveness and engage in a number of other practices that can enhance their capacity for mental wellness and transformational resilience will be another very important foundational area RCCs will need to focus on during the long climate emergency.

These practices are important because, as discussed in Chapter 3, a public health approach to preventing mental health and psycho-social-spiritual problems involves ongoing systematic efforts to alter norms, attitudes, habits, and behaviors. As residents build social connections, refurbish local physical/built, economic, and ecological conditions, and increase their literacy about mental wellness and resilience, healthy thinking and behaviors can be enhanced by regularly engaging in specific practices research shows can help people remain mentally well and resilient during persistent adversities.

Several different practices boost the capacity for mental wellness and transformational resilience. However, research shows that some of the most important practices include forgiveness, finding simple joys, laughing often, being grateful, continual learning, and caring

DOI: 10.4324/9781003262442-14

Figure 10.1 Regular Engagement in These Practices Can Support Mental Wellness and Transformational Resilience

for our physical health (Figure 10.1). RCCs can make engagement in these important practices a stand-alone focus. They should also integrate partaking in the practices into the other foundational areas they focus on.

PRACTICE FORGIVENESS

Long before the COVID-19 pandemic, a survey by the Fetzer Institute found that 62 percent of American adults said they needed more forgiveness in their lives.[2] The percentage is likely even higher today. Similar numbers of Europeans and people in other parts of the world undoubtedly also feel this way.

The need to practice forgiveness is certain to grow as the climate emergency plays out because people will often become furious at individuals, organizations, and industries that continue to damage the planet and harm society. In addition, the traumatic stresses generated by the climate emergency will cause many people—include each of us—to say and do things that are offensive or hurtful to family, friends, or others.

The wounds can produce lasting feelings of anger, bitterness, and resentment. When those who were harmed continue to embrace these feelings, they often end up being the ones who pay the greatest costs. The anger and bitterness can pervade every relationship they have and damage their connections with others. The unreleased emotions can also cause people to become anxious or depressed, lose meaning and purpose in life, and experience physical health problems.[3]

Forgiveness is not about forgetting that someone hurt you, downplaying the harm they caused, excusing or letting the perpetrators off the hook, or making up with them. It is about those who were hurt choosing to let go of their feelings of resentment and desire for revenge. The harmful acts will likely always be with you, and you might never speak to the offenders again. But you make the decision to let go of feelings of anger, hurt, and desire for retribution to heal yourself. Practicing forgiveness can release unhealthy anger and resentment. This can lead to healthier relationships and improved mental wellness. It can also lower blood pressure, increase immune functions, and in other ways, improve your physical health.

Forgiveness toward others takes work. But it can be achieved by recognizing how it can improve our life, identifying who needs to be forgiven and for what, and making a conscious decision to stop seeing oneself as a victim and release the control and power the perpetrator has over us. As this occurs, life will no longer be defined by the hurts one experienced, and people might even have compassion and empathy for those who harmed us, even if the individual refuses to acknowledge the harm they caused or change their behavior.[4]

Forgiving ourselves for our own transgressions will also be vital during the long climate emergency because each of us is likely to say or do hurtful things. This can be more difficult that forgiving others because it requires acknowledging unpleasant and unhealthy thoughts and emotions that caused us do things that harm other people or ecological systems and species. But it will be very hard to remain mentally well and resilient unless we make the choice to forgive ourselves.

Self-forgiveness involves understanding how traumatic stressors pushed you outside your Resilient Growth Zone, caused you to become stuck in a high or low zone, and led to poor decisions about how to think and act. It also involves having compassion and empathy for yourself because you were doing the best you could at the time given the information you had and the condition you were in. It then requires making a deliberate choice to develop greater awareness of what is happening within you when you are stressed, and striving to avoid harm to others or nature. Enhancing our ability to make these choices will be an essential resilience mechanism during the long climate emergency.

Examples of How RCCs Can Promote Forgiveness in Their Community

*   *Organize Community "Forgiveness Blitzes"*: A two-week "Community Forgiveness Blitz" was operated on the entire Luther College campus, located in Decorah, Iowa. The interventions included guest speakers from outside the university on forgiveness, chapel talks on the topic, requests to professors to assign projects related to forgiveness, group activities such as Movie nights where students watched and discuss forgiveness-themed movies such as *Les Misérables* and *You Got Mail*, student poster competitions, and more. The short campaign led to significant feelings of forgiveness among students. The researchers concluded that community-based approaches are a viable method of promoting forgiveness because they can be less intense, but more easily disseminated, and a less costly approach to promoting forgiveness than traditional modalities of psychological treatment.[5]
*   *Organize Youth Forgiveness Education Programs*: It takes practice to understand and become skilled in expressing forgiveness. Starting in childhood is an excellent way to do this because it gives people the most time to practice. A program operated by the International Forgiveness Institute took this approach. They believed that if a majority of students in a community were educated in forgiveness, then as they transition to adults they will practice forgiveness with their family, where they worked, and in other community contexts. Forgiveness Education Programs were run in Milwaukee, Wisconsin, in the US, and in Belfast, Ireland, that produced positive results. These communities were chosen because both were challenged by poverty and violence. The educational programs included comprehensive curriculum guides for use by teachers of pre-kindergarten through twelfth grade students. Research completed on both initiatives showed very positive results. The program continued for over ten years in Ireland. In Milwaukee, it eventually reached more

than 25,000 students in numerous Wisconsin communities and spread to communities in 17 US states, and 30 countries around the world as well.[6]

RCCs can use these examples to design strategies that encourage residents to practice forgiveness when they are angry or want revenge for harmful actions.

Other Ways RCCs Can Promote Forgiveness

*   *Model Forgiveness During RCC Meetings and Events*: It will be important for RCCs to practice forgiveness during all its meetings and events. For example, when a coalition member makes a mistake or communicates poorly with others, forgiveness can be explained and then expressed. Similarly, when someone in the community does something that harms others, the climate, or ecological systems and biodiversity, the RCC can engage residents in a similar process. These practices will help RCC members maintain their capacity for mental wellness and transformational resilience even in difficult times. And, because many residents will be watching how the RCC operates, it will also provide a model that others in the community can follow.

*   *Promote the Enright Model of Forgiveness*: One approach an RCC can use to promote forgiveness is the four-phase process developed by Robert Enright. In the Uncovering phase, the person who was harmed seeks to understand the offense and its impact on their life. In the Decision phase, the person is taught about forgiveness and then decides if they want to commit to forgiving. In the Work phase, the victim seeks to understand the offender and potential reasons why the offender might have acted hurtfully. This helps a person rethink the offense and see the offender in a new light as a fallible human. In the Deepening phase, the person who was impacted seeks to find a sense of meaning or purpose in their suffering. They might also decide if they want to re-engage with individuals. The result is that the person often feels less sad, anxious, and suspicious, and experiences greater purpose in life.

*   *Utilize the REACH Approach*: Another method an RCC can use is Everett Worthington's "REACH Forgiveness" approach. REACH is an acronym for a five-step process that demonstrates that forgiveness involves both a decision to forgive and an emotional transformation for the person who practices it. It also helps them to see that there are physical, health, psychological, relational, and spiritual benefits to forgiving. The five steps include R = Recall the hurt; E = Empathize with your offender; A = make an Altruistic gift of forgiveness; C = Commit to forgiveness; and H = Hold onto forgiveness for the long-term.[7]

*   *Employ the Forgive for Good Method*: Still another approach an RCC can use to engage residents in forgiveness is Frederic Luskin's "Forgive for Good" method. This is a nine-step process in which participants are taught to reframe the experience of victimhood and transform it into a story of resilience. Participants also learned self-regulation skills to help modulate the stress and anxiety that accompanies addressing hurtful events from one's past.[8]

*   *Other Resources*: The Fetzer Institute offers some excellent tools to help people engage in forgiveness.[9] The International Forgiveness Institute also has very good suggestions and examples that RCCs can use.[10] In addition, The Forgiveness Project provides helpful information and tools.[11] And, Edward Worthington's report on *The Science of Forgiveness*, which was written for journalists, offers excellent recommendations.[12]

FIND SIMPLE JOYS

Back in 2015, researchers found that 93 percent of Americans wanted to experience more joy in their daily lives.[13] Like forgiveness, the COVID-10 pandemic is likely to have increased that number. The lack of joy will undoubtedly be aggravated by the constant adversities generated during the long climate emergency. Research shows, however, that when people take the time to find joy in small things when they are distressed, their nervous system is calmed, blood pressure is reduced, stress is relieved, and more oxygen is released to the brain which activates the release of endorphins and helps them feel more positive.[14]

In his book *Awakening Joy*, my longtime friend and colleague at Spirit Rock Mediation Center, James Baraz, describes how to cultivate simple joys during difficult times to promote health and wellness.[15] People can find simple joys by taking a moment to relish ordinary experiences like playing with pets, watching wildlife or flowers, staring up at the stars at night, or simply marveling at being alive. Celebrating good news—successes and accomplishments—with others, no matter how large or small, also helps people find joy in the present moment. Becoming engaged in activities that are virtuous and meaningful, rather than being obsessed with those that feel good but offer no meaning, is also important. In addition, reminiscing with family and friends about past experiences can bring joy and contentment, and help strengthen relationships with them, which again will be the most vital protective factor one can have during the long climate crisis.[16]

You can also help others, such as family, friends, and isolated and elderly people, find simple joys by sending them letters, poems, and drawings. This will not only give the receiver joy, it will also give you, the author, a sense of fulfillment. Running errands for friends and making someone else laugh are other ways to find simple joys. Cultivating these and other ways to find simple joys can help temper the struggles people experience during ongoing climate adversities.[17]

Examples of How RCCs Can Promote Simple Joys

- *Action for Happiness Campaigns:* This approach was created by the Young Foundation in the UK. It brings people together from all walks of life and helps them take practical steps to create more joy and happiness around them. They offer monthly "10 Keys to Happier Living" calls and support the formation of groups that promote happiness campaigns in communities throughout the UK. Happiness Campaign groups also exist in other locations in Europe, the US, Canada, Mexico, and other nations. For example, a group in Brighton, England created a Happy Café that led to the establishment of a Happy Café in East London. There are now over 100 similar cafés in the UK and around the world. Stan Rosenthal, a co-organizer of the Brighton group and the brains behind the Happy Café idea said, "I hope the UK's first Happy Café will become a beacon of happiness in Brighton to reinforce and inspire people in their search for well-being."[18]

- *Spread Joy Through Neighborhood Art:* A project in Green County, Missouri, in the US found that good art can create social connections and bring joy. They launched a project during the COVID-19 pandemic to help residents get to know their neighbors through joyful art. The started by helping everyone learn their neighbor's name. When that happened, the entire community changed. People took their new relationships to a higher level by asking neighbors to draw "large and inspiring" chalk art on their sidewalk or driveway for residents to view as they walked the neighborhood. Residents of one community organized a "Chalk Art Walk." A group of women in another area went even further to create different weekly chalk art themes for a month. They sent out fliers and organized a neighborhood Facebook group to let families know about the themes. One week focused on "quotes and sayings," and another had an "egg hunt" theme in which residents were asked to decorate their yard, landscaping, or home with colored eggs so children could have a visual egg hunt while walking with their parents. Another adopted an "art walk" theme that encouraged neighbors to create and put unique art in their windows or yards. One resident said, "We know that this virus is contagious, just like panic and anxiety. But kindness, joy, and optimism can also be contagious."[19]

RCCs can use these examples to innovate and create their own unique ways to promote simple joys within the community.

Other Ways RCCs Can Help Residents Find Simple Joys

- *Take Time to Celebrate Simple Joys During RCC Meetings and Events*: RCCs can practice finding simple joys during its meetings and events. For example, coalitions can take time when they gather to allow members to share things they found joy in during the day. This will help participants calm their body, mind, and emotions during adversities. As with the other practices described in this chapter, doing so will also provide a model other community members can follow.

- *Encourage Residents to Create Joyful Street Art*: In Seattle, Washington, in 2015, a rogue designer painted colorful new crosswalks on several streets. Neighbors loved them and, rather than removing them, the city made them permanent. This led to a community crosswalk program that allowed other neighborhoods to create their own colorful street art. It not only brought joy to residents, it enhanced community pride, and increased pedestrian visibility and safety, all of which enhanced social connections. The simple act spurred cities like Atlanta, Los Angeles, and others to adopt similar programs.[20] RCCs can promote similar types of joyful innovations by community members.

- *Urge Local Groups and Organizations to Promote Simple Joys*: RCCs can also urge local groups and organizations to find ways to help their staff, customers, clients, members, and stakeholders find simple joys. At Lenox Hill Hospital in New York City, for example, the song "Here Comes the Sun" was played every time a coronavirus patient was discharged or recovered enough to breathe without the help of a ventilator. RCCs can urge other local organizations to find ways to practice similarly joyful things.

- *Include Simple Joys in Community Activities*: RCCs can also work with local governments, schools, and other organizations to make it easy for residents to engage in activities that promote simple joys. For example, gardening at a community garden or park can be made available to everyone, street or park clean ups can be organized, and in other ways RCCs can make it easier for residents to engage in activities that can be joyful.

LAUGH OFTEN

Abraham Lincoln is quoted as saying, "With the fearful strain that is on me night and day, if I did not laugh, I should die."[21] The writer and poet Khalil Gibran remarked, "In the sweetness of friendship let there be laughter and sharing of pleasures. For in the dew of little things the heart finds its morning and is refreshed."[22]

Both Lincoln and Gibran had it right. Closely connected with finding simple joys is the need to keep laughing. Continual laughter and humor will be more important than ever during persistent climate adversities. Although it cannot prevent or heal all problems, a growing body of evidence indicates that laughter lightens our psychological and emotional load, and helps activate our body's natural capacity for wellness and healing.

Research has found many near-term benefits to laughter. It can, for example, relieve physical tension and stress and relax muscles. It can decrease stress hormones and increase immune cells and infection-fighting antibodies, thus improving the body's resistance to disease. Laughter can also activate the release of endorphins that promote an overall sense of well-being and even relieve pain for a short time. In addition, laughter can improve the function of blood vessels and increase blood flow, which helps protect against a heart attack and other cardiovascular problems. Further, laughter can diffuse anger and help resolve conflicts.[23]

The long-term benefits of constant laughter include reduced stress and greater ability to prevent health problems because negative thoughts are replaced by positive ones that release neuropeptides into the body.[24]

In short, laughter can be a "powerful relief from suffering." This is what Steve Wilson told me. He is a psychologist who calls himself a "Joyologist" and is "Cheerman of the Bored" of the World Laughing Tour.[25] This organization trains people in how to help others laugh and relieve distress.

All Joking Aside: Examples of How RCCs Can Promote Continual Laughter

- *Laughing Allowed Physical Comedy*: One great way to promote laughter during adversities was developed by a group in Victoria, Canada, as part of a neighborhood resilience project. The group came together in 2014 to explore how they could "find ways to turn the ups and downs they experienced in their neighborhood into a way to laugh often." Over a six-week period, participants were trained in theatre and physical comedy and together developed a show called *Laughing Allowed! The Slapstick World of Neighbourhood Activism*. The show itself is hilarious, and out of it they developed "A How-to Guide for Making a Physical Comedy Show to Build Neighbourhood Resilience."[26] RCCs can obtain the guide on their website and distribute it widely.
- *Go!Clowns Promotes Therapeutic Laughter*: The Gesundheit! Institute was organized by Dr. Patch Adams, who was made famous by a movie about his life that starred Robin Williams. Its "Go!Clowns" program is a leader in the therapeutic role of clowning in healthcare settings and distressed communities worldwide. In 1985, Adams and his team started traveling the world offering "clowning"—which they define as "spontaneous improvisational play"—to communities in distress. Since then Go!Clowns has brought thousands of volunteer clowns from many nations to many of the world's most distressed regions. The volunteers usually clown at two to three sites during the day, and then share, learn, and have fun together in the evening. They cultivate therapeutic alliances while "combining healthcare with clowning, collaborative play, music, and art." They also "build clinics, provide humanitarian and medical care, and engage communities in collaborative community development projects." RCCs can invite Go!Clowns to their community or develop the own version of the program.

RCCs can widely share these approaches with residents, and encourage them to invent their own way to keep laughing during the long climate emergency.

Other Ways RCCs Can Help Residents Find Simple Joys

*   *Take Time to Laugh During RCC Meetings and Events:* It will be important for RCC members to continually laugh during all its meetings and events to release stress and tension. Finding ways to enable constant laughter during RCC events will also help community members see that it is possible to laugh even when things are distressing.
*   *Promote "Guerrilla Humor":* This can be done, for example, by empowering residents to place funny art in public spaces, put humorous pictures on billboards or sidewalks, and in other ways find ways to surprise people with guerrilla humor. A great example was provided by Vancouver, British Columbia resident and comedian, Tanya Horne. During the COVID-19 pandemic, every Tuesday and Thursday, weather permitting, she operated a "sit-down" comedy stand from 11:30 a.m. to 1:30 p.m. in front of her home where she dished out jokes to people passing by.[27] Many other types of guerrilla humor are possible.
*   *Sponsor Laughter Clubs:* RCCs can use the approach developed by Steve Wilson and the World Laughing Tour to promote Laughter Clubs in business spaces, fitness centers, nursing homes, and community settings. A laughter session is organized around a laughter therapy program designed to help participants relieve stress, have fun, and stay healthy. Trained Laughter Club leaders facilitate the sessions, and they use visual aids, playful activities, laughter meditation, and other approaches to activate laughter. Other benefits for those who attend are the development of social connections and discussions about important issues.[28]
*   *Train Community Members to Promote Therapeutic Laughter:* RCCs might also consider urging residents to attend trainings by the World Laughing Tour in how to promote therapeutic humor.[29] The organization runs a training called "How to Create Therapeutic Laughter" that educates participants to become a qualified leader in Laughter Clubs and other therapeutic activities. During the training, participants learn about the science of laughter, as well as the theory, philosophy, and psychological aspects of therapeutic laughter. For other resources on promoting laughter, including research on the topic, RCCs can connect with the Association of Applied and Therapeutic Humor,[30] the International Society for Humor,[31] and the Institute for Emotionally Intelligent Learning.[32]

As it promotes continual laughter, RCCs will want to make it crystal clear that laughter should never occur at the expense of others and that inappropriate forms of humor should never take place because it can diminish the wellness and resilience of both those who are laughed at and those who engage in this demeaning practice.

BE GRATEFUL

At 2:00 a.m. in the morning, as the Tubs wildfire burned close to her home in Sonoma County, California, writer Michelle Ule paused for a moment as she was preparing to evacuate to be grateful. "I'm so grateful my writing life is backed up offsite," she said to herself. "The kitten was in her cage in the car, ready to go. Our son had room for the whole family at his house. We had time to get there." It turned out the wildfire prevented her from going to her son's house. But she and her family found safety in her brother's coastal cabin.

A year after the fire ended, she wrote about how gratitude helped her during the disaster. The gratitude she felt for the assistance her neighbors and brother offered, "swept away fears" she said, "soothed their emotions," and helped her realize that "people are more important than things."[33]

The benefits Ule experienced from gratitude are not surprising. The dictionary defines gratitude as "the quality of being thankful; readiness to show appreciation for and to return kindness." Roman philosopher Cicero is reported to have said: "Gratitude is not only the greatest of virtues, but the parent of all others."[34]

As the climate emergency accelerates gratitude—or thankfulness and appreciation— will be another vital antidote and resilience mechanism to counter the distresses generated by the mixture of cascading disruptions to essential systems and persistent disasters. Gratitude is an affirmation of the good things in life and the benefits we have received from them. It is also the recognition that most of the gifts we have experienced emerged from family, friends, or others, from the earth's ecological systems, or if you are a spiritual person, from a higher power or other powerful sources. Being grateful does not mean that life is perfect, or that you do not have problems or burdens. It means we make the effort to identify the goodness that also is present in our lives and in the world around us.

Research has found that people who practice gratitude consistently report numerous psychological and emotional benefits, including greater ability to become more present, block toxic negative emotions, and resist stress. Gratitude also generates a greater sense of self-worth, and more optimism and happiness in life. In addition, people who regularly practice gratitude typically experience significant prosocial benefits including being more helpful, generous, compassionate, forgiving, and outgoing toward others. This is particularly important because gratitude helps us see how we have been affirmed and cared for by other people, and helps us establish and maintain social connections that will be vital during the long climate emergency.[35]

Research has also found that people who constantly practice gratitude are less materialistic. They tend to avoid compulsive purchases that typically result from the desire for immediate pleasure.[36] Less materialism, of course, will be vital to reduce the climate crisis to manageable levels.

Further, gratitude generates many physical benefits such as a stronger immune system, less aches and pains, lower blood pressure, better and longer sleep, and the ability to exercise more and take better care of one's health.[37]

It will be essential for RCCs to promote the ongoing practice of gratitude to build universal capacity for mental wellness and transformational resilience during persistent climate hardships. This can bring people into direct positive relationships with others, and increase both the giver's and the receiver's a sense of wellbeing. It can also help isolated individuals connect with others, which will build and strengthen both "strong" and "weak" social ties. The new trusting connections can unify people and motivate them to work toward the common purpose of enhancing everyone's capacity for mental wellness and transformational resilience as they engage in solutions to the climate crisis.

Examples of How RCCs Can Promote Gratitude

- *The Newport News, Virginia, "Attitude of Gratitude Campaign"*: In 2021, the city of Newport News pushed the idea that November is a month of thanks by launching an "Attitude of Gratitude" campaign. Mayor McKinley Price said the "campaign was created to inspire residents to adopt a grateful spirit and uplift others in word and deed." … "I find this especially important to remember as we reflect upon the challenges and losses we experienced throughout the pandemic." The campaign included contests and activities, as well as daily social media postings and weekly giveaways, which were placed on the city's Facebook and Instagram pages. Residents were also encouraged to pick up a free yard sign from any Newport News Public Library branch, write what they are grateful for, and post it in their yard. Community members could also enter the "Attitude of Gratitude" Video Contest, where they posted a one-minute clip of what they are grateful for. The videos with the most views were posted on the city's social media pages and the creators won prizes. Mayor Price said, "By encouraging everyone to pause and give thanks, we are creating a healthier, happier, more unified community."[38]

- *Say Something Nice Day*: In 2011, the President and CEO of the Charleston, South Carolina Speech and Hearing Center, Mitchell Carnell, published a book called *Say Something Nice: Be a Lifter!*[39] It focused on the health benefits of lifting others up, instead of tearing them down. The book germinated the idea of setting aside a day to give appreciation to others. In 2006, the idea was officially recognized by the Mayor of North Charleston who proclaimed June 1 as, "Say Something Nice Day." Many local organizations joined in. The idea grew, and although it is not widely known, there is now a national "Say Something Nice Day" in the US when people are encouraged to say something nice to everyone they encounter throughout the day or send kind words to friends and family who need it most. Communities can celebrate the national day or schedule their own appreciation days.

RCCs can use both examples to design their own unique community gratitude campaigns.

Other Ways RCCs Can Promote Gratitude

- *Practice Gratitude During RCC Meetings and Activities*: As with forgiveness, finding simple joys, and laughing often, an RCC can promote gratitude during coalition meetings and events and offer a sincere welcome to people when they join the coalition. Whether 3 or 30 people attend a meeting, they should be openly thanked and shown gratitude for their presence. When people feel welcome, they are more likely to feel safe and cared for. They will also be more inclined to bring their friends and colleagues to future events. RCCs should also make it a point to show deep appreciation for people who volunteer their time to organize and run RCC activities, and for residents who participated in them. Sharing appreciation for funders will also be important.

- *Encourage Personal Gratitude Practices*: RCCs can also continually promote the personal benefits of practicing gratitude to residents. They can, for example, encourage people to keep a gratitude journal, regularly give a sincere verbal "thank you" to others, or send emails or letters of thanks. They can also inform the community that a smile or firm handshake is a form of gratitude, and that many people find praying or other forms of devotion are the highest form of gratitude. In addition, an RCC can encourage people to take the time to be thankful for having food to eat, a roof over their head, clothes to wear, and other necessities. Further, an RCC can urge people to show appreciation for those in their bonding, bridging, and linking social support networks.

- *Appreciate Different Local Cultures*: Learning about and showing appreciation for the different cultures that exist in the neighborhood or community is another way RCCs can practice gratitude. This can be done, for example, by offering culturally appropriate foods at different times of the year during gatherings, and holding rituals and events that reflect the cultural, religious, or spiritual backgrounds of different populations.

- *Hold Gratitude Celebrations*: RCCs can embed gratitude within their strategies to enhance universal capacity for mental wellness and transformational resilience by holding regular informal and formal celebrations that give out awards and in other ways recognize the efforts of different people, groups, or organizations that have given to the community. They can also take photos or videos of people as they engage in RCC activities (with their permission) and post them on websites and other places, take "before" and "after" shots of physical/built or ecological conditions residents have restored, and in other ways show appreciation for what people have done.

- *Organize "Gratitude Circles"*: RCCs can make gratitude an explicit part of its strategy by engaging neighborhoods, groups, and organizations in the formation of Gratitude Circles. These are groups of 5–100 people or more who come together to share gratitude for any other participant in the group they want to appreciate. A variation of this is called a Gratitude Fishbowl in which a person who is to be the recipient of gratitude sits in the middle of a circle (the fishbowl) and listens to the group share their appreciation without commenting on it. Both processes can take from 10 to 60 minutes and be held any time of day. Engaging in Gratitude Circles and their many variations can be powerful ways for communities to increase universal capacity for mental wellness and transformational resilience during the long climate mega-emergency.[40]

KEEP LEARNING

Researchers have found that if employees engage in on-the-job learning when they are stressed, they engage in fewer unproductive behaviors than when they used relaxation exercises. Learning buffered workplace stress, while relaxation exercises did not.[41] Another study found that reading for just six minutes can reduce stress levels by 68 percent, and still other research found that people who read for more than 3.5 hours per week live longer.[42] Maximizing the benefits of continual learning will be necessary to sustain mental wellness and transformational resilience during the long climate crisis.

Humans have a relentless drive to learn because it is what allows us to survive difficult experiences. Research has found that learning is good for our brains because it keeps the synapses performing well. Staying curious also helps reduce and manage stress because it leads to a drop in stress-related hormones, a better sense of control and self-efficacy, and reduced anxiety. In addition, engagement in new learning opportunities can lead to more social interactions because people can engage with others they might not know. Learning new things can also encourage risk-taking and lead to new adventures, which can produce feelings of joy. In addition, ongoing learning has been found to act as a protective factor against depression and various forms of dementia.[43]

People tend to focus on learning different things in each developmental stage of their lives. Young children focus on learning things that are distinct from what people learn when they are adolescents, working age, and older adults. For working-age adults, continual learning also promotes social mobility, which is particularly important in the current context of rapid technological change, as it can increase employability during the longer working lives people experience.

As previously discussed, to remain mentally well and resilience during the long climate emergency, it will be especially important for everyone to learn how traumatic stresses can affect their body, mind, and emotions, as well as the thinking and behaviors of groups, and how those reactions can be prevented and healed. It will also be important for everyone to learn how the climate and ecological systems work, how human activities can damage those systems, and how they can be regenerated.

Most importantly, continued learning will be essential to build a population that is capable, entrepreneurial, empowered, and engaged in their neighborhood and community to sustain mental wellness and transformational resilience as they engage in activities that help reduce the climate emergency to manageable levels.

Examples of How RCCs Can Help Residents Keep Learning

- *Rural Residents Learn About Trauma Cycles Through Systems Mapping*: Chapter 5 described how the residents of Edgecombe County, North Carolina, engaged in systems mapping to learn how vicious cycles of trauma are transmitted throughout their community by the continued use of punishment and isolation, and how healing and resilience can be fostered by changing those practices. The process facilitated by the Rural Opportunity Institute created a learning community where residents continued to discover how certain actions activated changes elsewhere that increase suffering, and how constructive responses to what initially appears to be problem behaviors among young people can stimulate feedbacks that lead to healing and resilience.

- *The UNESCO Global Network of Learning Cities (GNLC) Promotes Lifelong Learning*: In 2012, UNESCO organized the GNLC to help local governments develop life-long learning strategies. Over 230 member cities from 64 countries now participate. The city of Belfast, in Northern Ireland, for instance, now promotes learning to tackle inequalities and improve quality of life. The city's "Learning Charter" provides employment training academies for unemployed and hard-to-reach groups. Life-long learning in Wyndham, Australia, is promoted by a broad network that includes schools, the private sector, city government, and local residents. One of the focuses has been "Learning Festivals" that help people learn how to find employment and contribute to local social and economic well-being. Through a comprehensive learning strategy that prioritizes equity and inclusion, the city of Huejotzingo, Mexico, has transformed itself from an agricultural community to an industrial powerhouse in the state of Puebla. The city has implemented 140 learning projects over the past ten years that has decreased illiteracy by 50 percent, expanded access to the internet and new technologies, and supported 1,000 female entrepreneurs to organize projects. The city's first-ever Festival of Learning engaged more than 25 percent of the 90,000 plus residents.[44]

  RCCs can use these examples to develop innovative ways to help residents keep learning about how to respond to the climate crises and improve local social, physical/built, economic, and ecological conditions as a way to increase their own capacity for mental wellness and transformational resilience.

Other Ways RCCs Can Help Residents Keep Learning

- *Model Continual Learning During RCC Meetings and Events*: One of the most important ways an RCC can promote continual learning is to demonstrate it during coalition meetings and events. Members can share new insights they gained through their work or through recent conversations with others. They can also describe new perspectives they gained by reading books or documents and how it has affected their thinking or practices. In addition, they can continually acknowledge there is much they do not know and that they want to keep learning new things.

- *Raise Public Awareness of the Importance of Continual Learning*: RCCs can motivate residents to keep learning during the long climate emergency by continually raising public awareness of how important it is. This can include the value of listening to people with different perspectives, reading new and interesting books and articles, or looking for new and challenging things. It can also include taking cooking, art, language, computer, or other classes, joining a book or film club, learning how to play a musical instrument, or trying a new form of physical activity.

- *Connect People Who Want to Learn Similar Things*: Much like Abundant Community Edmonton does, RCCs can link together people who have similar interests to allow them to learn from each other. For example, people who might want to learn woodworking, music, art, or other skills can be connected with others who are interested in the same activity and are happy to share what they know.

- *Advocate for Equitable Access to Quality Education*: Another important step RCCs can take is to lobby for equitable access to quality education. This will be essential to prepare everyone for the long climate emergency. It can also promote social justice, peaceful relationships, and ecological regeneration. Unfortunately, many BIPOC and low-income residents, migrants, and other marginalized children and adults, as well as people living in rural areas, often do not have access to quality education. To change this, RCCs can advocate for universal, free, quality early childhood, primary, lower and upper secondary education, and higher education. Access to education will enable everyone to constructively contribute to their community, achieve their potential as human beings, and inspire them to engage in solutions to the climate crisis.

- *Advocate for Adult and Community Education*: Equally important, RCCs can promote Adult and Community Education (ACE), also referred to as "community learning." This covers a wide range of learning opportunities designed to help adults gain new skills, prepare for higher levels of education, return to learning, or develop interest in new subjects.[45] There are very few public policies dedicated to ACE, which is primarily delivered by voluntary neighborhood and community organizations and continuing education programs. To promote continued learning, RCCs can lobby public education institutions to offer ACE programs. They can also urge provincial/state and local/municipal governments to adopt policies that support and fund ACE programs.[46]

CARE FOR PHYSICAL HEALTH

As previously stated, it is difficult to maintain good physical health without good mental health. A 2019 BuzzFeed News article included 19 stories about how people used exercise to address mental health and physical health problems. They ranged from how walking the dog helped an individual deal with the stress of unemployment, to a person who used exercise to cope with panic attacks, and a woman who started running to manage stress and feel more in control at college.[47] Later that same year, National Public Radio in the US ran a story about research that found eating a healthy diet that includes plenty of fruits and vegetables and limits highly processed foods can help reduce symptoms of depression.[48]

Although these stories made the news, there is not much new here. It has long been known that getting regular exercise and eating healthy diets improves mental wellness. The fact that physical health problems can affect mental health has also long been understood. This underscores that the adversities generated during the long climate crisis will make it vital for RCCs to inspire residents to care for their physical health.

There are many ways to enhance physical health. For example, getting the right amount of sleep, and consuming modest amounts of alcohol are important. However, two actions that will be particularly helpful during the long climate emergency are getting regular exercise and eating healthy food, and I will focus on those two practices here. Both are likely to become more problematic as the mixture of cascading disruptions to essential systems and acute disasters accelerate, which means that RCCs should emphasize the importance of both during the long climate mega-emergency.

Promote Regular Physical Activity

Exercise makes you feel good and keeps your body healthy. It not only increases aerobic capacity and muscle size, but it can also trim your waistline, increase the sense of wellness and resilience, and add years to your life. Physically active people feel more energetic throughout the day, sleep better at night, have sharper memories, and feel more relaxed and positive about themselves. Regular activity has also been found to relieve stress and have positive impacts on depression and anxiety. Research indicates that even modest amounts of physical activity help improve mental and physical health. This can be difficult today as more and more people sit at their desks much of the day, isolated from others, staring at a computer screen, but RCCs must make this a priority.

Promote Access to Health Eating and Healthy Foods

Healthy diets have several dimensions. One is to eat regularly, as this can stop your blood pressure from dropping, which can leave you feeling tired and in a foul mood. Another is to have a balanced diet of whole grains, vegetables, fruit, and proteins, and the right balance of fats. The human body needs vitamins and minerals as well as healthy fats such as those found in olive oil, milk, avocados, and other foods. Trans fats and lots of sugar should be avoided, such as those found in processed or packaged food, as they can affect the heart. Some protein is good with every meal since it contains amino acids that help regulate moods. Limiting the amount of meat one eats is also important because overconsumption of the energy and fat it contains can produce excess weight and obesity and increase risk of chronic diseases such as cardiovascular disease and type 2 diabetes (and, as stated in Chapter 1, industrial meat production is also a major source of methane emissions that are disrupting the earth's climate system). Be aware of when you are eating too much because it is often a harmful coping mechanism for psychological, emotional, and spiritual distress. At the same time, the amount of caffeine consumed in soft drinks, coffee, and other products should be carefully monitored.[49]

Having access to healthy food and healthy eating is often difficult for low-income communities and people of color. The mixture of cascading disruptions to essential systems and acute disasters generated by the climate crisis will often aggravate these problems by creating more food insecurity. This is why RCCs must make this a priority.

Example of How RCCs Can Encourage Residents to Care for Their Body

- *Four Rural Counties Promote Healthy Eating to Reduce Obesity*: Haywood, Humphreys, Lake, and Lauderdale counties in western Tennessee in the US had adult obesity rates greater than 40 percent. So they joined a four-year community-based participatory initiative to address the problem. All four counties placed a major focus on promoting healthy food choices and physical activity. Residents were seen as equal partners in the entire process. The Community Coalitions for Change (C3) initiative emphasized building relationships between community members and developing mutual trust and equality. It was ultimately embraced by 67,400 community members and 67 organizations. During the first year, coalition members discussed the need to return to long-held traditions of collective community engagement and action to address rural obesity rates. In response, 25 community gardens were established, and ten existing gardens were supported. As a result, 8,300 community members received garden produce. Policy changes were also made, such as allowing children to carry water bottles at school. In addition, environmental changes were made, such as promotional and motivational signage in restaurants, grocery stores, and corner stores, along with the installation of food storage and display equipment. Overall, 61 percent of survey respondents reported being more physically active as a result of participating in the programs, 59 percent reported eating more fruit, and 66 percent reported eating more vegetables.[50]

- *"Play Streets" Help Youth Stay Physically Active*: Play Streets is the name often used to describe the work of local coalitions to promote physical activity and active play for youth by using streets as a neighborhood asset. This involves temporarily closing selected streets in different neighborhoods to create safe places for active play for a specified length of time, which usually means three to five hours. The approach has mostly been used during summer months, when youth do not have the opportunity to engage in school-based physical activity. Play Streets are free to all youth, which helps prevent inequities. Seattle, San Francisco, and other US cities have implemented Play Streets. Chicago has organized PlayStreets since 2012 in collaboration with neighborhood groups and residents. They involve a single-day parking and traffic restriction imposed on a residential block for at least three hours in a lower-income neighborhood with high obesity rates and a lack of public places to be active. Researchers found that the Chicago's PlayStreets provide youth with opportunities for physical activity in neighborhoods where they are rare. They concluded that local policies that facilitate temporarily closing streets and support opportunities for physical activity can advance health equity in cities.[51]

  RCCs can use these examples to innovate and craft strategies to engage community members in actions that promote physical health.

Other Ways RCCs Can Motivate Residents to Care for Their Body

- *Practice Movement and Healthy Eating During RCC Meetings and Events*: Every RCC should role model how to care for physical health by engaging members in physical activity and eating healthy foods during all coalition meetings and events. Breaks should be taken during meetings to allow people to get up and move around. Fast foods should be avoided, and whenever possible, locally grown organic fresh fruits and vegetables should be provided as snacks and meals.

- *Promote a Variety of Physical Activities*: RCCs can urge residents to set goals and establish routines that can include regular: running; fast or slow walking; stretching; sports and games; strength training; swimming, exercise classes; water aerobics; yoga; Pilates; dancing; bowling; bocce ball; gardening; bicycling; play with grandchildren (for older adults); and other forms of physical movement.[52]

- *Create "Walksheds"*: RCCs can urge residents to create their own "walksheds." This involves measuring and drawing a two-mile or so radius map around their residence that provides an easy 30- to 40-minute walk. Most people can walk two miles in about 40 minutes, and in addition to getting good exercise, by regularly following their walkshed, they are likely to meet new people, discover local amenities, and support local businesses.[53]

- *Promote Bike Sharing*: RCCs can support bike sharing, and if they live near a stream or lake, "paddle sharing." In the US city of Minneapolis, for example, a paddle share system lets commuters travel down the Mississippi River between two stations located on the river. The system connects people with the city bike share system, which allows commuters access to both modes of transportation.[54]

- *Create Mobile Produce Markets and Healthy Local Food Stores*: As previously mentioned, many low-income neighborhoods where BIPOC residents live are food deserts. RCCs can change this by using the approach developed by the Fresh Moves Mobil Market to help these neighborhoods get access to the same farmer's market produce found in other parts of a city.[55] RCCs can also partners with local farmers and other organizations to provide funding, training, and resources to help existing store owners stock and promote healthy foods and recruit the development of new health food stores.

- *Support Farm-to-School Programs*: These can range from buying food from local farmers to serve at schools, to farm field trips, hands-on learning in a garden, cooking demonstrations, and integration of food-related information into classroom curricula.

- *Promote Community-Supported Agriculture (CSA) and Farmers Markets*: RCCs can promote CSAs, as they are often called, that provide members with a box or a share of the fresh food they produce and harvest on a weekly basis. Farmers markets are locations in communities where local farmers can sell the food they produce. CSAs and Farmers Markets can both increase access to fresh, healthy foods, support local farmers, and keep food dollars circulating in the local economy.

- *Tap into the Approaches Offered by Common Threads, Fresh Roots, and Slow Food International*: Common Threads provides cooking and nutrition programs to underserved communities across the US. They take a hands-on, family-centered approach to education on nutrition, healthy eating, sustainability, and garden development.[56] Fresh Roots, located in Vancouver, Canada, cultivates school gardens and provides food education at schools across Vancouver. They also turn school gardens into educational sites, mentor youth at garden clubs and summer programs, and in other ways empower students to grow their own food.[57] Slow Food International works in more than 160 countries to help people gain access to good, clean, and fair food. They are also focused on combatting the environmental consequences of our food choices.[58]

- *Utilize the Expertise Offered by Healthy Places by Design, the Center for Advancing Health Communities, and America Walks*: Healthy Places by Design partners with communities to design place-based strategies to ensure health and well-being for all.[59] The Center for Advancing Healthy Communities "provides technical assistance and training for program implementation while expanding capabilities and resources, promoting healthful policy and environmental change, and collaborating to foster mutually beneficial partnerships."[60] America Walks offers training and technical assistance programs to help communities "create safe, accessible, equitable, and enjoyable places to walk and move."[61]

RCCS SHOULD ESTABLISH HEALTHY PRACTICES RESILIENCE INNOVATION TEAMS

To motivate residents to engage in the practices described in this chapter that enhance their capacity for mental wellness and transformational resilience, RCCs can establish a Healthy Practices Resilience Innovation Team composed of residents, civic, nonprofit, private, and public organizations. The team should continually innovate to develop new ways to engage residents in each of the six practices that support mental wellness and resilience.

RCCs can use the checklist provided at the end of this chapter to assess the extent to which it has taken steps to motivate community members to engage in the six key practices described in this chapter.

Even when residents are engaging in these practices and the other three core foundational areas previously discussed, as the climate emergency accelerates, many people will still become distressed and others will become traumatized by relentless adversities. It will therefore be crucial for RCCs to establish ongoing opportunities for people to heal their distress and trauma. The next chapter discusses how this can be approached.

CHECKLIST

For motivating residents to engage in practices that help enhance their capacity for mental wellness and transformational resilience

	Yes	No	Comments
Did the RCC investigate and implement simple ways to motivate residents to practice forgiveness?			
Did the RCC investigate and implement simple ways to motivate residents to find simple joys?			
Did the RCC investigate and implement simple ways to motivate residents to laugh often?			
Did the RCC investigate and implement simple ways to motivate residents to be grateful?			

	Yes	No	Comments
Did the RCC investigate and implement simple ways to motivate residents to keep learning?			
Did the RCC investigate and implement simple ways to motivate residents to care for their physical health?			

NOTES

1   Reneau A. (July 2019). A 3-year old gave her mom a 25-word master class on what forgiveness really means. *Upworthy*. Obtained at: https://www.upworthy.com/3-year-old-lessons-in-forgiveness
2   Fezter Institute. *Fetzer Survey on Love and Forgiveness in American Society*. Obtained at: https://fetzer. org/resources/fetzer-survey-love-and-forgiveness-american-society
3   Weir K. (January 2017). Forgiveness and improve mental health and physical health. *CE Corner, American Psychological Association*, 48(1). Obtained at: https://www.apa.org/monitor/2017/01/ce-corner
4   Worthington Jr. E. (April 2020). *The Science of Forgiveness*. John Templeton Foundation; and Weir, K. (Jan 2017). Forgiveness can improve mental and physical health: research shows how to get there. *CE Corner, American Psychological Association*, 48(1).
5   Brandon G. et al. (2019). Evaluating the effectiveness of a community-based forgiveness campaign. *The Journal of Positive Psychology*, 14(3), 354–361. Obtained at: https://www.tandfonline. com/doi/abs/10.1080/17439760.2018.1437464
6   Enright R. (July 2010). *Renewing Communities through Resilience Education: A Prospect for Peace*. University of Wisconsin-Madison and the International Forgiveness Institute. Obtained at: https://internationalforgiveness.com/wp-content/uploads/2021/02/Renewing   Communities Through Forgiveness Education-1.pdf
7   Worthington E. (2003). *Forgiving and Reconciling: Bridges to Wholeness and Hope*. InterVarsity Press.
8   Luskin F. (2002). *Forgive for Good: A Proven Prescription for Health and Happiness*. HarperCollins.
9   The Fetzer Institute. *Resources on Forgiveness*: https://fetzer.org/resources/resources-forgiveness
10 International Forgiveness Institute: https://internationalforgiveness.com/
11 The Forgiveness Project: https://www.theforgivenessproject.com/stories/
12 Worthington E. (April 2020). *The Science of Forgiveness*. John Templeton Foundation. Obtained at: https://www.templeton.org/wp-content/uploads/2020/06/Forgiveness_final.pdf
13 Edelman (April 2015). *New Edelman Study Reveals Americans Face a Dilemma in their Pursuit of Wellbeing*. Obtained at: https://www.edelman.com/news-awards/new-edelman-study-reveals-americans-face-dilemma-their-pursuit-well-being
14 Murphy C. (August 2018). This is how joy affects your body. *Healthline*. Obtained at: https://www. healthline.com/health/affects-of-joy
15 Baraz J. and Alexander S. (2012). *Awakening Joy: 10 Steps to Happiness*. Parallax Press.
16 Gable S. and Reis H. (2010). Good news! Capitalizing on positive events in an interpersonal context. *Advances in Experimental Social Psychology*, 42, 195–257. Obtained at: https://labs.psych.ucsb. edu/gable/shelly/publications/422
17 Paquett J. (June 2009). *Awestruck: How Embracing Wonder Can Make You Happier, Healthier, and More Connected*. Shambhala Books; Thrive Global Staff. (July 2018). *Why Experiencing Wonder Can Do Wonders For Your Well-Being and Productivity: Science Shows There Are Clear Benefits to Nurturing What We Think of as Childlike Qualities*. Thrive Global.
18 Action for Happiness: https://www.actionforhappiness.org/10-keys-groups
19 Burton D. (April 3, 2020). *Neighborhood Art Can Spread Kindness and Joy in a Community to Combat Isolation and Loneliness*. University of Missouri Extension. Obtained at: https://extension.missouri. edu/news/neighborhood-art-can-spread-kindness-and-joy-in-a-community-to-combat-isolation-and-loneliness-4455
20 Keeley S. (August 2015). We live in the golden age of multicolored Seattle crosswalks. *Curbed/Vox Media*. Obtained at: https://seattle.curbed.com/2015/8/7/9932774/seattle-crosswalk-red-black-green-central-distruct

21 *Humor That Works.* Obtained at: https://www.humorthatworks.com/benefits/why-dont-you-laugh-abraham-lincoln-and-the-seriousness-of-humor
22 BrainyQuote. Obtained at: https://www.brainyquote.com/quotes/khalil_gibran_162061
23 Robinson L. et al. (July 2021). Laughter is the best medicine. *HelpGuide.* Obtained at: https://www.helpguide.org/articles/mental-health/laughter-is-the-best-medicine.htm
24 Ibid
25 Personal interview, March 1, 2022.
26 *A How-to Guide for Making a Physical Comedy Show to Build Neighbourhood Resilience.* https://www.resilientneighbourhoods.ca/wp-content/uploads/2017/03/Laughing-Allowed-How-to-Guide.pdf.
27 Humphrey M. (November 14, 2020). The comedian is in: peanuts-inspired stand delivers sidewalk comedy to pandemic-weary Vancouverites. *CBC News.* Obtained at: https://www.cbc.ca/news/canada/british-columbia/laughter-best-medicine-1.5799408
28 World Laughing Tour Inc.: https://www.worldlaughtertour.com/clubs/
29 Ibid.
30 Association of Applied and Therapeutic Humor: https://www.aath.org/
31 International Society for Humor Studies: https://www.humorstudies.org/
32 Institute for Emotionally Intelligent Learning: http://www.teacheq.com/
33 Ule M. (November 14, 2018). Lessons on gratitude learned from a natural disaster. *AllMomDoes.* Obtained at: https://www.allmomdoes.com/blog/lessons-on-gratitude-learned-from-a-natural-disaster/
34 Meta-Inspired. Obtained at: https://meta-inspired.com/the-power-of-gratitude-advice-from-a-great-roman-philosopher
35 Guerzon T.D. (December 9 2020). The power of gratitude: building mental resilience during tough times. *ParentMap.* Obtained at: https://www.parentmap.com/article/power-gratitude-building-mental-resilience-during-tough-times
36 Keltner D. and Marsh J. (January 8, 2015). How gratitude beats materialism: new studies reveal how to deliberately cultivate gratitude in ways that counter materialism and its negative effects. *Greater Good Magazine.* Obtained at: https://greatergood.berkeley.edu/article/item/materialism_gratitude_happiness
37 Emmons, R. (2013). *Gratitude Works!: A 21-Day Program for Creating Emotional Prosperity.* Jossey-Bass; and Sacks. O. (2015). *Gratitude.* New York, NY: Alfred A. Knopf.
38 News Staff. (November 1, 2021). Newport News launches "Attitude of Gratitude" campaign. *13 News Now.* Obtained at: https://www.13newsnow.com/article/news/community/newport-news-attitude-of-gratitude-campaign/291-88ddfe97-7473-4284-abd8-6d6c92e44110
39 Carnell M. (July 31, 2011). *Say Something Nice: Be a Lifter.* Charleston Publishing, Charleston, NC.
40 See for example: *Hosting Transformation* at: https://www.hostingtransformation.eu/methode/gratitude-circle/#; Gratitude Plus at https://www.gratitudeplusapp.com/about; and the *UK Mentally Health Schools Appreciation Circles*: https://www.mentallyhealthyschools.org.uk/resources/appreciation-circles-celebrating-ourselves-and-others/
41 Zhang C. et al. (Sept 4, 2018). To cope with stress try learning something new. *Harvard Business Review.* Obtained at: https://hbr.org/2018/09/to-cope-with-stress-try-learning-something-new
42 *Reliefweb* (April 17, 2020). Continuous learning can boost your health and enhance your social life. Obtained at: https://reliefweb.int/training/3606404/continuous-learning-can-help-boost-your-health-and-enhance-your-social-life#
43 Hammond C. (2007). Impacts of lifelong learning upon emotional resilience, psychological and mental health: Fieldwork evidence. *Oxford Review of Education*, 30(4); and UN Reliefweb (April 2020). Continuous learning can help boost your health.
44 UNESCO Global Network of Learning Cities: https://uil.unesco.org/lifelong-learning/learning-cities
45 UNESCO. (2016). Community-based lifelong learning and adult education: role of community learning centres as facilitators of lifelong learning. Obtained at: https://unesdoc.unesco.org/ark:/48223/pf0000246742
46 For more information, see the American Association for Adult and Continuing Education at: https://www.aaace.org/
47 Tamkins T. (January 16, 2019). 19 Moving stories from people who used exercise to change their life. *BuzzFeed News.* Obtained at: https://www.buzzfeednews.com/article/theresatamkins/how-exercise-can-save-your-life
48 Aubrey A. and Chatterjee R. (October 9, 2019). Changing your diet can help tamp down depression, boost mood. *NPR.* Obtained at: https://www.npr.org/sections/thesalt/2019/10/09/768665411/changing-your-diet-can-help-tamp-down-depression-boost-mood

49 UK Mental Health Foundation (January 2022). *Diet and Mental Health*. Obtained at: https://www.mentalhealth.org.uk/a-to-z/d/diet-and-mental-health and enhance your social life.
50 Wallace H. et al. (2019). Community coalitions for change and policy, systems, and environmental model: a community-based participatory approach to addressing obesity in rural Tennessee. *Preventing Chronic Disease*. Obtained at: https://www.ncbi.nlm.nih.gov/pmc/articles/PMC6745929/
51 Pollack Porter K. et al. (September 2019). Transforming city streets to promote physical activity and health equity. *HealthAffairs*. Obtained at: https://www.healthaffairs.org/doi/10.1377/hlthaff.2019.00454
52 See for example: Kandola A. et al. (2018). Moving to beat anxiety: epidemiology and therapeutic issues with physical activity for anxiety. *Current Psychiatry Reports*, 20(8), 63. Obtained at: https://pubmed.ncbi.nlm.nih.gov/30043270/; and Kandola A. A. et al. (2020). Individual and combined associations between cardiorespiratory fitness and grip strength with common mental disorders: a prospective cohort study in the UK. *BMC Medicine*. Obtained at: https://bmcmedicine.biomedcentral.com/articles/10.1186/s12916-020-01782-9
53 Walksheds: https://walkshed.org/
54 Minneapolis Paddle Share Program: https://www.paddleshare.org/ank. *BMC Medicine*, 18(1), 303.
55 Fresh Moves: https://freshmoveschicago.wordpress.com/
56 Common Threads: https://www.commonthreads.org
57 Fresh Roots: https://freshroots.ca/
58 Slow Food International: slowfood.com
59 Healthy Places by Design: https://healthyplacesbydesign.org/who-we-are/
60 Center for Advancing Healthy Communities: https://chronicdisease.org/the-center-for-advancing-healthy-communities/
61 America Walks: https://americawalks.org/programs/

CHAPTER 11

Establish Ongoing Opportunities for Residents to Heal Their Distresses and Traumas

The morning of November 8, 2018, promised to be a beautiful one in the town of Paradise, California. So it surprised Carol Holcomb to hear what sounded like raindrops dropping on her roof. When she went outside to investigate, she saw chunks of pine bark drifting down from the sky with billowing smoke. It was her first glimpse of the wildfire that incinerated 90 percent of the homes in her community.

"Everyone who experienced this went through trauma," said Linnea Duncan, a licensed clinical social worker who fled the rapid-moving firestorm from her home in Magalia, a community just north of Paradise. Debilitating nightmares and flashbacks are common after these types of events, as are anger, irritability, hypervigilance, sleep problems, as well as post-traumatic stress disorder (PTSD).[1]

For the majority of people who do not experience another traumatic event like Holcomb experienced soon after the previous one, the impacts eventually fade away. Even then, however, about 10 percent can experience continual symptoms of PTSD or other mental health problems. But if people soon find themselves in another extremely stressful or traumatic situation such as a flood, extreme heat event, or other disaster, or if they do not acknowledge and surfacing their despair, the symptoms may affect them for years.

Holcomb got help for her PTSD and started to heal. But she was so traumatized that she decided to look for a home in a farming community. "I can't live in the forest again," said Holcomb. "I just can't."[2]

As this story illustrates, even if communities successfully engage residents in each of the other four foundational areas involved with building universal capacity for mental wellness and transformational resilience, the cascading disruptions to essential systems and acute disasters generated during the long climate emergency will distress almost everyone, and seriously traumatize many others. Establishing ongoing opportunities for people to heal their traumas will therefore be another vital protective factor RCCs will need to emphasize.

ENGAGEMENT IN THE OTHER FOUR FOUNDATIONAL AREAS WILL OFTEN FOSTER SELF-HEALING

As previously stated, the long climate emergency is certain to cause millions of people to experience anxiety, depression, anger, grief, hopelessness, and other distressing emotions. However, for most people, these feelings will not be symptoms of psychopathology. They will be normal reactions to dysfunctional and often frightening external conditions. Again, rather than pathologizing people, it will be important for RCCs to help everyone understand the distress they feel is perfectly natural given the state of the world. Helping people engage in the other four foundational areas involved with enhancing universal capacity for mental wellness and transformational resilience will enable many to heal themselves.

Self-healing will occur, for example, when people gain emotional support from close family, friends, or others in their community, join with fellow residents to build healthy, safe,

DOI: 10.4324/9781003262442-15

just and equitable climate resilient local built/physical, economic, and ecological conditions, and when they develop good mental wellness and resilience literacy. People can also self-heal when they engage in specific therapeutic practices such as forgiveness, finding simple joys, laughing a lot, being grateful, learning new things, and caring for their physical health. And self-healing can occur when people transform experiences that previously caused them to harm themselves, others, or the natural environment, into opportunities to learn, grow, and find positive new sources of meaning, purpose, and healthy hope.

At the same time, millions of people are certain to require more to heal the traumas they experience. It will therefore be essential for RCCs to establish ongoing opportunities for residents to obtain safe and emotional supportive ways to journey through the healing process.

Healing can often be difficult because distressed and traumatized people can fail to understand what they are experiencing or how to deal with it. Often all they can do is attend to their basic needs, such as finding shelter or getting food on the table. This is why it is crucial for RCCs to take the lead to organize ongoing healing opportunities. As Ruben Cantu from Prevention Institute told me during an interview, "It only takes one person or group to recognize the need for people to heal, and they are usually leaders of their community."[3]

HEALING CLIMATE TRAUMAS

Establishing opportunities to heal traumas does not mean the threatening events or circumstances that traumatized residents experience will disappear or be forgotten. This will often be impossible as the climate emergency accelerates because people are likely to directly experience additional traumas, know family or friends who are impacted, or witness from afar incidences or conditions that are similar to those that caused their original suffering. For many, there will be no post-disaster calm period that gives them time to grieve, recover, and move on with their lives as they would typically do after a "normal" single-event catastrophe that ends. Adversities will often be ongoing and produce roller-coaster-like ups and downs with no easy fix or closure.

This does not mean that people who are traumatized by climate impacts cannot recover and live meaningful, fulfilling lives. Healing is possible. If people don't deny what is happening and can surface, share, and release the trauma they experienced, they can learn to manage their distress in ways that allow them to regain control of their lives without being overwhelmed by thoughts and feelings about the past or fears about the future. This will allow people to feel good, function well, and find new sources of meaning, purpose, and healthy forms of hope, despite the ongoing adversities they and others experience or witness.[4]

Healing is possible because the human mind can be considered a great garden in which many types of seeds can grow. Said differently, the mind can be thought of as a field of wildflowers. Under certain conditions some wildflowers grow, when conditions change others wither away and die, and still others will take their place and grow again. In neuroscience this is called neuroplasticity, which means that at the neurological level the human brain has the capacity for flexibility, dynamic growth, and change.[5]

A countless variety of seeds exist within our brains. Some are positive, such as the seeds of compassion, empathy, joy, fairness, and happiness. Others can sow harmful outcomes, such as seeds of delusion, anger, jealousy, greed, and willful ignorance. Some of the seeds that grow in our minds are innate and others are passed down by our evolutionary and more recent biological ancestors. Other seeds are sown when we were in the womb and when we are young children. And still others are planted by the norms that dominate the social networks we existing within, and by the economic, religious, and political ideologies we are exposed to, and the structural conditions and policies they create.

What is important to understand is that no matter when and where our seeds originated, the quality of our lives—our capacity for mental wellness and transformational resilience—depends on which seeds we choose to nurture and grow.

Neuroplasticity means the neurons of the human brain have the capacity to learn, adapt, and grow. To grow positive seeds—which helps heal trauma—requires making deliberate efforts to nourish the seeds that allow us to feel good, function well, and find meaning, purpose, and healthy hope, and not water the toxic seeds.[6] Because repressed anxiety, fear, depression, anger, grief, and other distressing emotions become imbedded in the nervous system and produce symptoms of psychological pain, as well as physical illnesses, healing requires releasing those emotions, which will, over time, dissipate the symptoms.

The starting point in the healing process is to develop some level of clarity about what happened in the past and what is occurring now within us. Developing the capacity to identify, recognize, and acknowledge what we experienced, and our reaction to it, opens the space within us required to begin the healing process. Processing internalized trauma in this way releases it from the nervous system and allows it to surface and be processed. Continued healing involves constant effort to nourish the seeds that enhance mental wellness and transformational resilience, while allowing those that generate suffering to dry up and wither away.

When traumatized people feel emotionally safe and supported by those around them, and have good guidance, they can share their trauma experience with others and describe in their own words how they reacted at the time of the event or circumstances. When they are ready, they can then share what they have thought about and how they have acted since the events, and why they have been unable to let go of the thoughts and emotions that accompany them. Allowing people to share their trauma story with others in this way helps them make sense of it, and receives the validation needed to move forward with the grieving process.[7]

Elisabeth Kübler-Ross described five stages of the grieving and healing process for serious loss: denial, anger, bargaining, depression, and final acceptance. The coauthor of two of her books, David Kessler, eventually added a sixth stage: finding meaning in the loss. Although the stages are described sequentially, the reality is that the grieving process is not linear. People will not necessarily go through all the stages or follow a specific order. Each person is different and will experience the grieving and healing process in their own unique ways.[8]

HEALING CIRCLES AND OTHER COMMUNITY-BASED THERAPEUTIC METHODS

One therapeutic approach that will help community members move through the grieving process and heal during the climate crisis is "healing circles." As I briefly mentioned in Chapter Six, the approach is derived from practices of Native Americans, First Nations, and indigenous people. The circles, which can involve 5–100 people or more, emphasize the formation of relationships that allow people to share their trauma stories as equals with others who have experienced painful experiences in a safe and supportive environment, and then engage in dialogues. They are called "circles" because participants usually sit in a circle. The process is usually facilitated by trained peers and takes place over two-to-three hours. The facilitators provide the guidance and support people need to move through the process of healing their distress and traumas.

Healing circles are widely used today to support people with cancer, those who have lost loved ones, and individuals who have experienced racism or been subjected to many other types of systemic oppressions. An important element of healing circles is the focus on strength-based dialogues that enable people to identify the assets and resources that enabled them to survive a harmful ordeal. They also emphasize community-building in a shared environment which creates solidarity, collective healing, and the proliferation of resilience.

The way people relate to memories of past traumatic events is a vital part of the healing process. The more they focus on the strengths and resources they used to endure the adversities, the more likely they are to realize they had some degree of control during the experience. This understanding allows them to transform their experience into a vision of the future that includes new possibilities and new sources of healthy hope, based on new ways to utilize their skills, strengths, and resources. This type of approach, which is the focus of most Healing Circles, enhances their resilience by opening the door to a new approach to life, new social connections, and an enhanced sense of self-efficacy.

OTHER FORMS OF HEALING OPPORTUNITIES

It will also be important for RCCs to help establish ongoing therapeutic art, theatre, written dialogues, journaling, drawings, different forms of mindfulness, connecting with nature, and other healing opportunities. The approaches an RCC pursues should be shaped by the age, demographic, and cultural make-up of the neighborhoods and communities they are engaged with (Figure 11.1).

Figure 11.1 Examples of Age and Culturally Accountable Healing Opportunities for the Climate Crisis

HEALING THROUGH MENTAL HEALTH TREATMENT

Individualized mental health treatment will also remain important. As previously discussed, however, the number of certified clinicians will never be sufficient to assist all of the people who will be traumatized as the climate emergency accelerates. In addition, most of the trained professionals that do exist are usually found in wealthier urban centers, not low income or BIPOC communities or rural areas. Further, due to fears of being stigmatized, treated inequitably, and other reasons, many people will not engage in mental health treatment services. Clinicians themselves will often be severely distressed or traumatized by climate impacts, which can reduce their effectiveness, minimize their availability, or cause them to leave the field altogether. For this reason, it will be important for clinicians themselves to regularly engage in healing methods.

In addition, as discussed throughout this book, it will be important to remember that not all of the problems people experience can be traced back to internal personal or family dynamics. The social, cultural, physical/built, economic, and ecological conditions people exist within can cause significant mental health and psycho-social-spiritual problems. Mental health treatments might help some people deal with these forces a little better. But treating individual symptoms of pathology may not work very well when ever-present social-ecologically generated traumas and toxic stresses exist and are reinforced by unhealthy, unsafe, and unjust social norms, economic practices, and government policies. This is why engagement in community-based healing events, and the other four foundational areas involved with enhancing universal capacity for mental wellness and transformational resilience, must be a priority.

THE THERAPEUTIC IMPORTANCE OF MEMORIAL EVENTS AND RITUALS

In addition to direct healing opportunities, when communities are traumatized by climate-related events, it will also be therapeutic for residents to come together to hold public rituals and ceremonies that memorialize what happened and honor those who were injured, lost, or seriously affected. These types of events often spring up spontaneously when people organize vigils that can include the placement of pictures, cards, or flowers in symbolic locations. Planning other types of memorial events in advance will ensure people throughout the community are aware of them and can attend.

This might sometimes be challenging during ongoing climate adversities. However, a continual series of community rituals and memorial events can help residents connect with each other, share their grief, develop mutual support, gain collective strength, and water the positive seeds that can help them begin the healing process.

Memorial ceremonies will also be important to keep the adversities alive in the public eye, highlight the need to support the survivors, and pressure elected officials, business leaders, and others to adopt practices and policies that reduce the climate emergency to acceptable levels. At the events, people will often come up with catchy slogans and narratives that promote healing, prevention, and transformational resilience that can be widely distributed through the media and local social support networks. Community rituals and memorial events can also serve as a venue for victims to demand justice from perpetrators and seek redress. Further, they can be a powerful way to help people learn lessons from what occurred and take collective action to prevent future traumas and improve local conditions.

Examples of How RCCs Can Establish Culturally Accountable Healing Opportunities

*   *Convivencia Gatherings in Sonoma County, California*: Following the 2017 Tubbs Fire discussed in Chapter 10, some people were traumatized every time an ambulance siren blared near their homes in Santa Rosa. Things got even worse after the Kincade Fire, which blazed through Sonoma County two years later. To cope, many Latinos began to attend a *Convivencia*, or community gathering, organized by Humanidid Therapy and Educational Services. Convivencia essentially means "gathering." They are a type of healing circle but were not promoted that way. They looked more like a family picnic or potluck. Wildfire survivors gathered in a local park to discuss their experiences with a bilingual therapist over hot chocolate, coffee and bread. The facilitator walked them through deep-breathing exercises, stretches, and stress-reduction techniques in Spanish. By placing the focus on socializing and sharing personal stories, the cultural stigma of mental-health treatment that is prevalent in the Latino community was overcome. After attending these free group sessions for several weeks, people realized they were not alone and began to heal.[9]

*   *The Neighborhood Resilience Project in Pittsburg, Pennsylvania*: A different form of healing is offered by this wonderful organization. The Neighborhood Resilience Project (NRP) is run by staff and volunteers and uses a Trauma-Informed Community Development Framework to assist residents of the city's poorest neighborhoods. This approach helps people "be healthy enough to sustain opportunity and realize their potential." The NRP starts its work by providing community support to local residents. This includes an emergency food pantry that provides residents with enough food to get through the month, meals to children on weekends, medical care, counseling, help to recover lost identification cards, clothing to those who need it, and weekly bus passes to people who obtain jobs but do not have means to travel to the workplace. After people become engage in these activities, the NRP engages them in a year-long healing process. They build meaningful relationships among residents that lead to community-based networks that introduce and reinforce healthy interventions that enhance health and wellness. The interventions include free primary, behavioral, and dental care offered by volunteer professionals for people who are under or uninsured. It also includes several microcommunity interventions. As people begin to heal, they are asked to become leaders to foster positive change in their community by helping their brothers and sisters. Their service to others is a strong indication of healing and can produce significant change in the community. This NRP describes it as knighting "the oppressed in order to attain true personal and community transformation."[10]

    RCCs can learn a great deal from the Convivencia Gatherings and Neighborhood Resilience Project about how ongoing healing initiatives can be organized in their community.

Other Ways RCCS Can Establish Ongoing Healing Opportunities

*   *Model Healing Practices During RCC Meetings and Activities*: Many members of the RCC board/steering committee and Resilience Innovation Teams are certain

to be distressed, and others will be traumatized as the climate emergency plays out. In addition to encouraging them to participate in formal healing events, simple healing practices can take place during meetings and events. For example, an RCC might start every event with a one to two minute "Resilience Pause" when participants practice a resilience skill and take time out for one or two additional Resilience Pauses throughout the session. Modeling how a broad and diverse coalition can engage in healing will also influence others in the community.

- *Organize Trauma Healing Resilience Innovation Teams*: RCCs can also form a Trauma Healing Resilience Innovation Team composed of neighborhood groups, volunteer organizations, faith-based, nonprofit, private, and public organizations that work together to plan and organize a wide range of ongoing age and culturally accountable opportunities for residents to heal their trauma. The Innovation Teams should organize affordable, easy-to-reach healing gatherings for every age group and population in the community. Here are some examples of the healing methods RCCs can organize:

  ○ *Establish Ongoing Integrative Community Therapy (ICT) Gatherings*: ICT is a therapeutic approach that enhances social connection and fosters emotional solidarity. It was created by Dr. Adalberto Barreto to build psychological and emotional literacy and support communities in crisis in poor neglected neighborhoods in Brazil called favelas. There are 40,000 trained facilitators in Brazil and ITC has become part of the Brazilian primary health system. It is also now used across Latin America, Africa, Asia, and in Europe as well. The method derives its conceptual basis from Paulo Freire's work, cultural anthropology, resilience theory, systems thinking, and communication theory. RCCs can connect with Dr. Barreto's organization, or with the Visible Hands Collaborative, which is promoting the approach in the US, to offer ITC programs in their community.[11]

  ○ *Establish Other Types of Group Healing Opportunities*: There are several other approaches to group healing that RCCs can utilize. Some are called Restoration Circles, and are being used by communities in many parts of the US and numerous other nations. Healing Circles Global offers information about how to form and facilitate these gatherings. They also train people in how to facilitate healing circles. In addition, they offer online Coming Together circles, which are incubators for specific circles that address topics such as people living with cancer, grieving together, sexual orientation, gender, race, healing through the arts, and life transitions. And, they offer circles for people who live in the same part of the world but speak different languages.[12]

  ○ *Offer Culturally Accountable Healing Gatherings*: RCCs should ensure that the healing opportunities offered in their community are culturally accountable. Some organizations RCCs can connect with include:

    □ *The National Compadres Network*: It provides training and technical assistance to organizations and system leaders who are looking for tangible ways to support Chicano, Latino, Native, Raza, and other communities of color address issues of racial inequity and heal from intergenerational and present day traumas. Its culturally based transformational health and healing philosophy recognizes that within an individual's, families, and

community's authentic cultural values, traditions, and indigenous practices exist that offer a pathway to healthy development, restoration, and
life-long well-being. They offer a variety of trainings as well as consulting
options and have networks composed of individuals and organizations
that have participated in the NCN's Healing Generations efforts or La
Cultura Cura curriculum certification trainings throughout the US.[13]

▫ *Emotional Emancipation Circles for People of Color*: EE Circles help Black people heal from centuries of white racism and superiority. Originated by
the Community Healing Network, and developed in collaboration with
The Association of Black Psychologists (ABPsi), EE Circles are evidence-
informed, psychologically sound, culturally grounded, and community-
defined self-help support groups designed as "liberatory spaces in which
Black people share stories; deepen our understanding of the impact of
historical forces on our sense of self-worth, our relationships, and our
communities; and learn essential emotional wellness skills to help us be at
our best as individuals and as a people."[14]

▫ *The Community Healing Network*: In addition to the Emotional Emancipation Circles, this network mobilizes Black people to "heal from the trauma
caused by centuries of anti-Black racism, to free ourselves of toxic ste-
reotypes, and to reclaim our dignity and humanity as people of African ancestry." They offer Community Healing Days, Rapid Response
Unbuntu Healing Circles, and other services to help Black people heal
from trauma.[15]

• *Organize Ongoing Somatic, Mindfulness, Art, Music, Writing, Dance/Movement, Drama,
and other Therapeutic Opportunities*: RCCs should also consider healing opportunities that focus on: somatic skills such as body scan, tracking, grounding,
shaking, and dancing; mindfulness skills such as soft-belly breathing, six second breathing, guided meditation, and mindful eating and walking; cognitive
skills such as awareness of thinking distortions, guided imagery, dialogues with
symptoms, and meetings with the wiser self; and other healing techniques.[16]
For example, RCCs can connect with the The Pocket Project, based in the EU,
that offers programs to promote trauma-informed leadership to heal individual, ancestral, and collective trauma.[17] They can also contact the International
Expressive Arts Therapy Association to obtain names of certified expressive
therapists, artists, educators, consultants and others "using integrated, multi-
modal arts processes for personal and community growth and transformation."[18]
The American Association of Art Therapy supports a mental health approach
offered by certified art therapists who can engage participants in painting, drawing, sculpting, photography, digital art, creative journaling, music, dance and
other art forms.[19]

• *Engage Residents in Nature-Based Healing*: Also called ecotherapy, this is an umbrella
term for the practice of being in nature to promote healing. There are different
types of nature-based healing programs including: exercising outside in green
spaces; wilderness therapy, animal-assisted therapy; using natural materials for
arts and crafts; therapeutic farming; and therapeutic horticulture (see the sub-
section "*Utilize Innovations Like Social and Therapeutic Horticulture*"). When engaging
in these practices, it is important for participants to leave their smart phones

and other technological devices behind so they actually are present and connect with nature. When people go into nature it will also be vital to take great care to not beat down or in other ways damage ecosystems or harm biodiversity, as large groups can easily do this. A number of universities and organizations offer Ecotherapy Certificate Programs. Dr. Patricia Hasbach, who for 13 years co-directed the Lewis and Clark Ecotherapy Program, has written an excellent book about it titled *Grounded: A Guided Journal To Help You Reconnect with the Power of Nature and Yourself.*[20]

- *Utilize Innovations Like Social and Therapeutic Horticulture:* Thrive Birmingham, located in Birmingham, England, uses an approach called "social and therapeutic horticulture" where therapists help people with specific health, social, or educational needs work with plants and others to improve their mental and physical health, as well as communication and thinking skills. The program works in small groups, on a 1-1 basis, and in larger groups to facilitate social interaction, engage in discussions, and support group learning. The work takes place in a public park, but the gardens where they run their program offer a safe, secure, and private space for "client gardeners" to work with volunteers and therapists. They also run several outreach projects in the broader community as well as "Sow and Grow," a 12-week course in seasonal gardening for people over 50-years old.[21]

- *Organize Peer-to-Peer Trainings and Healing Opportunities:* Many residents will not participate in healing programs offered by trained mental health professionals. They will, however, be willing to engage when services are facilitated by people like them. And, as previously stated, people who have healed from trauma are often the best to help others heal. Peer-to-peer healing programs will be an important way for an RCC to help residents normalize their stress reactions, reduce stigma and other barriers to engagement, and increase the social connections needed to heal the traumas they experience during the long climate mega-emergency. The programs typically offer regular people the opportunity to become educated in one or more of the three aspects of mental wellness and resilience literacy discussed in Chapter 9. The training programs often end with a certification. After an individual is trained and certified, they join with others who have similar training to offer support services to their fellow residents. This can include facilitating different types of healing circle, peer-level crisis counseling, community support groups, community outreach, home visits, and other services. The National Empowerment Center offers a range of educational materials, workshops, and other resources on how to organize peer-to-peer healing programs. As you read in Chapter 5, the Center for Mind-Body Medicine and Trauma Resources Institute offer peer-to-peer training programs in many locations worldwide.[22]

- *Organize Neighborhood Resilience Healing Hubs:* As discussed in Chapter 7, a number of communities are establishing neighborhood-focused resilience hubs to provide services during and after disasters. In addition to San Francisco, California, and Victoria British Columbia, for example, the US cities of Baltimore, Minneapolis, Miami, and Washington DC have created hubs that strive to coordinate services by a number of government agencies and nonprofit organizations during disasters, including the provision of culturally sensitive, multilingual services.[23] The hubs can provide services, such as safe shelter during a disaster, a distribution center for food and water, and source of multilingual information for diverse groups of residents.

Most hubs are located in churches, libraries, civic centers, or other facilities trusted by local residents. Although many of the existing resilience hubs offer services delivered by local agencies and institutions and thus have a top-down emphasis, RCCs can establish grass-roots organized Trauma Healing Hubs that offer residents ongoing age and culturally accountable opportunities to connect with neighbors and engage in practices that help heal their suffering.[24]

- *Organize Resilience Centers*: A slightly different approach RCCs can use is to establish Resilience Centers in their community. The Israel Trauma Coalition (ITC) uses this approach. It allows area residents to receive both trauma therapy and participate in workshops that strengthen and build community resilience. By establishing the Resilience Centers, they found that "the focus changed from victim-based trauma to a proactive community approach which places a focus on strengths, resources, and a culture of preparedness and mutual help." The coalition has seen that the approach "has contributed to the resilience of communities not only in times of crisis but also in times of relative calm and routine." RCCs should examine the ITCs approach and see how it can be replicated in their community.[25]

- *Organize Memorial Events and Rituals*: Because disasters will become commonplace as the climate mega-emergency worsens, ongoing anniversary events, rituals, and symbols will contribute to the healing process. The National Mass Violence Victimization Resource Center (NMVVRC) offers helpful information about how to organize memorial events and rituals for any type of emergency or disaster. The events should let people know where support can be found and engage them in healthy, safe, and equitable responses. Memorial events that are initiated and led by residents are typically most beneficial to survivors, which is why an RCC should play a key role in organizing and supporting them.[26]

There are many other approaches to healing that RCCs can promote as well. The point is that trauma healing opportunities should be made available on a regular basis to people of all ages, backgrounds, and cultures during the long climate mega-emergency. The healing opportunities should be integrated into the RCCs efforts to engage community members in each of the other four foundational areas involved with building universal capacity for mental wellness and transformational resilience.

RCCs can use the checklist provided at the end of this chapter to determine the degree to which it has considered the different ways to offer ongoing healing opportunities to community members. To implement and sustain these opportunities, as well as each of the other four foundational areas involved with building universal capacity for mental wellness and transformational resilience, RCCs will need to continually evaluate its progress, learn, and improve their offerings. Coalitions will also need to plan ahead to ensure its activities can be sustained during the challenging times that lie ahead. The next chapter will discuss how these, and other needs, can be addressed.

CHECKLIST

For establishing ongoing opportunities for residents to heal climate distresses and traumas.

	Yes	No	Comments
Did the RCC find ways to support the efforts of residents to self-heal their distresses and traumas?			
Did the RCC consider establishing different types of age and culturally accountable healing circles?			
Did the RCC consider establishing age and culturally accountable somatic, art, writing, mindfulness, movement-based, nature-based, and other types of healing options?			
Did the RCC establish innovative therapeutic opportunities like therapeutic horticulture?			
Did the RCC find ways to support memorial events and rituals that emerge spontaneously in the community during or after an emergency?			
Did the RCC develop a strategy to hold a regular series of memorial events and rituals to commemorate previous disasters and emergencies?			

NOTES

1 O'Neill S. (April 8, 2019). Mourning paradise: Collective trauma in a town destroyed by fire. *Kaiser Health News*. Obtained at: https://patch.com/california/across-ca/mourning-paradise-collective-trauma-town-destroyed-fire
2 Ibid.
3 Personal interview December 3, 2021.
4 Boss P. (1999). *Ambiguous Loss: Learning to Live with Unresolved Grief*. Boston, MA: The President and Fellows of Harvard University, 8–25.
5 Voss P. et al. (October 2017). Dynamic brains and the changing rules of neuroplasticity: implications for learning and recovery. *Frontiers in Psychology*. Obtained at: https://www.frontiersin.org/articles/10.3389/fpsyg.2017.01657/full
6 This description of the trauma healing process combines my background in neuroscience with the simple way Buddhist psychology explains it. See for example: Nhat Hahn T. (2002). *Understanding Our Mind: 50 verses of Buddhist Psychology*. Parallax Press, Berkley, CA; Hanson R. (2013) *Hardwiring Happiness: The New Brain Science of Contentment, Calm and Confidence*. Rodale, Emmaus, PA; and Doidge N. (2015). *The Brain's Way of Healing: Remarkable Discoveries and Recoveries from the Frontiers of Neuroplasticity*. Viking Press, New York, NY.
7 Boss P. (1999). *Ambiguous Loss: Learning to Live with Unresolved Grief*. Boston, MA: The President and Fellows of Harvard University, pp. 8–25.
8 Kessler D. (2019). *Finding Meaning: The Six Stages of Grief*. New York, NY: Scribner Books.
9 This story was retrieved from: Cattel M. (August 25 2020). Community gatherings offer healing for emotional wounds after disasters. *Center for Public Integrity*. Obtained at: https://publicintegrity.org/environment/hidden-epidemics/community-gatherings-offer-healing-for-emotional-wounds-after-disasters/
10 Community Healing Network: https://communityhealingnet.org/
11 Visible Hands Collaborative: https://www.visiblehandscollaborative.org/
12 Healing Circles Global: https://healingcirclesglobal.org/#top

13 National Compadres Network: https://www.nationalcompadresnetwork.org/about/mission-and-purpose/
14 Emotional Emancipation Networks. Obtained at: https://communityhealingnet.org/emotional-emancipation-circle/
15 Ibid.
16 This is a sampling of healing techniques offered by the Center for Mind-Body Medicine, The Trauma Resource Institute, my Transformational Resilience healing programs, and other organizations. However, it does not represent a complete list of all the healing methods that are available.
17 The Pocket Project: https://pocketproject.org/
18 International Expressive Arts Therapy Association: https://www.ieata.org/
19 American Art Therapy Association: https://arttherapy.org/becoming-art-therapist/
20 To obtain the book go to: https://www.simonandschuster.com/books/Grounded/Patricia-H-Hasbach/9781507218105
21 I first heard about Thrive Birmingham during a personal interview with Dr. Antonis Kousoulis from the Mental Health Foundation in the UK. More information can be obtained at: Thrive Birmingham, https://www.thrive.org.uk/how-we-help/regional-centres-and-programmes/birmingham
22 The Trauma Resource Institute: https://www.traumaresourceinstitute.com/
23 Rogerson B. and Narayan M. (June 22, 2020). Resilience hubs cam help communities thrive--and better weather disasters: Baltimore and Minneapolis among cities trying new approach to better coordinate critical services. *The Pew Charitable Trusts*. Obtained at: https://www.pewtrusts.org/en/-research-and-analysis/articles/2020/06/22/resilience-hubs-can-help-communities-thrive-and-better-weather-disasters
24 For more information about Resilience Hubs, see: Baja K. (2019). *Guide to Developing Resilience Hubs*, Urban Sustainability Directors Network. Obtained at: http://resilience-hub.org/wp-content/uploads/2019/10/USDN_ResilienceHubsGuidance-1.pdf
25 Israel Trauma Coalition Resilience Centers: http://israeltraumacoalition.org/in-israel/
26 The National Mass Violence Victimization Resource Center (NMVVRC). *Remembering*. Obtained at: https://www.nmvvrc.org/community-leaders/rebuild-your-community/remembering/

CHAPTER 12

Continually Track Progress, Learn, Improve, and Plan for the Long Term

After the strategies developed by an RCC have been implemented for a year or so, it will be imperative to regularly evaluate progress and learn what works and what does not. The RCC should use this information to adjust the assumptions, beliefs, and thinking that shaped its logic model, and continually improve its goals, strategies, and action plans. Regular evaluation will also help local residents understand what the RCC is doing, what has been accomplished, what the outcomes are, and how they came about. This will help increase the support and engagement of community members.

In addition, after a few years of implementing and evaluating its strategies, the RCC should begin to plan for the long term. This involves establishing methods to ensure the RCC can continue to learn, innovate, and improve its efforts to strengthen and sustain the entire population's capacity for mental wellness and transformational resilience during ongoing climate adversities.

In this chapter, I explain both of these focuses. It is not intended to be an all-inclusive description of either issue. The purpose is to provide enough basic information to help an RCC understand how it can move forward and craft its own approach.

THE IMPORTANCE OF ONGOING TRACKING AND EVALUATION

The purpose of tracking and evaluating an RCC's activities and progress is to improve its effectiveness and inform future planning and implementation.[1] The process involves four overall steps:

1 The RCC develops its logic model and strategies (as described in Chapter 6).
2 After the strategies have been implemented for a year or two, information about the process and results is gathered.
3 The data are analyzed and interpreted.
4 The findings and conclusions are published in a report.

The four steps should be done in a collaborative way that involves RCC members, as well as other residents, groups, and organizations from across the community. When done well, the process will tell the story of the RCC's approach and strategies to everyone involved and those who are observing from the outside.

Taking the time to develop a well-planned and executed evaluation process will provide many more benefits for the RCC, and the community, than an assessment completed in haste or as an afterthought. RCC members might think they lack the time, resources, and expertise to complete this type of evaluation. However, taking the effort to learn about and carefully plan evaluations will help everyone understand what has gone well, and what has not, which will enable coalition members to continually improve their strategies. In addition,

DOI: 10.4324/9781003262442-16

a good evaluation will allow funders to see evidence that the RCC's approach is working, which can lead to continued and possibly additional funding.

THE EVALUATION PROCESS

One way an RCC can evaluate the progress of its activities is to monitor changes seen in the indicators it selected as part of its logic model. In Chapter 6, the need to use indicators that are good proxies for measuring mental wellness and transformational resilience in a community was discussed. For example, one indicator of the degree to which residents have good Bonding and Bridging social connections might be the number of individuals who say they now have people they can count on for emotional support and practical assistance during an emergency. Another might be how frequently a resident contacts their friends or neighbors either face-to-face, electronically, or by phone.

RCC members can track changes in these indicators every 6–12 months to see what, if any, shifts are occurring. Or, if they can raise funds, they can hire a consultant or work with a university to complete the monitoring.

EVALUATION THINKING

RCCs will often benefit by more in-depth evaluations that involve what is called "evaluative thinking."[2] This approach focuses on much more than just determining if the RCC's activities performed as expected. Evaluative thinking involves constant discussion, reflection, learning, and improvement. It involves surfacing and openly discussing the underlying assumptions and beliefs coalition members hold about the nature of the populations and sectors they are engaged with, and the challenges they face. It also involves asking thought-provoking questions about the changes that should be expected when the RCC engages in its work. The entire process should always be carried out in a culturally accountable manner to ensure the assessment process is not shaped by beliefs or assumptions that are prejudiced or in any other way will lead to limited or biased conclusions.

In short, evaluative thinking involves constant learning, growth, and improvement. The process should become embedded within the culture of the RCC and shape all its activities.

DEVELOPING AN EVALUATION PLAN

The first step in developing an evaluation plan involves determining what type of evaluation is needed. The type of assessment should be determined by the stage the RCC's activities are in. Different types of evaluations are more helpful during the early stage of an initiative, compared to those used three to five years down the road.

There are three overall types of assessment processes. Each serves a specific function and answers different questions:

1. *Process (or implementation) evaluation* seeks to determine if the RCC's strategies are being implemented as planned and according to schedule. It also assesses if the strategy is producing the intended outcomes, and identifies its strengths and weaknesses. An

RCC should employ this type of assessment early on in its operations to determine what, if any changes, are needed in its strategies and action plans.

2. *Outcome (or summative) evaluation* seeks to determine if the RCC's strategy achieved the desired outcomes and what made it effective or ineffective. It also determines if the approach is sustainable and replicable. An RCC should consider this type of evaluation after it completes one to two years of implementing its strategies and action plans to determine the outcomes.

3. *Impact evaluation* determines any broad long-term changes that have occurred as a result of the RCC's activities. The impacts constitute the net effects for individuals, families, a neighborhood, groups (such as informal clubs), organizations (such as schools), and the community as a whole. This type of evaluation is likely to make the most sense three to five years after the RCC starts its work.

After the RCC has determined the specific type or combination of assessment methods it wants to use, the next step is to determine the approach to evaluation it will employ. Four approaches can be considered:

1. *Culturally responsive evaluation* recognizes that cultural beliefs, values, and context lie at the core of any evaluation process. It ensures that people who have been historically excluded are fully integrated into the design, planning, and implementation of the assessment process.

2. *Developmental evaluation* supports innovation. It recognizes that innovative initiatives like an RCC is engaged in will be continually adapting to new information and challenges. It therefore emphasizes using information to continually learn and innovate in the face of change.

3. *Empowerment evaluation* can provide an RCC with tools and knowledge that helps participants improve their efforts through constant self-reflection and evaluation. RCC members are involved in facilitated discussions, often led by the evaluators, to clarify priorities for the assessment process to determine the evidence necessary to determine success.

4. *Systems-based evaluation* views the RCC's activities as part of social-ecological systems that are affected by the many interlocking cultural, economic, ecological, and political systems in which it operates. It emphasizes boundary conditions, relationships, and feedbacks within and across the systems of the community in which the RCC operates.

After the evaluation approach is chosen, the methodology that will be used to gather information and assess progress should be determined. This can include:

- *Case studies* that assess, in-depth, one specific RCC activity, or elements of an activity, with the goal of generalizing the findings to other programs. Cross-case studies can also be used to compare patterns found in a variety of case studies.

- *Experimental and quasi-experimental design (or randomized control) studies* that assess the effects seen by comparing a group involved with the RCC's activities with a group that was not involved.

- *Outcome mapping* that assesses how an RCC's strategy affected the individuals, groups, and organizations it was designed to influence or interact with. The outcomes can include changes in social connections, activities, behaviors, actions of individuals and groups, and other characteristics.

AN EXAMPLE

Let us say, for example, that the RCC has implemented a strategy to build social connections across boundaries in the community and now wants to evaluate it. It secures funding from a local donor and hires an external consultant or works with a university to complete the assessment. The RCC decides to only hire evaluator(s) who are skilled in culturally responsive evaluation because the RCC's activities take place within a racially and culturally diverse community.

Through discussions with the evaluator(s), the RCC might decide the first step will be to conduct a process and outcome evaluation to help the RCC understand the extent to which its strategy was implemented as planned, and achieved its intended outcomes.

Following this, discussions with the evaluator(s) might lead the RCC to determine that it will benefit from the combination of a case study and quasi-experimental design methodology. This could, for instance, compare the changes in social connections found in four different neighborhoods, with an in-depth case study of one or two neighborhoods to understand in greater detail what, if any, changes occurred and how they came about. Combining the two methodologies will generate different types of information that help the RCC understand what happened and tell its story in greater depth. However, this approach will also require more funding and other resources, and the evaluation team will need expertise in both methodologies.

The evaluator(s) would then work with the RCC to craft an easy-to-read report, complete with simple graphics, that describes the extent to which the RCC did what it intended to do, and the changes that have be observed as a result. The information should then be widely shared with residents, groups, and organizations community-wide. It should also be used by RCC members, including people involved with the Resilience Innovation Teams, to learn what worked and what did not, reassess the assumptions and beliefs that shaped their logic model, and improve their strategies.

To enhance and sustain universal capacity for mental wellness and transformational resilience during the long climate emergency, RCCs should continually develop an evaluation strategy, collect information, analyze and interpret the data, report the findings, and learn and improve its offerings. The process should be repeated every year or so.

CONTINUAL EVALUATION HELPS TROUBLESHOOT PROBLEMS

By continually evaluating its work, an RCC will have greater capacity to understand why certain things succeed as intended and others fail. Some of the common troubles the RCC might experience include:

- Lack of suitable spaces to hold meetings and events;
- Inability of key groups and organizations to engage due to lack of time, transportation, or financial resources;
- Reluctance of certain populations to participate due to fears about their safety, stigmatization, lack of cultural relevance, or inequities and injustices;
- Insufficient funding or other key resources;
- Lack of skilled staff or sufficient staff time to support the RCCs activities;
- Insufficient number of volunteers to assist with events;
- Burnout by RCC members due to having too much on their plate;

- Tensions or conflicts over approaches to enhance mental wellness and transformational resilience;
- Minimal age and culturally accountable resilience-building activities;
- Participants sporadically attending meetings and events, or leaving early;
- Continual disruptions due to persistent climate impacts.

These are common troubles every new coalition is likely to face. Continual evaluation will help an RCC spot these problems early on. Coalition members can then engage in candid discussions about what might be causing them and how they can be addressed.

RCCS SHOULD BECOME LEARNING COMMUNITIES

I have just described a traditional way RCC's activities can be evaluated. However, there is another closely related way to regularly evaluate progress: become a true learning community.

After the RCC engages in dialogues and activities with residents, it should have learned quite a lot about the community. Members should have discovered, for example, what people see as deeply valuable, what they see as the community's core strengths, resources, and protective factors, and what they believe will help strengthen and sustain their capacity for mental wellness and transformational resilience and engage in climate solutions. RCC members should also have a good sense of how residents describe these issues, which will be in their own unique way, using terms that some RCC members might not be familiar with.

If the RCC commits itself to being a true learning community, coalition members will engage in ongoing discussions about these issues to reflect on their meaning and significance. For example, members can determine who really names the community's concerns and how these issues are framed. They can also discern how decisions about priorities are actually made in the community, how resources are allocated, what really gets done, and who benefits. Coalition members can also identify the groups and organizations residents trust and respect, where they are all located, and what they do, and those that are not well valued or seen as untrustworthy (are not assets). Further, RCC members can determine how different neighborhoods, populations, and the community as a whole overcame major adversities in the past and how they remain resilient today. And, they can understand what factors undermine their capacity for wellness and resilience.

Answers to these questions should lead RCC members to candid discussions to determine if they truly understand their community. Coalition members can, for example, determine if they have accurately defined the challenges facing different populations and sectors? Have they correctly captured what is most important to them? Do they have a good understanding of the frictions that exist between different groups or neighborhoods, and does the RCC see a satisfactory pathway through them? Equally important will be candid discussions to determine if the RCC has actually identified and tapped into all of the community's strengths, capabilities, resources, and other protective factors? Have they thoroughly assessed how those assets can be mobilized to enhance everyone's capacity for mental wellness and transformational resilience as the climate emergency intensifies, or are they missing key ingredients?

Continually posing and openly discussing these questions will enable the RCC to become a true learning community. As the RCC implements its strategy, and coalition members continue to engage with the community, they are likely to notice shifts in how people see and define issues, who they connect with, and how they respond to adversities. This information can be used to regularly refine and improve the strategies and action plans developed by the different RCC Resilience Innovation Teams. This type of evaluation will frequently be as or more valuable than the more formal evaluations.

RCCS MUST ALSO PLAN FOR THE LONG TERM

After the RCC has engaged in its activities for one to three years, it will behoove the coalition to take steps to ensure that it can continue to function over time as the climate emergency accelerates.

Currently, most voluntary, civic, nonprofit, private, and public organizations are operating with limited understanding about the type, scale, and consequences of the wicked distresses and traumas that will emerge during the long climate emergency. Consequently, very few are prepared for the magnitude of what is speeding their way.

RCCs will need to motivate community members to deepen their understanding and adopt new and expanded approaches to prevent and heal the wicked multifaceted mental health and psycho-social-spiritual problems generated during the long climate crisis. At the same time, RCCs will need to develop internal organizational plans to ensure their efforts can be sustained over the long term.

EMBED MENTAL WELLNESS AND RESILIENCE IN LOCAL ORGANIZATIONAL PRACTICES AND POLICIES

To ensure that everyone in the community can enhance and sustain their capacity for mental wellness and transformational resilience over the long term, organizations of all types will need to incorporate the practices and policies into their operations. This can be accomplished by asking the organizations that are involved with the RCC to issue public declarations and/or sign a Memorandum of Understanding (MOU) describing their commitment to implement principles and practices that foster and sustain mental wellness and transformational resilience among the people involved in their enterprise.[3]

It will often take time for groups and organizations to decide to engage in this way because it may require examining and altering their existing goals, norms, and practices. But it can be a very important step forward. When RCC member organizations make this commitment, they should be publicly congratulated and widely publicized it in local newspapers, social media, and other communication mediums.

Peace4Tarpon in Tarpon Springs, Florida, has used this approach very successfully. Members sign an MOU pledging to attend monthly meetings, serve on at least one workgroup or committee, complete ACE and resilience questionnaires, sign on to PACEs Connection, and practice trauma-sensitivity among friends, family, and coworkers.[4] "Our slogan is 'Offer the Peace/Piece You Can,'" cofounder Robin Saenger told me. "We ask people to commit to this work at a very personal level."

The Community Resilience Initiative in Walla Walla Washington also uses this approach. They ask all types of local organizations to sign an MOU describing the actions they will take to embed trauma-informed resilience principles and practices into their staff training and program operations.

The New Hanover County Resilience Task Force (RTF) in North Carolina uses a variation of this approach. They ask local organizations to sign a "Belief Statement" developed by the RTF that includes a set of principles they agree with, beliefs they embrace, and list of actions they will commit to as a member of the RTF.[5]

RCCs should use the public proclamations or MOUs signed by organizations to encourage even more organizations to take the same steps. Over time, the number of organizations and institutions that have publicly committed to incorporating mental wellness and resilience-building principles and practices into their operations will grow to the point that it shifts the culture of the community.

DEVELOP LONG-TERM STRATEGIC PLANS

In addition to embedding mental wellness and resilience protocols in local organizational operations, after a few years of operation, an RCC should develop strategic plans to sustain its operations for a long period of time.[6]

Although they are related, a strategic plan differs from an operational plan. An operational plan involves planning day-to-day work to execute a current strategy. In contrast, a strategic plan clarifies where the RCC wants to be at some point in the future, and how it is going to get there. The strategic aspect of the planning process also relates to looking into the future to identify what is likely coming down the pike and determining how the RCC can prepare for it. Ideally, an RCC should develop a strategic plan for three to five years out into the future. The plan can address issues such as:

- Three-to-five-year income projections and options for raising funds;
- Methods to expand who is involved with the coalition to include more populations and sectors;
- How to facilitate transitions of RCC members and (if they exist) staff;
- How to continue delivering its services in the midst of emergencies and disasters;
- Other locally relevant big-picture issues.

The RCC should review the strategic plans on a regular basis to track progress and make needed adjustments. RCCs can think of their long-term strategic plans as a GPS system. Members can use the plan to steer the coalition's operations from one year to the next, determine the best course of action as challenges arise (as they certainly will), and use it to navigate major shifts that occur in the neighborhood or community in which they work.

Having this type of strategic plan demonstrates that the RCC is committed to sticking around for the long term. When members know where they want to be in three to five years, they can make better decisions about short-term actions. A long-term plan also gives members something to shoot for as well as a way to measure and review progress.

RCCs can develop a long-term strategic plan by following these steps[7]:

- Complete an "environmental scan" that involves a deep and wide look around at what's going on outside and within the community, including issues such as the climate emergency and how they might affect the RCC;
- Identify opportunities the RCC might be able to capitalize on, as well as threats to its operations (including but not limited to those posed by the climate crisis);
- Examine the RCC's internal resources and strengths as well as its limitations (perhaps using a SWOT analysis);

- Establish the internal organizational goals the RCC wants to accomplish during the coming three-to-five years based on what it perceives to be occurring within and around the community and its strengths and limitations (which might include issues such as funding, staffing, and program expansion);
- Identify how those goals will be reached, highlighting strategies, objectives, responsibilities, and timelines.

Completing this process is likely to influence some of the RCC's core functions such as:

- The strategies and specific activities the RCC engaged in and how they are designed;
- The organizational structure used by the RCC;
- The staffing the RCC needs to operate effectively;
- How the RCC can organize and implement fundraising efforts;
- How the RCC should respond when emergencies and disasters occur.

Each of these issues is important. However, I will address three in more detail here that are particularly important: devising strategic plans for transitions of RCC members and staff, developing a long-term funding plan, and preparing for disasters and emergencies.

RCC MEMBER AND STAFF TRANSITIONS

Over time, some RCC members will transition out of the coalition, and new people will become engaged. Similarly, staff will leave and new ones will need to be hired. Transitions like these can be challenging for any coalition. They will often require existing members to shift their responsibilities or add new ones, or for some activities to be put on temporary (or possibly permanent) hold. It will therefore be helpful for the RCC to develop transition plans before these changes occur. This type of plan can be thought of as involving six basic steps.[8]

1   *Nominate an RCC member transition coordinator and one for staff transitions*: They can be two different people, or the same person can handle both roles.

2   *Ask for assistance by the person who is leaving*: For example, the individual leaving the RCC can be asked to contact an individual or organization that is engaged with the same population or sector as they have worked with to request a replacement. Similarly, a staff member who is transitioning out can be asked for suggestions on who the RCC can contact about replacing them.

3   *Determine what individuals, populations, and sectors should be informed about the transition*: No one should be surprised to hear of a change. People should be informed before a transition occurs. This includes all RCC members and participants, including those involved with the different Resilience Innovation Teams, as well as other key neighborhood and community leaders.

4   *Identify temporary replacements*: Clarifying ahead of time who within the RCC will temporarily assume the roles that will be vacated will prevent significant disruptions.

5   *Hold exit interviews and feedbacks*: Getting feedback from the person who is leaving about how they perceive the RCC, and their role in the coalition, will help in many ways.

6   *Ensure that people leave on a positive note*: Doing whatever is possible to ensure the coalition member or staff who is transitioning out does so on a positive note will enhance everyone's morale.

DEVELOP A LONG-TERM FUNDING PLAN

Establishing long-term financial sustainability can be challenging for nonprofits. Creating a strategic long-term funding plan can help an RCC address the challenges. It typically involves seven steps.[9]

1   *Organize a fundraising planning team*: After a year or so of operations, the RCC should form a team to help the coalition think through the options and decide on a long-term fundraising plan. The team can be composed of board/steering committee members, Resilience Innovation Team members, and others in the community, such as people from different organizations, consulting firms, or academic institutions.

2   *Examine existing activities and project the amount of funding that will be needed to engage all residents*: After a year or two of work, the RCC should assess how many people and sectors the coalition has been able to engage given the funds it has raised, and then project the total finances that will be needed to engage the entire population in the future. This should lead to a long-term fundraising goal.

3   *Assess past and current fundraising efforts*: Determine the amount of money the RCC has raised in the past from all sources, including residents, members, large donors, foundations, businesses, and governments. Knowing where most funds are coming from and how the different funding sources have varied can provide a picture of year-to-year fluctuations.

4   *Analyze the successes and failures of your funding strategies*: Examine the past and current fundraising efforts and determine: what has worked well and what has not; which areas can be modified to become more effective; which aspects should be abandoned; which sources of funds are most reliable; and which sources seem to have the greatest potential for expansion.

5   *Examine a variety of nonprofit funding strategies*: Look around to see if there are fundraising options the RCC has not yet considered using to raise long-term funds.

6   *Craft a long-term fundraising plan*: After thinking through the best approach with the fundraising team, a long-term plan should be developed that includes specific financial goals, activities, and an evaluation process.

7   *Get buy-in from the RCC board/steering committee*: This is essential. The RCC's steering committee/board and members of the Resilience Innovation Teams should all be kept informed about the long-term fundraising plan and approve it.

CONTINUING ITS OPERATIONS DURING DISASTERS AND EMERGENCIES

As the climate crisis accelerates, communities everywhere are certain to experience more frequent, extreme, or prolonged disasters or other types of emergencies. The calamities will sometimes make it impossible for an RCC to hold regular meetings or in other ways prevent it from continuing its activities. Looking ahead to prepare for these events should be another important focus of the RCC's long-term strategic plan.

To get prepared before disasters strike, RCC members should learn about the six phases commonly seen in disasters and emergencies that were discussed in Chapter 3. With this information in mind, a plan should be crafted that spells out what coalition members will do in each of the phases.[10] The six common phases of disasters, and the role RCC members can play, are:

1. *The Pre-Disaster Phase*: As a reminder, this often includes years or days of warnings about potential emergencies. During this phase—meaning *now* regarding the climate crisis—each RCC member should develop a household disaster preparedness plan. It should include emergency evacuation procedures, evacuation routes, how to mitigate risk for family members and facilities, directions for emergency communications (with names and contact information), and more. Each RCC member should also create an emergency supply kit that includes spare clothing, sleeping bags and mats, several days of food and water, manual can openers, sanitation products, needed medications, first-aid kits, flashlights, a hand-cranked or battery-operated radio, pet transportation crates and food, whistles, dust masks, and local maps.[11] In addition, the RCC should help *all residents* create evacuation procedures and emergency kits. If people do not have sufficient materials, or for other reasons are unable to create a kit, the RCC can partner with local agencies to provide them with needed materials, and also assist them to develop their procedures and kits.

   In addition, the RCC's predisaster plan should identify all the key functions coalition members will play during the impact phase, and all phases that follow. One key function should be to organize a team of RCC members who will provide emotional support and practical assistance to other coalition members through all phases. This can help people self-heal and enable RCC members to continue to support other community members.

   Another key function should be to organize teams that will support the different Bonding, Bridging, and Linking social support networks, and Neighborhood Resilience Hubs the ITRC has helped organize. This can include in-person, phone, email, or other types of assistance, connecting members to others in the community who can provide practical assistance, or linking them with organizations that can provide food, water, shelter, and other basic needs. In addition, the RCC might install solar panels and batteries in key locations with charging stations that members can use to power their cell phones and computers to enable them to continue to communicate with each other.

   All RCC members should also have a list of the teams that will perform different functions, with their names, titles, phones, emails, street addresses, ages, and any special services they can offer. This will enable the RCC to facilitate ongoing communications and coordination during emergencies.

2. *The Impact Phase*: This is the period during and immediately after a major disaster or emergency occurs. During this phase, the first priority of RCC members should be to work with emergency responders to save lives. Again, this may include helping residents find water, food, or shelter, organizing or participating in rescue efforts, providing medical services to those in need, and create access to other services. The second priority should be to protect property, pets, other animals, and the natural environment.

   Still another important function RCC teams can fulfill during and immediately after the impact phase is to offer disaster resilience services. This can include psychological first aid to help stabilize people.[12] Even more importantly, they can help people use simple Presencing skills to calm their body, mind, and emotions, which can include somatic, breath, movement/shaking, cognitive, and other practices. This should all be approached using the same methods RCC teams have utilized from the start: respectfully acknowledging and reinforcing of the skills, strengths, and capabilities residents have to respond constructively to the adversity, while recognizing and being sensitive to the traumas they have experienced. At times more will be required, such as hand-holding and other forms of emotional support or linking seriously traumatized people with licensed mental health professionals.

3. *Community Cohesion Phase*: This phase occurs after the impacts of a disaster have moderated or ended, and strangers come together to provide each other with practical assistance, emotional support, and other types of help. RCCs should have a plan for this phase that supports the Neighborhood Resilience Hubs that exist in the community and, in other ways, help people connect with the Bonding and Bridging and Linking social support networks. The plan should also include engaging residents in simple Presencing and Purposing skills, and having trained peers facilitate healing circles and other types of therapeutic gatherings. In addition, RCC members should know how to connect severely traumatized residents with trained mental health professionals.

4. *The Disillusionment Phase*: Again, this period can last for months or years and is when most mental health and psycho-social-spiritual problem appear. The RCC's plan for this phase should be to continually offer culturally accountable gatherings that enable healing and resilience. RCCs should also bring residents together for community rituals and memorial events so they do not feel alone or become isolated and allow collective efficacy to emerge. Residents should also be engaged in rebuilding efforts, and the RCC should continue to engage them in the other foundational areas involved with building mental wellness and transformational resilience. The ultimate goal should be to help the entire community rekindle its spirit and build on its strengths, resources, and other protective factors in order to use the emergency as a transformational catalyst to help everyone find positive new sources of meaning, purpose, and healthy hope. The RCC should also plan for the likelihood that some people are likely to remain traumatized for quite some time.

5. *The Recovery Phase*: Recall that during this phase people slowly rebuild their lives and recover their capacity for mental wellness and resilience. The plan an RCC develops for this phase should include intensifying their efforts to engage residents in each of the five foundational areas involved with building their capacity for mental wellness and transformational resilience. Special attention and resources should be allocated to help prevent regression on the anniversary date of previous disaster(s) or when new emergencies appear, and help people continue to recover.

6. *The Bounce Back and Transformational Resilience Phases*: As discussed in Chapter 3, if people do not experience another major disaster, most will eventually return to some semblance of their precrisis condition. But returning to previous states is often not a safe or healthy place for many people, nor is it what people need to meaningfully engage in solutions to the climate emergency. RCCs should have a plan in place for the recovery stage to teach everyone how to turn toward and use the adversity as a catalyst to learn, grow, envision, and move toward a new and more positive future. When this occurs, people throughout the community can experience transformational resilience and find new meaning, purpose, and healthy hope, which should be the RCC's ultimate goal.

The checklist offered at the end of this chapter can be used by an RCC to determine the extent to which it has addressed the many aspects involved with continually tracking progress, learning, improving, and planning for the long term.

The global climate emergency will continue for decades. It is therefore essential for RCCs to be established in communities and rural areas throughout industrialized nations and worldwide. This will require transformational leadership, the formation of learning communities and communities of practice, and the enactment of policies and funding streams to support efforts to enhance and sustain the entire population's capacity to prevent and heal climate distresses and traumas. The conclusion of this book addresses these issues.

CHECKLIST

Has the RCC developed means to track progress, continually improve, and plan for the long term?

	Yes	No	Comments
Did the RCC develop a strategy to track and evaluate its progress in building universal capacity for mental wellness and transformational resilience?			
Did the RCC use "evaluation thinking" throughout the entire process?			
Has the RCC become a true "learning community?"			
Has the RCC developed ways to get local organizations to commit to incorporating mental wellness and resilience principles and practices into their operations?			
Has the RCC developed a long-term strategic plan to address member and staff transitions?			
Has the RCC developed a long-term strategic funding plan?			
Has the RCC developed a long-term strategic plan to prepare coalition members to respond effectively during each of the six common phases of a disaster?			

NOTES

1 Patton, M. Q. (1987). *Qualitative Research Evaluation Methods*. Sage Publishers, New York, NY. Obtained at: https://aulasvirtuales.files.wordpress.com/2014/02/qualitative-research-evaluation-methods-by-michael-patton.pdf

2 Much of the information provided in this section is adapted from: W.K. Kellogg Foundation. (2017). *A Step-By-Step Guide to Evaluation: How to Become Savvy Evaluation Consumers*. Obtained at: https://evaluationguide.wkkf.org/

3 See, for example, the MOUs used by Peace4Tarpon in Tarpon Springs, Florida (https://www.peace4tarpon.org/), and The Community Resilience Initiative in Walla Walla, Washington (https://criresilient.org/).

4 Peace4Tarpon's MOU can be obtained at: https://www.peace4tarpon.org/wp-content/uploads/2015/07/MOU-March2015.pdf

5 Hanover County Resilience Task Force: https://www.nhcbouncesback.org/systems-change

6 The information provided here is adapted from *Strategic Planning for Non-Profits* by the National Council of Non-Profits. Obtained at: https://www.councilofnonprofits.org/tools-resources/strategic-planning-nonprofits

7 Ibid.

8 This material is adapted from: National Institutes of Health. (2015). *Workforce Planning Tool Kit: Using a Transition Plan to Ensure Continuity of the Mission*. Obtained at: https://hr.nih.gov/sites/default/files/public/documents/workforce/workforce-planning/pdf/14-stafftransitionplanoverview.pdf; and Bridges W. (2004). *Transitions: Making Sense of Life's Changes*. New York, NY: Lifelong Books, Hachette Book Group.

9 Information in this section is adapted from: Sontag-Padilla L. et al. (2012). *Financial Stability for Nonprofit Organizations: A Review of Literature*. Rand Corporation. Obtained at: https://www.rand.org/content/dam/rand/pubs/research_reports/RR100/RR121/RAND_RR121.pdf; The Non-Profit Academy. (Undated). *Ten Steps to Creating Your Fund Development Plan*. Obtained at: https://thenonprofitacademy.com/ten-steps-fund-development-plan/; and Landes Foster W. et al. (2009). Ten Non-Profit Fundraising Models. *Stanford Social Innovation Review*. Obtained at: https://ssir.org/articles/entry/ten_nonprofit_funding_models#

10 Information provided in this section is adapted from: Ready.gov. *Community Preparedness Toolkit*. Obtained at: https://www.ready.gov/community-preparedness-toolkit; Keep Safe, *Inspiring Post Disaster Planning for Community*. Obtained at: https://keepsafeguide.enterprisecommunity.org/en/-inspiring-post-disaster-planning-community; and Mercy Corps Northwest. (2021) *Community-Based Organization Disaster Response Preparedness Toolkit*. Obtained at: https://nonprofitoregon.org/sites/default/files/uploads/file/Disaster-Response-Preparedness-Toolkit-for-CBOs-March-2021.pdf

11 FEMA (September 16, 2021). *10 Items to Include in Your Emergency Kit*. Obtained at: https://www.fema.gov/blog/10-items-include-your-emergency-kit

12 World Health Organization. *Psychological First Aid: Guide for Field Workers*. Obtained at: https://www.who.int/publications/i/item/9789241548205

CONCLUSION The Need for a Global Movement to Enhance Universal Capacity for Mental Wellness and Transformational Resilience for the Civilization-Altering Climate Emergency

Take a moment to reflect on what things will be like in 2030. Even if global emissions are significantly reduced, average global surface temperatures will likely still have risen close to, or possibly slightly more than, 2.7 degrees Fahrenheit (1.5 degrees Celsius) above pre-industrial levels. All of humanity will experience significant distresses and traumas due to the mixture of cascading disruptions to the ecological, social, and economic systems they rely on for basic needs, and more frequent, extreme, and prolonged storms, wildfires, floods, heat waves, droughts, and other disasters.

What steps can you envision taking now to prepare for these challenges? For example, are there members of your Bonding, Bridging, and Linking social support networks that you can begin to discuss the issues with? As you do so, can you identify other individuals, groups, and organizations that could be engaged in the dialogues? Who has the trust of different populations and sectors? Is there an organization or network of groups that can take the lead in addressing the issues, or is a new coalition needed? How can you help organize and participate in these efforts?

As I have continually emphasized, no single organization, profession, or program can prevent or heal the distresses and traumas generated by the wicked climate-ecosystem-biodiversity mega-emergency. Prevention and healing will be needed at every level of society because the personal, family, social, economic, and ecological problems we face are all interconnected. This will require that many long-standing orthodoxies be jettisoned. We must think and act through a population and holistic lens, not an individualized siloed and fragmented one.

Accordingly, entire communities must be engaged in preventing and healing distresses and traumas and in solutions to the climate emergency, and the best way to do this is to form a Resilience Coordinating Coalition (RCC). The RCC will need to coordinate numerous semi-independent initiatives that continually engage the different populations and sectors of their community in the five foundational areas discussed in this book. The problems generated by the climate crisis will continue for decades, so the work of the RCCs must be ongoing.

Again, only a few of the community-based initiatives I examined are specifically focused on the climate emergency. And none address all five of the foundational areas that will be essential to enhance universal capacity for mental wellness and transformational resilience during the climate emergency. Most emphasize just one or two of the core foundational areas in ways that make sense given the issues they were originally organized to address in their community, be it violence, adverse childhood experiences, or disaster preparedness. But to enable people to remain mentally well and resilient during the decades or longer climate crisis and reduce their community's contribution to the emergency, the existing initiatives will need to expand their focus, and thousands of new comprehensive holistic ones will need to be organized in communities throughout industrialized nations and other parts of the world.

DOI: 10.4324/9781003262442-17

Indeed, organizing culturally accountable RCCs must become a top international priority and a global movement is needed to establish these initiatives. Here are some important actions that can help grow the movement.

GALVANIZE TRANSFORMATION LEADERSHIP

Effective leadership is required for any positive change to occur. The climate mega-emergency requires leaders who can motivate people to make deep-seated changes faster, and with more acumen, than ever before.

It is a common misperception to think of leaders as people at the top with authority such as a CEO or elected official. However, pressure for change usually comes from the middle and grassroots levels of organizations and communities and those at the top merely announce and implement what others propose or demand. Equally importantly, the belief that leadership comes from the top allows people without formal authority to disregard their responsibility to drive positive change.

The wicked problems generated by the climate crisis require that people at all levels of society–especially those of us without formal authority–respond to its complex challenges in ways that stimulate deep-seated transformational changes. This can only occur when people are equipped with the mindset and competencies called transformational leadership, which is a leadership approach that stimulates positive fundamental change in individuals, groups, and social systems. It can be defined as the ability to respond to rapid disruptive changes with personal integrity, insight, vision, agility, and commitment that inspires others to build a new positive future for all.[1]

Transformational leadership has four primary characteristics. First is the degree to which the leader seeks out and listens to the concerns of others and attends to their needs, not their own. Second is the degree to which the leader challenges long-held assumptions and beliefs and encourages people to think differently and identify new and more effective ways to respond to challenges. The third characteristic is the degree to which a leader articulates to others a coherent and inspiring vision of what is possible. This involves communicating both realism and optimism, and providing meaning and a strong sense of purpose in the actions required to bring about positive change. The fourth characteristic of transformational leaders is their ability to serve as a role model by exhibiting high ethical and moral standards that generate trust and respect from others.[2]

Researchers in the field have described Martin Luther King Jr., Rose Parks, and Steve Jobs as transformational leaders. People who worked with them said they constantly inspired everyone to challenge their assumptions and beliefs and think in new and different ways to produce outcomes they never thought were possible.[3]

No human is perfect. Everyone makes mistakes. But the more people understand the characteristics transformational leaders embody, the greater the number that will seek to embrace the qualities and mobilize their communities to build universal capacity for mental wellness and transformational resilience and engage in climate solutions. Transformational leaders can be found at all levels of society, and it will be vital to inspire all of them to lead efforts to respond to the climate emergency.

ESTABLISH TRANSFORMATIONAL LEADERSHIP LEARNING EXCHANGES

One action that will help expand the number of people who embody the characteristics of a transformational leader is to establish "learning exchanges" around the world.[4] A number of non-profit organizations and universities offer transformational leadership webinars, courses, and certificate programs that teach participants what transformational leadership involves, and how they can embody the core characteristics.[5] However, much more is needed for the climate emergency. Learning exchanges are needed to help people from all walks of life learn the core principles and practices of transformational leadership and enhance the skills they need to mobilize their fellow residents to organize and operate community-based initiatives to address the wicked nature of the individual, family, community, and societal challenges speeding our way.

In addition to examining their personal assumptions and enhancing their skills, an important focus of the learning exchanges should be to inform participants about the change process. Big changes don't happen in a smooth linear way. They typically occur through chaotic, confusing, and even contradictory processes that include a mix of large and small setbacks and successes. If people remain focused and persistent, however, things can eventually come together and change can occur. Participants need to understand this so they know how to handle and lead the chaotic process of change with confidence and resolve.

Related to this is the need for participants to learn that big social changes come about only when people work together to pursue it. Not many people are willing to spend time trying to do something that will have minimal effects. Humans become motivated when they feel they are engage in something really important that is larger than themselves. Participants should learn about the change process and how to bring people together to work toward big fundamental changes.

People involved with learning exchanges often become actively engaged in the issues they learn about. This means that establishing Transformational Leadership Learning Exchanges throughout the world will help grow a movement of people committed to leading transformative change in their community.

ORGANIZE MENTAL WELLNESS AND TRANSFORMATIONAL RESILIENCE COMMUNITIES OF PRACTICE

Communities of Practice (CoPs) will also be needed to help people who are already engaged in community-based wellness and resilience-building initiatives enhance their understanding and skills. This requires continual learning, reflection, and improvement.[6]

People who are not committed to constant learning, growth, and advancement often abandon their work when they experience a significant setback. Failure causes them to give up. In contrast, people who are committed to continual learning and improvement don't stop when they experience a setback. They see failures as challenges that offer the opportunity to learn, adapt, and develop better ways to address issues.

To foster this type of mindset, CoPs should be organized around the globe. A mental wellness and transformational resilience CoP will be a group of people who share the common goal of helping their community come together to continually learn, improve, and develop effective strategies to build universal capacity to prevent and heal distresses and traumas as they engage in solutions to the climate emergency. Guest speakers can be invited to offer different perspectives, share research, and teach practices and skills. The goal of a CoP should be to engage participants in deep-seated dialogue and reflection to examine their core assumptions and beliefs, and develop new insights, knowledge, and innovative ideas to advance their work.

THE NEED FOR NEW POLICIES

New policies are also needed to grow a global movement to build universal capacity for mental wellness and transformational resilience.

One type of policy needed is the "Community Mental Wellness and Resilience Act" (CMWRA). It was developed by my organization, the International Transformational Resilience Coalition (ITRC), for federal/national and state/provincial governments. Congressman Paul Tonko (D-NY) introduced the CMWRA in the US Congress with Representative Brian Fitzpatrick (R-PA) and a number of co-sponsors in October 2022 and Senator Ed Markey (D-MA) then introduced it in the Senate.

At the federal level in the US, for example, the CMWRA would make the prevention and healing of mental health and psycho-social-spiritual problems through community-based initiatives a top priority. It would accomplish this by establishing a new federal grant program to fund community-based initiatives that use a public health approach to enhance the entire population's capacity for mental wellness and resilience. The policy would establish smaller planning grants to allow community groups to get organized, as well as larger implementation grants to enable the development of community-based initiatives. Information about the CMWRA can be found on the ITRC website.

The information, skills, and methods involved with building population-level capacity for psychological, emotional, and spiritual wellness and resilience were developed for non-climate-related traumas. This means the CMWRA will help prevent and heal individual, community, and societal traumas resulting from many types of human-caused and ecologically generated emergencies, disasters, and toxic stresses.

Similar policies are needed at the state and local levels in the US. Other nations and provinces will benefit by enacting their own version of the CMWRA. The ITRC developed a "model" CMWRA policy that other nations, states/provinces, and municipalities can use to design their own policy. It can be found on the ITRC website.

Another piece of legislation that should be enacted everywhere can be called "Resilience in All Policies" (RiAP). This is an adaptation of the Health in all Policies (HiAP) policy promoted by the World Health Organization (WHO) and other organizations. They describe it as "an approach to public policies across sectors that systematically takes into account the health implications of decisions, seeks synergies, and avoids harmful health impacts in order to improve population health and equity."[7]

RiAP legislation would expand the WHOs proposal to emphasize that all policies and actions adopted by governments should examine their impact on, and ensure that they enhance, and do not undermine, individual and collective mental wellness and resilience.

Many other new policies are needed as well. The list is too long to include here, so I will offer just a few examples:

- The most important policies, of course, will mandate the swift phase out of fossil fuels in all sectors of the economy, and scale-up of clean renewable energy as well as the protection and regeneration of vast swaths of ecological systems and biodiversity and make a rapid transition to a healthy, just and equitable climate-resilient cradle-to-cradle economic system.

- All climate mitigation, ecological regeneration, physical adaptation, and disaster management policies should explicitly require a just transition.
- Preventing and healing climate traumas should be integrated into all mental and behavioral health policies to enable everyone to prepare for them.
- Mental and behavioral health policies should be expanded to support multisystemic community-based initiatives that strengthen the entire population's capacity for mental wellness and transformational resilience.
- Healthcare policies should be changed to ensure equity in all mental health services and require that mental health and physical health services be integrated into a mind-body holistic system.
- Educational policies should be changed to require all staff, teachers, and students to become literate about mental wellness and resilience, and also learn about climate science, systems thinking, and the other aspects of mental wellness and transformational resilience described in this book.
- In addition to these and many other new national policies, similar policies will be needed at the state/provincial and local levels.

CLOSING THOUGHT

When I wrote this book, the COVID-19 pandemic continued to create despair in many parts of the world. Millions of people were also struggling with heightened racism, violence, poverty, lack of food, water, and shelter, drug and alcohol addiction, adverse childhood experiences, and other adversities. These problems make it hard to think about or deal with issues such as the climate crisis. But it is essential to not let these important daily challenges distract us from the far greater threats posed to every individual, family, community, and civilization as a whole by the accelerating climate-ecosystem-biodiversity mega-emergency.

No matter how quickly emissions are reduced, the long global climate crisis will change the course of human history. Life will not end. But every person alive today, located in every part of the world, and all future generations, will be impacted in ways that generate significant distresses and traumas. The consequences will close the door to many of the ways society functions today. Yet, we should never forget that the crisis will also open the door to new pathways.

It will not be easy. But we *can* address these challenges. By returning the responsibility for preventing and healing distresses and traumas to neighborhoods and communities where it naturally belongs, everyone can enhance their capacity for mental wellness and transformational resilience. In doing so, people will be inspired to create innovative solutions to the climate emergency and many other challenges.

Organizing community-based initiatives across the globe won't solve all our problems. But it will mitigate many of them and spur new thinking, approaches, and policies that can put humanity on a safer, healthier, just, and equitable regenerative path.

NOTES

1 This definition is based on my own experience leading organizations and movements, and is an adaptation of the definition provided by: Bass B. M. and Riggio R. E. (2008). *Transformational Leadership*. Mahwah, NJ: Lawrence Erlbaum Associates, Inc.; and Choi S. L. et al. (2016). Transformational leadership, empowerment, and job satisfaction: The mediating role of employee empowerment. *Human Resources Health*, 14, 1–14.

2 Cherry C. (March 2020). Transformational leadership: a closer look at the effects of transformational leadership. *VeryWellMind*. Obtained at: https://www.verywellmind.com/what-is-transformational-leadership2795313

3 See for example: *Transformational Change Leadership: Stories of Building a Just Future*. Center for Transformational Change. Obtained at: https://tcleadership.org/introduction/#:~:text=%E2%80%9CTransformational%20change%20leadership; and Fontein D. (February 17, 2022). Your guide to transformational leadership in education. *ThoughtExchange*. Obtained at: https://thoughtexchange.com/blog/transformational-leadership-in-education/

4 Information in this section was adapted from: The Kettering Foundation. *Learning Exchanges*. Obtained at: https://www.kettering.org/shared-learning/learning-exchanges; and Alternative Roots. *Learning Exchanges*. Obtained at: https://alternateroots.org/arts-activism-tools/learning-exchanges/

5 See, for example: The Interaction Institute for Social Change online program; University of Texas at Dallas Transformational Leadership Academic Certificate; and The American Management Association seminar on the topic.

6 Information in this section was adapted from: Edmonton Regional Learning Consortium. *Creating Communities of Practice*. Obtained at: https://www.communityofpractice.ca/background/what-is-a-community-of-practice; and Centers for Disease Control and Prevention, Communities of Practice (CoPsa). Obtained at: https://www.cdc.gov/publichealthgateway/phcommunities/communities-of-practice-cops.html

7 World Health Organization. *What You Need to Know About Health in All Policies, Geneva, Switzerland*. Obtained at: https://www.who.int/social_determinants/publications/health-policies-manual/key-messages-en.pdf

INDEX

Note: **Bold** page numbers refer to tables; *italic* page numbers refer to figures and page numbers followed by "n" denote endnotes.

Abernathy, P. 60, 117, 172
ABPsi *see* Association of Black Psychologists (ABPsi)
Abundant Community Edmonton (ACE): approach to asset mapping 111–112; goals of 117; keep learning 195; Resource Guide 138; social connections, building 138–139; vision of 111
access to health eating, promotion of 196
access to quality education 195
activities-based approach 119
Adams, P. 189
Adult and Community Education (ACE) 195
adults, trauma-informed 173
Adverse Childhood experiences (ACE) 112
adversity-based growth 57
Albee, G. 11
Aldrich, D. 130, 131
Amazon 155
American Dream 50
American Society of Adaptation Professionals (ASAP): Climate Access communications forum 15n10; Climate Masters program 15n10
America Walks 198–199
AMOC *see* Atlantic Meridional Overturning Circulation (AMOC)
Anda, R. 102
Arrhenius, S. 20
ASAP *see* American Society of Adaptation Professionals (ASAP)
asset mapping 102–103, 107–108; ACE approach to 111–112; development of 108–109, *109*; into draft "Community Resilience Profile," integrating 110
Association of Applied and Therapeutic Humor 190
Association of Black Psychologists (ABPsi) 210
Atlantic circulation, slowing 27–28
Atlantic Meridional Overturning Circulation (AMOC) 28
"Attitude of Gratitude" campaign, Newport News, Virginia 191–192
Australia: climate overshoot 21; wildfires 26
Awakening Joy (Baraz) 187

Baraz, J.: *Awakening Joy* 187
Barila, T. 80, 103
Barreto, A. 209
bathtub analogy 23–25, *24*
Bearded Fishermen project 177–178
be grateful 190–193
Belgium, flooding in 21
Be the Bridge 177
Biden, J. 5, 23; Administration 17
bike sharing 198
biodiversity extinction 28
Bloom, S. 102
bounce back phase of disaster 59, 225
BRING: Construction Materials Recovery and Reuse Program 159
Buddhism 7
Building and Using Conceptual Diagrams (National Ecosystem Services Partnership) 124
Building Resilient Neighborhoods, Victoria, British Columbia, Canada 140–141; operating principles 88
business-as usual 36–38

C3 *see* Community Coalitions for Change (C3)
Cantu, R. 77, 100, 204
carbon dioxide (CO_2) 19–20
carbon footprint 159
Carnell, M.: *Say Something Nice: Be a Lifter!* 192
case studies 217, 218
CBR *see* Community Bill of Rights (CBR)
Center for Advancing Healthy Communities 198
Center for Mind-Body Medicine (CMBM) 101; peer-to-peer healing training programs 211
CFCs *see* chlorofluorocarbons (CFCs)
Chalk Art Walk 188
checklist: community capacity, building 114–115; healing 212–213; just transition 165–166; motivating residents to engage in practices 199–200; Resilience Coordinating Coalition 96–98, 125; social connections, building 143; tracking

of RCC 226–227; universal literacy, cultivation of 180–181

China, drought 29

chlorofluorocarbons (CFCs) 20

Chrastil, J. 41

Cicero 191

civilization-altering mega-emergency: humanity and 32; impacts of 26

CLI *see* Climate Leadership Initiative (CLI)

climate crisis: cascading disruptions to essential systems with disasters and 6–7; and historic trauma 47–50; and intergenerational trauma 47–50; and societal trauma 46–47; transformational resilience for 12–13, 17–18; *see also* climate emergency

climate disruption: human consequence of bio-physical impacts of 28–31; US National Academy of Science on 24

climate distress, preventing and healing 9–11

climate-ecosystem-biodiversity mega-emergency 25, 26, 32, 44; bio-physical impacts of 26–28

climate emergency: and community trauma 44–46; and hopelessness 44; and individual distress/trauma 41–42; as symptom of unresolved trauma 50–51; *see also* climate crisis

Climate Leadership Initiative (CLI) 3, 15n10

climate mega-emergency 2, 6, 12, 13, 17, 18, 21, 25; civilization-altering impacts of 26

climate overshoot 5–6, 19–32, 36–38, 40; bathtub analogy for 23–25, 24; drivers of 19–21; impact of 21–22; Paris Agreement and 22–23; population growth and 25

climate resilient 2, 13, 38, 39, 70, 149–165, 204, 232; housing, healthy, safe, just, and equitable 150–151; local ecological conditions, healthy, safe, just, and equitable 160–163; local economic conditions, healthy, safe, just, and equitable 154–160; public spaces, healthy, safe, just, and equitable 151; transportation infrastructure, healthy, safe, just, and equitable 149–150

climate science 89–90

CMBM *see* Center for Mind-Body Medicine (CMBM)

CMWRA *see* Community Mental Wellness and Resilience Act (CMWRA)

Coalition to End Social Isolation and Loneliness 142

coastline restore, Louisiana 161

collective efficacy 40, 61, 109, 130, 136

collective trauma *see* societal trauma

Colussi, M. 141

Common Threads 198

Communities of Practice (CoPs) 38, 230–231

community-based initiatives, organizing and operating 73–76, *75*

community-based therapeutic methods 206

Community Bill of Rights (CBR) 158

community capacity for mental wellness and transformational resilience, building 100–115; ACE approach to asset mapping 111–112; asset mapping (*see* asset mapping); checklist 114–115; Community Resilience Portrait 102–110; Community Resilience Profile (*see* Community Resilience Profile); modified approach 102; Resilience Snapshot 105–108, 110; ROI systems mapping approach to trauma 112, *113*; trauma healing gatherings 100–102; university students, assistance of 111

Community Coalitions for Change (C3) 197

community cohesion phase of disaster 57–58, 225

community farms, growth of 159

"Community Forgiveness Blitz" 185

Community Healing Days 210

Community Healing Network 210

community learning *see* Adult and Community Education (ACE)

Community Mental Wellness and Resilience Act (CMWRA) 231

Community Resilience Coalition, Walla Walla, Putnam County (CRC) 79–82; core values of 87; mission of 86; training 177; vision of 87

Community Resilience Initiative, Walla Walla (CRI) 80, 81, 102, 103, 220; objectives of 117, *118*

Community Resilience Model (CRM) 100, 177

Community Resilience Portrait: collection of information 104–105; creation of 102–103; development of 103–110; geographic boundaries, clarifying 104; identity paths forward 110

Community Resilience Profile 121–122; draft, integrating information and asset maps into 110; reengage residents in discussions to finalize 110

Community-Supported Agriculture (CSA) 198

community trauma 7–9, 112; climate emergency and 44–46

Connections Matter 177

Convivencia Gatherings, Sonoma County, California 208

CoPs *see* Communities of Practice (CoPs)

COVID-19 pandemic 6, 8, 9, 17, 20, 28, 47, 80, 178, 184, 187, 190, 232
cradle-to-cradle economic system, local businesses transition to 155–156
CRC *see* Community Resilience Coalition, Walla Walla, Putnam County (CRC)
CRI *see* Community Resilience Initiative, Walla Walla (CRI)
CRM *see* Community Resilience Model (CRM)
crowdfunding platforms 94
CSA *see* Community-Supported Agriculture (CSA)
culturally responsive evaluation 217

developmental evaluation 217
disaster: bounce back phase of 59, 225; community cohesion phase of 57–58, 225; disillusionment phase of 58, 225; impact phase of 57, 224–225; pre-disaster phase of 57, 224; recovery phase of 59, 225; transformational resilience in 57–60, *58*, 224–225
disillusionment phase of disaster 58, 225
distress 7–9, 26; climate 9–11; climate emergency and 41–42
Duncan, L. 203

Eaton, W.: *Public Mental Health* 54
eco-anxiety 41
ecological disasters 47
ecological environment 147–166
ecological footprints 25, 151, 156–163
Economic Development Logic Model (U.S. Economic Development Administration) 124
economic environment 147–166
Ecotherapy Certificate Programs 211
eco-village, Taomi 160–161
Edgerton, J. 49
EE *see* Emotional Emancipation (EE) Circles
Eisenman, D. 42
Emotional Emancipation (EE) Circles 210
empowerment evaluation 217
Environmental Protection Agency (EPA): on climate overshoot 21
EPA *see* Environmental Protection Agency (EPA)
equity 87, 89, 150, 151, 159, 194
Erickson, K. 47
Europe, drought 29
European Union (EU) 210; ecological footprints 25
evaluation of RCC 215–219; continual 218–219; importance 215–216; plan development 216–217; process 216; thinking 216

evidence-based approaches, pros and cons of 120–121
experimental design 217

Farmers Markets 198
farm-to-school programs 198–199
Fetzer Institute 184, 186
First International Conference on Health Promotion (1986) 54
Fitzpatrick, B. 231
focus groups 107
"Forgive for Good" method 186
forgiveness 184–186, 192
Forgiveness Project 186
Foundation for Social Connection 142–143
The Framework Institute 136
Frankl, V.: *Man's Search for Meaning* 7
Freire, P. 209
Fresh Moves Mobil Market 198
Fresh Roots 198
Fund Local Program, Washington state 159

Garbarino, B. 80, 177
Germany, flooding in 21
Gesundheit! Institute 189
Gibran, K. 188, 189
Global Footprint Network 25
Global Initiative on Loneliness and Connection 143
GNLC *see* UNESCO Global Network of Learning Cities Promotes Lifelong Learning (GNLC)
"Go! Clowns" program 189
GoFundMe 94
Gordon, J. 101, 172
gratitude 191–193
Gratitude Circles 193
Gratitude Fishbowl 193
Great Depression 49–50
Green, H. 50
Grounded: A Guided Journal To Help You Reconnect with the Power of Nature and Yourself (Hasbach) 211
Groundswell Northwest 159, 162
Groupthink 46
guerrilla humor 190

habitat degradation 28
Habitat for Humanity 147
habitat loss 28
habitat regeneration teams, organization of 162
Hacienda Community Development Corporation 147
Hanover County Resiliency Task Force 78
Happiness Campaign 187

Happy Café 187
Hasbach, P. 211; *Grounded: A Guided Journal To Help You Reconnect with the Power of Nature and Yourself* 211
healing 203–213; checklist 212–213; circles 206; climate traumas 204–206, *204*; culturally accountable opportunities 208–210; group 209; opportunities (*see* healing opportunities); self-healing 203–204; through mental health treatment 207
Healing Collective Trauma (Hubl) 46
healing opportunities: culturally accountable 204, *204*, 208; forms of 206; group-minded 209; ongoing 208–213; trauma 74, 212
Health in all Policies (HiAP) 231
health service professionals: in RCC, roles of 92
healthy foods, promotion of 196
healthy hope 44, 45, 57, 60, 206
Healthy Places by Design 149, 198
Healthy Practices Resilience Innovation Team 199
Henriquez, L. M. 133
HiAP *see* Health in all Policies (HiAP)
historic trauma, climate crisis and 47–50
Holcomb, C. 203
Homsey, D. 140
hopelessness, climate emergency and 44
"How to Create Therapeutic Laughter" 190
Hubl, T.: *Healing Collective Trauma* 46
humanity, and civilization-altering mega-emergency 32
human rights 89
Hurricane Katrina 170
Hurricane Sandy 15n11

impact evaluation 217
impact phase of disaster 57, 224–225
India, drought 29
individual trauma 7–9, 44, 45, 51; climate emergency and 41–42
Industrial Revolution 21
Institute for Emotionally Intelligent Learning 190
Institute for Local-Self-Reliance (ILSR): climate-resilient local economic conditions, recommendations for 158
Integrative Community Therapy (ICT) gatherings 209
intensive (indicative) prevention 64, *64*
intergenerational trauma: climate crisis and 47–50
Intergovernmental Panel on Climate Change (IPCC): climate-ecosystem-biodiversity

mega-emergency, bio-physical impacts of 26; on climate overshoot 5, 22, 23
International Forgiveness Institute 186
International Society for Humor 190
International Transformational Resilience Coalition (ITRC) 4, 172, 231
IPCC *see* Intergovernmental Panel on Climate Change (IPCC)
Israel Trauma Coalition (ITC) 212
ITC *see* Israel Trauma Coalition (ITC)
ITRC *see* International Transformational Resilience Coalition (ITRC)

Japan, ecological footprints 25
Jobs, S. 229
just transition 13, 70, 147–166, *148*, 232; checklist 165–166

K-12 school Resilience Innovation Team 93, 94
Kessler, D. 206
King, M. L., Jr. 229
Kübler-Ross, E. 206

Latin America, mass migration 30
laughing 188–190
Laughing Allowed! The Slapstick World of Neighbourhood Activism 189
Laughter Clubs 190
Lawrence, H. 10, 112
learning 193–195
learning communities 219–220
Les Misérables 185
Lewis and Clark Ecotherapy Program 211
Leyland, M. 177–178
life-course approaches 63–67, *66*
Lincoln, A. 188, 189
Listing Logic Models on Health Education 124
Living Cully coalition, Northeast Portland, Oregon 147
local watershed councils, formation of 162
logic model: development of 120; outcome-based 119, *119*
The Longest Table, Tallahassee, Florida 142
long-term plan 220; funding plan, development of 223; strategic plans, development of 221–222
Luskin, F. 186

Making Connections Initiative 142
Man's Search for Meaning (Frankl) 7
McKnight, J. 139
"Meet Me Downtown" program 142
Memorandum of Understanding (MOU) 220, 221

memorial events, therapeutic importance of
    207–212
mental health disorder 37
Mental Health First Aid 177
mental health professionals: in RCC, roles
    of 92
mental health treatment, healing through 207
mentally well and resilient communities 60–61
mental wellness 2–4, 10–14, 17–19, 38, 39,
    41, 44, 51–52, 77, 78, 82, 86, 89–95,
    100–115, 116, 118–121, 123, 125,
    127–130, 132–136, 142, 148–151, 153,
    154, 158, 164, 165, 183–200, 203–205,
    207, 211, 212, 215, 216, 218–221, 225,
    228–232; Communities of Practice
    230–231; community-based initiatives,
    organizing and operating 73–76, 75;
    community capacity, building 100–115;
    definition of 56; engagement in specific
    practices, fostering 183–200, 184;
    enhancement of 56–57; global movement
    to enhance universal capacity for 228–232;
    in local organizational practices and
    policies 220–221; population-level 51–52;
    population-level capacity for, building
    17–18; protective and risk factors to
    62–63; public health approach to 54–70;
    and resilience literacy 170; universal
    capacity for, building 12–13, 70; universal
    literacy, cultivation of 170–181; see also
    individual entries
methane (CH$_4$) 20
#MeToo movement 135
Metrics for Healthy Communities 124
MOU see Memorandum of Understanding
    (MOU)
Mt. Baker Community Coalition 78
Mycelium Youth Network 133

National Compadres Network (NCN)
    209–210
National Empowerment Center 211
National Mass Violence Victimization
    Resource Center (NMVVRC) 212
The National Storytelling Network 136
Native American Youth and Family Center
    147
nature-based healing, residents engagement
    in 210–211
NCN see National Compadres Network
    (NCN)
Neighborhood Empowerment Network, San
    Francisco, California (NEN): Empowered
    Communities Program 140; Neighborfest
    Program 140; social connections, building
    139

neighborhood resilience dialogues 107–108
neighborhood resilience healing hubs
    211–212
Neighborhood Resilience Hubs 224, 225
Neighborhood Resilience Project (NRP),
    Pittsburg, Pennsylvania 172, 208
neighborhood tree planting and park
    development events, organization of 162
neuroplasticity 205
neuroscience 89–90
New Hanover County North Carolina
    Resiliency Task Force (RTF) 85, 86,
    220–221; core values of 87; organizational
    structure 94
New Homeland Foundation 161
new policies, need for 231–232
Nextdoor 142
nitrous oxide (N$_2$O) 20
NMVVRC see National Mass Violence
    Victimization Resource Center
    (NMVVRC)
NOAA National Centers for Environmental
    Information: on economic damage 29
North Carolina Healthy and Resilient
    Community Initiative: core values of 87;
    goals of 116–117; mission of 86; operating
    principles 88–89; vision of 87
NRP see Neighborhood Resilience Project
    (NRP), Pittsburg, Pennsylvania

Oakridge National Lab projects 7
ocean acidification 27
Oluo, I.: So You Want to Talk About Race 49
Ottawa Charter 54
Otto, F. 19
outcome-based approach 119
outcome (or summative) evaluation 217
outcome mapping 217
Overseas Development Institute 28
ozone pollution 20

Paris Agreement 22–23
Parks, R. 229
participatory leadership 89
Patterson, J. 135, 165
Peace4Tarpon, Tarpon Springs, Florida 94,
    111; goals of 116
peer-to-peer healing trainings 211
Perpetual Purpose Trusts 158–159
personal interviews 106–107
PGZ see Resilience Growth Zone (PGZ)
physical/built environment 147–166
physical health, care for 195–199; access to
    health eating, promotion of 196; healthy
    foods, promotion of 196; regular physical
    activity, promotion of 196

Pinderhughes, H. 45
Play Streets 197
The Pocket Project 210
population growth, and climate overshoot 25
population-level 2, 4, 11, 14, 17–18,
    56, 62–66, 73, 77, 91, 134, 172, 231;
    mental wellness 51–52; prevention 63–65,
    64; transformational resilience 51–52
post-traumatic growth 57
post-traumatic stress disorder (PTSD) 1, 3,
    45, 58, 203; societal 46
pre-disaster phase of disaster 57, 224
"Presencing" (or self-regulation) skills
    4, 40, 59, 61, 62, 164, 176, 179; self-
    administrable 173–174
Prevention Institute 45, 100, 142
Price, M. 191–192
process (or implementation) evaluation
    216–217
proportionate universalism 63–65, *64*
PTSD *see* post-traumatic stress disorder
    (PTSD)
public health approach to mental health 12,
    17, 18, 54–70, 92, 111, 183, 231; common
    community-level protective factors 68,
    69; common community-level risk factors
    69, *70*; common protective factors for
    individuals 66–67, *67*; common risk
    factors for individuals 67–68, **68**; elements
    of 61–62; life-course approach 65–66, *65*;
    mentally well and resilient communities
    60–61; population-level prevention
    63–65, *64*; protective and risk factors,
    identification of 62–63; universal capacity
    for mental wellness and transformational
    resilience, framework for building 70
public health response 12–13
Public Mental Health (Eaton) 54
"Purposing" (or adversity-based growth)
    skills 4, 40, 59, 61, 62, 164, 176, 179; self-
    administrable 174–175

quasi-experimental design 217, 218

R4R *see* Resources for Resilience (R4R)
racial trauma 48, 49
rainbow model 54
randomized control studies 217
RAP *see* resilience action plan (RAP)
Rapid Response Unbuntu Healing Circles
    210
RCC *see* Resilience Coordinating Coalition
    (RCC)
"REACH Forgiveness" approach 186
Reconnect for Resilience 177

recovery phase of disaster 59, 225
Regan, M. 21
regenerative transformation 38–40
regular physical activity, promotion of 196
residents involved with activism, supporting
    163–164
resilience 38–40; definition of 56;
    enhancement of 56–57; literacy 124,
    170, *171*, 172, 173, 175–180, 204, 211; in
    local organizational practices and policies
    220–221; policy 137; practices 183–200;
    transformational (*see* transformational
    resilience); *see also individual entries*
Resilience Centers 212
Resilience Coordinating Coalition (RCC)
    14, 74–98, 100–108, 110, 111, 112, 114,
    127–144, 149–166, 183–200, 203, 204,
    206, 208–213, 215–229; action plans,
    development of 124; basic education
    and training for members, offering 92;
    benefits of forming 78–79; checklist
    96–98, 125; communication 85–86;
    conflict resolution skills 85–86; core values
    87–88; effective community leaders and
    staff, identification of 90–91; evaluation
    of (*see* evaluation of RCC); evidence-
    based approaches, pros and cons of
    120–121; expanding participation in
    83–85; funding 94–95; goals of 116–117;
    gratitude, promotion of 191–193; health
    service professionals, roles of 92; Healthy
    Practices Resilience Innovation Team
    199; learning communities 219–220;
    life-course approach 65; local businesses
    transition to cradle-to-cradle economic
    system 155–156; local healthy, safe, just,
    and equitable climate-resilient physical/
    built conditions, building 152–154; logic
    model, development of 120; long-term
    funding plan, development of 223;
    long-term plan 220; long-term strategic
    plans, development of 221–222; member
    and staff transitions 222; members, roles
    of 82–83; mental health professionals,
    roles of 92; mission and vision 86–87;
    new coalition, starting 83; objectives of
    117, *118*; operating principles 88–90;
    operations disasters and emergencies
    223–226; organizational structure,
    selection of 92–94, *93*; organization of
    79–82; outcome-based logic model 119,
    119; progress, tracking and evaluation
    of 124–125; regenerative transformation
    38–40; Resilience Innovation Team, logic
    model development by 123–124; selecting

indicators 121–123, *122, 123*; strategies, development of 117–120; tracking of 215–216, 226–227; universal literacy, cultivation of 170, 175, 177–181; working through existing organizations and networks 83
resilience action plan (RAP) 139–140
Resilience Growth Zone (PGZ) 42–43, *43*, 59, 64, 173, 179, 185
Resilience Hubs 39, 141, 142, 162
Resilience in All Policies (RiAP) 231
Resilience Innovation Teams 39, 91, 94, 117, 162, 208, 218, 220, 222; Healthy Practices Resilience Innovation Team 199; logic model development 123–124; regenerative economy 157–159; Social Capital Resilience Innovation Team 141–142; Trauma Healing Resilience Innovation Teams 209–210
Resilience Network of the Gorge 102
Resilience Snapshot 105–108
Resources for Resilience (R4R) 101, 177
rewilding 162–163
Rhode Island Health Equity Zone Initiative 78
RiAP *see* Resilience in All Policies (RiAP)
ring team approach 93, *93*, 94
rituals, therapeutic importance of 207–212
Roberts, R. 177–178
Rockström, J. 22
Rodgers, A. D. 121
ROI *see* Rural Opportunity Institute (ROI)
RTF *see* New Hanover County North Carolina Resiliency Task Force (RTF)
Rural Opportunity Institute (ROI): learning community 194; systems mapping approach to trauma 112, *113*

Saenger, R. 79, 94
Sanctuary Model 102
San Francisco Department of Emergency Management 139
San Francisco Neighborhood Enhancement Network (NEN) 111
Save the Bay 162
Save the Children: "Journey of Hope" trainings 177
Say Something Nice: Be a Lifter! (Carnell) 192
"Say Something Nice Day" 192
The Science of Forgiveness 186
Seattle Ballard Neighborhood 162
self-healing 203–204
Senate Preparedness Committee, Oregon 137

servant leadership 89
Servin-Lacy, N. 100–101
sheltered in place (SIP) 140
simple joys 187–188, 190
SIP *see* sheltered in place (SIP)
Skiva, J. 174
slavery 48–49
Slette, K. 79
Slow Food International 198
social and therapeutic horticulture 211
social capital 129; core elements of *132*
Social Capital, Health, and Wellbeing: A Planning and Evaluation Toolkit (Health Inequalities Standing Group of Edinburgh, Scotland) 123
Social Capital Resilience Innovation Team 141–142
social connections, building 129–144, *131*; BIPOC residents 132–134; checklist 143; collective efficacy 136; communicating with peoples of different psychological frames 137–138; importance of 129–132; other ways 141–143; storytelling 134–136; strong and weak 138–141; today's polarization, overcoming 137–138; youth 132–134
social-ecological model 55, 56, 61, 69, 89, 129
"Social-Ecological" model 55–56, *55*
social justice 89
social support networks 45, 58, 85, 119, 120, 123, 130, 131, *131*, 134–136, 142–143, 192, 207, 224, 225, 228
societal trauma 7–9, 37, 44, 46–47, 50, 51, 231; climate crisis and 46–47
Soul Fire Farm 159
Southeast Asia, mass migration 30
Southeast Florida Regional Climate Change Compact 15n10
"Sow and Grow" 211
So You Want to Talk About Race (Oluo) 49
Sterman, J. 23
stigmatization 176
storytelling 134–136
Storytelling For Good 136
structural trauma 45
sub-Saharan Africa: drought 29; mass migration 30
Sustainable Ballard 159
SWOT analysis 221
systems-based evaluation 217
systems thinking 89–90

targeted (selective) prevention 64, *64*
Theory of Change approach 118

Thiaw, I. 24
Thrive Birmingham 211
Tonko, P. 231
town hall resilience meetings 107
transformational leadership 229; learning exchanges 230
transformational resilience 2–4, 10; for climate emergency 11–12, 17–18; Communities of Practice 230–231; community-based initiatives, organizing and operating 73–76, *75*; community capacity, building 100–115; framework for building universal capacity for 70; global movement to enhance universal capacity for 228–232; for long climate crisis 12–13; in phases of disaster 57–60, *58*, 225; population-level 51–52; protective and risk factors to 62–63; public health approach to 54–70; *see also individual entries*
transgenerational trauma *see* intergenerational trauma
Trauma, ACEs and Resilience diagram (Oregon MCH Tile IV) 123
Traumacene 1, 7, 31, 32, 38, 40, 51, 62; drivers of *31*; multisystemic causes of *51*
trauma healing gatherings 100–102
Trauma Healing Hubs 212
Trauma Healing Resilience Innovation Teams 209–210
trauma-induced growth 57
Trauma-Informed Community Development Framework 208
Trauma Resources Institute (TRI) 42, 100, 174, 177; peer-to-peer healing training programs 211
TRI *see* Trauma Resources Institute (TRI)
Tyndall, J. 19

UNESCO Global Network of Learning Cities Promotes Lifelong Learning (GNLC) 194
United Nation's Convention to Combat Desertification (UNCCD) 24
United Nations Office for the Coordination of Humanitarian Affairs 7
United States (US): Agriculture Department 6; coal industry 147; drought 29; ecological footprints 25; mental health disorder 37; Substance Abuse and Mental Health Services Administration (SAMHSA) 87; Surgeon General 132; wildfires 26
United Women of East Africa Support Team 142
universal literacy about mental wellness and resilience, cultivation of 170–181, *171*, 180–181; increasing 176–180; stigmatization 176; usefulness of 175–176
universal (primary) prevention 64, *64*
University of Oregon (UO): Climate Leadership Initiative (CLI) 3, 15n10
Using Logic Models Grounded in Theory of Change to Support Trauma-Informed Initiatives to Build Resilience in Children and Families (U.S. Department of Health and Human Services) 123
US National Academy of Science: on climate disruption 24

Visible Hands Collaborative 209

Wagner, B. 170
walksheds 198
Walmart 155
Whatcom Family & Community Network 78; core values of 87; mission of 86; operating principles 88; vision of 87
Whatcom Prevention Coalition 78
white supremacy 48, 49
WHO *see* World Health Organization (WHO)
wicked problem 2, 25
wildfires 1, 26, 44–45, 190
Wilson, S. 190
World Health Organization (WHO) 54; on climate-resilient housing 150; Health in all Policies (HiAP) 231; mental wellness, definition of 56
World Laughing Tour 190
World Meteorological Organization: on climate overshoot 5, 22–23
World Vision 28
Worthington, E. 186
written resilience surveys 106

You Got Mail 185
youth, trauma-informed 173

9781032200200